THE ARDEN SHAKESPEARE

GENERAL EDITORS:
RICHARD PROUDFOOT, ANN THOMPSON,
DAVID SCOTT KASTAN AND H.R. WOUDHUYSEN

WITHDRAWN

CORIOLANUS

THE ARDEN SHAKESPEARE

ALL'S WELL THAT ENDS WELL	edited by G. K. Hunter*
ANTONY AND CLEOPATRA	edited by John Wilders
AS YOU LIKE IT	edited by Agnes Latham*
THE COMEDY OF ERRORS	edited by R. A. Foakes*
CORIOLANUS	edited by Philip Brockbank*
CYMBELINE	edited by J. M. Nosworthy*
HAMLET	edited by Harold Jenkins*
JULIUS CAESAR	edited by David Daniell
KING HENRY IV Parts 1 and 2	edited by A. R. Humphreys*
KING HENRY V	edited by T. W. Craik
KING HENRY VI Part 1	edited by Edward Burns
KING HENRY VI Part 2	edited by Ronald Knowles
KING HENRY VI Part 3	edited by A. S. Cairncross*
KING HENRY VIII	edited by Gordon McMullan
KING JOHN	edited by E. A. J. Honigmann*
KING LEAR	edited by R. A. Foakes
KING RICHARD II	edited by Peter Ure*
KING RICHARD III	edited by Antony Hammond*
LOVE'S LABOUR'S LOST	edited by H. R. Woudhuysen
MACBETH	edited by Kenneth Muir*
MEASURE FOR MEASURE	edited by J. W. Lever*
THE MERCHANT OF VENICE	edited by John Russell Brown*
THE MERRY WIVES OF WINDSOR	edited by Giorgio Melchiori
A MIDSUMMER NIGHT'S DREAM	edited by Harold F. Brooks*
MUCH ADO ABOUT NOTHING	edited by A. R. Humphreys*
OTHELLO	edited by E. A. J. Honigmann
PERICLES	edited by F. D. Hoeniger*
SHAKESPEARE'S POEMS	edited by Katherine Duncan-Jones and H.R. Woudhuysen
ROMEO AND JULIET	edited by Brian Gibbons*
SHAKESPEARE'S SONNETS	edited by Katherine Duncan-Jones
THE TAMING OF THE SHREW	edited by Brian Morris*
THE TEMPEST	edited by Virginia Mason Vaughan and Alden T. Vaughan
TIMON OF ATHENS	edited by H. J. Oliver*
TITUS ANDRONICUS	edited by Jonathan Bate
TROILUS AND CRESSIDA	edited by David Bevington
TWELFTH NIGHT	edited by Keir Elam
THE TWO GENTLEMEN OF VERONA	edited by Clifford Leech*
THE TWO NOBLE KINSMEN	edited by Lois Potter
THE WINTER'S TALE	edited by J. H. P. Pafford*

* Second series

THE ARDEN EDITION OF THE
WORKS OF WILLIAM SHAKESPEARE

CORIOLANUS

Edited by
PHILIP BROCKBANK

The general editors of the Arden Shakespeare have been
W.J Craig and R.H. Case (first series 1899-1944)
Una Ellis-Fermor, Harold F. Brooks, Harold Jenkins and
Brian Morris (second series 1946-82)

Present general editors (third series)
Richard Proudfoot, Ann Thompson, David Scott Kastan and H.R. Woudhuysen

This edition of *Coriolanus,* by Philip Brockbank, first published 1976 by
Methuen & Co. Ltd

© 2007 Cengage Learning

Visit the Arden website at **www.ardenshakespeare.com.**
For your lifelong learning solutions, visit **www.cengage.co.uk**

Printed in China

Arden Shakespeare is an imprint of Cengage Learning

Cengage Learning, High Holborn House, 50-51 Bedford Row, London WC1R 4LR

Cengage Learning products are represented in Canada by Nelson Education, Ltd.

For product information and technology assistance, contact
emea.info@cengage.com.

For permission to use material from this text or product, and for
permission queries, email Clsuk.permissions@cengage.com

ISBN 978-0-17-443627-0 (hbk)

ISBN 978-1-903436-64-6 (pbk)
NPN 10 – 10 09 08

FOR
DOREEN

CONTENTS

	PAGE
PREFACE	ix
ABBREVIATIONS	xi

INTRODUCTION

I. The Text
I   The Printing of the Folio   1
II   The Copy   2
III   Spelling and Punctuation   7
IV   Lineation   9
V   Act and Scene Divisions and Locations   16
VI   Stage-directions and Speech-headings   18
VII   Anomalies of the Folio Text   21

II. The Play
I   Date of Composition   24
II   Sources   29
III   The Tragedy of Coriolanus   35
IV   The Language of the Play   68
V   The Play on Shakespeare's Stage   71
VI   Coriolanus in the Theatre   74

THE TRAGEDY OF CORIOLANUS   91

APPENDIX
1. North's Plutarch, 'The Life of Caius Martius Coriolanus'   313
2. Extract from Camden's *Remaines*   369

PREFACE

WORK on the New Arden edition of *Coriolanus* was begun by the late A. P. Rossiter a year or two before his death. He left a draft for the first three acts of the text, together with material for a paper that has since been published in *Angel with Horns* (edited by Graham Storey, 1961). It was not possible to make use of his text for the present edition as it was prepared with the intention of conserving some of the Folio's irregular lineations while eliminating many of its distinctive elisions; from a few surviving jottings it appears that he found the lineations expressive and the elisions archaic. The paper (first delivered as a lecture in Stratford-upon-Avon in 1952) offers a characteristically searching and vital account of the play which might, in happier circumstances, have served as a ground for his critical introduction. 'Real states', says Rossiter, 'are dynamic', and the comment serves alike for his analysis of the play's politics and for his response to its language; it is good that his virtues still 'lie in th'interpretation of the time'.

I have assimilated much from the 1922 Arden edition by W. J. Craig and R. H. Case. Case, who was responsible for completing the text and commentary and for writing the introduction, brought immense reading and discernment to bear, but it would not have been appropriate to take over more than a few of the hundreds of parallels that his philological enthusiasms supplied. Some of his glosses have been quoted with acknowledgement while others have been silently adapted or modified. Elsewhere, the commentary and apparatus recognize the many who have contributed to the rich editorial tradition of the play.

I have more than formal reason to express my gratitude to the general editors, Professor Harold Brooks and Professor Harold Jenkins, for a vigilance and assiduity that have saved me from many lapses and inconsistencies, and for suggestions that have prompted many acquiescent improvements and a few necessary clarifications of my own convictions.

As for the many friends, colleagues, and students who have

either answered my importunate questions or listened to my
obsessive talk of Rome, I hope that they will accept my general
recognition that I have 'great cause to give great thanks'.

University of York   J. PHILIP BROCKBANK
1975

ABBREVIATIONS

Abbreviated titles of Shakespeare's plays are as in Onions, *A Shakespeare Glossary*; line references, except those to *Coriolanus* which are to this edition, are from the Cambridge edition of Clark and Wright as in Peter Alexander's edition of the *Complete Works*, 1951.

1. *Editions*

Alexander	Shakespeare, *The Complete Works*, ed. Peter Alexander, 1951.
Ard.¹	*Coriolanus*, ed. W. J. Craig and R. H. Case (Arden Shakespeare), 1922; text and apparatus are mainly Craig's, but the commentary is by Case.
Brooke	*Coriolanus*, ed. C. F. Tucker-Brooke (Yale Shakespeare), 1924.
Brower	*Coriolanus*, ed. Reuben Brower (Signet Classic Shakespeare), 1966.
Cam.	*Works of Shakespeare*, ed. W. G. Clark and W. A. Wright (Cambridge Shakespeare), 1865; 2nd edn, 1892.
Capell	*Works of Shakespeare*, ed. Edward Capell, 1768.
Case	See above, Ard.¹
Chambers	*Coriolanus*, ed. E. K. Chambers (Warwick Shakespeare), 1898.
Collier	*Works of Shakespeare*, ed. J. P. Collier, 1844; 2nd edn, 1858. (Some readings of the 1858 edn are anticipated in 1853, see below, Collier².)
Craig	*Works of Shakespeare*, ed. W. J. Craig (Oxford Shakespeare), 1892.
Deighton	*Coriolanus*, ed. K. Deighton, 1891.
Delius	*Shakespeares Werke*, ed. N. Delius, 1854; 3rd edn, 1872.
Dyce	*Works of Shakespeare*, ed. Alexander Dyce, 1857; 2nd edn, 1866.
Furness	*Coriolanus*, ed. H. H. Furness Jr. (New Variorum Shakespeare), 1928.
Globe	*Works of Shakespeare*, ed. W. G. Clark and W. A. Wright (Globe Shakespeare), 1864.
Gomme	*Coriolanus*, ed. A. H. Gomme (Shakespeare Workshop), 1969.
Hanmer	*Works of Shakespeare*, ed. Thomas Hanmer, 1744.
Harrison	*Coriolanus*, ed. G. B. Harrison (Penguin Shakespeare), 1947.
Hibbard	*Coriolanus*, ed. G. R. Hibbard (New Penguin Shakespeare), 1967.
Hudson	*Works of Shakespeare*, ed. H. N. Hudson (Harvard Shakespeare), 1880.

Kittredge   *Works of Shakespeare*, ed. G. L. Kittredge, 1936.
Knight   *Works of Shakespeare*, ed. C. Knight, 2nd edn, 1865.
Johnson   *Plays of Shakespeare*, ed. Samuel Johnson, 1765.
Leo   *Coriolanus*, ed. F. A. Leo, 1864.
Malone   *Plays and Poems of Shakespeare*, ed. Edmund Malone, 1790.
Munro   *Works of Shakespeare*, ed. John Munro (London Shakespeare), 1958.
Pope   *Works of Shakespeare*, ed. Alexander Pope, 1723; 2nd edn, 1728.
Rowe   *Works of Shakespeare*, ed. Nicholas Rowe, 1709; 2nd edn, small 8°, 1709; 3rd edn, 1714.
Singer   *Dramatic Works of Shakespeare*, ed. S. W. Singer, 1826; 2nd edn, 1856.
Sisson   *Works of Shakespeare*, ed. C. J. Sisson, 1954.
Staunton   *Plays of Shakespeare*, ed. H. Staunton, 1858.
Steevens   *Plays of Shakespeare*, ed. George Steevens, 1793.
Theobald   *Works of Shakespeare*, ed. Lewis Theobald, 1733; 2nd edn, 1740.
Var. '73, '78, '85 *Plays of Shakespeare*, 'with the Corrections and Illustrations of Various Commentators', ed. Samuel Johnson and George Steevens, 1773; 2nd edn, 1778; 3rd edn, 1785.
Verity   *Coriolanus*, ed. A. W. Verity (Student's Shakespeare), 1905.
Warburton   *Works of Shakespeare*, ed. W. Warburton, 1747.
White   *Coriolanus*, ed. R. G. White, 1861.
Wilson   *Coriolanus*, ed. John Dover Wilson (New Shakespeare), 1960.
Wright   *Coriolanus*, ed. W. A. Wright (Clarendon Press Series), 1878.

2. *Commentaries*

Collier²   J. P. Collier, *Notes and Emendations to the Text of Shakespeare's Plays*, 1853.
Edwards   T. Edwards, Canons of Criticism, 3rd edn, 1750.
Keightley   T. Keightley, *Shakespeare Expositor*, 1867.
King   A. H. King, 'Notes on Coriolanus', *English Studies*, XIX–XX, 1937–8.
Leo   F. A. Leo, *Shakespeare Notes*, 1885.
Sisson, *New Readings* C. J. Sisson, *New Readings in Shakespeare*, 1956.
Tyrwhitt   T. Tyrwhitt, *Observations on Shakespeare*, 1766.
Whiter   W. Whiter, *Specimen of a Commentary on Shakespeare*, 1794.

3. *Other references*

Abbott   E. A. Abbott, *A Shakespearian Grammar*, 1869, etc. (References are to paragraph numbers.)
Bullough   Geoffrey Bullough, *Narrative and Dramatic Sources of Shakespeare*, vol. 5, 1964.
Brooke, *Sh.Apoc.* C. F. Tucker Brooke (ed.), *The Shakespeare Apocrypha*, 1908, 1919.

Cotgrave	Randall Cotgrave, *A dictionarie of the French and English tongues*, 1611; 2nd edn (ed. Robert Sherwood), 1632.
Dodsley	*Dodsley's Old English Plays*, ed. W. C. Hazlitt, 1876.
E.D.D.	*English Dialect Dictionary*, ed. Joseph Wright, 1905.
Kökeritz	Helge Kökeritz, *Shakespeare's Pronunciation*, 1953.
M.S.R.	Malone Society Reprint.
Noble	Richmond Noble, *Shakespeare's Biblical Knowledge*, 1935.
North	*Plutarch: The lives of the noble Grecians and Romanes*, translated out of French by Thomas North, 1579, 1595, 1603, 1607.
North (S.H.P.)	*Plutarch's Lives of the Noble Grecians and Romans* (1579), Shakespeare Head Press, 1928.
O.E.D.	*Oxford English Dictionary*, 1933.
Onions	C. T. Onions, *A Shakespeare Glossary*, 1911, 1919 (last corrected impression, 1946).
Schmidt	A. Schmidt, *Shakespeare–Lexicon*, ed. G. Sarrazin, 2 vols, Berlin, 1902.
Sherwood	See above, Cotgrave.
Tilley	M. P. Tilley, *A Dictionary of Proverbs in England in the Sixteenth and Seventeenth Centuries*, Ann Arbor, 1950. (References are to numbered proverbs.)

4. Periodicals

J.E.G.P.	*Journal of English and Germanic Philology.*
M.L.R.	*Modern Language Review.*
N.&Q.	*Notes and Queries.*
P.M.L.A.	*Publications of the Modern Language Association of America.*
R.E.S.	*Review of English Studies.*
S.Q.	*Shakespeare Quarterly.*
T.L.S.	*Times Literary Supplement.*

INTRODUCTION

I THE TEXT

I. THE PRINTING OF THE FOLIO

The Tragedy of Coriolanus reaches us through the Folio of 1623; there is no quarto, and no evidence to suggest that there ever was one. Working from technical evidence (including the identification of type from different cases) Charlton Hinman has shown that the text was set up by two compositors, conventionally called A and B, in a number of recognizable stints.[1] The following table simplifies Hinman's findings but serves to identify the compositor responsible for the Folio counterparts of the present edition:

I. i. 1–I. viii. 15	Compositor B	F pp. 1–6 (aa1–aa3ᵛ)
I. ix. 1–I. x. 9	Compositor A	F p. 7 (aa4)
I. x. 10–II. i. 94 S.D. 1	Compositor B	F p. 8 (aa4ᵛ)
II. i. 94 S.D. 2– II. ii. 153	Compositor A	F pp. 9–11 (aa5–aa6)
II. ii. 154–II. iii. 115	Compositor B	F p. 12 (aa6ᵛ)
II. iii. 116–III. i. 74	Compositor A	F pp. 13–14 (bb1, bb1ᵛ)
III. i. 75–III. i. 190 (Sicinius)	Compositor B	F p. 15 (bb2)
III. i. 190 (Hear)– III. i. 261	Compositor A	F p. 16 (bb2ᵛ) to l. 93.
III. i. 261 S.D.–III. ii. 64	Compositor B	F p. 16 (bb2ᵛ) l. 94– p. 17 (bb3)
III. ii. 65–III. ii. 121	Compositor A	F p. 18 (bb3ᵛ) column 1
III. ii. 122–V. vi. 153 S.D.	Compositor B	F p. 18 (bb3ᵛ) column 2–p. 30 (cc3ᵛ)

Only 7¼ of the Folio's 30 pages were set by A, but his contribution may be a particularly significant one, for it is generally agreed that he was apt to follow his copy more meticulously than B, and is likely to give a better indication of its character.[2]

The numbering of its pages shows that *Coriolanus* was meant to stand at the head of the tragedies, but it is preceded by

---

1. Charlton Hinman, *The Printing and Proof-reading of the First Folio of Shakespeare*, 1963, II, pp. 134–48, 154–66, 182–94.

2. See Hinman, *First Folio*, I, pp. 10–12; also Alice Walker, *Textual Problems of the First Folio*, 1953, pp. 11–12. I think it easy to dramatize the differences between A and B, and that E. E. Willoughby's account (*The Printing of the First Folio of Shakespeare*, 1932, pp. 61–9) still has its value.

Troilus and Cressida (whose printing was interrupted, occasioning its displacement in the Folio order).

Coriolanus is not among the plays significantly affected by proof corrections in the course of printing the Folio. Hinman finds only one instance: the form *blocke head* is corrected to *blocke-head* in some copies (at II. iii. 28).[1]

II. THE COPY

Editors have variously abused the text of *Coriolanus* for its corruption ('the worst printed play in the whole First Folio', says R. G. White) and commended it as 'a distinguished one' (Reuben Brower). In the present edition it has been found necessary to emend some forty words of the text, a dozen speech attributions, and about twenty apparent errors in punctuation. Over three hundred lines of the edited text have been recast to regularize lineation, and many small interventions (e.g. marking exits, clarifying stage-directions, refining punctuation) have been found expedient. There is force in G. S. Gordon's indictment of the play's early editors: 'Much less has been done to improve the text than their foot-notes give out, and much less was needed than has been done. They found the play abrupt and irregular, full of fierce rapidities of speech and cultural dissonance of metre. They have left it, after two centuries of tidying, not yet quite neat, but neater and tidier certainly than it ever left its author's hands.'[2] Editors have risked making smooth what was meant to be rough; but the nature of the roughness needs to be understood.

There is a temptation (unresisted by Gordon) to attribute to the state of the copy some of the characteristics of the play's language—the speed, vehemence, and grammatical enterprise manifest in such lines as 'His Pupill age / Man-entred thus, he waxed like a Sea'. One is predisposed to accept arguments that bring the text close to Shakespeare's foul papers, for the confidence and singleness of purpose of much of the writing are consistent with the impression that the firstlings of Shakespeare's thought were the firstlings of his hand. But there is no necessary continuity between the first draft and the final effect; the immediacy of impact may be laboriously won, and faults of transmission may look like signs of spontaneity. The evidence that the text is close to Shakespeare's foul papers is nevertheless strong if not decisive, and it deserves analysis. It depends upon (1) the character of the stage-directions and the several inconsequential variations in

1. See Hinman, *First Folio*, I, pp. 284–5.
2. *Coriolanus*, ed. G. S. Gordon, 1911, p. xviii.

speech-headings, (2) the occurrence of certain idiosyncratic spellings, at least one of which is identifiable as Shakespearean, (3) the absence from the text of all but a few of the signs of scribal work, and (4) the persistence in F of anomalies that a scribe might have been expected to eliminate.

The stage-directions are offered by W. W. Greg as the main evidence for his claim that F is from 'a carefully prepared author's copy'.[1] They are in the playwright's style, not the prompter's, made with the live theatre in prospect but not exigently present. They are fully discussed below (pp. 18–21) together with the interestingly various speech-prefixes (e.g. *Pat.*, *Noble*) which would have been regularized by most scribes, if not by the book-keeper. More trivial inconsistencies in speech-prefixes (*Cor.*, *Corio.*, *Coriol.*, *Menen.*, *Mene.*) are also perhaps unusually common and are a feature of those pages of the *Sir Thomas More* manu-script believed to be Shakespeare's and known as Hand D (Lin-colne, Linco, Linc, Lin).

Of the idiosyncratic spellings, much the most important is the form *Scicinius*. Compositor A's stint retains the form or its con-tractions, apparently from the copy, some thirty times.[2] That he was rendering Shakespeare's hand is strongly suggested by the occurrence of *sc* for *s* in *scilens* (*silence*) in Hand D, l. 50, *Scilens* for *Justice Silence* in the speech-prefixes of *2 Henry IV* (Q) and *Scicyon* for *Sicyon* in *Antony and Cleopatra* (I. ii. 115 F etc.). The form *scilens* may not be unique to Shakespeare (Partridge finds instan-ces of *scylens* and *scilence* elsewhere)[3] but it remains characteristic. The spelling was too eccentric for the taste of Compositor B, who uses *Sicinius* and its contractions some ninety times, with only two lapses into the copy's *Scicinius*. Were it not for the lapses and for the Shakespearean analogues, one might have suspected the mannerism to be Compositor A's, but I can find no evidence of such a mannerism elsewhere.[4] Other spellings which may indicate Shakespearean idiosyncrasies in the copy are *shoot* for *shout* (I. i. 213, I. ix. 49, V. v. 4), *strooke* for *struck* (I. vi. 4, IV. i. 8, IV. ii. 19, IV. v. 222), *god* for *good* (III. i. 90), and *too* for *to*,

1. W. W. Greg, *The Editorial Problems in Shakespeare*, 3rd edn, 1954, p. 148, and *The Shakespeare First Folio*, 1955, pp. 404–7.

2. See *Oxford Shakespeare Concordances*, ed. T. Howard Hill, *Coriolanus*, 1972.

3. A. C. Partridge, *Orthography in Shakespeare and Elizabethan Drama*, 1964, p. 62.

4. Compositor A is not responsible for *Scilens* in *2 Henry IV* (Q) or for *Scicyon* in *Antony and Cleopatra* (set by B). The form *Sceneca* for *Seneca* occurs in *Hamlet*, II. ii. 395 (Q2), and could be Shakespeare's. There are no other similar intrusive *c*s in the Folio.

particularly in the form *too't*, which occurs nine times. The forms *shoold* and *woold*, however, used exclusively in Hand D, do not occur in F. Shakespeare's readiness to use severely abbreviated forms and to employ the nasal vowel õ may account for the misreading *tongue* for *toge* (Malone) in II. iii. 114, *Through* for *Throng* (Theobald) in III. iii. 36, and *lamention* for *lamentation* in IV. vi. 34 (F2).

Whether or not a transcript intervened between Shakespeare's foul papers and the printer can never be finally determined; Shakespeare himself may have made a fair copy of some pages and left others; a slavish scribe may have retained all the anomalies and accidents of his original. Philip Williams, however, appears to have concluded that the copy for *Coriolanus* has specific characteristics of transcript; unfortunately he was unable to develop his argument fully, but as far as it goes it fails to convince.[1] Following Alice Walker,[2] he supposes the first three acts of *King John* to be from foul papers and the last two from promptcopy, and he notices that the first three acts prefer *O* to *Oh* while the last two prefer *Oh*. He therefore takes *Oh* for a sign of transcript and feels able to allude to the *Coriolanus* copy as scribe's work. It is true that *Oh* occurs forty times in F and *O* only twelve, and that Compositor A, with a reputation for fidelity to copy, uses only *Oh* (eight times). But Compositor B (said by Hinman to be 'remarkably consistent' in the use of his chosen forms)[3] has a dozen *O*s alongside his three dozen *Oh*s, and this is quite enough to unsettle confidence in the evidence.

The frequency in F of colloquial contractions such as *th'*, *toth'*, *o'th*, *a'th*, *by'th*, *y'are*, *wee'l*, *ta'ne*, has also been taken as a sign of transcript. Partridge argues that this 'highly developed dramatic orthography' is capable of three explanations: Shakespeare had learned from others (such as Jonson) the 'new technique of colloquial clipping'; or the foul papers had been copied or edited by the company scribe; or the copy was 'revised by the supervising editors of the publishers themselves'.[4] But Partridge himself accepts his first explanation as probable, and colloquial contractions are in any case found in Hand D (including *thoffender*,

1. Philip Williams, 'Textual Problems in Shakespeare', *Studies in Bibliography*, VIII, 1956, p. 6. Fredson Bowers (*On Editing Shakespeare and the Elizabethan Dramatists*, 1955, p. 109) endorsed Williams's findings in advance of their publication.

2. *Apud* Greg, *Editorial Problems*, p. 143 note.

3. Hinman, *First Folio*, I, pp. 180–93. Hinman does not find the *Oh* and *O* distinction significant for compositor identification.

4. Partridge, *Orthography in Shakespeare*, p. 116.

tooth ports, byth, weele, youle, and *tane*—but all without apostrophes).
One may add that F's contractions are very variously spelt
(e.g. *I'th, i'th, ith*), the mixed forms occurring in both compositors' stints; a scribe sophisticating the orthography might have
been more consistent.

There is some evidence for the intervention of the book-
keeper at some stage in the transmission, but it is not decisive.
Crompton Rhodes alleges it in I. iv. 45 and 46 where Martius
enters the gates and is shut in for the second time;[1] but Shakespeare may have written a general direction for the action in
I. iv before making it specific. Greg wonders about the addition of
Cornets after *Flourish*, at I. x. S.D. and II. i. 202; but in a play very
thoroughly attentive to musical effects in its stage-directions
(and even its dialogue) the refinement could be the playwright's,
and at II. ii. 154 the direction reads *Flourish Cornets* (without an
intervening stop) and there is no reason here to suppose *Cornets* an
afterthought—either Shakespeare's or the book-keeper's.[2] Dover
Wilson suspects *Coriolanus stands* at II. ii. 36, but this could be
Shakespeare's ordering of the scene. The difficulty, as elsewhere
in the later plays, may be owed to Shakespeare's readiness to act
almost as his own book-keeper; for it remains true that Shakespeare's manuscript is made almost ready for use in the theatre,
but not quite ready—as the irregular speech-headings testify
(see p. 20). Another possible sign of a book-keeper's hand is the
reading *with Cumalijs* at III. iii. 135 S.D. (F). Since Compositor B
failed to recognize the Latin form and promoted it to a proper
name, it must have stood in the copy along with other Latin
directions (see p. 19 below). But as *cum alijs* is rare in Shakespeare,[3] it may be the note of a book-keeper trying to clarify an
illegible direction for his own use.

The anomalies that survive in F, apparently from foul papers,
are separately discussed (pp. 21–4) as they may have implications
beyond the nature of the copy. They include the confusions
over Titus Lartius—the spelling of his name, and his movements between Rome and Corioli; the irregular ordering of the
names *Caius Martius Coriolanus*; and the muddle about the conspirators in V. vi. A scribe, one feels, would have put things

1. R. Crompton Rhodes, *Shakespeare's First Folio*, 1923, pp. 132–3.
2. See Greg, *First Folio*, p. 406. Support for the theory might be adduced
from *The Merchant of Venice*, where the several cornet flourishes are prescribed
in F only, possibly owing to access to prompt-book (see *Mer. V.*, ed. J. R.
Brown, II. vii. 1 S.D. note).
3. There are instances in *Hamlet*, I. ii. S.D. (Q) and II. i. S.D. (F); the first
could be Shakespeare's, but not the second. See Greg, *First Folio*, pp. 310–11.

right. Honigmann would include among the significant anomalies
the references to *Cominius the Generall* at II. i. 160 and *Cominius the
Consul* at II. ii. 36;[1] but the second is the common form in North
and it looks as though Shakespeare reverted to it—another tiny
sign of the closeness of the copy to the playwright's first thoughts.

McKerrow once wondered that ten folio pages of a book
printed by Jaggard in 1619 exhibit 'eighteen errors, of which
only one is at all serious' and asked why the F text of *Coriolanus*
should 'in some 3,400 lines contain, apart from many errors or
irregularities in punctuation and line arrangement, at least
twenty-one passages in which conservative modern editors have
had either to emend the text or admit their inability to do so'.[2]
If we suppose a copy for *Coriolanus* that in certain respects re-
sembled Hand D of the *Sir Thomas More* manuscript, the inadequacies are not surprising and are within the ordinary expectation of error in the printing of the plays. The incidence of
minim errors is much the same, for example, as in *Timon of
Athens* and *Antony and Cleopatra*, both commonly held to be from
Shakespeare's autograph in the same decade.[3] These and similar
errors, however, while they convey some impression of the orthographic character of the copy, do not enable a distinction to be
made between autograph and transcript.[4] Certain characteristics
thought by Dover Wilson to be Shakespearean idiosyncrasies—

1. E. A. J. Honigmann, *The Stability of Shakespeare's Text*, 1965, pp. 147–8.
He claims that the discrepancy 'confirms that the two adjacent scenes were not
originally written one after the other'.

2. R. B. McKerrow, 'The Elizabethan Printer and Dramatic Manuscripts',
The Library, XII, Dec. 1931, pp. 253–75.

3. Cf. *Antony and Cleopatra*, ed. J. D. Wilson, 1950, pp. 124–7, and *Timon of
Athens*, ed. J. D. Wilson and J. C. Maxwell, 1957, pp. 90–2.

4. They include: I. i. 109 F, taintingly (tauntingly F4), I. iii. 43 F, *Contenning*
(contemning *Leo*), I. vi. 70 F, Lessen (Lesser F3), III. i. 285 F, one (our *Theobald*), IV. iv. 23 F, haue (hate *Capell*), and v. iii. 152 F, change (charge *Theobald*). See also II. i. 184 F, begin (begnaw *Craig*), I. ix. 46 F, Ouerture (ovator
this edn.), and III. ii. 21 F, things (thwartings *Theobald*, taxings *Sisson*, crossings
Hibbard). Slightly more ambiguous cases, where errors may be owed to misreading, may be found at I. i. 91, I. i. 238, I. vi. 53, III. ii. 32, III. iii. 55, IV. v. 194,
v. iii. 63, v. iii. 48. At I. iv. 57 *Cato's* (*Theobald*) was misinterpreted as *Calues*,
perhaps from the copy form *Catoes*. The apparent misattributions at III. i. 229
and 235 could be minim confusions of *Com.* and *Cor.*, but like others in the play
(e.g. at III. i. 236, involving *Men.* and *Cor.*) they are likely to be misinterpretations of illegible or ambiguously aligned speech-headings in the margins of the
copy. There remain a few errors that could be either misreadings or misprints:
I. i. 217 F, unroost (unrooft = unroof'd *Theobald*), I. iii. 98 F, *Carioles* (*Corioles*),
IV. v. 192 F, carbinado (carbonado), v. iii. 149 F, fiue (fine *Johnson*), IV. vii. 39
F, detect (defect F2). The odd form *Cominisn* at I. i. 225 S.D. is owed to a
turned ligature. See also I. ii. 82–4 n.

the confusion of *one* and *on*, the arbitrary use of a capital C—are in fact not uncommon and could be found in a transcript; they remain consistent, however, with autograph. A sparse punctuation resembling Hand D's would account both for the comparative lightness of the pointing in F and for the occasionally bewildering interventions of the compositors. The frequent mislinings in F (discussed below, pp. 9–16) are likewise a probable inheritance from copy which, like Hand D, would have no capital letters to make the lineation, and might have carried a number of short and long lines, together with marginal insertions and corrections.

It is consistent with the evidence to suppose that F was set up from autograph copy, at least partly prepared by the playwright for the theatre. It is not possible to be sure that the book-keeper had or did not have a casual, occasional hand in it. Compositors A and B were responsible for adapting their copy to the reading conventions of the Folio, and in particular to the exigencies of its double-column format. Modern editors can at best seek to minimize the damage done in the process to Shakespeare's expressive intentions.

III. SPELLING AND PUNCTUATION

The assumption that the text is close to Shakespeare's hand encourages a conservative treatment. From the conviction that they represent Shakespeare's practice in writing this play, the forms *th'*, *i'th'*, *o'th'*, *to th'* and *by th'* have been retained throughout in both verse and prose, with such related ones as *toth'* and *ith* silently normalized. The form *a'th'* (= of the) is commoner in the text than *o'th'* but the more modern one (also usual elsewhere in Shakespeare) has been used throughout.[1] It is easy to exaggerate the effect of these contractions upon the pace of the dialogue, but it may be cumulatively sensed by eye and ear, and locally recognized in such lines as:

> Even to the court, the heart, to th'seat o'th'brain.

For the sake of consistency certain other archaic contractions are retained too: *th'have* (they've), *th'other* (t'other), *thou't* (thou wilt), *y'are* (you're), and *ha't* (have it). The form *and* = 'if' has throughout been preferred to the equally archaic *an*, which is not used in the text of F. Among the anomalies F's *ha's* at I. iii. 59 is

1. The *Oxford Concordance, Coriolanus,* shows *a'th* and variants used 27 times, *o'th* 16.

rendered '*has* (= he has) and not *has*; similarly the omission of
the pronoun at both III. i. 160 (F, *Has*) and 161 (F, *H'as*) is
indicated by '*Has*.

Modernizations in the present edition which may digress from
Shakespeare's preferred forms include *vile* for *vilde* (I. i. 183),
vilely for *vildly* (III. i. 10), *boils* for *biles* (I. iv. 31), *osprey* for *aspray*
(IV. vii. 34), and *wedged* for *wadg'd* (II. iii. 28). More routine
modernizations of interest include, *bisson* for *beesome* (II. i. 63–4),
faucet for *fosset* (II. i. 70), *pother* for *poother* (II. i. 216), *choired* for
quier'd (III. ii. 113), *poll* for *Pole* (III. iii. 10), *Requite* for *Requit*
(IV. ii. 12), *cement* for *ciment* (IV. vi. 86), *clip* for *cleep* (IV. v. 110),
errand for *arrant* (v. ii. 59), *hautboys* for *hoboyes* (v. iv. 49 S.D.), and
cymbals for *Symboles* (v. iv. 51). In IV. v. 192 F's *carbinado* is
probably a misreading, as the correct form *carbonado* occurs in
2 Henry IV, v. iii. 55 Q (also from foul papers). The modern form
digest and the older one *disgest* both occur in F (see I. i. 149 note).
Slightly archaic forms are retained at I. i. 249 (*mutiners*), III. iii. 32
(*hostler*), and v. ii. 43 (*dotant*). At IV. i. 36 the unique *exposture* is
kept, but to avoid eccentricity *clock'd* is changed to *cluck'd*
(v. iii. 163) and *Flatter'd* to *Flutter'd* (v. vi. 115). The echoic words
hollow (I. viii. 7) and *Hoop'd* (IV. v. 79) are given as *Holloa* and
Whoop'd.

Many inconsistencies persist in F's spelling of proper names
(suggesting again that any scribe must have been of the servile
kind). In the present text most have been normalized to accord
with North's Plutarch: the commonest F form *Corioles* (as in
North) is preferred to alternatives (*Carioles, Corialus, Coriolus*)
throughout; North's *Volsces* displaces F's *Volces* and *Volcies*, and
Volscians is used both for *Volceans* and *Volcians*. F's *Martius* has
been retained in conformity with North, and not corrected to
Marcius.

If Hand D is a reliable guide, Shakespeare's punctuation was
startlingly light and much in the transmitted text is likely to be
the responsibility of the compositors.[1] We cannot be sure, however, that Shakespeare always left his manuscripts scantily
pointed, or that the compositors were other than conscientious in
interpreting his intentions; for the punctuation of F is usually
good. It is possible to distinguish rival theories of punctuation in
Shakespeare's time, with some mixed practices. 'The breath',

1. Willoughby (*First Folio*, p. 68) says of Hand D that had the passage
'been printed in the Folio with the usual proportion of punctuation to words, it
would have contained not 36 marks but 215'. Five out of six marks in *Coriolanus*
would by this analogy be owed to the compositors.

says Puttenham, 'asketh to be now and then releeved with some pause or stay more or less', and 'the very nature of speach (because it goeth by clauses of severall construction and sence) requireth some space betwixt them with intermission of sound, to th'end they may not huddle one upon another so rudly and so fast that th'eare may not perceive their difference.'[1] In practice, particularly in the theatre, the demands of 'breath' are not always easily reconciled with those of 'construction and sense'. Jonson, in his carefully groomed and expressive texts of *Volpone* and *The Alchemist*, was much concerned with what Puttenham calls 'the commodious and sensible distinction of clauses'; but Shakespeare may have preferred what Partridge calls 'a *partly* rhythmical system, or what Mulcaster in his *Elementarie* called "right and tunable uttering"'.[2] The compositors did their not unworthy best, but it is not possible to find behind their text a fully coherent system or style. The present text is fairly conservative of F's punctuation but includes several dozen silent editorial changes. Changes thought significant are recorded in the apparatus and occasionally discussed. There is a high incidence in F of colons and brackets (none in Hand D); most colons have been given as periods or commas and most brackets have been silently replaced with commas. All quotation marks in the present text are editorial. Occasionally F's punctuation has been retained in passages where repointing would prematurely mask a difficulty (e.g. v. i. 67–9).

IV. LINEATION

If the lineation of F were followed uncritically there would be some awkwardness but no significant loss of clarity or effect. Readers would occasionally notice, players would (with some embarrassments) adapt, and audiences would be untroubled. Lineation is an importunate problem only for editors; it nevertheless asks for a solution.

Since the beginning of the eighteenth century editorial tradition has intervened in more than a hundred and twenty passages to make adjustments affecting over three hundred line-divisions in the edited text. A few of these interventions may modify our impression of speech-movement and the pace of exchanges between speakers, but many simply affect the look of the page and are matters of printing convention merely. Editorial tradition

1. George Puttenham, *The Arte of English Poesie*, ed. G. D. Willcock and A. Walker, 1936, p. 74.
2. Partridge, *Orthography in Shakespeare*, p. 130.

has often worked in the confidence that Shakespeare meant to honour the pentameter model in his verse, and that apparent failures to do so are owed to oversight or to want of refinement in the processes of transmission. That confidence has occasionally been called into question. G. B. Harrison, for example, whose edition follows the Folio very closely, invites us to 'assume as a matter of common sense that the arrangement of the verse lines in the Folio follows the original copy unless some very good reason can be found for supposing otherwise.'[1] By his account an edited text of certain plays of Shakespeare's maturity (including *Coriolanus, Antony and Cleopatra, Macbeth,* and *Timon of Athens*) should demonstrate to the reader Shakespeare's willingness occasionally to abandon blank-verse patterns in favour of freer and more flexible forms.

The text of *Coriolanus* (like that of *Antony and Cleopatra*[2]) offers resistance to both the decorous and the liberal approaches to its line-divisions: some can be held expressive, some infelicitous or perverse, and many defy technical explanations appealing to the accidents of transmission. The technical problems of the compositor are most likely to affect lineation when he finds a line overriding his measure, or finds that owing to an error in casting-off he needs either to crowd the page to accommodate his copy or to spread his copy to fill the page. On about a dozen occasions a long line appears to have been divided into two merely in order to accommodate it into F's column.[3] At II. iii. 164, for example, F reads,

> *3. Cit.* Hee said hee had Wounds,
> Which he could shew in priuate:

which Pope recasts as one line. Such divisions are not uncommon elsewhere in Shakespeare, and may sometimes have been a feature of the copy as well as of the printed text.[4] Crowding and spreading are more difficult to identify. Crowding may be alleged in about thirty passages where a slight saving of space is effected,

1. G. B. Harrison, 'A Note on Coriolanus', *J. Q. Adams Memorial Studies,* ed. J. G. McManaway, etc., 1948, p. 241.

2. For a discussion of the lineation of *Antony and Cleopatra,* see J. D. Wilson's introduction to his 1929 facsimile edition.

3. I. iv. 1, 25, I. ix. 77, II. iii. 164, III. i. 279, 302, III. iii. 33, 40, IV. ii. 11, IV. v. 5, IV. vi. 24. More dubious cases, perhaps involving split lines, are at I. vi. 57–9 and III. ii. 52–6.

4. Greg (*First Folio,* p. 401) notices the many half-lines in *Antony and Cleopatra,* and acquiescently quotes Chambers's view that 'Shakespeare sometimes split a line in the middle of a speech to indicate a pause'.

but in half of these it may be doubted if the saving was deliberate.[1]
Among the more convincing instances, F at III. i. 116 reads,

> I say they norisht disobedience: fed, the ruin of the State

while editors, following Pope, usually read,

> I say they nourish'd disobedience, fed
> The ruin of the state.

Compositor B apparently saves one line on a crowded page (bb2) which happened to be the last of that stint. Anomalously long lines, however, can occur in MS. (compare Hand D ll.94–5 with *Coriolanus*, v. iii. 40–2 F). The clearest instances of spreading would appear to be the work of Compositor A on pp. 9 and 10 (aa5 and aa5ᵛ) of F, where three speeches that together take up sixteen lines in a regularized text are made to take up twenty-one (see textual notes, II. i. 180–90, 198–200), with two further lines needlessly added in other passages (II. i. 208–9, 235–6). Another half-dozen passages could be regarded as spreading, but they are trivial and dubious.[2]

The largest single group of adjustments of the Folio lineation in modern texts (about forty) consists of transitions between speeches, often short ones and sometimes mixing prose and verse.[3] Attempts to regularize transitions often affect the lines that follow, and it would be rash to claim that anything resembling the regularized text actually stood in the copy. For instance, II. i. 234–41 F reads,

> Toth' People, begge their stinking Breaths.
> *Scicin.* 'Tis right.
> *Brutus.* It was his word:
> Oh he would misse it, rather then carry it,
> But by the suite of the Gentry to him,
> And the desire of the Nobles.
> *Scicin.* I wish no better, then haue him hold that purpose, and to put it in execution.
> *Brutus.* 'Tis most like he will.
> *Scicin.* It shall be to him then, as our good wills; a sure destruction.

---

1. I. v. 19–20, I. ix. 44–50, 64–5, II. i. 167–70, II. ii. 54–66, 129–30, 132–5, 138–43, II. iii. 56–8, 157–8, 203–6, 215–17, 224–30, 252–3, III. i. 79–84, 85–7, 89–90, 116–17, 189–90, 229–30, 238–9, 273–6, 326–7, III. iii. 9–10, IV. ii. 5–8, 25–8, IV. v. 55–8, IV. vi. 11–12, 115–16.
2. I. iii. 71–2, 103–7, II. i. 157–8, II. iii. 164, III. iii. 33, 40.
3. E.g. I. i. 92–4, 258–62, II. iii. 203–6, IV. vi. 56–7.

Attempts at regularization by Steevens, Pope, and Rowe yield,

> To th'people, beg their stinking breaths.
> *Sic.*   'Tis right.
> *Bru.* It was his word. Oh, he would miss it rather
>   Than carry it but by the suit of the gentry to him
>   And the desire of the nobles.
> *Sic.*   I wish no better
>   Than have him hold that purpose, and to put it
>   In execution.
> *Bru.*   'Tis most like he will.
> *Sic.* It shall be to him then, as our good wills,
>   A sure destruction.

The passage occurs on p. 10 (aa5ᵛ) of F, where Compositor A has to try to fill the space at his disposal; he would therefore appear to have a motive for spreading the first four lines, but none for crowding Sicinius' verse into prose. It therefore seems likely that something close to A's version stood in the copy and that Shakespeare, as elsewhere in the speeches of the tribunes and the citizens, hesitated between verse and prose and left the text undivided. Compositor A may have stuck doggedly to confused copy, but more probably he intermittently recognized verse in the exchanges and intermittently failed to do so (compare I. i. 92–4, where Compositor B mistakenly sets the citizen's prose as verse). The edited version cannot here be justified either as an approximation to copy or as a recovery of the author's intention; it is rather an interpretation of an intention imperfectly achieved. Shakespeare, the implicit claim has it, would have transcribed into verse had he been making a fair copy; but being free to emend, he would have made a better job of it than his editors. Certain infelicities (e.g. l. 236 of the edited text above) are the expected inheritance from autograph first draft.

If Compositor A was responsible for the line-divisions in the passage above, they may be held characteristic of his handling of the lineation elsewhere. Although he set less than a quarter of the text, Compositor A is behind five-twelfths of its irregular lines, including those admired most for their expressiveness. Act I, Scene ix, for example, is taken by Harrison to exemplify the Folio's 'subtle touches', the 'pauses, the silences, and the rushes', effaced by most editors in obedience to the metronome.[1] Consider A's rendering of I. ix. 13–23,

> My Mother, who ha's a Charter to extoll her Bloud,
> When she do's prayse me, grieues me:

---

1. 'A Note on Coriolanus', *Adams Memorial Studies*, p. 249.

I haue done as you haue done, that's what I can,
Induc'd as you haue beene, that's for my Countrey:
He that ha's but effected his good will,
Hath ouerta'ne mine Act.
   Com. You shall not be the Graue of your deseruing,
Rome must know the value of her owne:
'Twere a Concealement worse then a Theft,
No lesse then a Traducement,
To hide your doings, . . .

Most editions, following Pope and Hanmer, divide: mother, / . . . blood, / . . . done / . . . induc'd / . . . country. / . . . will, / . . . be / . . . know / . . . concealment / . . . traducement, / . While it is possible to acquiesce in Harrison's account of what is happening, it is also apt to observe that A's lineation shows a reluctance to detach words from clauses at the end of a line, and that each line pauses on a punctuation mark. Because it attends to syntactical units rather than to metrical ones, it conveys the speech movement with clarity and emphasis (it is not hard to imagine actors' parts written out in this fashion), but it forfeits the measure.

   Similarly, in i. ix. 44–50 F reads,

Made all of false-fac'd soothing:
When Steele growes soft, as the Parasites Silke,
Let him be made an Ouerture for th'Warres:
No more I say, for that I haue not wash'd
My Nose that bled, or foyl'd some debile Wretch,
Which without note, here's many else haue done,
You shoot me forth in acclamations hyperbolicall . . .

Compositor A here neither gains nor loses space and the lineation must belong either to the copy or to A's editorial initiative. Modern editors usually follow Theobald, dividing: grows / . . . made / . . . say, / . . . bled, / . . . note / . . . forth / . . . hyperbolical. The Folio again renders the speaking movement accurately but loses control of the metrical ground, while Theobald's version recovers the metre but relies on punctuation to convey the pace of the voice.

   The third sustained passage of irregular division occurs on the first page of Compositor A's stint aa5 to aa6, one that shows some symptoms of 'spreading'; ii. i. 182–8 F reads,

     Mene. A hundred thousand Welcomes:
     I could weepe, and I could laugh,
     I am light, and heauie; welcome:
     A Curse begin at very root on's heart,
     That is not glad to see thee.

> Yon are three, that Rome should dote on:
> Yet by the faith of men, we haue
> Some old Crab-trees here at home,
> That will not be grafted to your Rallish.
> Yet welcome Warriors:

Pope reduces the ten lines to seven by dividing: weep, / . . . welcome: / . . . heart, / . . . three, / . . . men, / . . . not / . The first six F lines gain in fluency and excitement by the recasting, in which the pentameter pulse can again be felt; the powerful speech movement of the last sentence, however, rides against the pentameter and leaves Pope's lines verses for the eye only. On this occasion too, the copy may have been undivided and therefore have invited Compositor A's syntactical intervals. If he was 'spreading' badly cast-off copy, it may be significant that all but one line ends with a punctuation mark. The same disposition to work in clauses may account for the twelve occasions (all but one in A's stint) when a modern editor finds it necessary to move *And* from the beginning of one line to the end or later part of the previous one.[1] For example, where the Folio at II. i. 245–6 reads,

> Haue made them Mules, silenc'd their Pleaders,
> And dispropertied their Freedomes; holding them,

Pope corrects to,

> Have made them mules, silenc'd their pleaders and
> Dispropertied their freedoms, holding them

None of A's lines ends in *and*; but several in B's stint do (e.g. v. vi. 39, 75), and where they begin with *and* they are correct (e.g. v. vi. 20, 51). If this is a significant circumstance, the displaced *ands* were either a characteristic of the copy transmitted by Compositor A and corrected by B, or they were introduced by A.

Compositor B's apparent mislinings occur predominantly in transitions between speakers and between verse and prose. In two longer passages, however, it will be seen that the syntactical principle at work in A's lineation is not operating in B's. At I. vi. 56–9 F, we find,

> By all the Battailes wherein we haue fought,
> By th'Blood we haue shed together,
> By th'Vowes we haue made
> To endure Friends, that you directly set me
> Against *Affidious*, and his *Antiats*.

---

1. II. i. 245–6, 260–1, II. ii. 37–8, 84–5, 142–3, II. iii. 137–8, 186–7, 204–5, III. i. 60–1, 66–7, 262–3. The instance in B's stint is at IV. ii. 6–7.

Pope reduces the lines to four by dividing: fought, / . . . vows / . . . directly / . . . Antiats. We may be uncertain whether it was Shakespeare or Compositor B who was anxious to preserve the symmetry of the oath by beginning three lines with *By*; but the halting half-line pays a heavy price, and does not quieten the suspicion that the compositor was either deliberately spreading the text or that he was tricked by the repetition into setting a third *By* at the start of a line. The Folio page (6, aa3ᵛ) is at the end of B's first stint, and its ample spacing of stage-directions is another symptom of 'spreading'.

It happens that the second long irregular speech in B's work is placed at the end of a page (p. 17, bb3) immediately before A took over one column from the stint. III. ii. 51–6 F reads,

> It stands in like request.
>   *Corio.* Why force you this?
>   *Volum.* Because, that
> Now it lyes you on to speake to th'people:
> Not by your owne instruction, nor by'th'matter
> Which your heart prompts you, but with such words
> That are but roated in your Tongue;
> Though but Bastards, and Syllables

Editors, in the wake of Malone, divide: this? / . . . speak / . . . instruction, / . . . you, / . . . in / . . . syllables. Neither awkwardness of transition (for Coriolanus nicely divides a verse with Volumnia) nor speech-movement of the kind recognized in A's lineation, can account for *Because, that*. Nor would any of the edited lines be too long for the column. Again, it would seem, the need to make a line to fill space has infected the lineation, and we may assume that something close to Malone's division stood in the copy.

Elsewhere, in both B's stint and A's, fortuitous short-lines attend upon some mechanical adjustment of the text, e.g. F at II. i. 208–9 reads,

> Clambring the Walls to eye him:
> Stalls, Bulkes, Windowes, are smother'd vp,
> Leades fill'd, and Ridges hors'd

which Pope divides: windows, / . . . hors'd. Pope's first line would not have fitted the Folio column.

Local analysis, however, cannot in itself be decisive. The editor who wonders what respect should be accorded F's departures from conventional lineation must set the question in a larger perspective and recognize:

(1) that while over three hundred lines are irregularly divided, over two thousand are within the pentameter norm;

(2) that while transitions are often a problem, the greater number are regular;

(3) that the higher incidence of apparent mislinings is in A's stint;

(4) that A, more markedly than B, tends to set irregular verse in syntactical rather than metrical units.

From (1) it would seem that Shakespeare chose to confine his allegedly freer style to three, four, or five of the longer speeches (depending upon the weight allowed to qualifying technical evidence); (2) suggests that Shakespeare may have been negligent about transitions (especially across short speeches) but that he was not in principle and in this play indifferent to them. The other points need to be pursued in relation to the practice of both compositors elsewhere.[1] But A's reputation for fidelity makes it likely that the copy itself had occasional eccentricities which were better disguised by B. These would include undivided passages where Shakespeare was moving between verse and prose rhythms; and mannerisms acquired by A in the course of dividing them may have sometimes infected his treatment of the formal verse.

In the present edition, therefore, the irregularities of F's lineation have been largely effaced and brought into some conformity with the dominant practices established by the text itself. Wherever a metrical pattern can be discerned, however faintly, it is represented to the eye; while the speech-movements, often powerfully dissenting from the pentameter ground, are measured by the punctuation.

V. ACT AND SCENE DIVISIONS AND LOCATIONS

The Folio text is correctly divided into acts but, beyond *Actus Primus. Scæna Prima*, not into scenes. The act divisions may not be Shakespeare's (*Antony and Cleopatra*, the companion text, is without them) but the play evidently received some of the attention due to its planned position as first of the tragedies. Scene divisions were introduced by Rowe, augmented by Pope (following French conventions), and modified by Capell. Modern

---

1. See, for example, *Julius Caesar*, I. iii. 57–9, where A appears to be responsible for mislining similar to that in *Coriolanus*; but a full analysis would be complex and extensive.

editions follow Capell except in distinguishing Act v, Scenes v
and vi, which are owed to Dyce.

No locations are given in the Folio, but they are usually clear
from the text. Brief ones (*Rome, Coriolus, The Walls of Coriolus*)
were supplied by Rowe, and slightly more circumstantial ones
(*A Street in Rome*) by Pope. Capell and others pursued refinements
which have been followed with inconsequential variations in
modern texts. Locations of this kind are usually innocent but
superfluous; they are not given in the present text but are discussed in the headnotes to each scene. Shakespeare has been
solicitous in charting the city and the territory in stage-direction
and dialogue. Thus in I. i. 45–6 we are made aware by '*shouts
within*' of 'The other side o'th'city', and learn that we are some
distance from the Capitol and that the crowd is on its way there.
The directions in I. ii. and I. iii set the scene with economy and
immediacy. In I. iv they specify '*the city Corioles*', '*the walls of
Corioles*' (l. 12), the '*trenches*' (l. 29), and the '*gates*' (l. 42). The
direction at I. iv. 62 proleptically locates I. v in the city, and the
dialogue at I. v. 11–14 sets one scene that we do not see (in the
market-place of Corioles) and another that we do see with Cominius
in the field (I. vi). Some of Shakespeare's locations are theatrical
rather than topographical (e.g. I. viii. S.D.), but the attention to
topography can be highly evocative; Aufidius, for example, confesses his isolation from the centre of power in I. x. 30–2:

> I am attended at the cypress grove. I pray you—
> 'Tis south the city mills—bring me word thither
> How the world goes . . .

The festive street scene when Martius returns to Rome is reported
by Brutus (II. i. 203–19), but the routinely prosperous scene
described by Sicinius (IV. vi. 7–9) could be theatrically realized.
Coriolanus' arrival in Antium is so promptly and disarmingly
announced before the house of Aufidius (IV. iv. S.D.) that the effect
might be thought naive, were it not for the momentous directness
of purpose that consists with it. The traditional editorial locations
can occasionally mar a Shakespearean effect. Thus it is better
both in the theatre and in the reading to wait for Adrian the
Volscian to tell us he is a day's journey from Rome than to have
the location prematurely and (as in Capell's direction) mis-
leadingly proclaimed. Similarly, Shakespeare's concern to
establish the market-place as an element in the city's political
topography (e.g. II. ii. 159, III. ii. 131) is frustrated by locations,

following North and Pope, at *The Forum* in II. iii and III. iii, although the meaning is the same.

VI. STAGE-DIRECTIONS AND SPEECH-HEADINGS

Since the directions show, in Greg's words, a high degree of graphic elaboration and are 'clearly designed for the producer', they are important not only for what they tell about the copy[1] but also for what they reveal of Shakespeare's craft. They mediate between the Rome of Plutarch and the Elizabethan stage, attending to domestic matters (*Enter Volumnia and Virgilia, mother and wife to Martius: They set them downe on two low stooles and sowe*, I. iii), to stage business (*Enter at one Doore Cominius, with the Romanes: At another Doore Martius, with his Arme in a Scarfe*, I. ix. I), and to the source in North (*Holds her by the hand silent*, V. iii. 182). One direction has the amplitude of narrative: *Titus Lartius, having set a guard upon Carioles, going with Drum and Trumpet toward Cominius* (I. viii). Greg thinks that this, and *Enter Martius Cursing* (I. iv. 29), mảy have been 'copied in from the author's plot or scenario'. Shakespeare may, however, have simply staged the event to the mind's eye. Consider, for example, North's account of Coriolanus' covert entry into Antium:

> For he disguised him selfe in suche arraye and attire, as he thought no man could ever have knowen him for the persone he was, seeing him in that apparell he had upon his backe . . .
> It was even twy light when he entred the cittie of Antium, and many people met him in the streetes, but no man knewe him. So he went directly to Tullus Aufidius house, and when he came thither, he got him up straight to the chimney harthe, and sat him downe, and spake not a worde to any man, his face all muffled over. They of the house spying him, wondered what he should be, and yet they durst not byd him rise. For ill favoredly muffled and disguised as he was, yet there appeared a certaine majestie in his countenance, and in his silence: whereupon they went to Tullus who was at supper, to tell him of the straunge disguising of this man. Tullus rose presently from the borde, and comming towards him, asked him what he was, and wherefore he came. Then Martius unmuffled him selfe . . .

All the theatrical potential here is fully realized in stage-direction and dialogue: '*Enter Coriolanus in meane Apparrell, Disguisd, and*

1. See above, p. 3. J. D. Wilson finds the elaborate directions 'perhaps necessitated' like those of *The Tempest* 'by the author's absence in Stratford at the time the play was being rehearsed' (*Coriolanus, A Facsimile of the First Folio Text*, 1928).

muffled . . . A goodly city is this Antium . . . Then know me not . . .
I will not hurt your hearth . . . What would'st thou? thy name?
Why speak'st not?' It is at this point (IV. v. 55) that Capell adds,
very fittingly, the direction from North, '*Unmuffling*'.

The relationship between stage-directions, dialogue, and situation often witnesses to the playwright's art and insight. The
resonantly ceremonious one at II. i. 160, for example, *A Sennet.
Trumpets sound. Enter Cominius the Generall, and Titus Latius:
betweene them Coriolanus, crown'd with an Oaken Garland, with
Captaines and Souldiers, and a Herauld*, is muted in advance by
Volumnia's response to the trumpets, 'These are the ushers of
Martius: before him he carries noise, and behind him he leaves
tears'. Similarly, the processional entry at II. ii. 36 expresses in its
order and its grouping the unstable relationships of the state:
*A Sennet. Enter the Patricians, and the Tribunes of the People, Lictors
before them: Coriolanus, Menenius, Cominius the Consul: Scicinius and
Brutus take their places by themselves: Coriolanus stands*. The procession
enters in due order, divides into factions, and leaves Coriolanus
isolated. The present edition retains the indecorous order of entry
at I. i. 225 and does not, following Malone and the class-conscious
editorial majority, recast to keep the tribunes in the rear. Another
ironic and politically expressive direction announces Coriolanus'
return to Antium at V. vi. 70: *Enter Coriolanus marching with
Drumme, and Colours. The Commoners being with him.*

The directions show Shakespeare more than usually conscious
of the sounds and movements of the spectacle, both formal and
spontaneous. The clamour of protest, riot, and war often fill the
theatre: *Enter a Company of Mutinous Citizens* (I. i), *Showts within*
(I. i. 45), *They Sound a Parley . . . Drum afar off* (I. iv. 12, 15), *They all
shout and wave their swords, take him up in their Armes, and cast up their
caps* (I. vi. 75). Popular noise and martial noise are ironically resolved in Rome, 'Tabors and cymbals and the shouting Romans /
Make the sun dance. Hark you!' (V. iv. 51–2), and in Antium,
Drums and trumpets sounds, with great shouts of the people (V. vi. 49).
And the play's clamour lends significance to its silence.

Stage-directions are conserved in the present edition as fully
as its conventions allow. There are a few slight repositionings and
emendations recorded in the apparatus.[1] Additions to directions
are enclosed in square brackets.

The form *manet* has been changed to *remain* at I. i. 250, II. ii. 154,
and V. ii. 92. *Omnes* is omitted from the stage-directions at I. ii. 37
and III. i. 333, and given as *All* in the speech headings at I. ix. 66

1. E.g. II. i. 155, III. i. 171, III. iii. 30, 137, IV. iv. 6.

and as *Citizens* in that at IV. vi. 140. The curious error at III. iii. 135 where *cum alijs* is taken for a name has been noticed already (p. 5).

Speech-headings present an abnormal number of difficulties, sometimes occasioned by apparent misreadings, sometimes by misinterpretations of alignment, and sometimes perhaps by lack of clarity in the playwright's intentions; errors could also arise from the compositor's anticipating the wrong speech-heading or by eye-skip in the margin of the copy. Speech-headings are emended at I. i. 34, 56; II. i. 179; III. i. 229, 235, 236, 303; IV. i. 37; IV. ii. 15. They have been added at I. vi. 76; III. i. 184, 238; and multiple prefixes (e.g. *All*) have sometimes been clarified (e.g. *All Pleb.*). F's ascriptions at I. i. 27, III. i. 47, and III. i. 202 have been challenged but are retained in the present text. The high incidence of this problem in III. i (affecting both stints) suggests that the margin of the copy here may have been damaged and the speech-headings therefore illegible.

There are occasional discontinuities between directions and prefixes, owing apparently to Shakespeare's inconsistent naming of the social groups and classes of Rome. In a dozen directions and twenty-five speech-headings the term *Citizen* or its contractions is used (in both stints and in the first four acts); four directions, however, speak of *Plebeians* (II. iii. 152, 253, III. i. 178, III. iii. 38), with one speech-heading *All Ple.* at III. i. 213. The anomaly is of interest, suggesting that Shakespeare thought of the citizens collectively as *Plebeians* when they were making their presence felt as a political faction (*Enter a rabble of Plebeians*); it is therefore admitted into the present edition. A more complex situation might arise out of Shakespeare's apparently indiscriminate use of the terms *Patricians*, *Senators*, and *Nobles*. All three are named by Nicanor (IV. iii. 14–15) as enemies of the people, and senators and patricians are separately named at V. iv. 54. *Patricians* are named in one direction (II. ii. 36) and *Patri.* in two prefixes (III. i. 252, 259). *Senators* and related contractions are much commoner, occurring in six directions and sixteen prefixes. *Patricians* is clearly meant to be the more comprehensive term, and Shakespeare uses it much as, for example, it is used in Holland's Plutarch when it is asked why it was not lawful for 'the Patricians or nobles of Rome to dwell upon the mount Capitoll'.[1] Some patricians were senators, Shakespeare supposes,

---

1. Plutarch's *Moralia*, trans. Philemon Holland, 1603, p. 877. This is no. 81 of the Roman Questions, and Plutarch speaks only of Patricians. 'Patricians and nobles' is an explanatory tautology which also occurs in North's Plutarch (see Appendix, p. 328, etc.).

and some were consuls, and some were neither; there is no evidence that he weighed the constitutional roles closely. F's terms have been retained, with some amplifications of *All* to *All Pat.*, to distinguish from *All Pleb.* in III. i. In III. ii. S.D. the term *Nobles* is retained in the direction (meaning 'Patricians') but *Noble* is changed to *Pat.* in the prefix to l. 6 to keep it consistent with III. i. 259. In IV. i. S.D. the curious term *the young Nobility* is retained because it suggests that Coriolanus had a militant young following (perhaps the same nobles as at III. ii. S.D.). At III. i the stage-direction specifies *all the Gentry*, giving an expressively English flavour for which Shakespeare must be responsible; there is no ambiguity.

The play's thematic preoccupation with names lends more than casual significance to Shakespeare's change of prefix from *Martius* to *Coriolanus*; in F this occurs in Act II, but this edition follows Steevens in making the change at the moment of proclamation (I. ix. 66). Reversions to *Martius* in the play's last stage-directions are retained from the conviction that Shakespeare was responsible for them.

The present edition includes a number of editorial directions (usually traditional) indicating the character addressed; there are none in the Folio.

VII. ANOMALIES OF THE FOLIO TEXT

A few of the play's slight anomalies have been thought to carry implications about the order of its writing or about possible editorial interventions prior to printing. The first concerns Titus Lartius. He features in four of the first eight scenes (all in B's stint) described in stage-directions as *Titus Lartius* (I. i. 225, I. iv, I. vii) and *Titus* (I. v. 3) and in prefixes as *Tit.* (3) and *Lar.* or *Lart.* (12). At I. i. 238 he is mistakenly addressed as 'Titus Lucius'. In I. ix (A's stint) he figures as *Titus* in the opening direction and as *Titus Lartius* or *Lartius* in the prefixes; at the end of the scene (I. ix. 73–4) he is sent back to Corioles to further negotiations. When he reappears at II. i. 160 (also in A's stint) it is as *Titus Latius*, a mute but essential participant (see l. 185) in the ceremonies of triumph. Finally, he appears with Coriolanus at the start of III. i as *Titus Latius*, with all five prefixes *Latius*—again in A's stint.

The variant spelling *Lartius / Latius* would be of little consequence (compare *Surrey* and *Sury* in Hand D) were it not (1) for the consistency of their use in III. i, and (2) for their occurrence in the 1595 and 1603 texts of North's Plutarch. E. A. J. Honigmann finds in these circumstances 'one of the best examples of "irregular composition" in Shakespeare'.[1] He argues that II. i. 161 ff. and III. i, and possibly parts of I. i, were written before Shakespeare spotted the misprint in his Plutarch, and that the other relevant parts of Act I were therefore written later. Honigmann, however, does not take the compositors into account, and the result of doing so is ambiguous. Compositor A's sustained use of *Latius* in III. i is proof that it stood in the copy here, and strongly suggests that it did so at II. i. 160. It is not proof that *Lartius* was consistently used elsewhere—B may have ironed it out, as he virtually did the form *Scicinius* (see above, p. 3). The strongest evidence for an inconsistent spelling in the copy is offered by A's consistent use of *Lartius* in I. ix; yet it remains possible that A began his stint by regularizing to *Lartius* on aa4 of F but reverted to *Latius* (as in the copy) when he resumed on aa5 after handing over 114^v to Compositor B.[2]

Honigmann may be right to claim that Shakespeare did not always compose his scenes in the sequence in which he left them, and it would be interesting to know that he wrote early a crucial scene of his own invention—the triumphant return to Rome. The suggestion, however, creates its own difficulties. The misprint *Latius* occurs in the text of the 1595 North at the point where Cominius divides his armies into two commands, while the marginal gloss reads *Lartius*;[3] all the immediately relevant scenes of the play (I. i, iv, v, vii) have the correct form. Further episodes concerning Lartius are of Shakespeare's making; for North says nothing of the special duties in Corioles (I. ix. 73–6), reports only the ovation at Corioles (cf. I. ix) and not that at Rome (II. i), and has no occasion to make Lartius the bearer of news from Corioles (III. i). That Shakespeare thinks of Lartius as still in Corioles is shown by II. ii. 38 where Menenius speaks of a determination to send for him. Moreover, the opening twenty lines of III. i, giving Lartius special knowledge of the Volscians and concluding with a 'Welcome home' from Coriolanus, link the scene directly with I. ix. 73–6. Thus I. ix and III. i are consistent in plotting but not in spelling, I. ix and II. i are inconsistent in both plotting and spelling, and II. i and III. i are consistent in spelling but not in plotting. No valid conclusions about the order of

1. E. A. J. Honigmann, *The Stability of Shakespeare's Text*, 1965, pp. 146–7.

2. See p. 1 above, and Hinman, *First Folio*, II, p. 141. The spelling *Latius* is not used by B, but Greg thought *Lucius* at I. i. 238, possibly misread from *Latius* in the copy.

3. The 1603 edition has *Latius* in both text and margin, but *Lartius* in the index; see Appendix, p. 321.

composition can be drawn from this evidence; and we are forced to assume that the appearance of Lartius at Rome in II. i was a lapse on Shakespeare's part, and that the spelling variant has no special significance.

A second anomaly concerns the several irregular renderings of the names *Caius Martius Coriolanus*. Dover Wilson wonders if they are 'due to some editorial interference in the F. text'.[1] The reading *Marcus Caius Coriolanus* occurs twice (I. ix. 64, 66), *Martius Caius Coriolanus* twice (II. i. 164 F, II. ii. 46), and *Martius Caius* once (II. i. 163); all are in A's stint. Most editors follow Rowe in emending the order to the correct Roman one explained in North (see I. ix. 64 note). But Shakespeare's responsibility for the name-order is suggested by all three occurrences of the full name being in the same irregular order, and by Volumnia's treatment of the names in the like order at II. i. 171–3, passing from the familiar *Martius* by the less familiar *Caius* to the addition *Coriolanus*. By a kind of tactical mistake, Shakespeare treats *Martius* as a more intimate name than *Caius* (cf. II. i. 99, 'my boy Martius'), while still allowing it a general familiarity and currency; an extensive use of *Caius* in the play would have been needlessly perplexing. It is, moreover, hard to find a motive for the aberrant meddling alleged by Dover Wilson; only a pedant would intervene, and he should set things right. Compositor A is unlikely to be to blame, for he too would lack motive, and like B he sets *Caius Martius* elsewhere. The two misreadings, *Marcus* for *Martius*, are probably a slip, but they could be owed to an editorial attempt to correct to *Marcius*; the extra-metrical repetition of *Martius Caius* could only be a slip, as a misinterpreted correction would not have repeated the same name-order.[2]

Finally, there are the anomalies relating to the conspirators announced in the direction at v. vi. 8 F, *Enter 3 or 4 Conspirators of Auffidius Faction*. In the following dialogue 1. *Con.*, 2. *Con.* and 3. *Con.* are specified in the prefixes; another prefix (l. 130) specifies *All Con.*, but the direction that immediately follows reads, *Draw both the Conspirators, and kils Martius, who falles, Auffidius stands on him*. It could be that the two directions were by different hands. The first exemplifies what Greg calls the permissive or petitory direction in which 'an author shows his hand most clearly';[3] the second could be ascribed to the book-keeper,

---

1. *Coriolanus*, ed. Dover Wilson, p. 170.

2. Unless a marginal *Caius Martius* was treated as an addition, rather than a correction, and then reversed for the sake of consistency!

3. *Shakespeare First Folio*, p. 135.

witnessing to a performance that made do with two conspirators. The second, however, has still the amplitude and circumstance that suggest the author; and the book-keeper would have little motive for inserting *both*—if he were clarifying the number he would have written 'the two'.

II. THE PLAY

I. DATE OF COMPOSITION

While there is a wide measure of agreement that *The Tragedy of Coriolanus* was written after 1605 and before 1610, there is no decisive evidence to determine its year. The manifest maturity of its verse and its political insights strongly recommend a late date, and lend to a number of trivial circumstances more weight than they would otherwise carry.

That the play is not likely to have been made before the publication of Camden's *Remaines* in 1605 is indicated by a number of verbal parallels between Menenius' fable of the belly (I. i. 95–153) and the version attributed to Adrian IV by Camden under the heading of 'Wise Speeches'. The parallels (discussed below, p. 29) cannot be fortuitous, and since Camden closely follows the Latin of John of Salisbury he is unlikely to owe key words, sequences, and concepts to Shakespeare.[1] But, tantalizingly, the evidence is not quite decisive: since the dedicatory epistle of the *Remaines* is dated June 1603, a version of the manuscript must have been ready by then, and we cannot be certain that Shakespeare had not seen it.[2]

Malone, who noticed the debt to Camden, was also the first to remark the occurrence in Ben Jonson's *Epicœne* (v. iv. 227) of a phrase that seems mockingly to be borrowed from *Coriolanus*, 'you have lurch'd your friends of the better halfe of the garland, by concealing this part of the plot'. The construction *lurch'd . . . garland* is without parallel (although *lurch* is common as a gamester's term) other than in Cominius' words at II. ii. 101, 'He lurch'd all swords of the garland'. Shakespeare's heroic context lends comic point to Jonson's unheroic one, and the allusion looks like a sly glance at the characteristic rhetoric of *Coriolanus*. *Epicœne* was performed late in 1609 or early in 1610. If Truewit's jest was meant to be public, Shakespeare's play must by then have

1. For Camden's version, see Appendix, p. 369; his source is John of Salisbury, *Policraticus*, VI, p. 24.

2. Camden was among Shakespeare's admirers and counted him among the 'most pregnant witts of these our times' (*Remaines*, 1605, *Poems*, p. 8); that they knew one another is probable.

been staged; if it was covert, then Jonson had enjoyed privileged access to the manuscript. But in either case, *Coriolanus* was a live topic in 1609/10.

The 'coal of fire upon the ice' in I. i. 172 is generally agreed to hark back to the great frost of 1607/8, when the Thames was frozen over and it was reported that 'in the middle of the river' some were 'ready with pans of coals to warm your fingers'.[1] The play's image does not strictly need an occasion (it couples easily with 'hailstones in the sun') but the memory of a recent hard winter would keep the effect easy and familiar rather than odd and paradoxical. The only comparable frost in Shakespeare's time was in 1564/5, but memories of it would be remote and allusions to it do not speak of fire.[2] Another topical glance has been alleged at III. i. 95-6 where Coriolanus, fearing the diversion of power to the plebeians, warns the patricians of Sicinius, 'he'll turn your current in a ditch / And make your channel his'. It is known that in February 1609 a goldsmith, Hugh Middleton, began a scheme to bring fresh water from Hertfordshire to London and met 'many causeless hindrances and complaints of sundry persons through whose ground he was to cut his watery passage'.[3] Again, a specific occasion is superfluous but acceptable, and the image may be more complex in its sources than in its effects; Shakespeare may have known, for example, that Plutarch tells how Caius Marius compelled the plebeians to yield to him by cutting off 'the pipes and conduits by which the water ran into the Capitol'.[4] A more bizarre attempt (first made by Malone) to derive a date from a metaphor appeals from III. ii. 79, 'Now humble as the ripest mulberry', to the royal proclamation encouraging the growth of mulberries, issued on 19 January 1609. Shakespeare's earlier mulberries, however, in *A Midsummer Night's Dream* (III. i. 153) and *Venus and Adonis* (1103), make it unlikely that he was subliminally assisting the king to promote the culture of silk-worms.[5]

Some have adduced the death of Shakespeare's mother in September 1608 as a motive for the play's preoccupation with what Georg Brandes, the great Danish critic, called the 'sublime mother-form' of Volumnia. But certain hyperbolic claims about

1. From 'The Great Frost' [By Thomas Dekker?]; for relevant extracts see Bullough, v, pp. 560-3.
2. See Stow's account in Bullough, v, pp. 559-600.
3. See G. B. Harrison, 'A Note on Coriolanus', *Adams Memorial Studies* pp. 239-40.
4. See North, 'Life of Caius Marius', S.H.P., III, p. 397.
5. See III. ii. 79 note.

the virtue of Volumnia are of interest to the psychiatrist and sociologist rather than the critic,[1] and those who do not allow them would find the play strange and inept as a memorial to Mary Arden. In the quick forge and working-house of thought there must be strong links between intimate experience and public creation, but we cannot, from the nature of the evidence, hope to know what they are.

More comprehensively, many points of contact have been alleged between the political concerns of the play, and events and attitudes in the first decade of the century. Although the corn-riots were taken by Shakespeare from Plutarch, he could not have been unaware of their closeness to his own time. Food shortages in the towns and peasant discontents in the country were commonplace both in Elizabeth's reign and James's, owing to the displacement of tillage by pasture and to the wide-spread enclosure of common land. Among the several insurrec-tions, particular attention has been drawn to the Oxfordshire rising of 1597 and the Midlands disturbances of 1607/8.[2] Neither, however, is close enough in circumstance to be of service in dating the play. Shakespeare's decision to make a single crisis out of the demonstration against usury which in Plutarch preceded the episode at Corioli and the corn-rising that followed it is sufficiently vindicated by its dramatic and political fitness, without appeal to contemporary events. The play's contemporaneity is not of the kind that concerns the chronicler, as distinct from the historian, of the Jacobean scene. Nor does it offer much to the biographers. Some have tried to recognize in Martius an image of Raleigh, or Essex, or even of King James himself. It is indeed true that Raleigh supported the repeal of the Statute of Tillage with the argument that all nations abounded with corn, but that was in 1601, long before he was to record in his Remains that two million pounds was spent on the import of corn in the dearth of 1608 to 1609.[3] Nor can any conclusions be reached from Martius'

1. E.g. Furnivall's in his Introduction to the Leopold Shakespeare, 1877, 'from mothers like Volumnia came the men who conquered the known world and have left their mark for ever on the nations of Europe . . . no grander, nobler woman, was ever created by Shakespeare's art'. See also, A. Henderson, 'Coriolanus and the Grief of Shakespeare', Shakespeare in the Southwest, ed. T. J. Stafford, Texas, 1969.

2. See Bullough, v, pp. 456–8, 553–8, and E. C. Pettet, 'Coriolanus and the Midlands Insurrection of 1607', Shakespeare Survey, 3, 1950, pp. 34–42.

3. For Raleigh and Coriolanus, see A. Brandl, Shakespeare, Dresden, 1894, G. Chalmers, Supplemental Apology, 1799, M. W. MacCallum, Shakespeare's Roman Plays and their Background, 1910, and Günter Grass, see below, p. 88.

dealings with the Volscians about Shakespeare's attitude to rumours of Raleigh's treasonous transactions with Spain. Such parallels have only a retrospective and accidental validity. They testify nevertheless to the contiguity of past and present, and cannot altogether be set aside. Thus it is good to know that the virtues and defects of Essex as a soldier ('one of the first that got over the walls' but 'of a nature not to be ruled') were much like those of Coriolanus,[1] and that divided command was a theme in Shakespeare's England as well as in ancient Rome.[2] As for King James, it may be true that *Coriolanus* was the work of a 'conservative observer of the contests between James and his refractory parliaments',[3] but there is nothing to indicate that it was prompted by those contests or that the conservatism can be transposed from the Tarpeian Rock to the Tower. Both Rome and England offered older precedents for conflict between king and commons.[4]

Of attempts made to determine which of the several editions of North's Plutarch was used by Shakespeare, only one would significantly affect the date of composition. This is Halliwell-Phillips's observation that the 1612 edition is closer than any other to v. iii. 97. Where the play has, 'How more unfortunate than all living women', the 1612 edition has, 'how much more unfortunate then all the women living', while earlier editions have *unfortunately* (sometimes followed by a comma). The slight grammatical advantage that prompted the 1612 correction, however, could also have prompted Shakespeare's, and the

1. See P. A. Jorgensen, 'Shakespeare's Coriolanus: Elizabethan Soldier', *PMLA*, LXIV, 1949, pp. 221–35, and *Shakespeare's Military World*, Berkeley, 1956, ch. VI. William Barlow in *A Sermon preached at Paules Crosse* (1601), sig. C3ᵛ, said of Coriolanus that he might 'make a fit parallel for the late Earle, if you read his life'.

2. See P. A. Jorgensen, 'Divided Command in Shakespeare', *PMLA*, LXX, 1955, pp. 750–61, and *Shakespeare's Military World*, pp. 50–4. He argues that Shakespeare highlights the joint operations of Cominius and Martius, and that the Elizabethans had known the problems of joint command under Essex and Howard at Cadiz. But the instabilities of command hinted at in I. i. 260–75 are not staged in the battle-scenes, in which Martius keeps a properly subordinate role. Livy, but not Plutarch, remarks that Martius 'much obscured and stopped the light of the Consull his fame' (Holland's translation, *apud* Bullough, V, p. 499). Plutarch in the *Life of Camillus* (S.H.P., I, p. 369) sees 'of how great importance it is, in daungerous times to have but one head and generall'. The point is perennial.

3. Garnett, *apud* Furness, Variorum *Coriolanus*, 1928, p. 604.

4. *Woodstock*, for example, is an Elizabethan play about such conflicts in the time of Richard II; there are many analogous instances in Plutarch's *Lives* (e.g. those of Theseus, Romulus, and Lycurgus).

play's metre is improved by the shedding of a syllable. There are, moreover, other minute correlations that appear to indicate an earlier edition (see below, p. 29).

Metrical tests, for what they are worth, agree on indicating a comparatively late date, between *Antony and Cleopatra* and *Pericles*. The incidence of feminine endings and pause-variations is comparable with that in *Cymbeline* and *The Tempest*.[1]

All the 'objective' evidence is vulnerable and would count for little were it not for its consonance with what pedantry might call a coenaesthetic response to the art and understanding of the play. It belongs appropriately to a late stage in Shakespeare's long engagement with Plutarch. This began before *Julius Caesar* was played in 1599, and continued with *Antony and Cleopatra*, not as a sequel (Shakespeare set aside a chance to make it so)[2] but as an apt and necessary successor. And it is imaginatively fitting that Plutarch's tale of the 'pestilent plague and mischief of Cleopatra's love' should carry within it the germ of *Timon of Athens*, 'a viper and malicious man unto mankind'. *Timon* in its turn looks forward to *Coriolanus* by way of the parallel Life of Alcibiades. This is not to allege a naive pattern in Shakespeare's reading; he could easily have read all the *Lives* before he wrote *Julius Caesar*, and it would be absurd to treat him as if he were innocent of this feat until proved guilty.[3] But the complex process by which Shakespeare takes more and more from Plutarch even while disengaging from Plutarch's Aristotelean sense of life does have its simpler aspect. Shakespeare could have recognized in North's version of Amyot's preface to the *Lives* an epitome of Plutarch's wisdom: 'it is a vertue of the mind which teacheth a man the mean point, between the two faulty extremities of too much and too little, wherein the commendation of all doings consisteth.' But he knew that tragedy cannot be shaped at this temperature, and his rendering of a choice of the *Lives* endows only those who run to 'extremities' with the intensity and stature that ask expression in tragic art. *Coriolanus* is a singleminded fulfilment and exposure of this insight, and it satisfies the imagination to suppose it the last.

Trusting, therefore, to the topicality of the unsure coals upon the ice, and allowing time for the play to be familiar to audiences

---

1. Chambers , *William Shakespeare*, II, pp. 400–1.
2. According to Plutarch, Antony first fell in love with Cleopatra when he summoned her to answer charges of assisting Cassius in the civil war.
3. I carry to an extremity a point made by J. C. Maxwell in the New Cambridge *Timon of Athens*, pp. xiii–xiv.

of *Epicœne*, we may acquiesce in Chambers's necessarily tentative conclusion that the play 'may have been produced early in 1608' and therefore suppose that it was Shakespeare's final tragedy.

II. SOURCES

Coriolanus is remarkable for its apparently close dependence upon one sovereign source: 'The Life of Caius Martius Coriolanus', in *The Lives of the Noble Grecians and Romanes*, translated 'out of Greeke into French by James Amyot' and 'out of French into Englishe by Thomas North'. If Shakespeare had had no access whatever to other accounts, the play, aside from one passage, need not have been noticeably different. Nor does it matter much which edition he used, although a number of variants between copies from 1579, 1595, 1603, and 1612 have encouraged attempts to find out. The play's word *unfortunate* (v. iii. 97) occurs in the 1612 edition where earlier ones have *unfortunately*, but as already observed (above, p. 27) the fact cannot be held significant. In favour of 1579 or 1595 it has been claimed that where the play at iv. v. 83 has *in mere spite* later editions omit the words *with spite*.[1] Against 1579, it has been noted that the Folio's *Conduits* (ii. iii. 240) corresponds with 1595 *conduites* and not with 1579 *conducts*.[2] Finally, a disposition in favour of 1595 may be established by the occurrence in that edition only of the two spellings *Latius* and *Lartius* which persist in the Folio (see p. 21, above).

The one passage that strays into specific source-texts outside the 'life of Coriolanus' is the fable of the belly (i. i. 95–153), where Menenius' deceptively colloquial ease proves on analysis to be composed of an intricate mosaic of Shakespearean recollections. It can readily be demonstrated from it that Shakespeare had read not only North's version but also Holland's Livy, Camden's *Remaines*, and William Averell's *A Marvailous Combat of Contrarieties* (1588). To Holland's Livy he owes the suggestion that the belly distributes blood through the veins into all parts of the body.[3] From Camden he offers a paraphrase of words borrowed in the first instance from John of Salisbury's Latin to describe the functions of the body's 'instruments',[4] and from Averell he seems to recall more than a dozen words (some rare or unique in

1. See M. W. MacCallum, *Shakespeare's Roman Plays and their Background*, 1910, p. 458.
2. F. A. Leo *apud Coriolanus*, ed. H. H. Furness, 1928, p. 614.
3. See i. i. 134–9 note.
4. See i. i. 100–2 note.

Shakespeare) and to take a sense of the tale's comprehensive significance.[1] Other alleged parallels are faint and trivial. Although, for example, it is possible that Shakespeare read the *Fables of Bidpai* in North's translation of 1570 (see I. i. 89 note) the occurrence in it of the phrase 'pretty tale' does not prove that he did so. Nor can our confidence that he read Sidney's *Apology* rest on the alleged echo of the common words, 'there was a time'.[2]

Outside the fable there are few identifiable traces of Shakespeare's wider reading, but it does not therefore follow that he did none. At a few points editors have found it convenient to illustrate a word or a concept from other *Lives* in North's Plutarch, but there is no decisive evidence of immediate debts.[3] While there is ample proof of the scope of Shakespeare's interest in the manners and the values of Rome and the ancient world, it must rest upon the play's insights and effects, not upon specific documentation. An apparently nugatory instance of how elusive and tantalizing documentation can be is afforded by Shakespeare's choice of the names Cotus, Nicanor, and Adrian. The first is given in the play to the First Servingman of Tullus' household and does not occur in North unless we admit the form 'Cotys', the name of a King of Paphlagonia in the 'Life of Agesilaus'. Nicanor and Adrian are the play's names for the Roman and the Volscian who meet on the road in IV. iii; there are two Nicanors in the *Lives*, including one who was in command of the Athenian garrison in the 'Life of Phocion', and there is an Adrian in the 'Life of Lucullus'. One might have supposed the names chosen at random (perhaps from an index)[4] were it not that the stories of both Cotys and Nicanor offer passing analogues with that of Coriolanus: Cotys switched his allegiance from the Egyptian to the Spartan alliance, while Nicanor was treacher-

1. See K. Muir, *Shakespeare's Sources*, 1957, p. 224. Muir instances *superfluity, crammed, malicious, viand, instruments, mutually, participate, cormorant, sink, rivers,* and *dissentious*. He thinks Shakespeare may have recalled *contrariety* and *malignantly* from Averell's title-page (see IV. vi. 74 note), and that Averell's *Pantrey* prompted Shakespeare's *cupboarding* and *store-house* in Menenius' tale. For the general influence of Averell, see below, p. 54.

2. See Bullough, V, p. 551.

3. See notes on I. i. 136, I. iv. 37, II. i. 54, II. i. 174, II. iii. 95. For a possible general debt, see F. Chappell, 'Shakespeare's *Coriolanus* and Plutarch's Life of Cato', *Renaissance Papers*, 1962, no. 914, pp. 9–16.

4. All three names occur in the texts of Holland's Plutarch's *Moralia* (1603) and in his Livy (1600); the 1603 index lists Cotys, Cothus, and Nicanor, that of 1600 Cotis only. None is named in the tables appended to the several editions of North's Plutarch.

ously treated by the Athenians and plotted 'to be revenged of the city'.[1] Very few in the audience would take the point of a calculated allusion, even if the point were worth making, but it is hard to dismiss the impression that Shakespeare at some point in his reading had noticed the parallels and was associatively enlisting them.

It has been claimed that Shakespeare also read Alexandre Sylvain's *The Orator* (1596) for the scenes in which Coriolanus confronts the tribunes.[2] It is true that there are resemblances between the scenes and Sylvain's account of the 'Declamation of Spurius Servilius, who defended himselfe against the people, being by them accused for his cowardly fighting at the hill of Janicola', but they witness to the continuity of Roman history rather than to Shakespeare's shaping of the play. The analogue is valid without being necessary; as Fluellen says of the rivers of Macedon and Monmouth, 'there is salmons in both'.

A few touches of Roman circumstance seem not to be owed directly to the immediate source. Some of them suggest that Shakespeare may have looked at Plutarch's *Moralia* in Holland's translation of 1603. There, in the section *Romane Questions*, he might have found that 'wax-lights' were lit at Roman weddings (I. vi. 32), that there were many temples of Diana (v. iii. 67), and that Roman priests were called Flamens (II. i. 211).[3] It is more probable, however, that Shakespeare had a grammar-school recollection of Roman custom without the opportunity or inclination to refresh it from the *Romane Questions*. Had he done so he would have been reminded that Roman brides (Plutarch says nothing of Volscian ones) would not be allowed to 'bestride' a threshold (see IV. v. 119) since tradition, perhaps looking back to the rape of the Sabines, required that they be carried across it.[4] He might have found that the tribunes alone among the leading officers of Rome wore no embroidered purple robes and were not preceded by 'ushers' or lictors carrying fasces because 'the Tribunate was an empeachment, inhibition, and restraint of magistracie, rather than a magistracie it selfe'.[5] As it is, the play's

1. In addition to some of the references discussed, B. Kytzler cites a 'Cottus' in Golding's *Eyght Bookes of Caius Iulius Caesar*, 1565, fol. 196 (see *Archiv für das Studium der Neueren Sprachen*, 204. Band, 1968, pp. 133–7).

2. See W. Nowottny, 'Shakespeare and *The Orator*', *Bulletin de la Faculté des Lettres de Strasbourg*, XLIII, no. 8, 1965, pp. 813–33.

3. *Moralia*, trans. Holland, 1603, pp. 850, 851, 867.

4. *Moralia* (1603), p. 852. The practice is also discussed in the Life of Romulus (S.H.P., I, p. 70).

5. *Moralia* (1603), p. 877.

allusions at II. i. 67–79 and III. i. 103 suggest that Shakespeare, following the terms of North, thought of the tribunes as indeed 'magistracy itself', if only in a petty and perverse form, and the direction at II. ii. 36 seems to make a single entrance of patricians and tribunes with 'Lictors before them'.

If Shakespeare's reading extended from North into other accounts of the life of Coriolanus, it has left no identifiable marks upon the play other than the memories of Livy in the belly-fable. Wherever Livy and Plutarch differ (for example, in the names given to the tribunes, to Martius' family and to the leader of the Volscians) Shakespeare follows Plutarch. Of the other relevant histories, Plutarch's most important source, the *Roman Antiquities* of the Greek historian Dionysius of Halicarnassus, was not widely known in Shakespeare's time and only appeared in English translation in the eighteenth century.[1] Similarly, the *Roman Histories* of another Greek historian, Dio Cassius, were not known to Shakespeare, and their fragmentary story of Coriolanus resembles the play only in its version of the belly-fable, which was apparently transmitted by way of John of Salisbury and Camden.[2] Fabius Pictor's work is known only from fragments, but his account of Coriolanus is used by Livy and includes the report that he died of old age in exile among the Volscians. Valerius Maximus and Florus, historians of the first century, were compilers whose stories of Coriolanus owe much to Dionysius and Livy respectively, but with small divergences of detail and judgement.[3] Appian's Roman History, partly translated into English in 1578 and a possible source of some passages in Shakespeare's *Julius Caesar* and *Antony and Cleopatra*, deals with Coriolanus only in the fragmentary second book, which Shakespeare would not have known.[4] For an understanding of Shakespeare's play there is no need to look for its narrative source outside the 'Life of Coriolanus'. It is as well to recognize, however, that Plutarch's own version takes its place in a scheme of *topoi* and *exempla*, through which, according to one account, he was undertaking to encourage his Greek readers to assume office in the Roman

1. Dionysius' version is fully discussed by Bullough, v, pp. 462–72. *Roman Antiquities* is edited by E. Cary, 1945, 7 vols.

2. Dio's version is in *Roman Histories*, ed. Cary, 1914, I, pp. 121–2.

3. See T. Mommsen, *Römische Forschungen*, Berlin, 1879, II, pp. 113–52, and J. L. Barroll, 'Shakespeare and Roman History', *M.L.R.*, LIII, 1958. Bullough v, pp. 549–50, prints extracts from E.M.B.'s translation of Florus, but the date is thought to be 1621 and the correspondences are faint.

4. The fragments are translated by H. White in *Appian's Roman History*, 1913, 4 vols., vol. I, 'Concerning Italy'.

empire.[1] The process of interpreting and refashioning the Coriolanus story for rhetorical and political ends, remarked by Cicero,[2]
had already begun, long before Shakespeare had a hand in it.

In shaping the Coriolanus material[3] Shakespeare had no
dramatic precedent to which he might have had access. Among
the many earlier Roman plays, there is no equivalent to Pescetti's
Il Cesare, for example, to *Caesar's Revenge*, the *Antonie* of Garnier,
or Daniel's *Tragedy of Cleopatra*. There was only Alexandre
Hardy's *Coriolan*, which was certainly not published and possibly
not played until after Shakespeare's death.[4] It has been well
observed, however, that Plutarch himself was for Shakespeare
'the channel or medium of the Greek tragic spirit'.[5] By strategies
of selection and emphasis, and a few inventions, Shakespeare
compels Martius' personal fate in Plutarch's account to assume a
maximum significance in the life of the city of Rome. To begin
with, he allows to figures who appear transiently, intermittently,
or tardily in the source a continuing presence in the play,
and endows each with an individuality and a representative
significance. Menenius, merely the senate's persuasive popular
spokesman early in Plutarch's story, is given a quasi-paternal
relationship with Martius and becomes the stage voice of an
accommodating patrician wisdom. Aufidius, unnamed by Plutarch
until Coriolanus goes to Antium, is made an intimate heroic
antagonist, a personal motive for war, and at the same time the
voice of soldierly policy and craft. Volumnia, named late in the
history, is acknowledged early (Martius was 'brought up under his
mother a widowe'); but the Roman matriarch with Spartan convictions is pre-eminently Shakespeare's, with her political and
rhetorical powers extended through the play from evidence the
source partly offers in the supplication speech. The silence of Virgilia, unremarked by Plutarch, who perhaps unnoticingly gives her

1. D. A. Russell, *Plutarch*, 1973, p. 109. Russell also offers an interesting
account of the comparison of Alcibiades with Coriolanus.

2. See below, p. 74.

3. For a more detailed account of Shakespeare's use of North and Camden
see the Appendix and its notes. The fullest and best survey of the material is in
Bullough, v, pp. 453–95.

4. See below, pp. 75–6.

5. J. A. K. Thomson, *Shakespeare and the Classics*, 1952, p. 243. See also Reuben
Brower, *Hero and Saint*, 1971, Eugene Waith, *The Herculean Hero*, New York,
1962, and H. D. F. Kitto, *Poiesis: Structure and Thought*, 1966. Kitto remarks the
play's resemblance to the *Ajax* of Sophocles. For commentary on the play in
relation to its classical and literary contexts see also T. J. B. Spencer, 'Shakespeare and the Elizabethan Romans', *Shakespeare Survey*, 10, 1957, and M. St
Clare Byrne, 'Classical Coriolanus', *National Review*, xcvi, 1931.

nothing to say, is also extended through the play, and made the more striking by Valeria's social graces. The consul Cominius is in North the commander at Corioli and the orator commemorating Martius' triumph; but it is Shakespeare's initiative that not only makes him the voice of fame but also counts him among Martius' 'familliar friendes' and shows him as an active, noble, but ultimately inadequate participant in subsequent events. Shakespeare is close to North in treating Brutus and Sicinius as the 'causers and procurers' of sedition, and takes only a slight liberty when he has the people hale Brutus up and down in the last act (v. iv. 38).[1]

In reordering the events of the narrative, Shakespeare's most important move was to make a single rising out of the usury riots which led to the creation of the tribunate in 494 B.C. and the corn riots three years later. He adapts the Corioli scenes (originally coming between the two risings) with a skill in compression learned in the English history-plays, and insinuates some elements of class invective and some of warrior solidarity; North's Martius enters the city 'with very fewe men to helpe him' while Shakespeare's enters alone. The popular welcome the stage hero receives on his return to Rome is not in Plutarch, and Shakespeare allows him to be chosen consul by the senate before he canvasses the support of the people. In the history Martius follows the customs and shows his wounds without protest, but provokes the hostility of the people by turning up on election day 'with great pompe' as if presuming on their support or coercing it; he has already alienated the people by appropriating the spoils of Antium and compelling them to colonize Vellitrae, and when he is refused the consulship he tries in pique to abolish the tribunate and stop the distribution of corn. Had Shakespeare followed his source here, Martius would have appeared pettily vindictive and his integrity would have been forfeited; as it is, his physical revulsion from vulgar display looks like a kind of hubristic modesty and is of a piece with his soldier's virtue. The play omits many of the formalities of arraignment and banishment, including the senate's measures of appeasement, and it generates its theatrical and political excitements out of the confrontation between Martius and the populace. The tribunes are

1. North speaks of great 'sturre and broyle betweene the nobilitie and people' (Appendix, p. 350). Shakespeare omits all suggestion that Coriolanus was out to revenge himself only on the people, not the patricians, and allows a measure both of class recrimination and of common distress among the Romans.

made to stage-manage the banishment with what the jargon of the 1970s calls 'situation politics', and the politics can extend into the play's performance.[1] The last phase of the play owes much to the source, its tragic outcome finely turned on North's 'you have wonne a happy victorie for your countrie, but mortall and unhappy for your sonne'. Conspicuously, however, Shakespeare ignores much in the last pages of Plutarch which might have suggested a play more like that which Bradley sees—one consonant with the 'latest works, in which the powers of repentance and forgiveness charm to rest the tempest raised by error and guilt.'[2] North's Plutarch muses much upon the wonders wrought by the 'omnipotence of God' and counts among them the salvation of Rome by women who communed with Fortuna; the casualness of the allusion to the temple of Fortuna which survives in the play[3] is proof that Shakespeare recognized in Plutarch a tragedy and not a mere miracle.

It has been observed by Kenneth Muir[4] that a number of Shakespeare's contemporaries shared Shakespeare's kind of interest in Coriolanus, including Dudley Digges in *Foure Paradoxes, or politique Discourses* (1604), Bodin in *Six Bookes of a Commonweale* (translated Knolles, 1606), and Edward Forset in *A Comparative Discourse of the Bodies Natural and Politique* (1606). Muir remarks Digges's admiration for the military hero, Bodin's critical analysis of democracy, and Forset's preoccupation with the diseases of the body politic and their remedies. Shakespeare, he observes, may have been commenting on the Warwickshire troubles, but he was also writing within a literary tradition.

III. THE TRAGEDY OF CORIOLANUS

In the year 1623, when *Coriolanus* was first published, Thomas Middleton designed for the City of London 'an vnparaleld Maister-peece of Art, called the *Cristall Sanctuary*, stilde by the name of the *Temple of Integrity*, where her Immaculate selfe with all her glorious and Sanctimonious Concomitants sit transparently seene through the Crystall'. London is modelled upon Rome, and the 'Graue and Honorable Senators of the City' including 'two worthy Consulls' are invited to recognize in the crystal emblematic proof that 'There's no disguise, or hypocritike vaile' to mask Integrity's actions 'for respect or fear'. Middleton,

1. See below, p. 84.
2. A. C. Bradley, *Shakespearean Tragedy*, 1904, p. 85.
3. See v. iii. 207, and Appendix, pp. 364–5.
4. Kenneth Muir, 'The Background of *Coriolanus*', *S.Q.*, x, 1959, pp. 137–46.

to borrow the language of *Coriolanus*, was helping to throng London's large temples with the shows of peace, to keep the chairs of justice supplied with worthy men, and to recall the people and governors of the state to 'that integrity which should becom't'.[1] The pageant honoured a civic occasion, however, and belongs to the celebrative, conforming traditions of art, keeping the system going. Shakespeare's tragic art is alive to the energies and stresses of the political life of Rome that were still promptly intelligible to a Jacobean audience because they still threatened the integrity of the state. It is an art that transposes political conflict into the *agon* or ritual conflict of the theatre, and it is attended by the historical insight that sustains political continuities over a span of two thousand years. It is because it reaches both Plutarch's Rome (itself a re-creation) and Shakespeare's England that it can be held in our own time to reach Milan or Paris or East Berlin.

Shakespeare's theatrical engagement with popular risings began with the Cade scenes of *2 Henry VI*, to be extended in *Julius Caesar* and *Sir Thomas More* and consummated in *Coriolanus*. All offer ironic analogies between fact and fiction which witness to the elusive intricacy of the relationship between life and art. In the play of *Sir Thomas More*, for example, a fictional Earl of Shrewsbury speaks of the 'frowning vulgare browe' and the 'displeased commons of the cittie' while More, in a scene of Shakespeare's making, invites the mutinous apprentices to submit to the King's mercy or to persist to 'present death'.[2] Some six years after the fiction a living Earl of Shrewsbury wrote to the Earl of Kent about the 'tumultuous rable of people' assembled in the Midlands to throw down 'thos late inclosures which made them of the porest sorte reddy to pyne for want', telling of the persuasions used to disperse them—'that his Highness wolde promis to reform thos abuses' if they would return home, and of the threats to set upon them with the force proper to 'rebells and traytors'. The persuaders would have standing by 'some 40 or 50 horses well apoynted, which will run over and cutt in peeces a thousand of such naked roges as thos are'.[3] Specific debts are not in question. We need not assume that the Earl had read *Sir Thomas More, Henry VI*, or *Jack Straw*. *Sir Thomas More* looks back to events reported by Hall; it was never printed and probably

1. See III. iii. 33–6 and III. i. 158.

2. *Sir Thomas More*, ed. Tucker Brooke (*Shakespeare Apocrypha*), I. iii. 4, 8; II. iv. 173.

3. Bullough, v, p. 556.

never performed after Henry Tilney had officially enjoined its
makers to 'Leaue out the insurrection wholy and the cause
thereoff . . . att your own perrilles'.[1] A few words from its insurrection scene, where men like ravenous fishes 'woold feed on one
another', were nevertheless to find their way into *Coriolanus* to
characterize, in Rome as in London, the self-destructive potentials
of human society.[2] They survive in Bertolt Brecht's version, which
the Boss in Günter Grass's Berlin tragedy is represented as rehearsing, while the Party's tanks (like the Earl's well-appointed
horses) wait in the wings.[3]

The self-destructive potentials treated in *Coriolanus* will not,
however, yield to an exclusively political analysis. Shakespeare
perceived that in the history as Plutarch presents it the personal
crisis coincides with the political one. Hence a bleak and deso-
lating consistency of purpose manifests itself in the political
argument of the play, in its tragic catharsis, in its idiom and its
spectacle. 'He did it to please his mother,' says the first citizen,
talking of Martius' battle-service, 'and to be partly proud, which
he is, even to the altitude of his virtue' (I. i. 37–9). The wisdom
that cries out in the streets contributes much to our understanding
of Martius, but it includes the second citizen's answer, 'What
he cannot help in his nature, you account a vice in him' (I. i. 40–1).
The quick, expendable exchanges of the plebeians intimate the
comprehensive structure of the play. Pride is the essence of
Martius' nature, at once his vice and his virtue, the instrument
of his service to the Roman state and the source of his bond with
his mother. The tragedy requires, however, that the multiple
nature of the virtue and the pride be fully experienced until its
human possibilities are exhausted, both in the state and in its
hero.

For Martius, pride is co-extensive with those patrician preroga-
tives of honour and power that must not be forfeited:

> Your dishonour
> Mangles true judgement, and bereaves the state

1. See R. C. Bald, '*The Booke of Sir Thomas More* and its problems', *Shakespeare Survey*, 2, 1949, p. 50. The politics of the play are admirably discussed by
R. W. Chambers in A. W. Pollard (ed.), *Shakespeare's Hand in Sir Thomas More*,
1923.

2. See I. i. 187, and note; and *More* (ed. Brooke), II. iv. 106–7. Shakespeare,
characteristically for this play, omits the fishes. Cf. Breughel the Elder, 'Big
Fish Eat Little Fish' (*Graphic Worlds of Peter Breughel*, ed. H. A. Klein, New
York, 1963, p. 137).

3. See 'The Uprising of June 17, 1953' by Uta Gerhardt, in Günter Grass,
The Plebeians Rehearse the Uprising, 1967.

Of that integrity which should becom't,
Not having the power to do the good it would
For th'ill which doth control't.   (III. i. 156–60)

But the significance of the indictment cannot be weighed without recognizing that it is one contribution among many to the play's probings of the integrity of the state.

Our understanding of the unity of the state is initially dominated by Menenius' celebrated parable of the belly, which is an exquisite piece of political and theatrical tactics. Menenius' wit and histrionic skill, comparing the senators to the belly and the citizens to the mutinous limbs, subdue the stage audience of rebels to silence and awaken the theatre audience to a more than usual alertness to a range of metaphors still to come. The fable is so designed and elaborated that Shakespeare at a glance can recall the analogue of state and body that underlies it. Thus the 'navel of the state' is threatened (III. i. 122), the people are 'this bosom multiplied' (III. i. 130), the tribunes are the people's 'mouths' told to rule their 'teeth' (III. i. 35), Coriolanus is a gangrened limb (III. i. 304), the country is 'cankered' (IV. v. 92), and war will be poured like a purgative 'Into the bowels of ungrateful Rome' (IV. v. 131).

Shakespeare's contemporaries had inherited from many sources the conviction that the state is, or ought to be, a unity made from a variety of functions, a system of mutual responsibilities. The organic theory of the state, which finds a model for such a system in the human body, is at least as old as the fables of Bidpai and still flourishes in the positivist traditions of sociology. Shakespeare found his fable in Plutarch but was interested enough to pursue it in the versions of Livy, Camden, and William Averell.[1] He makes the Roman workmen familiar with the postulates (their ringleader 'speaks', to Menenius' ironical satisfaction, of 'the kingly-crowned head, the soldier-hand and the counsellor-heart'), and the apprentice in his theatre might have known them too—transmitted from John of Salisbury by the sermons and homilies that taught the subject to know his place.[2] But it does not therefore follow that Shakespeare vindicates the Menenius of the play. For the art that establishes the fable in the theatre also constrains it within the play's political structure.

1. See above, p. 29.
2. The most accessible edition of the homilies is by John Griffiths, *The Two Books of Homilies Appointed to be Read in Churches*, 1859; the best account of their influence is Alfred Hart, *Shakespeare and the Homilies*, Melbourne, 1934.

The protest in Plutarch's account at this point is occasioned not
by famine (that comes later) but by war and usury, and by trans-
posing the story Shakespeare puts it under a severe strain. Its
claim is inept, food is clearly and literally not being distributed
and the people, not the patricians, have to make do with the
bran. Menenius in the play momentarily saves the situation not
by his wisdom but by his wit, silencing the most thoughtful of the
citizens (the great toe of the assembly) with comic abuse. Plutarch allows Menenius and his tale not a greater significance but
a greater dignity. He tells how the people 'offering no creature
any hurt or violence' leave Rome and camp upon the Holy Hill.
Menenius comes as emissary from the senate to pacify them with
a formal oration 'knit up with a notable tale'; conditions are
made and tribunes appointed 'whose office should be to defend
the poore people from violence and oppression'. Thus Plutarch's
Menenius established the mood in which responsible political
thinking can begin. Remembering Shakespeare's Thomas More
at St Martin's gate, where enlightened authority confronts the
innocent inhumanity of the crowd, we may imagine the play
much closer to the source. As it is, the tribunes are appointed at
the other side of the city by 'the other troop', while Menenius
side-steps the grievance of the people and, as one of them puts it,
fobs off their disgrace with a tale. His adroit and disingenuous
deployment of a great and valid political parable establishes his
character but subtly diminishes his wisdom. The spectacle
ironically makes Menenius himself a conspicuous belly among
mutinous members (idle and unactive, a gulf, making the flesh
smile) and, finding the crowd still restless after his performance,
he betrays his private conviction in the sour apostrophe that
announces the entrance of Martius:

> Rome and her rats are at the point of battle;
> The one side must have bale.   (I. i. 161–2)

Since the 'limbs' have become the 'rats' (rats to gnaw the garners
as Martius has it) the collaborative functioning of the state is a
fable only. Menenius reverts to the raw naiveties of class conflict;
Rome for him is the patricians while for the tribunes it is the
people, 'What is the city but the people?' (III. i. 197). For Martius,
as events will prove, it is neither.

The people, taunted by Menenius to make ready their 'stiff
bats and clubs', find themselves confronted by the figure and the
wrath of Martius, a very different body. The spectacle realizes a
formidable presence already insinuated into the verse:

> you may as well
> Strike at the heaven with your staves, as lift them
> Against the Roman state, whose course will on
> The way it takes, cracking ten thousand curbs
> Of more strong link asunder than can ever
> Appear in your impediment.   (I. i. 66–71)

The description of the Roman state is a proleptic invocation of
Martius. The body-politic is here the Achillean body, a war-
machine, a destructive, neutral, advancing *thing*, yielding to no
human obstacle. By this commanding metaphor Rome and its
hero are indivisible, but the body of Martius cannot be accommo-
dated into the mood of the tale and his presence is not an en-
dorsement of its moral-of-state but a challenge to it.

There is much in Plutarch about figures, like Lycurgus, Numa,
Aristides, and Cato, who 'by their only vertue and wisdom' have
been 'governors in their common wealth' and have 'thereby
achieved to great honor and estimacion'.[1] They are admired for
possessing and promoting precisely the qualities of civility which
Martius is said to be without.[2] From one point of view, the socially
tolerant one that Menenius is made to represent, the defect is of
manners merely; he is 'bred i'th'wars' and 'ill school'd / In bolted
language', like Shakespeare's Henry V or Plutarch's Marius. But,
more radically, he is committed to a different relationship to the
state and to a different mode of virtue. North's Plutarch offers the
necessary clue:

Now in those dayes, valiantnes was honoured in Rome above
all other vertues: which they called *Virtus*, by the name of
vertue selfe, as including in that generall name, all other
speciall vertues besides.

Valiantness, as the long procession of the *Lives* reveals, was for the
cities and states of the ancient world not only a cult but also a
condition of survival. Those who create a commonwealth must be
prepared to defend and perhaps to extend it, but there are many,
like Pelopidas and Marcellus, 'valiant, painful and noble-
minded',[3] whose prerogative and special responsibility it is to kill
and to die for their countries. Martius is among them. But
Shakespeare brings to Plutarch an answering conviction, more
intimately felt, acquired in the course of his long re-creation of the
Wars of the Roses, that the habit of violence in war generates

1. 'The Comparison of Aristides with Marcus Cato' (S.H.P., III, p. 205).
2. See North, Appendix, p. 314.
3. 'The Comparison of Marcellus with Pelopidas' (S.H.P., III, p. 103).

a destructive self-effacing form of heroic commitment, best
expressed in the figure of the young Clifford at St Albans:

> Let no soldier fly.
> He that is truly dedicate to war
> Hath no self-love; nor he that loves himself
> Hath not essentially, but by circumstance,
> The name of valour.   (*2H6*, v. ii. 36–40)

Shakespeare's Martius is truly dedicate to war, has in Clifford's
sense 'no self-love', and would win essentially and not by circumstance the 'name of valour'. Cominius' words directly recall
Plutarch's,

> It is held
> That valour is the chiefest virtue and
> Most dignifies the haver.   (ii. ii. 83–5)

But they do not exhaust the possibilities of their claim on the
ethical imagination; only Martius' experience does that.

The 'name of valour' is by ancient and renaissance tradition
the commemorative end of heroic endeavour, and the play
Coriolanus is in this perspective the tragic history of a name:

> For what he did before Corioles, call him,
> With all th'applause and clamour of the host,
> Martius Caius Coriolanus!   (i. ix. 62–4)

It is a fortuitous irony that at the climax of its acclamation the
strict Roman form of the name a little miscarries, tempting editors
to emend to 'Caius Martius Coriolanus'. But there is no mis-
carriage of effect. As D. J. Gordon puts it, 'Name is Fame, is
Honour, and is won by deeds; in Rome, by deeds in war.'[1]

The conviction that valour is the whole of virtue informs the
terse logic by which Coriolanus (the 'addition' is apt) indicts the
populace. Where there is no valour there can be no desert—no
right to eat, let alone to govern:

> being press'd to the war,
> Even when the navel of the state was touch'd,
> They would not thread the gates: this kind of service
> Did not deserve corn gratis.   (iii. i. 121–4)

That implacable movement of argument and syntax constitutes,
in one aspect, the integrity of Coriolanus; his *virtus* demands

1. In G. I. Duthie (ed.), *Papers Mainly Shakespearian*, 1964, p. 4. See also
L. F. Dean, 'Voice and Deed in *Coriolanus*', *University of Kansas City Review*,
xxi, 1955.

the inexorable satisfaction of a military ideal. Menenius in contrast represents the mature patrician awareness that the state
must somehow be kept whole, saved from disintegration. The
tragedy discovers that the rival martial and political virtues
sustaining the city of Rome can be reconciled only in its hero's
death.

Coriolanus is 'too absolute' (III. ii. 39) and will not dissemble
with his nature. He will not honour the wisdom that Amyot
looks to find in a man 'experienced in the affairs of the world',
nor exercise 'the good judgement to discern what is to be said,
and what to be left unsaid, and what would do more harm to have
it declared, than do good to have it reproved or condemned'. The
'true drift' of such a man, says Amyot, 'ought to be to serve the
commonweal'.[1] In the play the politic traditions are variously
represented by Menenius, Cominius, and Volumnia, with Plutarch's judgement upon Coriolanus largely assigned to Aufidius
(IV. vii. 35–53). The tragedy requires, however, that the imper-
sonal stresses of the Roman state be acted out in the relationship
between the Roman mother and her Roman son.

Plutarch's Volumnia appears late in the story, to speak less
about her son's 'former valiancy and glory' than about the
'common misery' that he has brought upon the 'common weal'.[2]
It is Shakespeare's imaginative initiative that identifies her with
Roman heroic tradition and attributes to her tutelage the youth-
ful Martius' inclination to the wars that Plutarch reports in his
early pages. His play and his schooling are, as it were, retro-
spectively prefigured in the one son that Shakespeare allows him
(North speaks of 'children'), and attested in a wry valedictory
tribute:

> You were us'd to load me
> With precepts that would make invincible
> The heart that conn'd them.   (IV. i. 9–11)

Volumnia's heroic precepts are not attributable to her character
merely, nor to her role as mother (even widowed mother), but to
the matronly disciplines of Rome and Sparta.[3] Yet her indulgent
delight in the name of valour ('Coriolanus, must I call thee?')
is to be much tempered by political sagacity, and the exchanges

1. 'Amyot to the Readers' (S.H.P., I, pp. xx, xxi).
2. See North, Appendix, p. 360.
3. See particularly Holland's Plutarch, *Moralia* (1603), pp. 479–82, 'The
Apophthegmes of Lacedaemonian Women'; also pp. 443–79, for other apophthegms, customs, and ordinances. Much of the material is found scattered in
the *Lives*, especially those of Lycurgus and Agesilaus.

of Act III witness to an intimately transmitted education in public values that has gone awry:

> I talk of you.
> Why did you wish me milder? Would you have me
> False to my nature? Rather say I play
> The man I am.   (III. ii. 13–16)

In ways that recall *King John*,[1] Shakespeare enlists sympathy for the *virtus* that disdains compromise. Volumnia, like Menenius, knows what the time craves as physic (III. ii. 33) and has a brain that can lead her use of anger 'To better vantage' (III. ii. 31):

> O sir, sir, sir.
> I would have had you put your power well on
> Before you had worn it out.   (III. ii. 16–18)

She is skilled in what the Bastard of the earlier play calls 'commodity', and behind her fashioning it is possible to detect Shakespeare's mastery of the politics of English history.

Roman history, as North tells it, however, offers example and precept enough to vindicate her, even when she recommends policy to the warrior.[2] We are left only a little to wonder how Volumnia, pursuing the tactics of class-warfare, can attribute a soldier's cunning to Martius himself:

> I have heard you say,
> Honour and policy, like unsever'd friends,
> I'th'war do grow together.   (III. ii. 41–3)

Some interpretations of stage convention claim that no character offers false data that cannot be checked from the evidence of the play. But Volumnia is convicted of an error of judgement; the Martius of the staged events at Corioli can hardly be conceived as a politic warrior. It is only in the play, not in the source, that he is left 'himself alone, / To answer all the city' (I. iv. 51–2). Moreover, it is his uncomplicated, even uncontaminated, valour that prevails. While the parallel with Essex (the first to scale the walls of Cadiz) is an interesting one, it cannot be taken as a warning to irresponsible adventurers. Nor can it make Barnaby Rich's

---

1. E.g. *King John*, II. i. 561–98.
2. In the 'Comparison of Alcibiades with Martius Coriolanus', Plutarch finds both to be 'wise and politick in the wars'. In the *Moralia* we are told that the Spartans sacrificed an ox to Mars in celebration of a victory by stratagem and a cock for one gained by 'fine force', 'by which meanes, they occasioned their leaders to be not only valiant, but also politicke warriors' (trans. Holland, 1603, p. 477).

point that 'Many mo fieldes have been lost for want of pollicy than for want of strength'.[1] When Martius 'sensibly outdares his senseless sword' (I. iv. 53) he is not displaying the military good sense that allows Cominius to retire to win his purpose (I. vi. 50), but he therefore prevails to become 'lord of the field' and to do the state some service.

When Coriolanus dismisses his mother's appeal with contempt ('Tush, tush!') and accedes to it only with ironic reluctance, he may be counted among those followers of the wars described by Thomas Churchyard who 'knowe not how to flatter and faune, or crouch and coursie for commoditie'.[2] But Shakespeare's realizations cannot be reached even by Churchyard's lively Elizabethan prose. Volumnia's plea for commodity ('Go to them with this bonnet in thy hand') is persuasive in gesture and in argument, but Coriolanus' acquiescence does not surrender his convictions either as a soldier or as a patrician:

> I'll mountebank their loves,
> Cog their hearts from them, and come home belov'd
> Of all the trades in Rome. (III. ii. 132–4)

His patrician contempt for tradesmen features the politic patrician as a mountebank, a charlatan in the market-place.

The tragic conflict within the Roman state is poised proleptically upon Volumnia's sardonic recantation, 'Come all to ruin' (III. ii. 125), and Coriolanus' insight into the stress imposed upon his own nature, 'You have put me now to such a part which never / I shall discharge to th'life' (III. ii. 105–6). The provisional resolutions of the history plays, through the resourceful Bastard, the 'vile politician' Bolingbroke, and the 'princely hypocrite' Prince Hal, are frustrated in the market-place and forum of Coriolanus' Rome. Because Coriolanus cannot dissemble with his nature and win the uncritical good will of the populace, the tribunes are able to turn his choleric and destructive energies back upon himself.[3] His performance collapses under the taunt of 'traitor' (the word

1. Cited Jorgensen, *PMLA*, LXIV, 1949, p. 224, who also reports the Essex exploit at Cadiz (p. 222).

2. Cited Jorgensen, *PMLA*, LXIV, 1949, p. 227.

3. For the 'choleric' disposition of Martius as reported in North, see Appendix, pp. 342 and 354. For the general use of the psychological type see L. B. Campbell, *Shakespeare's Tragic Heroes*, 1930, and for specific applications to Coriolanus, O. J. Campbell, *Shakespeare's Satire*, 1943, and J. W. Draper, 'Shakespeare's Coriolanus: a Study in Renaissance Psychology', *West Virginia University Bulletin*, III, 1939. The earliest known *Coriolan* play has 'Ira' for prologue (see below, p. 75).

is not in North). How can he be a traitor? To serve Rome is to
fight for Rome. Rome is an ideal of military virtue. What is
Rome but the valorous? How can cowards hold power in Rome?
But they can, of course. His heroic logic confronts the incantatory
manifestation of the people's malevolent power ('It shall be so, it
shall be so'), but the most valiant and therefore the most complete
Roman is banished the city by the cowardly and therefore un-
Roman rabble.

The engagement and alienation of the audience's sympathies
are so regulated that it is not easy wholly to acquiesce in Coriolanus' sense of the significance of his banishment or wholly to
resist it. Had he played his civil role to the general satisfaction,
what then? Politic good sense, of the kind displayed by the wiser
Elizabethan theorists, like Sir Thomas Smith,[1] might answer that
all would have been well. But within the mood of the play both
Coriolanus' tragic sense of life and Shakespeare's compel us to
recognize that a compliant hero would not then have played the
man he was, and would have been false to the nature that tri-
umphed at Corioli. As his valedictory imprecation proclaims
(III. iii. 120–35), the ignorant have the power to banish their
defenders, but the *virtus* to which the city owes its survival cannot
without catastrophe be precipitated from the Tarpeian rock,
cast into exile, or tamed in the market-place. We therefore admire the disinherited Roman who cries 'There is a world elsewhere' far more than we could the conforming mountebank.

The admiration is not, however, unconditional. Shakespeare
measures the increasing distance between sympathy for Martius
and the common range of human sympathies:

> You common cry of curs! whose breath I hate
> As reek o'th'rotten fens, whose loves I prize
> As dead carcasses of unburied men
> That do corrupt my air: I banish you!   (III. iii. 120–3)

The peculiar revulsion that the rhetoric expresses and provokes
is not wholly contained by the ugly political situation; it is more
than defiance of a lynching mob. To distinguish it from a less

1. *De Republica Anglorum*, 1583. Smith represents the government of England
as a mixed constitution, allowing degrees of authority to both King and
Parliament. For a full account of the idea (which goes back to Lycurgus) and
for its relevance to the play, see C. C. Huffman, *Coriolanus in Context*, Lewisburg,
1971. While the play and its source can provide material for those who advo-
cate 'balanced co-existence', however, I do not believe that the play is an
exercise in such advocacy. See also J. E. Phillips, *The State in Shakespeare's
Greek and Roman Plays*, New York, 1940.

obsessive indignation we may recall Alcibiades (Coriolanus' counterpart in Plutarch) from *Timon of Athens*:

> Banish me!
> Banish your dotage! Banish usury
> That makes the Senate ugly.   (III. v. 98–100)

Alcibiades' wrath is of the moral kind, the acquisitive corruption of the Athenian senate being manifest to normal humane judgement. But Coriolanus apparently recoils from bad breath. In Jack Cade's London the breath that 'stinks with eating toasted cheese' offends within the compass of Shakespearean good humour.[1] But here the breath that moves the 'cry of curs' is the reek of death, and a symptom of the reversion of the louts to their craven animal nature. Elsewhere the 'mutable rank-scented meinie' are rats, geese, crows, curs, and a beast with many heads.[2] Characteristically, Martius' physical nausea reaches us as a judgement—that of the triumphant body upon common carcasses. It is another manifestation of pride, and our response to it may well depend less on our ethical and political dispositions than on the commonness of our own carcasses.

The language and the central experiences of the play compel more than usually physical intensities of reaction. The effects are both general and local. By making Coriolanus shrink from displaying his wounds to the people (in Plutarch he readily goes through with it) Shakespeare focuses further action and spectacle upon the hero's body, and much of the thought and metaphor is attentive to the unity of body and mind. It is 'integrity' in yet another sense: we are under pressure to realize that all qualities of the spirit have a physical manifestation. Thus Aufidius speaks of 'thought' being 'brought to bodily act' (I. ii. 5), and Volumnia, in extravagant pantomime, tells Coriolanus that 'Action is eloquence' (III. ii. 76) when she briefs him for the market-place. But it is Coriolanus himself who, in refusing to bow or kneel, makes the most uncompromising claim upon the idea:

> I will not do't,
> Lest I surcease to honour mine own truth,
> And by my body's action teach my mind
> A most inherent baseness.   (III. ii. 120–3)

The claim is that a quality can be physically struck into the mind by acting the gesture that expresses it. In this regard, as in

1. *2 Henry VI*, IV. vii. 10–11.
2. I. i. 248, I. i. 171, III. i. 138, I. i. 167, IV. i. 1–2.

others, the play offers an ultimate expression of certain impulses in the heroic tradition that Rome inherited from Sparta, proclaiming the precedence of deeds over words.[1]

The body's action teaches the mind, and the accomplished pupil is composed wholly of power and motion, as in this resolution of harvester and soldier:

> His bloody brow
> With his mail'd hand then wiping, forth he goes
> Like to a harvest man that's task'd to mow
> Or all, or lose his hire.   (I. iii. 34–7)

And Shakespeare is still thinking of the motion of sickle and sword-arm when Volumnia awaits the triumph in Rome:

> Death, that dark spirit, in's nervy arm doth lie,
> Which, being advanc'd, declines, and then men die.
>   (II. i. 159–60)

What is offered for our admiration strikes coldly upon our ordinary affections, but it is nevertheless fully consonant with the invincible movement of the play.

Shakespeare, to cull Cominius' phrase, does not lack voice to utter the deeds of Coriolanus:

> as weeds before
> A vessel under sail, so men obey'd
> And fell below his stem: his sword, death's stamp,
> Where it did mark, it took; from face to foot
> He was a thing of blood, whose every motion
> Was tim'd with dying cries.   (II. ii. 105–10)

The language of the play sometimes reverts to the more familiar conventions of heroic theatre ('If any think brave death outweighs bad life'), but at its representative best it moves with implacable weight—its every motion timed with dying cries. The authority of Cominius' tribute owes everything to Shakespeare's art, but what he makes he unmakes, through processes

1. Plutarch both in the *Moralia* and in the lives of Lycurgus and Agesilaus often reports the Spartan plainness of speech in the service of war. He tells how the Spartan kings did sacrifice to the muses before battle, so that 'the Muses should present themselves before the soldiers' eyes, to prick them forwards to do some noble acts of worthy memory' ('Life of Lycurgus', S.H.P., I, p. 144.) For the larger claims for the unity of mind and body compare Florio's Montaigne, bk. II, ch. xvii, 'Of Presumption': 'The motions and actions of the body, give life unto words. . . . The body hath a great part in our being; and therein keepes a special rancke' (ed. Seccombe, 1908, II, pp. 452–3). See also III. ii. 76 note.

that gather momentum when Coriolanus, by the voice and breath of the people, has been 'whooped out of Rome'.

The intricate connections between breath, voice, name, and fame have been admirably charted by D. J. Gordon[1] and already touched upon in an earlier context. They relate the physical values and revulsions to the play's politics. It may be doubted if Shakespeare with any precision was keeping track of either Roman or Elizabethan election procedures,[2] but there is no mistaking his recognition that the distances between judging, voting, voicing, and shouting are slight when it comes to the exercise of popular power, and the tribunes contrive to close them: 'with a din confus'd / Enforce the present execution / Of what we chance to sentence' (III. iii. 20–2). Thus the 'stinking breaths' that Coriolanus is obliged to beg in the market-place are those that whoop him out of Rome.

The play also evokes ranges of physical response of quite other kinds, more obliquely connected with its central conflicts. Among the voices silenced by the cry of the people, that of Cominius pleads a love for his country 'more tender, / More holy and profound, than mine own life, / My dear wife's estimate, her womb's increase / And treasure of my loins' (III. iii. 112–15). The impulse extinguished here by the impatience of the tribunes is one that the play makes familiar elsewhere. It values the sensual satisfactions of dedicated violence above those of the nuptial and family affections. It first makes its presence felt in the third scene, with an art that reconciles cruel ecstasies with domestic solicitude:

> I pray you, daughter, sing, or express yourself in a more comfortable sort. If my son were my husband I should freelier rejoice in that absence wherein he won honour, than in the embracements of his bed, where he would show most love.
> (I. iii. 1–5)

A slight suggestion for the family setting might be found in the immediate source,[3] but for comparable outrage upon quotidian values we may amplify Plutarch's Rome from his Sparta, where the women rejoice to hear their sons have been killed in battle

1. 'Name and Fame: Shakespeare's Coriolanus', in *Papers Mainly Shakespearian*, ed. G. I. Duthie, Aberdeen University Studies, 147, 1964.

2. Referred to by Gordon and fully described by J. E. Neale, *The Elizabethan House of Commons*, 1949, pp. 87 ff. For the Roman procedures see Bullough, v, pp. 467–9.

3. See Appendix, p. 359, where the ladies call upon Volumnia and find her with her daughter-in-law.

and are capable of murdering them if they survive.[1] The heroic rapture blights the very sources of creative life:

> The breasts of Hecuba
> When she did suckle Hector, look'd not lovelier
> Than Hector's forehead when it spit forth blood
> At Grecian sword contemning. (i. iii. 40–3)

Life is transmitted from body to body in the service of death: 'Thy valiantness was mine, thou suck'st it from me' (iii. ii. 129). But valiantness offers other intimate satisfactions, felt when Martius embraces Cominius outside Corioli ('As merry as when our nuptial day was done') and when Aufidius takes him 'hotly' in his arms more 'rapt' than on his wedding night. The effect directly contrived at some moments of the play is subliminally felt at others:

> We have been down together in my sleep,
> Unbuckling helms, fisting each other's throat—
> And wak'd half dead with nothing. (iv. v. 125–7)

It is not surprising that *Coriolanus* has had its share of attention from psychoanalytical critics.[2]

The displacement of the values of peace by those of war registers both viscerally, as the life-sustaining affections are metamorphosed into state-sustaining obsessions, and at the level of social comedy in the gossip of Aufidius' kitchen:

> Let me have war, say I. It exceeds peace as far as day does night: it's sprightly walking, audible, and full of vent. Peace is

1. See *Moralia* (1603), pp. 479–82. The stories include one of particular relevance to the play in i. iii: 'A ladie there was of *Ionia*, who bare herselfe verie proud of a worke in tapistrie which she herselfe had made, most costly and curiously; but a Laconian dame shewed unto her, foure children, all verie well given and honestly brought up; Such as these (quoth she) ought be to the works of a ladie of honour, and herein should a noble woman in deed, make her boast and vaunt herselfe' (p. 481).

2. See especially, Charles K. Hofling, 'An Interpretation of Shakespeare's *Coriolanus*', *American Imago*, 14, 1957, pp. 411–31 (partly reprinted in *Twentieth-Century Interpretations of Coriolanus*, ed. J. E. Phillips, 1970). Hofling sees Martius as a 'phallic-narcissistic character' whose need for 'exhibitionistic, pseudo-masculine behaviour', owed to his morbid relationship with his mother, is finally displaced by 'a partial emotional maturation' nourished by the silent relationship with Virgilia. See also Robert J. Stoller, 'Shakespearean Tragedy: *Coriolanus*', *Psychoanalytic Quarterly*, xxxv, 1966, pp. 263–74. Stoller is pre-occupied with the 'muscular and psychological hardness' of Coriolanus 'who can scarcely help himself from penetrating everyone he meets either by his explosive words or his weapons'. For a more socially directed analysis see M. D. Faber, 'Freud and Shakespeare's Mobs', *Literature and Psychology*, xv, 1965, pp. 238–55. For historical and biographical accounts, see above, p. 26.

a very apoplexy, lethargy; mulled, deaf, sleepy, insensible; a
getter of more bastard children than war's a destroyer of men.
(IV. v. 228–32)

Plutarch tells how a certain Aetolian asserted that for real men
war is better than peace and was answered by Zeuxidamas, 'By
Heaven, no; but for such men death is better than life.'[1] Such
men are inhuman.

Coriolanus' inhumanity is felt in the play as a consummation
of his virtue. The integrity of the soldier destroys the integrity of
the man. The outcome is shadowed in the early battle scenes,
in the imagery (wounds may 'fester 'gainst ingratitude, / And
tent themselves with death'[2]) and in the episode, of Shakespeare's devising, in which Martius forgets the name of the
prisoner he had hoped to free and, in more senses than he intends,
his wrath overwhelms his pity.[3] He speaks slightingly of having
'foil'd some debile wretch' (I. ix. 48) and this sickeningly authentic phrase, offered in modesty, might be recalled when
Coriolanus in Rome is made to hear his 'nothings monster'd' in
the encomium of Cominius:

> his doubled spirit
> Requicken'd what in flesh was fatigate,
> And to the battle came he, where he did
> Run reeking o'er the lives of men, as if
> 'Twere a perpetual spoil.   (II. ii. 116–20)

After that, the tribute to his noble indifference to loot is un-
comprehendingly perverse:

> Our spoils he kick'd at,
> And look'd upon things precious as they were
> The common muck of the world.   (II. ii. 124–6)

The distant but distinct play upon 'spoil' is a presentiment
however, of Cominius' appalled sense of Coriolanus's virtue when
he returns to lead the Volscians against Rome:

> He is their god. He leads them like a thing
> Made by some other deity than nature,
> That shapes man better; and they follow him
> Against us brats, with no less confidence
> Than boys pursuing summer butterflies,
> Or butchers killing flies.   (IV. vi. 91–6)

Divinity manifests itself in the wanton destruction of life, whether
evanescent and vulnerable (the father like the son, pursuing

1. *Moralia* (1603), p. 458.   2. I. ix. 30–1.   3. I. ix. 80–9.

summer butterflies) or mean and pestiferous. By metamorphosis, as a grub into a butterfly, 'This Martius is grown from man to dragon: he has wings: he's more than a creeping thing' (v. iv. 12–14). Shakespeare recalls what was perhaps his first image of heroic man, used of Henry V at the beginning of *Henry VI*: 'His arms spread wider than a dragon's wings; / His sparkling eyes, replete with wrathful fire'.[1] Spenser, conjuring up the dragon that the Red Cross Knight encounters, invokes exactly the reciprocal image; its burning eyes are like beacons warning 'that enemies conspyre, / With fire and sword the region to inuade'.[2] But Henry's 'Virtue' takes him dragon-like into France and the early play is untroubled by the ironies of the metaphor. Coriolanus, in the terms of medieval romance, is the knight become the dragon. The terms, however, are not medieval; the dominant dehumanizing word is not 'dragon' but 'thing', from the hyperbole of Aufidius ('Thou noble thing') to the steep caricature of Menenius:

> When he walks, he moves like an engine and the ground shrinks before his treading. He is able to pierce a corslet with his eye, talks like a knell, and his hum is a battery. He sits in his state as a thing made for Alexander. What he bids be done is finished with his bidding. He wants nothing of a god but eternity, and a heaven to throne in. (v. iv. 18–25)

The 'thing made for Alexander' is an idol and image, the 'engine' a machine of war—unmoving and moving renderings of the same divine and brutish presence. The man has become the god, the machine, and the butcher; the protesting hyperboles belong both to the tragic and to the comic imagination. Cominius recognizes the god turned butcher destroying the life of Rome, and Menenius sees the grotesque outrage upon human dispositions and affections ('There is no more mercy in him than there is milk in a male tiger'). Without depending upon sententious reflection, Shakespeare diagnoses the great hubristic drive that moved those heroes of the ancient world whose god was Mars—an uncompromising ideal of military virtue. Aufidius' delighted greeting ('thou Mars') makes casual and familiar what is elsewhere formidable and alien, the metamorphosis of human into inhuman being.

It is yet another discovery of the tragedy, however, that such a metamorphosis cannot be sustained through the pupal phase of the encampment outside Rome. To pursue the metaphor, the

1. *1 Henry VI*, I. i. 11–12.   2. *Faerie Queene*, I. XI. xiv.

processes of histolysis destroying the human larva and those of histogenesis shaping the emerging dragon are finally arrested. In a sense, the processes have been at work from the beginning, with Rome itself the larva through which creeping things become flying things. It has been observed that the play works through a cumulative repetition of certain effects and experiences,[1] and most are related to the endeavour of the city community to contain its own hero: Menenius' tactical fable, the several attempts to groom Martius for the market-place and the forum, and the successive pleas for Rome outside its walls, all prefigure the last encounter between mother and son. Both the analogical structure of the play and its unflagging progress come to the same point of crisis, and only then are we made fully to realize their significance. The effect is more of Shakespeare's making than Plutarch's. North says that Coriolanus' 'chiefest purpose was, to increase still the malice and dissention between the nobilitie, and the communaltie' and reports the vaunt that 'Romaines were no men that would ever yeld for feare'.[2] Shakespeare in the last phase of the play attributes to Coriolanus no patrician allegiance and allows the Romans no significant residual powers of resistance.

As playwright and historian Shakespeare had long recognized the simplicities and complexities through which inhuman energies are generated from human commitments. Clifford's selfless dedication to war, already remarked, precipitates those atrocities at Wakefield to which the future Richard III responds with murderous valour:

> I cannot weep, for all my body's moisture
> Scarce serves to quench my furnace-burning heart;
> Nor can my tongue unload my heart's great burden,
> For self-same wind that I should speak withal
> Is kindling coals that fires all my breast,
> And burns me up with flames that tears would quench.
> To weep is to make less the depth of grief.
> Tears then for babes; blows and revenge for me!
> Richard, I bear thy name; I'll venge thy death,
> Or die renowned by attempting it.   (*3H6*, II. i. 79–88)

Some of the same elements (fire, tears, name, renown) coalesce with fresh intensity and finer control in Cominius' report:

---

1. Reuben A. Brower, *Hero and Saint, Shakespeare and the Graeco-Roman Tradition*, 1971, p. 378.
2. See Appendix, p. 356.

'Coriolanus'
He would not answer to; forbad all names:
He was a kind of nothing, titleless,
Till he had forg'd himself a name o'th'fire
Of burning Rome.   (v. i. 11–15)

It is a state of cruel transcendence. The fire in which names
(and swords) are forged will consume the life of Rome; where
Marlowe in *Tamburlaine* ('fiery thirster after sovereignty') had
proclaimed its aspiring energies, Shakespeare here finds its
destructive ones. Yet in a double sense the outcome is felt as the
end of an aspiration—a terminus and a point of arrival. The 'kind
of nothing, titleless' is held in the awe appropriate to a god: 'he
does sit in gold, his eye / Red as 'twould burn Rome'. The burning of cities, as Shakespeare knew from Plutarch and Holinshed,
is a commonplace of war, and an expected climax of victory, but
this burning will be a consummation and a purgation, the supreme proof of Martius' *virtus* and a cleansing from Rome of its
base elements.

In the astringent comedy of the dialogue these awesome truths
are, as it were, domesticated; the tribunes have 'wrack'd for
Rome / To make coals cheap' (v. i. 16–17), and the people are
'a pile / Of noisome musty chaff' that cannot be left unburnt 'For
one poor grain or two' (v. i. 27). Remembering the 'musty
superfluity' of an earlier scene, Shakespeare calls corn back into
the play without any cue from Plutarch. Beneath the colloquial
recriminations we sense the outrage upon human sanctities
together with ironic recognitions of the working of tragic laws:

we are the grains,
You are the musty chaff, and you are smelt
Above the moon. We must be burnt for you.
Sic.   Nay, pray be patient.   (v. i. 30–3)

The nature of the Roman community is evoked by the easy
movement of the dialogue past its points of bitter insight ('We
must be burnt for you') to Menenius' undertaking to plead for a
Rome that includes plebeians and patricians in a common human
predicament. We are reminded that Menenius is indeed a patrician and his attitude to the people is a fatherly one (see, for
example, III. ii. 87–9).

Rome, at the beginning of Act IV, Scene vi, is allowed momentarily to recover the routine tranquillities of city life ('Our tradesmen singing in their shops and going / About their functions
friendly'). The play thus offers us a glimpse of the first of the

rival traditions that Plutarch weighed when he looked from Rome
to Sparta in the Comparison of Lycurgus with Numa:[1]

> Furthermore, touching their severall kinde of government, and
> dividing of their people into states and companies: that of
> *Numa* was marvelous meane and base, and framed to the liking
> of the meanest people, making a bodie of a cittie, and a people
> compounded together of all sortes, as goldesmithes, minstrells,
> founders, shoemakers, and of all sortes of craftes men and
> occupations together.

Sicinius and Brutus in this sense represent the 'bodie of a cittie',[2]
and the city they bend their political wits to repudiate is patrician
and martial, like Lycurgus':

> But that of *Lycurgus*, was directly contrarie: for his was more
> severe and tyrannicall, in governing of the nobility, casting all
> craftes and base occupations upon bondemen and straungers,
> and putting into the handes of his cittizens the shield and
> launce, suffering them to exercise no other arte or science, but
> the arte and discipline of warres, as the true ministers of Mars:
> which all their life time never knew other science, but only
> learned to obey their captaines, and to commaund their
> enemies. For to have any occupation, to buye and sell, or to
> trafficke, free men were expressely forbidden: bicause they
> should wholy and absolutely be free.

In this perspective the play's mockeries of the 'apron-men' who
have 'crafted fair' expose the contrarieties (to borrow Averell's
word again) of the city. Averell's *Marvailous Combat*, addressed
to the Lord Mayor of London and written under the imminent
threat from Spain (1588), wants it both ways of course; the
mercantile city must defend itself through 'the strengthe of our
people, the unitie of our minde', for 'virtue is the common profit
of our Countrie'.[3] When Cominius in the play reports the
menacing presence of Martius outside the gates he is both the
scornful patrician and the dismayed minister of Mars, shocked
to see soldier turned butcher. The integrity of the state, much

1. North, S.H.P., I, p. 204.

2. For fuller comment on the tribunes see John Palmer, *Political Characters of Shakespeare*, 1945; also, K. Muir, 'In Defence of the Tribunes', *Essays in Criticism*, 4, 1954, and 'Shakespeare and Politics' in *Shakespeare in a Changing World*, ed. Arnold Kettle, 1964. An interesting early vindication of the democratic cause in the play is offered by Charles Gildon, *Remarks on the Plays of Shakespeare*, 1710; Gildon indicts Shakespeare for his readiness to 'flatter Arbitrary Power' and for representing 'the Commons of Rome, as if they were the Rabble of an Irish Village'.

3. William Averell, *A Marvailous Combat*, 1588, Dedication.

threatened by imminent cataclysm, is sufficiently recovered for a common approach to Martius to be agreed and a common humanity confessed. Thus Shakespeare's wit is very active when he has Menenius wait to accost Coriolanus 'Till he be dieted to my request' (v. i. 57). The wisdom of the belly returns in a new guise, to be applauded by Brutus. The accord of Menenius and the tribunes at this point offers the best perspective from which to plot the significance of their differences elsewhere. The Marxist critic Smirnov has good reason to see Menenius as an enemy of the people and to register the people's trust in him as part of their naivety.[1] But the trust is not unqualified and even where the hostilities of the rival demagogues, Menenius and the tribunes, are most in evidence, there is a degree of understanding and common purpose that almost constitutes a bond. It is a common human frailty, made up of the vanity and colic of the tribunes and the sociable indulgences of the 'giber for the table'.[2] Thus when Brutus, with slightly ingratiating politic courtesy, tells Menenius, 'You know the very road into his kindness', he is honouring the fundamental human affinity that the word 'kindness' often signified in Shakespeare's time. When he visits the Volscian camp Menenius mediates between the apprehensive humanity of the people and the inhibited humanity of Coriolanus. He speaks for the 'petitionary countrymen' and not for the patricians; but the patrician prerogative and pride are still the source of social comedy ('a Jack guardant cannot office me from my son Coriolanus') and of tragic affirmation of the Stoic kind: 'He that hath a will to die by himself, fears it not from another: let your general do his worst' (v. ii. 102–4).

In the opening scenes of the last act the great antinomies of the

1. A. A. Smirnov, *Shakespeare: A Marxist Interpretation*, translated Sonia Volochova, 1936, p. 78. Marxist studies have largely focused on continuities between Jacobean tensions and those of our own time; e.g. V. Komarova, 'Coriolanus and Social Contradictions in England at the beginning of the Seventeenth Century', *Shakespeare Miscellany*, ed. A. Anikst, Moscow, 1969; Wolfgang Wicht, 'Mensch und Gesellschaft in *Coriolanus*', *Shakespeare Jahrbuch* (Weimar), cii, 1966, pp. 245–97. A. V. Lunacharsky, however, finds in both England and Ancient Rome a distinction between the older kind of aristocrat, committed to personal honour, and the new kind, favouring compromise (*O teatre i dramaturgii*, ii, Zapadnojevropejskij teatr. Moscow, 1958, pp. 417–41). A very different account is offered by the Russian critic L. Pinsky, who sees in Shakespearean tragedy 'the destruction of the free individual as he clashes with inhuman society'; Coriolanus is an epic hero, but the 'disinterested servant of Rome becomes, blinded by passion, a traitor to his country' (see Miklos Szenczi, 'The Nature of Shakespeare's Realism', *Shakespeare Jahrbuch* (Weimar), cii, 1966, pp. 37–59).

2. See ii. i. 1–95.

play are modulated if not transformed. The contraries resolved by banishment were valour and policy; they give place to constancy and humanity, to be resolved in death. The modulations attend upon the changing situation, and some have already been intimated in Coriolanus' farewell to family and friends at the start of Act IV. The wit, the affection, and the ironic solicitude ('My hazards still have been your solace') do not mask the 'heart-hard'ning spectacle' of the scene. The metamorphosis of which Menenius will speak is under way; the man is becoming the 'lonely dragon that his fen / Makes fear'd and talk'd of more than seen', while his resolution to 'exceed the common' and the recognition that he may fall to 'cautelous baits and practice' are non-specific prefigurations of the last act. The brief soliloquy before Aufidius' house (IV. iv. 12–26) has disappointed some by its failure to offer a full account of the process of mutation.[1] But it is apt that there should be little beyond the first sentence ('O world, thy slippery turns!') to suggest imaginative reflection. The terse formulations that make inconstancy a routine law of life are meant to endorse a peremptory switch of allegiance: 'My birthplace hate I, and my love's upon / This enemy town'. They carry conviction because Coriolanus is diagnosing his own condition and deciding wilfully to persist in it, but they do not fully account for it. A. P. Rossiter sees it as a 'depressing paradox' that Martius' 'unyieldingness and would-be self-sufficiency make him so pliant to force of circumstance',[2] yet the unyieldingness and self-sufficiency make a kind of constancy which in the tragic process of the play is clearly related to the *virtus*. Thus Coriolanus tells Menenius, 'Mine ears against your suits are stronger than / Your gates against my force', and Aufidius will comment, 'You keep a constant temper'. Coriolanus perseveres in his own nature ('I play the man I am') against his human nature towards a frustrated metamorphosis.

In words that have no occasion in the source, Shakespeare has Coriolanus speak to the boy Martius, poignantly recalling the old values, constancy in valour, in the new situation:

> The god of soldiers,
> With the consent of supreme Jove, inform
> Thy thoughts with nobleness, that thou mayst prove
> To shame unvulnerable, and stick i'th'wars
> Like a great sea-mark standing every flaw
> And saving those that eye thee! (v. iii. 70–5)

1. E.g. A. C. Bradley (see below, p. 71, note 4).
2. *Angel with Horns*, 1961, p. 252.

It is a generous metaphor. The sparse observation tells us that the soldier who holds his ground on the mutable battlefield gives courage to his fellows; but here, its confident, measured extensions to Olympus, to an extremity of virtue ('To shame unvulnerable') and to a point of enduring stillness in a stormy sea win for the words 'And saving those that eye thee' an immense resonance. This is the commemorative voice or, to recover the cliché, the voice of resounding fame; as Keats said of Kean's Othello, 'from eternal risk, he speaks as though his body were unassailable' and in a voice that 'had commanded where swords were as thick as reeds'.[1] The young Martius 'by th'interpretation of full time' will be Rome's saviour, but in this new 'hearthard'ning spectacle' of Coriolanus confronting his family, the unmoving figure is not saving those who eye him, he is the god of soldiers poised to destroy them.

As in the source, so in the play, the spectacle constrains the dialogue and qualifies its effects. Coriolanus is moved first by what he sees, not by what he hears (v. iii. 22–33); gestures of submission (curtsying, bowing, nodding, kneeling) foil the unbending attitudes of a constant purpose, and words fall into ambiguous silences. The remarkable fidelity of much of the scene's verse to the prose narrative does not confine Shakespeare's effects to Plutarch's, for the structure and movement of the play, together with a number of local interventions, change its weight and significance. Memories may stir about the messenger's report of Martius' return from Corioli, for example, 'the nobles bended, / As to Jove's statue', but more urgently they remind us that Volumnia is trying for a second time to change the role of Coriolanus. The earlier scene (iii. ii), which has no counterpart in the source, is rich in subtle preparations for the later one, not only in the continuing preoccupation with what the body's action teaches the mind (iii. ii. 122) but also in attentiveness to the self-conscious theatre of personal identity and political design, from 'Come, come, we'll prompt you' (iii. ii. 106) to 'Like a dull actor now / I have forgot my part and I am out, / Even to a full disgrace' (v. iii. 40–2). Few would suppose Coriolanus wholly tempered by Volumnia's 'colder reasons' (v. iii. 86). He is exhausted and broken, in a process which begins before his mother speaks, and finishes in silence, by the heroic but hubristic endeavour of his own will:

> I'll never
> Be such a gosling to obey instinct, but stand

1. Cited by Sidney Colvin, *Life of John Keats*, 1918, p. 243.

> As if a man were author of himself
> And knew no other kin.   (v. iii. 34–7)

The effort to be unnatural is again essential to that kind of
integrity which the service of the 'god of soldiers' demands:
Martius had reviled those who fled from the Volscians as 'souls
of geese, / That bear the shapes of men', for no yielder can be a
man. He persists in being a 'thing / Made by some other deity
than nature, / That shapes man better' (iv. vi. 91–3) in defiance
of his contrary understanding when he sees Volumnia as 'the
honour'd mould / Wherein this trunk was fram'd' (v. iii. 22–3).
Volumnia's persuasions, whose arguments and tactics Shakespeare largely retains from North, closely following her first
speech there (v. iii. 94–125, 132–48) and considerably amplifying
the second (v. iii. 148–82), reach their climax in the stage-direction, *Holds her by the hand, silent.* Earlier silences are less auspicious ('Speak to me, son . . . Why dost not speak? . . . He turns
away'), variously marking responses to Volumnia's policy, her
invocation of fame, her chiding and her sentimental indulgence:

> When she, poor hen, fond of no second brood,
> Has cluck'd thee to the wars, and safely home,
> Loaden with honour.   (v. iii. 162–4)

It is not the 'pity to our prayers' that prevails, nor the disowned
kinship ('his child / Like him by chance'), but the silent, kneeling
submission:

> Yet give us our dispatch:
> I am husht until our city be afire,
> And then I'll speak a little.   (v. iii. 180–2)

Shakespeare defers to this crisis the breakdown reported earlier
in North: 'Nature so wrought with him, that the tears fell from
his eyes, and he could not keep himself from making much of
them, but yielded to the affection of his blood'. The silence is
broken by the 'boy of tears':

> O mother, mother!
> What have you done? Behold, the heavens do ope,
> The gods look down, and this unnatural scene
> They laugh at.   (v. iii. 182–5)

The Homeric gods look down from Olympus and laugh (as at
Hephaestus in Book i of the *Iliad*) and the 'scene' here is the
tableau in which the mother unnaturally kneels to the son; the
Volscians who saw it, says Dionysius, 'could not bear the unusual
sight but turned away their eyes'.[1] The gods of Erasmus' Folly,

---

1. *Roman Antiquities*, viii, 54, 1 (p. 157).

too, take malicious delight in the ironies of human situations—
'There is no show like it. Good God, what a theatre!'[1]—and the
play's audience can momentarily share their privilege. But
Coriolanus' meaning does not exhaust Shakespeare's. The scene
is the most 'natural' in the play when we recall from its prelude,

> my young boy
> Hath an aspect of intercession which
> Great nature cries, 'Deny not'. (v. iii. 31–3)

It is the 'aspect of intercession' which makes the scene, and great
nature's cry is most heard in the silence, a truth that registers in
the unnaturalness and the naturalness of the spectacles devised
by Poussin and Tiepolo.[2] The process by which the 'thing made
for Alexander', the 'thing of blood', yields to 'Great nature' is
arduous and silent, another metamorphic growth, a feat of maturation.[3] The words play a limited part, for it is not maturation on
Volumnia's terms, merely a response to those of her persuasions
which would lead him to 'frame convenient peace', but a breaking-
through into a new territory of value and of moral experience
which the words of the play can hardly visit. 'It is no little thing
to make / Mine eyes to sweat compassion', Martius says to
Aufidius, and Shakespeare seems slily to transpose into human
ordeal Plutarch's marvellings about stone images that seem 'to
sweat or weep' in Roman temples. The antique gods, we may
remind ourselves, are not indivisible; among those who might be
supposed to find the scene 'unnatural' are the gods whose graces
Martius imitated under his mother's tutelage—Mars and Jove
(see v. iii. 150).

It is no little thing to make our eyes sweat compassion either,
after our experience of the play. For in a theatre that for some
three hours has been turned into Rome we have been almost
denied nourishment for the sympathetic affections. Early in his
English histories Shakespeare had discriminated in his own way
between the range of qualities and feelings that Plutarch too
would like to assign to woman and those that belong more
properly to warrior-man; Richard of York weeps as Queen
Margaret flaunts the blood of his slaughtered son:

> Women are soft, mild, pitiful and flexible:
> Thou stern, obdurate, flinty, rough, remorseless.
> (*3H6*, I. iv. 141–2)

1. *Praise of Folly*, 24 (translated H. H. Hudson, 1941, p. 69).
2. See below, p. 89.
3. See H. C. Goddard, *The Meaning of Shakespeare*, 1951, ch. xxxii.

All that is 'soft, mild, pitiful and flexible' has been shut out in *Coriolanus* and flows back into the stage silence. What is excluded, however, has sometimes been prefigured, and Martius' silence as the women and the boy kneel before him recalls and perfects much that has gone before—other pleas, silences, intimacies, recognitions of kinship, and touches of nature. But earlier moments were compromised or contaminated: Volumnia's pleas were expedient, Virgilia ('My gracious silence!') was intimidated by the clamour of victory, Martius' embraces of Cominius and Aufidius were ecstasies of war-delight, his affection for Menenius was wilfully set aside, and at Corioli he forgot the name of the prisoner whose plight he remembered. In the intercession scene itself the evocations of sensibility are poignantly heard in discordant settings; he sees Virgilia as 'those doves' eyes, / Which can make gods forsworn' (v. iii. 27–8) and greets her with 'a kiss / Long as my exile, sweet as my revenge' (v. iii. 44–5); his apostrophe to Valeria, 'The moon of Rome' (v. iii. 65), honours the sanctity he is about to desecrate, and that to his son (v. iii. 70–5) sounds a valediction to the earlier self that defended Rome. Most significantly, he tries by a movement of the body to disengage himself from a spectacle which moves him more than the eloquence:

> Not of a woman's tenderness to be,
> Requires nor child nor woman's face to see.
> I have sat too long.   (v. iii. 129–31)

These, and other interrelated responses, keep the long silence of Martius articulate and expressive until it dominates the theatre. We do well to remember that Tacita, or *Lady Silence*, as North calls her, was counted among the Roman divinities.[1]

The yielding to tenderness has for Martius a tragic significance that it does not overtly have for his mother; his death was not meant to be a part of her bargain and she does not reply to his recognition that it will be so:

> O my mother, mother! O!
> You have won a happy victory to Rome;
> But for your son, believe it, O, believe it,
> Most dangerously you have with him prevail'd,
> If not most mortal to him. But let it come.   (v. iii. 185–9)

The words are finely caught from Plutarch, with the last four added by Shakespeare in a tragic mode which includes Hamlet's

1. See **II**. i. 174 note.

'the readiness is all . . . Let be'. It is a part of the play's integrity that the martial dialect should, with these brevities, make what it can of the event. The tragic and political movements of the history are reconciled with a surprising ease and naturalness. The scene's closing exchanges keep up the illusion of a diplomatic triumph of Volumnia's making, and Martius deliberately and courteously acquiesces, offering wine to the ladies and submitting to return with Aufidius in quest of the political solution that his tragic insight has already disdained.

Shakespeare's Rome, waiting for Volumnia's return, re-enacts on a public scale some of the intimate tensions of the intercession scene. Menenius' experience (powerfully invoked in his prose) gives one force to Sicinius' anxiety while that of the theatre audience recognizes another, 'Is't possible that so short a time can alter the condition of a man?' And, we may add, the condition of a city, for the recovery of life which attended Martius' silent yielding is now allowed full festive expression in another of the play's more generous metaphors,

> Ne'er through an arch so hurried the blown tide
> As the recomforted through th'gates. Why, hark you!
> *Trumpets, hautboys, drums beat, all together.*
> The trumpets, sackbuts, psalteries and fifes,
> Tabors and cymbals and the shouting Romans
> Make the sun dance. (v. iv. 48–52)

The festive community of shouting Romans, the flowers and the triumphant fires make of the play at this point a pageant, a supreme public rite, with the figure of Volumnia a processional symbol of 'the life of Rome' (v. v. 1).[1] But Shakespeare contrives ironies enough to assimilate the public rite that the Romans enjoy into the larger tragic rite enjoyed by those who watch the Romans. The 'tribes' are invited to 'Unshout the noise which banish'd Martius', but as the telling transition to Aufidius and the Volscians reminds us, Martius is now at the mercy of other voices.

The role of Aufidius, much amplified from the source, is designed by Shakespeare both as a vehicle for the measured, political judgements upon Martius which North's Plutarch advances and many of the play's critics would endorse,[2] and as

---

1. The importance of the pageant element in the play is recognized by A. S. Venezky, *Pageantry on the Shakespearean Stage*, New York, 1951.

2. E.g. E. K. Chambers, commenting on IV. vii. 28–57, finds the speech 'out of keeping with Aufidius' mood in this scene' and suggests that 'for once the dramatist, not the puppet speaks. On the eve of the catastrophe Shakespeare

vital proof that absolute virtue in the service of Mars cannot co-
exist with those skills and insights of expedience that in the play
he shares with Volumnia and the tribunes. In him the generous
martial hospitalities are visibly metamorphosed into a plausible,
state-sustaining malevolence, accommodating the people's power
(v. vi. 16, 55), building pretexts (v. vi. 20–6), nursing grievance
(v. vi. 31–41), diminishing and reviling his enemy's humanity,

> At a few drops of women's rheum, which are
> As cheap as lies, he sold the blood and labour
> Of our great action,   (v. vi. 46–8)

and finally treading upon his mangled body. The play's dis-
coveries about intimacies of feeling keep pace with its public
issues and find expression in the theatre of public events. Aufidius'
jealousy shapes the plot into a form that may be seen to satisfy
historical and tragic laws beyond his understanding: 'Therefore
shall he die, / And I'll renew me in his fall'. But his plot can work
only if he can divert the 'great shouts of the people' to his own
ends, exploiting the terrible instabilities of the situation described by the second conspirator:

> And patient fools,
> Whose children he hath slain, their base throats tear
> With giving him glory.   (v. vi. 52–4)

Like Brutus and Sicinius before him, he finds provocations to
touch the most vulnerable areas of Martius' sensibility:

> He has betray'd your business, and given up,
> For certain drops of salt, your city Rome,
> I say 'your city', to his wife and mother;
> Breaking his oath and resolution, like
> A twist of rotten silk, never admitting
> Counsel o'th'war: but at his nurse's tears
> He whin'd and roar'd away your victory,
> That pages blush'd at him, and men of heart
> Look'd wond'ring each at others.   (v. vi. 92–100)

Shakespeare's play weaves for Aufidius' purpose a web of sub-
liminal reverberations: 'Thy tears are salter than a younger man's'
(iv. i. 22); 'schoolboys' tears take up / The glasses of my sight!'
(iii. ii. 116–17); 'When he might act the woman in the scene, /
He prov'd best man i'th'field' (ii. ii. 96–7); 'His pupil age / Man-

---

pauses, to sum up his hero's career so far' (Warwick Shakespeare). Chambers
is reluctant to allow that insight and malevolence may co-exist in the one
character and indeed in the one speech.

enter'd thus' (II. ii. 98–9); 'Hence rotten thing! or I shall shake
thy bones / Out of thy garments' (III. i. 177–8); 'Thy valiantness
was mine, thou suck'st it from me' (III. ii. 129); 'It is a part / That
I shall blush in acting' (II. ii. 144–5); 'certain of your brethren
roar'd and ran' (II. iii. 55). The effect of these faint anticipatory
tremors is obscurely to prepare the audience for the *saeva indignatio*
with which Martius meets Aufidius' climactic taunt a little later,
'Name not the god, thou boy of tears!' (v. vi. 101); for Aufidius is
made a meaner version of what Martius once was among the
'men of heart' and is using against Martius the mode of invective
he has now outgrown. This way of putting it, however, leaves out
of account the deliberate, self-conscious, and histrionic nature of
the performances of both men. The Martius who earlier in the
scene plays with confidence his part (assigned to him by Volumnia) of triumphant warrior diplomat (v. vi. 71–84) could be
proof against the first of Aufidius' charges (although Livy's
history suggests that in the long run Volscian business was in
fact betrayed[1]); he is not proof against the devaluations of wife,
mother, and tears that are exactly calculated by Aufidius to
damage the newly discovered vulnerable self.

Martius' final utterances keep the weight of the play's experience behind them, adducing its earlier significances with
great economy. His retort to the indictment uses the scale of
Aufidius' mendacity to re-create the magnanimity of his own
virtue:

> Measureless liar, thou hast made my heart
> Too great for what contains it. 'Boy'! O slave!
> (v. vi. 103–4)

He recovers the word 'heart' from Aufidius' misappropriation of
it, to senses more fully and less austerely realized in *Antony and
Cleopatra*—the soldier's courage, the 'captain's heart, / Which in
the scuffles of great fights hath burst / The buckles on his breast'
(I. i. 6–8), and what might be called human capacity for life and
suffering, 'Heart, once be stronger than thy continent, / Crack
thy frail case' (IV. xiv. 40–1). The play charges the word 'boy'
with great intensities of public and intimate feeling, and hardly
less so the word 'slave',[2] for the manly virtue which saves the city

1. Livy reports the rapid decline of the Volscian cause after this setback. The
Aequi refused to accept 'Attius Tullius' as leader of the alliance wth the Volsci,
the two tribes fought and Rome was spared.

2. It is an abusive word in Martius' invective (I. i. 198, I. iv. 36, I. v. 7) but is
often so used in Elizabethan plays, including Shakespeare's histories. More
specific Roman significances occur at I. viii. 5 where Martius tells Aufidius that

from slavery is bred in the boy by the human and inhuman
devotion of the mother. Martius has carried the virtue to its
extremest point, with consequences both for himself and for the
city. His presumption of maturity expresses itself oddly and
amusingly in his apology to the Volscian patricians, "tis the first
time that ever / I was forc'd to scold' (v. vi. 105–6), and his
claims, setting a great distance between Aufidius' manhood and
his own, are almost judicially thrust home before they reach their
ecstatic sacrificial climax as he recovers his sovereign voice:

> Cut me to pieces, Volsces, men and lads,
> Stain all your edges on me. Boy! False hound!
> If you have writ your annals true, 'tis there,
> That like an eagle in a dove-cote, I
> Flutter'd your Volscians in Corioles.
> Alone I did it. Boy! (v. vi. 111–16)

'What his breast forges,' Menenius says of Martius earlier, as the
Roman rabble shouts for blood, 'that his tongue must vent'
(III. i. 256). Here Martius forges and vents the words that win
acquiescence in a re-created fame; or rather Shakespeare does
so, for it is a passage in which one is more than usually aware of
his mastery of blank-verse movement, making the symbolic
primacy of the eagle alive and immediate to tongue and breath.
Nothing is left of the lurching of the 'thing made by some other
deity than nature' or of the 'butcher killing flies'. The strongest
lines express a readiness to die, not a readiness to kill—a truth
which qualifies the otherwise hubristic flourish, 'Alone I did it';
for pride in the exercise of a pre-eminent human courage is not
the same thing as emulation of the gods, or as standing 'As if a
man were author of himself / And knew no other kin' (v. iii.
36–7). The most poignant lines are commemorative of a heroic
self now transcended, recovering for the 'annals' the 'stol'n
name / Coriolanus, in Corioles'; and the vaunt bids farewell to
life as well as to the old habit of reticence, the now dispensable
mark of true breeding.

The tragic laws operating in the play are retributive and sacrificial, related to the class conflicts of the city of Rome, to its

---

the first 'budger' will die the other's slave, and at iv. v. 78, where the 'voice of
slaves' whoops him out of Rome. The invented incident of the prisoner at
Corioli (i. ix. 80–9) may remind us of the common practice of enslaving the
citizens of defeated cities (e.g. Syracusa in the 'Life of Marcellus'). The use of
slaves as messengers accounts for the word in i. vi. 39 and iv. vi. 38, and as
servants in iv. v. 176. Plutarch has much to say of their treatment in his 'Life
of Coriolanus' (see Appendix, p. 347).

survival in an Italy that includes the Volscians, and to the purging of hubris, the pride of power, both from the state and from its hero. The key question asked Menenius by the Volscian guard, 'Can you, when you have pushed out of your gates the very defender of them, and, in a violent popular ignorance, given your enemy your shield, think to front his revenges with the easy groans of old women . . . ?' (v. ii. 38–41), is answered by Shakespeare with many insights and ironies. The 'violent popular ignorance' is muted to bewildered dismay: 'though we willingly consented to his banishment, yet it was against our will' (IV. vi. 145–6). And the expelled defender of the gates forfeits function, role, name, and identity, becomes 'a kind of nothing, titleless', before he is mammocked by the enemy populace, 'Tear him to pieces! Do it presently! He killed my son! My daughter!' (v. vi. 120–1). Shakespeare contrives to keep the dignity of a ritual death without diminishing or distancing the malevolent operations of personal jealousy and lynch-law. What is from one point of view a cruel and vindictive atrocity is from another the retributive recoil of natural feeling upon the 'thing' that once 'ran reeking o'er the lives of men'. Martius presciently saw that this might be so when he first came, in disguise, to Antium:

> A goodly city is this Antium. City,
> 'Tis I that made thy widows: many an heir
> Of these fair edifices 'fore my wars
> Have I heard groan, and drop. Then know me not:
> Lest that thy wives with spits, and boys with stones,
> In puny battle slay me.   (IV. iv. 1–6)

In the last phase of the play there is no disguise, and Coriolanus stages his own death with an effect contrary to that which Aufidius designed for it, making it a triumph, not a humiliation. Shakespeare does not allow us to forget that the outrage upon the Volscian cities is avenged by those who first split the air with noise (v. vi. 52) to welcome Martius' return; and the shout which finally fills the theatre, 'Kill, kill, kill, kill, kill him!', has no clear retributive focus, it is a war-cry and the cry of the hunter. The killers, as in Rome, cry havoc where they 'should but hunt / With modest warrant' (III. i. 272–3) and their 'tiger-footed rage' finds the 'harm of unscann'd swiftness' (III. i. 309–10). Yet the mob savageries have been enlisted for political ends. While the Volscian patricians, like their Roman counterparts, recognize in the victim the fit hero of the city-state, 'The man is noble, and his fame folds in / This orb o'th'earth' (v. vi. 124–5), political expediency of the kind Volumnia would understand is already making its own provision for the state's survival: 'let's make the best of it' (v. vi. 146). With the authority of Plutarch, and in consonance with the conventions of heroic drama, Shakespeare accords Coriolanus the hero's obsequies ('Trail your steel pikes') which he denies Othello.

In his first Roman play, *Titus Andronicus*, Shakespeare had shown an almost anthropological interest in ancient rites of human sacrifice,[1] and in his second, *Julius Caesar*, the interest persists in subtler form as Brutus sees himself as both conspirator and priest, purging from the realm the spirit of Caesar.[2] *Coriolanus* is more profoundly shaped to a sacrificial design which has no need of antique superstition or Roman religion.[3] The fame of Caius Martius witnesses to the end of those days when Rome could sustain itself with the belief that *virtus*, or valiantness, included 'in that generall name, all other special vertues besides'. He dies for a city that has made too much of the cult of the warrior but failed to recognize the nature of its dependence upon that cult. His death is deserved as a climax and consummation of a life which exhausts the possibilities of a mode of virtue, and as a punishment because such a life cannot be reconciled with the larger and more vulnerable claims of human community; that community itself is purged, chastened, shamed, and renewed.

Among the more significant moments of the history of *Coriolanus* may be recalled Gifford's attack upon Hazlitt for claiming that Shakespeare showed in the play 'a leaning to the arbitrary side of the question' and that 'the language of poetry naturally falls in with the language of power'. Keats finds Hazlitt in the right of it: the tendency to theatrical effect, he says, 'gives a Bias to the imagination often inconsistent with the greatest good, that in Poetry it triumphs over Principle, and bribes the passions to make a sacrifice of common humanity'.[4] The imagination that so acts, however, was at work in Roman history before it helped to

1. *Titus Andronicus*, I. i. 96–156. The mood of the play is closer to that of the earlier *Lives* of Plutarch (e.g. the death of Tatius in Lavinium as reported in the 'Life of Romulus').

2. Cf. *Julius Caesar*, II. i. 166–74, III. i. 106–11. The play's attention to Caesar as a sacrificial victim owes nothing to Plutarch.

3. See C. Kenenyi, *The Religion of the Greeks and Romans*, 1962, ch. v. For fuller discussion of tragic sacrifice see John Holloway, *The Story of the Night*, 1961, and Kenneth Burke, '*Coriolanus* and the Delights of Faction', *Hudson Review*, XIX, 1966–7, pp. 185–202. Burke remarks that in Athenian law 'hubris' was 'used to designate a civil offence, an insulting air of superiority deemed punishable by death'.

4. *Letters*, ed. M. B. Forman, 1947, pp. 308–9.

create Shakespeare's play. To Keats's question 'Is it a paradox of my creating that "one murder makes a villain, millions a hero"?', there could be many responses from Plutarch's pages, but none more apt than his report that Coriolanus was 'murdered in the city of Antium'. The paradox is created in antiquity, and the many that Martius slaughtered with his 'lawful sword' do not excuse in Aufidius 'a deed whereat valour will weep'. It is true that the conspirators, like the tribunes before them, make their occasion by putting Martius 'to choler straight' (III. iii. 25) and provoking the predictable vaunt ('Alone I did it'), but it does not follow that nothing has changed. Coriolanus is 'a deliberately minimized hero', says Brents Stirling, 'he loves war and detests plebeians at the beginning and he does so at the end'.[1] But the play's *peripeteia* ('But let it come') has opened a great space between the early arrogance and war-delight and the late, which continuities of response and circumstance cannot bridge. Between 'I banish you' (III. iii. 123) and 'Stain all your edges on me' (v. vi. 112) we must take account of the 'certain drops of salt' (v. vi. 93) that have saved Rome, and recognize that the tragic recovery of the old self is also a farewell to it. Shakespeare's Martius does not kill himself, but he surrenders to death, 'the offering of self is sealed', as Wagner writes of Beethoven's *Coriolan* overture, and 'the colossus crashes down'.[2] We may aptly recall the prophet Daniel's great image with 'legs of iron, his feet part of iron and part of clay', for an immense presumption of power has proved vulnerable.[3] But the clay is the human element forming 'the most noble corse that ever herald / Did follow to his urn'. Not that the ironies of the play's last words are in any way diminished:

> Though in this city he
> Hath widow'd and unchilded many a one,
> Which to this hour bewail the injury,
> Yet he shall have a noble memory.
> Assist.

1. *Unity in Shakespearian Tragedy*, New York, 1956, pp. 187–8. Like many 'moderate' critics he finds 'the discerning Menenius caught between unreasoning opposites' (p. 190).

2. Wagner's first account of Beethoven's overture is related to his memories of von Collin's *Coriolan* (see below, p. 85) but in a later one he uses *Coriolanus* to compare the art-forms of Beethoven and Shakespeare. In spite of some misunderstandings, Wagner's insight into the work is searching. See *Richard Wagner's Prose Works*, ed. W. A. Ellis, 1894, III, pp. 225–8, v, pp. 107–8.

3. See Daniel, ii. 33. For a fuller account of the play's imaginative relationship with the Book of Daniel, see J. L. Simmons, *Shakespeare's Pagan World*, 1973, pp. 58–64.

It is as good a resting place as any in the language for the word
'noble', but it keeps strange company.[1]

All Shakespeare's plays, the mature ones increasingly, put
pressure upon the resources of the language, tuning it to new notes,
compelling old words to fresh service, coining novel ones,
recovering forgotten ones. *Coriolanus* is no exception. About
twenty words are wrested from their ordinary functions, usually
the noun turned to verb or participle—'had I come coffin'd
home' (II. i. 175), 'my true lip / Hath virgin'd it e'er since' (v. iii.
47–8), 'Lov'd me . . . Nay, godded me indeed' (v. iii. 10, 11).[2]
This characteristic of the play's language consorts well with
qualities that we have had reason elsewhere to call Spartan.[3]
For Shakespeare's creativeness of language is not here of the
exuberant kind, it works under the constraints of its theme,
requiring breath and voice for invective, exhortation, suasion,
and for the amplification of a fame won by deeds of violence.
Gestures, conspicuous in the play's action, are assimilated into its
language. High gestures and low, public and intimate, are evoked
to dominate the imagination: 'The kitchen malkin pins / Her
richest lockram 'bout her reechy neck' (II. i. 206–7), 'the nobles
bended / As to Jove's statue' (II. i. 263–4), 'to show bare heads /
In congregations, to yawn, be still, and wonder' (III. ii. 10–11),
'We pout upon the morning' (v. i. 52), 'Let me twine / Mine
arms about that body' (IV. v. 107–8), 'Where great patricians
shall attend, and shrug' (I. ix. 4). Words of brute violence are

1. For the word 'noble' in the play, see notes on I. i. 162, I. iii. 67, II. ii. 14,
II. ii. 40. II. iii. 9, II. iii. 236, III. i. 24, III. i. 55, III. i. 152, III. i. 253, III. i. 323,
III. ii. 40–1, III. ii. 118. IV. i. 9, IV. ii. 21, IV. ii. 32, IV. v. 117, V. i. 17, V. iii. 121.
P. A. Jorgensen (*Redeeming Shakespeare's Words*, Berkeley, 1962, ch. VI) finds a
rich context for it in Renaissance literature of nobility. In this last speech,
however, the word keeps company with a reminiscence of Isaiah (see v. vi. 151
note).

2. Also I. i. 99 *cupboarding*; I. i. 192 *side*; I. i. 194 *feebling*; I. iv. 12 *fielded*;
I. iv. 38 *agued*; II. i. 209 *hors'd*; II. i. 246 *Dispropertied*; III. ii. 55 *roted*; III. ii. 116
Tent; V. i. 5 *knee*; V. i. 6 *coy'd*; V. ii. 61 *office*; V. ii. 81 *servanted*; V. iv. 25 *throne*;
V. vi. 40 *wag'd*; V. vi. 151 *unchilded*. E. K. Chambers supplies this list (Warwick
Shakespeare, p. 121). Sister Miriam Joseph, in *Shakespeare's Use of the Arts of
Language*, 1947, pp. 63–4, lists twenty-three Shakespearean instances of pro-
nouns, adjectives, and nouns used as verbs; six are from *Coriolanus*.

3. See above, p. 48. The Lacedaemonian habits of language, cultivating
aphoristic incitements to deeds, were much commented on by Plutarch (*Moralia*,
III), and have given us the word *laconic*. Volumnia's 'Then his good report
should have been my son' (I. iii. 20) is in the mode.

used with expected intensity (*clutch'd*, *lurch'd*, *crush*), but words of muscular power are also used figuratively, 'make us think / Rather our state's defective for requital / Than we to *stretch* it out' (II. ii. 49–51), and even clichés take on a physical weight, 'in what hatred / He still hath *held* them' (II. i. 243–4), 'Purpose so *barr'd*' (III. i. 147). This pressure upon style has yielded some unique usages. 'Your dishonour / *Mangles* true judgement' (III. i. 156–7), 'I hope / My words *disbench'd* you not?' (II. ii. 70–1), and '*shout* me forth' (I. ix. 49). Another score of instances where Shakespeare is using a word in a rare or unique sense are noted in the course of the play,[1] but the stresses imposed on the language by its theme are definitively caught in a single phrase in III. ii. 115–120:

> The smiles of knaves
> Tent in my cheeks, and schoolboys' tears take up
> The glasses of my sight! A beggar's tongue
> Make motion through my lips, and my arm'd knees
> Who bow'd but in my stirrup, bend like his
> That hath receiv'd an alms!

That extraordinary catachresis, *arm'd knees*, might be the linguistic hallmark of *Coriolanus*, but it is not isolated; it owes its rigour to a movement and syntax that gives comparable weight to *tent*, *motion*, *bend*, *bow'd*, and *stirrup* before reaching the perverse pun on *alms*. The speech is one of a number in the play too, where the dual sources of its linguistic power are manifest—its observations and idiom can glance at what is everyday and familiar, while its rhythms obey a martial, epic impulse. Shakespeare responds at once to the heroical resonances of an English in touch with Plutarch and the Roman annals, and to the human cadences of the market-place. It is possible to polarize the distinction and say with James Calderwood that, 'lacking a common set of values, feelings, allegiances, principles, and knowledge and hence lacking a viable language, Coriolanus and the plebeians can have no real dialogue'.[2] It is a partial truth to which the third citizen

1. See I. i. 98 *unactive*; I. i. 162 *bale*; I. i. 256 *Bemock*; I. iii. 65 *mammocked*; I. iv. 12 *fielded*; I. iv. 62 *fetch . . . off*;·I. ix. 49 *shout me forth*; II. i. 116 *empiricutic*; II. i. 206 *chats him*; II. i. 246 *Dispropertied*; II. ii. 71 *disbench'd*; II. ii. 101 *lurch'd*; II. iii. 28 *wedged* (*wadg'd*); II. iii. 137 *limitation*; III. i. 103 *palates*; III. i. 128 *native*; III. i. 260 *What the vengeance*; III. iii. 29 *looks*; IV. ii. 47 *unclog*; IV. vi. 119 *crafted*; V. i. 6 *coy'd*; V. i. 44 *grief-shot*; V. ii. 17 *verified*; V. vi. 151 *unchilded*.

2. J. L. Calderwood, '*Coriolanus*: Wordless Meanings and Meaningless Words', *Studies in Eng. Lit. 1500–1900*, VI, 1966, pp. 211–24. He remarks that 'the plebeians' bad words have driven out of circulation Coriolanus's good words', but that is a very patrician view.

disarmingly bears witness, 'We have power in ourselves to do it, but it is a power that we have no power to do. For, if he show us his wounds and tell us his deeds, we are to put our tongues into those wounds and speak for them' (II. iii. 4–8). The condition of Rome is such that its hero (true bred) will not show his wounds and tell his deeds, and would recoil in disgust from plebeians' tongues offering to touch him and speak for him. Yet the citizen's punning upon 'power', and his readiness to give and take, speak for a generous sense of community which deserves to be acknowledged, and will be acknowledged vicariously when Martius ('I melt, and am not / Of stronger earth than others') proves to be not 'a god to punish' but 'A man of their infirmity' (III. i. 80, 81).

If Shakespeare persuades us in *Coriolanus* that this is the direction the language would have taken had London been a warring city-state, it is because he has mastered not only its heroical cadences but also its heroical and patrician vocabulary—*noble, gentle, man, virtue, name, fame, deed, honour*. It is an advantage to recognize their ancestry in classical literature and to savour their safe arrival into Shakespeare's English.[1] 'Bear th'addition nobly ever!' says Cominius, and Martius undertakes 'To under-crest your good addition, / To th'fairness of my power'. Shakespeare borrows from North the word *addition*, but using it perhaps for the last time, he brings it to a point of maximum significance in his own art.[2]

The heroic idiom apart, there is often reason to admire the ordinary talk of the play, and its continuities from plebeian to patrician settings. Menenius' gift for talking to, if not listening to, the people, is owed to his being allowed something of Shakespeare's taste for proverb (no gentleman uses a proverb), domestic wit, and vulgar wisdom.[3] The citizens and the tribunes have something too of that dialectical skill, conspicuous in Menenius and Volumnia, which interests Shakespeare in the play and has

1. See R. A. Brower, *Hero and Saint, Shakespeare and the Graeco-Roman Tradition,* 1971, pp. 354–81; Herbert Howarth, 'Shakespeare's Gentleness', *Shakespeare Survey,* 14, 1961, pp. 90–7; P. A. Jorgensen, *Redeeming Shakespeare's Words,* 1962; P. F. Neumeyer, 'Not local Habitation nor a Name: *Coriolanus*', *University Review,* XXXII, 1966, pp. 195–8. See also D. J. Gordon, in Duthie, op. cit. p. 41 note above.

2. Compare particularly *Macbeth,* I. iii. 106, 'In which addition, hail, most worthy Thane!', and *Lear,* I. i. 138, 'Th'name, and all th'addition to a King'. See I. ix. 65 note.

3. E.g. II. i. 1–95. For a general account, see Charles G. Smith, *Shakespeare's Proverb Lore,* Harvard U.P., 1963; 'The Foundations of Elizabethan Language', by Muriel St Clare Byrne in *Shakespeare Survey,* 17, 1964; and G. D. Willcock, 'Shakespeare and Elizabethan English', *Shakespeare Survey,* 7, 1954.

prompted D. J. Enright to see it as more of a debate than a tragedy.[1]

The comparative austerity of the play's metaphors has not encouraged much attention to its 'imagery'. Charting what another critic called its 'unsavory figurative language', Maurice Charney has found that 'food and eating is perhaps the most extensive and important motif in the play', but much relates directly and unfiguratively to the dearth; there is much too about disease, animals, acting, and isolation.[2] The significance of the many references to animals has been fully analysed by J. C. Maxwell and pursued by F. N. Lees in the light of Aristotle's apophthegm that 'He that is incapable of living in a society is a god or a beast'.[3] It remains true that the distinctive imaginative effects of the play's language are articulatory and echoic, not figurative. It happens, too, that abstention from language— silence—has its own eloquence.

Wyndham Lewis in *The Lion and the Fox* (1927) allowed Coriolanus 'his portion of magnificent music' and Bradley found in the 'huge violent heart . . . a store, not only of tender affection but of delicate and chivalrous poetry'.[4] Their work, and that of Wilson Knight,[5] senses the tenderness within the violence which is poignantly and ironically recovered in Eliot's *Coriolan* poems.[6]

V. THE PLAY ON SHAKESPEARE'S STAGE

While there is no decisive evidence for a production in Shakespeare's lifetime, the stage-directions show the play ripe for the theatre, and Jonson's glance at its style in *Epicœne*, performed by the Children of the Revels, excuses those who have talked confidently of *Coriolanus* at the Globe.[7] The action is firmly

1. D. J. Enright, *'Coriolanus*: Tragedy or Debate?', *The Apothecary's Shop*, 1957.

2. Maurice Charney, *Shakespeare's Roman Plays*, Harvard U.P., 1963, ch. v. See also, 'Shakespeare and the Lonely Dragon', *University of Toronto Quarterly*, XXIV, 1955.

3. J. C. Maxwell, 'Animal Imagery in *Coriolanus*', *M.L.R.*, XLII, 1947; F. N. Lees, *'Coriolanus*, Aristotle and Bacon', *R.E.S.*, n.s., I, 1950.

4. British Academy Lecture, 1912; reprinted in *Studies in Shakespeare*, ed. Peter Alexander, 1964, and Bradley, *A Miscellany*, 1929.

5. *The Imperial Theme*, 1931.

6. For discussion of the poems see F. O. Matthiessen, *The Achievement of T. S. Eliot*, 1935, 1958, pp. 137–43; R. Taranath, *'Coriolanus*, *The Waste Land* and the *Coriolan* Poems', *Literary Criterion* (Mysore), VI, i, pp. 111–20; E. P. Bollier, 'A Broken Coriolanus: A Note on T. S. Eliot's "Coriolan"', *Southern Review*, III, 1962, pp. 625–33.

7. E.g. Irwin Smith, *Shakespeare's Globe Playhouse: A Modern Reconstruction*, New York, 1956, p. 12. The stage-directions are discussed by Sahae Yoshitomi,

located, sometimes by stage-directions and sometimes by the topography of the dialogue, and there is little difficulty in determining at any point where we are in Rome and where on the stage; Allardyce Nicoll finds it possible that Volumnia's entrance in v. v was made from the yard, suggesting that the play made unusually enterprising use of theatre space.[1] An early Italian pageant was played between two 'castles' representing Rome and Corioli,[2] while Alexandre Hardy's *Coriolan* (*c.* 1600) was designed for multiple staging from six 'mansions' or 'scenes', with a seventh location without scenery.[3] There is no occasion for such staging in *Coriolanus*. The façade of the tiring-house, serving for Rome in I. i, serves for Corioli in I. ii, for Martius' house in I. iii, and for Corioli again in I. iv. The direction at I. iv. 12, 'Enter two Senators with others on the Walles of Corialus', indicates the use of upper levels[4] as city walls in these scenes, but they seem not to be specifically required elsewhere in the play. The direction requiring Martius to enter the gates and be shut in (I. iv) indicates the use of a large, gated central opening, while in I. ix that requiring Cominius to enter at one door and Martius at another suggests two narrower openings widely spaced. The basic stage-design described by W. W. Lawrence, with a tarras across three doors, one wide and perhaps inset, would meet the minimal prescription.[5] As stage-furniture, Shakespeare calls for low stools in I. iii, and for 'Cushions, as it were in the Capitoll' in II. ii. These initiatives could license others (e.g. siege-ladders, tents) and a throne is prescribed by the dialogue, but not by the stage-directions, in the supplication scene.[6] As in other plays scenes vary in their need for an expressive location. Some are better for being vague until suddenly made specific (e.g. Coriolanus in IV. iv before the house of Aufidius), and proof of Shakespeare's intermittently expressive use of location is offered by the last scene,

---

'Stage Directions and the Tragedy of *Coriolanus*', *Kikan Eibungaku*, II, 1965, pp. 109–24.

1. See head-notes to each scene, especially v. v.

2. See G. R. Kernodle, *From Art to Theatre*, 1944, p. 78, and below, p. 75.

3. See below, p. 75.

4. For a general account, see R. Hosley, 'Shakespeare's use of a Gallery over the Stage', *Shakespeare Survey*, 10, 1957, pp. 77–89.

5. W. J. Lawrence, *The Physical Conditions of the Elizabethan Public Playhouse*, 1927, p. 16. His sketch is reproduced with comments by R. Southern, 'On Reconstructing an Elizabethan Playhouse', *Shakespeare Survey*, 12, 1959, p. 33. I agree with Southern that there should be scope for a projecting discovery-space to conceal and reveal (say) a throne.

6. See v. i. 63, 'he does sit in gold', and v. iv. 22, 'sits in his state'.

which appears at one point to be set in Antium and at another in Corioli.[1]

Act IV, Scene vi, opens with Sicinius commending a Rome of 'tradesmen singing in their shops and going / About their functions friendly', the craftsman's city that the patricians despise. The spectacle here might well have actualized some elements in Brutus' description in II. i. 203–16—the stalls, bulks and popular throngs, with strong side-accent and a busy stage-platform. When Martius sits in his 'state' or throne, 'like a thing made for Alexander', convention requires a strong centre-accent, and it is possible that at this point the symbolic potentials of the Jacobean theatre prevailed over the naturalistic ones, with the live inhuman image against the façade flanked with others, literally unmoved and unmoving—of Mars, Jupiter, Victoria, and even Tacita (North's 'Lady Silence').[2] In v. ii, the throne could be concealed by a tent-like canopy, with the soldiers on guard outside it, to be revealed and occupied at l. 57.

Throughout the play much importance is attached to the body's movements. As Florio's Montaigne proclaims, 'there is no motion, nor jesture that doth not speake, and speakes in a language very easie, and without any teaching to be understood', and this, he adds, must be 'deemed the proper and peculiar speech of humane nature'.[3] In large ways and small there are clear continuities with pageantry. Some effects have already been remarked—the domination of the stage by the differing Roman bodies of Menenius and Martius in the first scene, the confrontation between Martius (muffled) and Aufidius (the servants doubtless crouched in their inadequacies), the figures of the older and the younger Martius against the invocation of 'a great sea-mark'. But the effects are almost continuous. The essential relationships between Volumnia ('seen him stamp thus') and Virgilia, bent over her embroidery are quite fully expressed without recourse to words. Shakespeare's control of the spectacle is sometimes quite overt, as in the stage-direction and opening

1. See v. vi headnote.
2. I share Kernodle's confidence that the symbolic resources of the English Renaissance theatres were much like those cultivated elsewhere in Europe, and that the evidence must be sought in architecture and the visual arts rather than in the meagre surviving theatrical documents. All the figures named here are to be found, for example, in the carved screens (dated 1610) and mantels of Burton Agnes Hall, Yorkshire; Mars bears a sword and shield, Jupiter bestrides an eagle, Victoria wears a laurel wreath and stands upon a dragon, and Quiet carries a dove upon her head.
3. Ed. T. Seccombe, 1908, II, p. 175 ('An Apologie of Raymond Sebond').

speech of v. v, and supremely in the silent tableaux of kneeling
figures in the 'unnatural scene' the gods look down and laugh at.
Clamour and music, as well as silence, are thoroughly assimilated
into the play's unity of effect, so that heard from a distance some
elements of its design would register still—from the early shouts,
the drums and trumpets of battle and ovation, through the
incantatory chants of 'it shall be so', the routine street cries of
Rome at peace, fresh panic and commotion, quiet and tension,
to the 'sackbuts, psalteries and fifes' and the Romans unshouting
the cries that banished Martius; and, alone of the plays, it calls
specifically at the end for the sounding of 'a dead march'.

The probability that Roman plays were staged in at least a
partial Roman costume is sufficiently established by the celebrated 'Peacham Drawing' of Titus Andronicus (1595). From it
Dover Wilson concluded that the plebeians wore the equivalent
of modern dress while the patricians were renaissance Romans; a
full discussion of stage-practice, with many illuminating illustrations, is offered by Moelwyn Merchant.[1] Shakespeare's
Martius is, however, given a hat to wave in II. iii. (ll. 98, 165),
and it is hard to resist the impression that Shakespeare had in
mind the bonnet that Bolingbroke is said to have doffed to the
oyster-wench.[2] Pope emended to 'cap', but 'stinking, greasy caps'
are very plebeian properties elsewhere in the play.[3]

Little has been written specifically about Jacobean acting of
Coriolanus, but the testing role of Volumnia has been related
speculatively to the abilities of boy actors.[4]

VI. CORIOLANUS IN THE THEATRE

Shakespeare reordered events and characters purposefully
enough to have been perfectly at ease with Cicero's observation,
made about Coriolanus, that 'it is conceded to rhetoricians to
distort history in order to give more point to their narrative'.[5]
He could have known from Livy the circumstance to which
Cicero was referring—that some authorities reported Martius
killed by the Volsces while others had him die in exile of old age.
A comprehensive history of the Coriolanus myth would chart the
changing emphases and claims of the rival accounts and seek to

1. 'Classical Costume in Shakespearian Productions', *Shakespeare Survey*, 10,
1957, pp. 71-6. See also J. D. Wilson (ed.), *Julius Caesar*, I. ii. 264 note.

2. *Richard II*, I. iv. 31.

3. IV. vi. 132, II. i. 265, etc.

4. W. Robertson Davies, *Shakespeare's Boy Actors*, 1939, pp. 149-50.

5. Cicero, *Brutus*, translated G. L. Henderson, 1962, p. 47.

relate them to contemporary pressures and interests.[1] Its history in the theatre responds to the same kind of probing. As Odell says, 'Shakespeare's *Coriolanus* seemed destined to be launched, with new trimmings, during or after each of England's successive politico-civic upheavals; Dennis so set it forth after 1715, and Thomson after the '45.'[2] And not Shakespeare's *Coriolanus* only. The Coriolanus myth in the theatre moves through many decades of European history and in several languages, disclosing new potentials and changing kinds of relevance, from the days of the Condottiere to those of the urban guerrilla.

It is aesthetically and historically appropriate that the theatrical history of Coriolanus appears to begin in 1453 when, in the course of Francesco Sforza's campaign against the Venetians, a pageant of *Coriolan* was performed between castle structures representing Rome and Corioli in the cathedral *piazza* of Milan.[3] Its promoters were apparently recruiting civic support for the Duke with a show commemorating the virtues of strong, magnanimous leadership in a city state, and in a superb, festive setting commending to the people the excitements of war. In contrast, the earliest formally composed play on the theme was in a rival tradition, remote from pageant and triumph. This was *Coriolanus tragicomica*, by Hermann Kirchner, written in Marburg in 1599. Imitating Seneca's Latin and opening with a prologue by *Ira*, its postulates are moral rather than political and have to do with the damaging consequences of ungoverned passion.[4] Kirchner's play coincided with the start of a flourishing neoclassic vernacular tradition in France, from the time of Henry IV, through the Thirty Years War and the wars with Spain and Austria, up to and after the outbreak of the Revolution. Fifteen French versions of *Coriolan* were written, and most of them performed, between 1625 (when Alexandre Hardy's *Coriolan* was published) and 1821, when Levacher de la Feutrie's *Coriolan devant Rome* coincided with the year of Napoleon's death.[5] Hardy's *Coriolan* is a play of great

1. See Bernhard Kytzler, *Shakespeare, Coriolan, Dichtung und Wirklichkeit*, Frankfurt, 1965.

2. G. C. D. Odell, *Shakespeare from Betterton to Irving*, 1921, I, p. 59.

3. See *Archivio Storico Lombardo*, serie seconda, Vol. IV, Anno XIV, Milan, 1887, pp. 826–7.

4. Kirchner's play is described by Martin Brunkhorst, *Shakespeare's 'Coriolanus' in Deutscher Bearbeitung*, Berlin, 1973, pp. 4–6.

5. They comprise: Alexandre Hardy (1625), Chapoton (*Le Véritable Coriolan*, 1637), Chevreau (1637), Abeille (1676), Chaligny de Plaine (1722), Mauger (1748), Richer (1748), Gudin de la Brenellerie (1776), Balze (1776), Tronchin (1784), La Harpe (1784), Beffroy de Reigny (*Coriolinet, ou Rome sauvée*, 1786), Ségur (1787), Achille Goujon (*Coriolan chez les Volsques*, 1800), Levacher de la

elegance and some force, with many tantalizing but apparently independent resemblances to Shakespeare, in its selection of events from Plutarch (Amyot's translation) and in some of its amplifications. Although published a little after the 1623 Folio it was probably written before the turn of the century.[1] Hardy begins with Coriolan (already so named) reluctantly persuaded by Volomnie to submit to popular trial:

> Moy, flechir le genoüil devant une commune.
> Non, je ne le veux faire, et ne crains sa rancune.

He ends with the distress of Volomnie at finding herself her son's murderer:

> O Mere parricide! ô Mere criminelle!
> De ton sang innocent execrable bourrelle.
> O Dieux! ô Dieux cruels! que vous avez produit
> De ma peine pieuse un detestable fruict!
> Chetive! pour sauver le sac de ma patrie,
> J'immole mon enfant, j'ay ma race meurtrie.

The myth is ripe for treatment in the neoclassic tradition, and its history in the French theatre is at once aesthetic (inviting symmetry and economy of form), moral (focusing the dilemmas of duty), and political (touching the divided interests of the community). And it is charged with the emotional intensities that set tensions between *nature* and *honneur*, well fitted to sustained histrionic declamation. The succeeding French *Coriolan*s react to changing taste and changing political pressures until the distance between possible renderings is measured by two versions of the late 1780s, one performed in Catherine the Great's Hermitage theatre in Petersburg, and the other a 'Folie héroï-comique en vaudevilles' in the turbulent Paris of 1786.[2]

Feutrie (*Coriolan devant Rome*, 1821). They are noted or discussed by H. C. Lancaster, *A History of French Dramatic Literature in the Seventeenth Century*, 9 vols., Baltimore, 1929–66; *French Tragedy in the Time of Louis XV and Voltaire, 1715–1774*, 2 vols., Baltimore, 1950; *French Tragedy in the Reign of Louis XVI and the Early Years of the French Revolution, 1774–1792*, Baltimore, 1953.

1. For a full account of the relationship between Shakespeare's play and Hardy's, see H. C. Lancaster, 'A. Hardy and Shakespeare', Todd Memorial Volume, *Philological Studies*, ed. J. D. Fitz-Gerald and P. Taylor, 1930, pp. 3–6, and M. W. MacCallum, *Shakespeare's Roman Plays*, pp. 475–82. Quotations from Hardy are from the 1884 edition, edited by E. Stengel, vol. II.

2. Ségur's *Caius-Marcius Coriolan*, 'Représentée sur le Théâtre de l'Hermitage à Pétersbourg en 1787', was published in *Théâtre de l'Hermitage de Catherine II*, I, Paris, 1799. The vaudeville subtitle is of Beffroy de Reigny's *Coriolinet, ou Rome sauvée*, 1786.

There may be some truth in the claim that Shakespeare's pre-eminence discouraged others from attempting English versions of comparable enterprise and diversity through the same period,[1] but the London history of Coriolanus is nevertheless an eventful and various one. It begins with Nahum Tate's *The Ingratitude of a Common-Wealth*, a mangled and truncated version of Shakespeare's text with lurid appendages: Aufidius vows to violate Virgilia, who kills herself; Volumnia fells the Volscian conspirator Nigridius with a partisan; the young Martius is tortured before trying to wake his dead mother, and Coriolanus endures as a spectator to the end, flying to 'Death's calm Region' with his deceased family in his arms. In face of such effects it is impossible to take seriously the political circumstances of the dedication, which might otherwise have been interesting. Writing in the aftermath of civil war, and remembering that his patron's grandfather, the Marquess of Worcester, led the last garrison to hold out for the king, Tate proclaims that the moral of his scenes is to 'Recommend Submission and Adherence to Establisht Lawful Power, which in a word, is Loyalty'.[2] Tate's play was probably first performed in 1681 and in the following year it was put on ('Caius Martius with dancing and volting') to entertain the Moroccan ambassador;[3] there is no record of a revival and the *Coriolanus* played in Lincoln's Inn Fields in December 1718 was apparently Shakespeare's, restored to the stage by John Rich.[4]

In November of the following year John Dennis's version, *The Invader of His Country: or, The Fatal Resentment*, was acted three times at Drury Lane.[5] The Prologue confesses both Dennis's aesthetic concern to order the 'wild confusion' of his original 'upon Shakespeare's plan', and his political eagerness to point the analogy with the Pretender who 'Combin'd with Foreign Foes t'invade the State'. Neither the aesthetic nor the political ambitions are realized, and it is a play that Barton Booth, who played the lead, might well have blushed in acting. There are signs of Dennis's acquaintance with French versions ("Thy filial Piety has been thy Fate; / And I have kill'd my Son'), the belly-fable is omitted, Aufidius is killed by Martius, and Martius himself run through the back by a tribune. A curious

1. See MacCallum, *Shakespeare's Roman Plays*, p. 476.
2. N. Tate, *The Ingratitude of a Common-Wealth*, 1682 (Cornmarket Press Facsimile, 1969), A2ᵛ. See also Allardyce Nicoll, *Restoration Drama*, 1900, p. 173.
3. See, *The London Stage, 1660–1700*, pt I, pp. 303, 304.
4. Odell, op. cit., I, p. 227.
5. Published in 1720 (Cornmarket Press Facsimile, 1969).

but revealing feature of Dennis's preface is the resemblance he finds between the treatment of Coriolanus by the Roman rabble and that which he himself (and therefore also his patron, the Duke of Newcastle) suffered at the hands of 'insolent players' who allowed his work only three performances.[1] As soon as it was taken off, a play with the same title but 'written by Shakespeare' was put on at Lincoln's Inn Fields, and it appears that the subterfuge at Dennis's expense was repeated in January 1720.[2] By the end of the year, however, Shakespeare's *Coriolanus* was advertised again and performed, possibly with Quin in the title-role;[3] it was revived for three performances in 1721 and 1722.[4]

For nearly thirty years *Coriolanus* was neglected in the English theatre, a circumstance which may have encouraged James Thomson to try his hand with a neoclassic version based on Dionysius of Halicarnassus. After Thomson's death it was played for ten performances at Covent Garden (January 1749) as an act of piety and benevolence by Quin under the patronage of George Lyttelton, the considerable profits going to pay the author's debts. Veturia (in this play the mother of Martius, while Volumnia is his wife) was played by Peg Woffington. Thomson is nostalgically elegiac about antique nobility and his pen moves with Martius' sword:

> *Rome* is no more! that *Rome* which nurs'd my youth:
> That *Rome*, conducted by Patrician virtue,
> She is no more! My sword shall now chastise
> These sons of pride and dirt! Her upstart tyrants!
> Who have debased the noblest state on earth
> Into a sordid democratic faction.[5]

Veturia threatens suicide before Coriolanus capitulates to 'the powers of Nature' and the play ends with Galesus arresting Attius Tullus (who has conspired against Martius but not killed him) and telling the audience that 'Above ourselves our COUNTRY should be dear'. Thomson's play was never revived in its entirety but in February 1752 a hybrid version, *Coriolanus: or the Roman Matron*, 'taken from Shakespear and Thomson', was acted in Dublin and repeated, with changes, at Covent Garden in 1754.[6]

---

1. *The Invader of His Country*, 1720 (1969), A2ᵛ; see also Odell, I, p. 239.
2. See C. B. Hogan, *Shakespeare in the Theatre 1701–1800*, 1952, p. 101.
3. Genest's suggestion, accepted by Hogan, op. cit., p. 101.
4. Hogan, op. cit., pp. 101–2.
5. James Thomson, *Works*, ed. P. Murdoch, 6 vols., 1773, IV, p. 272.
6. The Covent Garden version was published in 1755 (Cornmarket Press Facsimile, 1969). For a full account of this and related versions see Esther K.

Thomas Sheridan, to whom the arrangement is attributed, retains only the third scene (the domestic one) of Shakespeare's first act and follows it with most of Shakespeare's second; his second act is made from Shakespeare's third, and his third from Thomson's first and second; the fourth act compounds Shakespeare and Thomson, and the last follows Thomson. The Advertisement to the 1755 edition finds Shakespeare's play 'ill calculated for representation' and Thomson's 'tedious in the acting'. It betrays its true appeal by featuring its 'universally admired' Roman Ovation 'performed to the sound of drums, fifes and trumpets' with a hundred and eight persons 'in the military Procession alone'.[1] Slightly anticipating Sheridan's Covent Garden production, Garrick revived Shakespeare's play at Drury Lane (11 November 1754) in a severely abbreviated but authentic text.[2] Comparing the two, a contemporary report commends the Drury Lane play as 'the most mobbing, huzzing, shewy, boasting, drumming, trumpeting Tragedy', and at Covent Garden finds the 'divine but nodding Shakespear, put in his Night-Gown by *Messire* Thomson'.[3] Garrick's production, however, enjoyed only eight performances and he never tried another, while Shakespeare in Thomson's nightgown took the stage again in 1758, 1759, 1760, 1765, and 1768, each time at Covent Garden. The mobbing and boasting were muted, and the age was persuaded to honour the hero of the earlier annals, 'Disinterested, just, with every virtue / Of civil life adorn'd',[4] who in the end forfeited his life to his country.

Another twenty years passed without a London production, but in February 1789 John Philip Kemble's staging of the play at Drury Lane began a generation of performances which have never been surpassed in celebrity. Usually with his sister, Mrs Siddons, as Volumnia, Kemble appeared in five further productions at Drury Lane, the last in 1797; and from 1806 to 1817 he played in five at Covent Garden, one in Edinburgh, and two in Bath. His

Sheldon, 'Sheridan's *Coriolanus*: An 18th-Century Compromise', *Shakespeare Quarterly*, xiv, 1963, pp. 153–61.

1. The Dublin version published in 1757 (Cornmarket Press Facsimile, 1969) claimed 'considerable additions' to the ovation at Covent Garden, with 'upwards of two hundred' participating.

2. Probably that printed in Bell's *Shakespeare*, 1773; see Odell, op. cit., i, p. 355.

3. See Odell, op. cit., i, p. 356.

4. From the 1755 edition, p. 78. The sentiment owes much to Dionysius of Halicarnassus, who is careful to say, however, that no man can have all the virtues (see *Roman Antiquities*, viii, pp. 60–2).

acting version, largely adapted from Sheridan's and published under much the same title, retained the ovation marking Martius' return from Corioli together with Volumnia's suicide threat and other contaminations from Thomson.[1] Kemble made no open attempt to focus the play on the politics of the Europe of his time, but it seems that he gave much thought to Rome. According to his biographer, James Boaden, he devoted himself 'with infinite solicitude, to the impersonation of the Roman character'.[2] Boaden's understanding of Kemble's interpretation rests on his recognition that 'the high patrician pride of that hero leads him to venture every thing for the Roman NAME' and that 'the sort of fame which exists but in popular breath, becomes at length despised from its certainty'. The role, he says, 'gave a *cognomen* to Kemble', the actor 'absolutely identified with the part'. Hence it happened that, confronting a riotous audience at Covent Garden, 'he did not . . . quite dismiss the character he played for the *manager*', and as a modern commentator has said, 'Kemble, defying for weeks the mob that besieged his theatre, is easy to think of as Coriolanus.'[3]

After Kemble the London theatre declined into what Odell calls its 'leaderless age', but Edmund Kean in January 1820 mounted a *Coriolanus* which offered 'to restore the text of Shakespeare, with omissions only'.[4] It ran for four days only and was coldly received, partly because of Kean's 'insignificance of figure' and partly because public taste had come to expect *The Roman Matron*. Hazlitt's comments leave the impression that Kean, knowing his limitations, chose to discard the monumental

1. *Coriolanus* ; *or, The Roman Matron. A Tragedy. Altered from Shakespeare*, 1789 (Cornmarket Press Facsimile, with introduction by Inga-Stina Ewbank, 1970). Another edition, 1806, calls itself 'A Historical Play' and directly attributes the 'additions from Thomson' to J. P. Kemble. As Inga-Stina Ewbank says in her introduction to the 1806 version (Cornmarket Facsimile, 1970) the changed subtitle 'reflects no new material or emphasis'; she describes such interventions as there are.

2. *Memoirs of the Life of John Philip Kemble*, 1825, II, p. 524. See also D. Rostron, 'John Philip Kemble's *Coriolanus* and *Julius Caesar*', *Theatre Notebook*, xxiii. i, pp. 26–34.

3. See Boaden's *Life of Kemble*, II, p. 428; A. C. Sprague, *Shakespearian Players and Performances*, 1954, p. 69; and Leigh Hunt on the 'O.P.' riots at Covent Garden, *The Examiner*, 24 Sept. and 19 Nov. 1809 (reprinted in George Rowell (ed.), *Victorian Dramatic Criticism*, 1971, pp. 165–170). Hunt says of the Covent Garden managers that in the new classical decor they had 'obeyed a certain aristocratic impulse of their pride', and remarked that the people would believe nothing about increased prices until they could inspect Kemble's accounts through 'an open and popular medium'.

4. Odell, *Shakespeare from Betterton to Irving*, II, pp. 150–1.

nobilitas carefully nutured by Kemble and descended into the common arena of man'.[1]

In the same season (November 1819) Macready at Covent Garden began his Coriolanus career. Conscious of Kemble's achievement, Macready tells us that he studied 'the various attitudes from the antique . . . intent on mastering the patrician's outward bearing, and under that giving vent to the unbridled passion of the man'.[2] His remaining performances included six at Drury Lane in 1824, 1831, and 1833, and at Covent Garden eight in 1838 and one in 1839. In 1838, says a contemporary account, Shakespeare's 'grand imaginings' were 'invested with reality, . . . the gowned nation, and the future masters of the world, whose eagles were to fly from furthest Ganges to extremest Thule are at last shown to us as the myriad-minded poet created them; simple, stern, barbaric, cooped up in the narrow field of their early struggles and conquests'.[3] Whatever the intimations of Victorian Empire and Victorian vulgarity, the production was, as John Forster reports, an eloquent historical pageant in a mode very different from Kemble's.[4] 'When Kemble played Coriolanus,' says Forster, 'his first appearance after his banishment was under worthy James Thomson's statue of Mars in the house of Aufidius'; Macready stood muffled and disguised before a starlit Antium with a distant level seascape 'interrupted only by a tall, solitary tower, the pharos, or watch-tower of Antium'—presumably the 'great sea-mark' of Martius' metaphor. The text was more fully Shakespeare's than any since Garrick, but Macready's own performance got a mixed reception and he himself was not always satisfied with it. Forster said of his Coriolanus that it was 'not an ideal abstraction of the dignities and graces, but a soldier of the early republic of Rome, a man of rough manners, but of fiery and passionate sincerity.'

Samuel Phelps, habitually cast in secondary parts by his jealous manager Macready, had played Aufidius to Vandenhoff's powerful Coriolanus in 1834. The play interested him and

1. See Hazlitt, *Works*, ed. P. P. Howe (1933), XVIII, pp. 290–1, for the article from the *London Magazine*, Feb. 1820; also pp. 199, 302, 308, and 377, and VI, p. 356.

2. Quoted by Furness (*Coriolanus*, p. 730). For a discussion of the 1837 production, see A. J. Basset, 'Macready's *Coriolanus*: an Early Contribution to Modern Theatre', *Ohio State University Theatre Collection Bulletin*, no. 13, pp. 14–26.

3. *John Bull*, 19 March 1838, cited by Odell, *Shakespeare from Betterton to Irving*, II, p. 211.

4. Forster's review, from *The Examiner*, March 1838, is reprinted in G. Rowell (ed.), *Victorian Dramatic Criticism*, pp. 67–71.

he was responsible for four of the eleven London productions from 1837 to 1860.[1] His first, which like the others respected Shakespeare's text, was much admired. It moved Henry Morley to say that 'the pride of Coriolanus is a virtue overgrown . . . associated with the utmost purity and tenderness of home affections'.[2] A continuity with the style of Kemble is suggested by the coincidence of Hazlitt's remark that Kemble's gesture to the lines, 'That like an eagle in a dove-cote, I / Flutter'd your Volscians in Corioles', gave 'double force to the image', with this on Phelps by Godfrey Turner:[3]

> A fine action of Phelps's accompanied his utterance of the word 'fluttered,' which came after a seemingly enforced pause, and with that lifted emphasis and natural break in his voice, remembered, I dare say, by all who admired him in his prime. Lifting his arm to its full outstretched height above his head, he shook his hand to and fro, as in the act of startling a flock of doves.

After Phelps the play was neglected in London for forty years but enjoyed a number of performances in New York, some with the distinguished American actor, Edwin Forrest, who is said to have turned upon the mob and 'calmly looked them reeling backwards'.[4] At Stratford there were productions in 1893 and 1898 with Frank Benson. Benson revived the play for London audiences at the Comedy Theatre in February 1901, to be followed by Irving two months later with a production at the Lyceum. The first was remembered mainly for Geneviève Ward's Volumnia, the second for Alma Tadema's sets, celebrated for their 'spectacular confrontations of space and distance'.[5] It was said of Benson that he was 'not big enough either in personality, in power, or inches',[6] and of Irving that 'his own personality was as unsuited for the part of Coriolanus as was that

1. I.e. 1848, 1850, and March and Sept. 1860, all at Sadler's Wells, where Phelps was manager; the others were played by Hamlin at Covent Garden (1837), Butler at Drury Lane (1837), Dillon at the Theatre Royal (1843), and by Anderson at Drury Lane (1851), the Britannia Theatre (1852), and the Standard Theatre (1852).

2. *Journal of a London Playgoer*, 1891, pp. 214–16 (quoted Furness, p. 733).

3. Quoted by A. C. Sprague, *Shakespeare and the Actors*, New York, 1963, p. 330.

4. Sprague, *Shakespeare and the Actors*, p. 329. See also Robert Speaight, *Shakespeare on the Stage*, 1973, pp. 76–7, who says of Forrest, 'If he could unloose the whirlwind, he was also the master of a monolithic repose'.

5. G. Reynolds, *Victorian Painting*, 1966, p. 123.

6. R. Dickins, quoted by Furness (p. 735).

of Miss Ellen Terry to Volumnia'.[1] Irving never resumed the role, but Benson included Coriolanus in six of his Stratford seasons from 1907 to 1919, the last being an abbreviated version curiously paired with a shortened *Merry Wives*;[2] his 1910 production was also put on in London at His Majesty's. Geneviève Ward continued with undiminished authority to play Volumnia through all the Benson productions, and again in 1920 to Charles Warburton's Coriolanus at the Old Vic. The producer on this last occasion was Robert Atkins, who revived the play in 1924 with Ion Swinley, again at the Old Vic. At Stratford George Skillan played Coriolanus in 1926, and the Irish actor of prodigious voice, Anew McMaster, in its next production in 1933. In the meantime the Marlowe Society of Cambridge staged a full Shakespearean text directed by Frank Birch (1928), Nugent Monck produced it with the Norwich Players at the Maddermarket, and William Poel offered a severely cut Napoleonic version on a platform stage in the Chelsea Palace (1931).[3]

The performance which has probably done most to set the standards and expectations of recent years was at the Old Vic under Lewis Casson in 1938, with Laurence Olivier and Sybil Thorndike. 'Olivier', says Trewin, 'was the arrogant patrician, a pillar of fire on a plinth of marble', while Sybil Thorndike, 'a thought too comfortably domestic in her early scene, was Rome personified during the Supplication'.[4] In 1939 Alec Clunes played in Iden Payne's Stratford production, which was the last at the Memorial Theatre until 1952, when Glen Byam Shaw's staging with Anthony Quayle occasioned at least one review of the play's politics.[5] The 1948 Old Vic production was distinguished not only for its Coriolanus (John Clements) but also for its Menenius, performed with great subtlety by Alec Guinness.[6] In 1953-4 Richard Burton and Fay Compton played under the

1. Austin Brereton, quoted by Furness (p. 736), who also quotes a commendatory comment by Arthur Symons. The most significant account of the production, based on the *Times* review, is given by Odell (II, pp. 456-7).

2. See J. C. Trewin, *Shakespeare on the English Stage 1900-1964*, 1964, pp. 297-9.

3. See R. Speaight, *William Poel and the Elizabethan Revival*, 1954, pp. 252-63. Speaight also comments on another Napoleonic version, by Langham, at Stratford, Ontario, 1961, in *Shakespeare on the Stage*, p. 237.

4. *Shakespeare on the English Stage*, p. 175. See also Speaight, *Shakespeare on the Stage*, p. 157.

5. See A. P. Rossiter, *Angel with Horns*, p. 237, who discusses the review which appeared in the *Daily Worker*.

6. Trewin, *Shakespeare on the English Stage*, p. 207.

direction of Michael Benthall at the Old Vic.[1] But it was another Olivier performance, in 1959 at Stratford under the direction of Peter Hall, with Edith Evans as Volumnia, that again vindicated the play in the theatre. It caught the arrogance and the violence but subdued them to the 'boy' under the sway of his Roman mother.

The play has since remained strongly established in the repertory. In 1963 Tyrone Guthrie put on a version in Victorian dress which made much of the emotional bond between Martius and Aufidius. At Stratford John Barton produced the play with Ian Richardson as Martius in 1967, and in 1972 all four Roman plays were 'performed in a group for the first time' with Ian Hogg as Coriolanus in Trevor Nunn's production. The same production, but with Nicol Williamson in the lead, joined the Royal Shakespeare Company's Aldwych season in October 1973. Williamson's performance gave great authority both to the rigour of the role and to the capitulation to natural feeling in 'It is no little thing to make / Mine eyes to sweat compassion'.

English productions could for the most part be held to witness to the truth of Coleridge's claim that the play shows 'the wonderful philosophic impartiality of Shakespeare's politics'—although not all accounts of that impartiality would be acceptable. The history of the play in Europe suggests that in translation some of the constraints and ironies that the play affords are less efficient, and that the propaganda potentials of its political myth can be more manifest. Thus it happened that a sequence of performances of a new translation by René-Louis Piachaud at the Comédie Française between December 1933 and February 1934 provoked fascist and royalist riots on a scale which led M. Daladier to dismiss the director and appoint the chief of the Sûreté in his place. Piachaud (a Swiss) was branded as 'a foreign fascist' and the play was suspended ('Coriolan en exil' said a newspaper), only to be resumed in March to renewed cheers for Martius' invective.[2] Robert Speaight records that the Maly Theatre in Moscow mounted in the following year a production which proclaimed a 'drama of individualism' showing 'a superman who

1. Described by Alan Dent as 'a mighty warming up of Shakespeare's coldest play'; see Speaight, *Shakespeare on the Stage*, p. 269.

2. See Rossiter, *Angel with Horns*, p. 236, and Speaight, *Shakespeare on the Stage*, p. 200. There are also brief comments by Henri Fluchère, 'Shakespeare in France: 1900–48', *Shakespeare Survey*, 2, 1949, p. 123, and by A. J. Axelrad, 'Shakespeare's Impact Today in France', *Shakespeare Survey*, 16, 1963, pp. 55–6. Pichaud's translation received further performances at the Comédie Française in 1957, and in the arena of Nîmes in 1955; they were politically uneventful.

had detached himself from the people and betrayed them',[1] and in 1960 an Army Theatre production of Saudek's translation in Prague is said to have represented Menenius as a 'rather nasty old loquacious fox of a politician' while the tribunes were 'wise, honest sincere, deep-thinking, class-conscious'.[2] There have been many other European productions, including an important one by Giorgio Strehler (Tofano's translation) in Milan where, in a sense, it all started.[3] In Italy, however, the story has usually been turned into opera,[4] and it is in Germany that the history of Coriolanus is most closely related to Shakespeare's theatre.

It begins with Kirchner's play in 1599 and reaches to Günter Grass's *Die Plebeier proben den Aufstand* (1966). It includes about a dozen significantly different translations, adaptations, and independent versions, which can often be shown to reflect intimately the political and cultural preoccupations of their time.[5] Thomson's *Coriolanus* was published in translation before Shakespeare's, in 1756, with a preface by Lessing; and for much the same public. Frederick the Great (who was another of Lessing's heroes) enlisted the great idea of Rome into the cause of national unity with an aria, 'Digli ch'io son fedele', for the opera *Coriolano* by Carl Heinrich Graun.[6] In 1789 Heinrich Joseph von Collin wrote his elevated version, in which Martius falls on his sword before the Volscian conspirators can reach him. It owes more to the French tradition than to Shakespeare and is now most remembered as the play to which Beethoven wrote his *Coriolan* overture.[7] Throughout the period the Coriolanus story afforded generous opportunities for the creative enterprise of both neoclassical and romantic makers and translators.[8]

1. *Shakespeare on the Stage*, p. 200.
2. Bretislav Hodek, *Shakespeare Survey*, 14, 1961, p. 118.
3. See Speaight, *Shakespeare on the Stage*, pp. 263–4.
4. See Max Friedlaender, 'Shakespeares Werke in der Musik', *Shakespeare-Jahrbuch*, xxxvii, 1901, p. 97. He names thirteen *Coriolan* operas, eleven Italian, but none is based on Shakespeare. Winton Dean notes two that are Shakespearean: A. Baeyens, *Coriolanus*, performed at Antwerp in 1940, and S. Sulek, *Koriolan*, at Zagreb in 1958; see 'Shakespeare in the Opera House', *Shakespeare Survey*, 18, p. 88.
5. A full account is given by Martin Brunkhorst, *Shakespeare's 'Coriolanus' in Deutscher Bearbeitung*, Berlin, 1973.
6. *Die Musik in Geschichte und Gegen-Wart*, 1955, iv, p. 958.
7. Von Collin's play is published in his *Werke*, 6 vols., Vienna 1812–14, vol. 1. Its relationship to Shakespeare is discussed by Wilhelm Münch in *Shakespeare Jahrbuch*, xli, 1906, pp. 22–44. There is no evidence that Beethoven's overture was ever performed with the play but see above p. 67.
8. They include an early undated MS. fragment by J. J. Kitt (1747–96), a celebrated, also unfinished, *Sturm und Drang* version by J. M. R. Lenz (1774), a

It is in the twentieth century, however, that the play has had its most distinctive life in Germany. Between the years 1911 and 1920 it seems to have been more often performed there than in England, perhaps because it has much to say about the relationship between military and democratic values.[1] Hans Rothe's translation of 1932 was broadcast in an emergent Nazi Germany, only to be banned a few years later and its author sent into exile. School editions of the 1930s, however, continued to offer Shakespeare's *Coriolanus* to the youth of Germany for its 'examples of valour and heroism' and for its illumination of the problem of populace and leader; the figure of Martius is said to tower over the falsely led people of a false democracy, offering to lead them to a healthier society 'as Adolf Hitler in our days wishes to lead our beloved German fatherland'.[2] The American authorities banned the play in the early years of occupation after the Second World War.[3] Its first post-war performance was at the Normark Landestheater at Schleswig in 1953, and there have been others. Most attention, however, has been attracted both within Germany and elsewhere by the version prepared by the Berliner Ensemble in 1963 from the unfinished adaptation by Bertolt Brecht.[4] Brecht, writing as he says, 'nach zwei idiotischen Kriegen', tried to diminish both the impact and the value of Martius' valour. His usefulness in the wars is recognized by the tribunes but it is not held in awe, and Brecht cuts from Shakespeare's poetry much of its heroic hyperbole.[5] Where the Volscian guard speaks of the Roman people banishing their defender 'in a violent popular ignorance' (v. ii. 39–40) Brecht characteristically suppresses the offending phrase, together with much in the play that

vigorous prose rendering by J. J. Eschenburg (1777), a neoclassic hybrid of Shakespeare and La Harpe by J. G. Dyke (1786), and an eclectic interpretation by J. F. Schink (1790). In the nineteenth century, the satirical poet Johannes Falk made the play a vehicle for anti-romantic polemic (1811), and Oswald Marbach adapted it to Hegel's rules (1866). The 'standard' translation is Dorothea Tieck's of 1831, challenged in recent years on the German stage by that of Richard Flatter.

1. Kytzler (*Shakespeare Jahrbuch*, LVII, 1921, p. 163) claims a 'Coriolan-Renaissance', with thirty-four performances in these years. His conclusions are put in perspective by Brunkhorst (op. cit., p. 157).

2. Brunkhorst, op. cit., p. 157.

3. See Dirk Grathoff, 'Dichtung versus Politik: Brechts "Coriolan" aus Günter Grassens sicht', *Brecht heute*, I, 1971, p. 169.

4. The text of the unfinished version, augmented by Tieck's translation, is in vol. XI (1959) of the *Stücke*, 14 vols., Frankfurt, 1953–7. It appends a study in dialogue form. Brecht began work on the play in 1951–2.

5. E.g. I. i. 66–71, II. ii. 86–7, v. iii. 70–4.

would seem to justify it—the excitement of the people's rage by slogans in III. iii, the sheepishness of the apprehensive citizens in IV. vi, the whipping of the slaves ordered by Sicinius, and the readiness of the people to lynch their leaders when things go badly. Similarly, the ampler claims of Martius' own kind of political wisdom are diminished or excised,[1] and the continuous simplification and occasional vulgarization of Shakespeare's effects leave little scope for a tragic outcome. Brecht's Martius asks that Rome should announce its capitulation with a smoke-signal, but Volumnia tells him that the smoke he sees from his camp is not a sign of surrender but rises up 'from forges where new swords are made for use against thee'.[2] He is no longer irreplaceable but merely a mortal threat to all in Rome. The political and historical discovery is that Rome has learned no longer to cherish such heroes, and the play closes with the tribunes presiding over a new popular order, with Brutus vetoing some modest proposals for mourning and commemorating Martius. Helene Weigel further heightened and simplified the struggle between plebeians and patricians, but she restored much of the Aufidius material which Brecht had cut and she represented the war with the Volscians as an episode in a feud whose motives were mere patrician honour.[3] She strengthens Brecht's presentation of a people refusing to fight until supplied with corn ('Kein Korn, kein Krieg') and follows him in requiring Martius to answer to the people about what he as consul would do with corn won from Volscian garners. Taking hints from Brecht she catches up material from other plays, allowing Martius to talk to a citizen-gardener about roses, recalling Macbeth's drunken porter into a conversation between Volscian officers, and borrowing odd lines from *Julius Caesar* and *Antony and Cleopatra*. Detailed comparison with Shakespeare's version reveals much about the subtleties of the original and about the brash nature of contemporary demands for 'relevance'.[4]

1. E.g. III. i. 89–111 is cut by Brecht, but restored, slightly shortened, by Helene Weigel.

2. Brecht, XI, pp. 374–5. The speech was featured in the London programme of the Berliner Ensemble (August 1965).

3. I owe my access to the *Bühnenfassung des Berliner Ensemble* to the Shakespeare Institute, Birmingham.

4. E.g. both Brecht and Weigel have the citizens greet the tribunes when they enter in Act I, and they instantly assume direction of the class struggle; Shakespeare insinuates them into the scene and allows them privately and independently to express their own assessments of Martius' position and character. Brecht cuts what Günter Grass oddly calls the talk of 'two benighted fools', while Weigel (but not Brecht) assimilates some of it into Volumnia's

Among the more interesting critics of Brecht's Shakespeare, Günter Grass was also sensitive to the ironies of Brecht's situation in East Berlin at the time of the uprising of 17 June 1953 when he continued without interruption his rehearsal of Strittmatter's *Katzgraben*. Grass's play (translated as *The Plebeians Rehearse the Uprising*) changes the production and shows the Boss (Brecht) rehearsing his *Coriolan* as news little by little reaches the stage about the progress of a Berlin rising against new work norms imposed by the Party and the Government.[1] The Boss uses the workers for the staging of his plebeian rising, and in the theatre the revolt prospers while in the streets outside it collapses. An adequate performance of Shakespeare's play would, one feels, leave an audience moved but unsurprised at the reported events of the Berlin of 1938, 1945, or 1953.

The Berliner Ensemble played at the National Theatre in 1965 and in the same year a production is said to have drawn huge, enthusiastic audiences in Central Park, New York. In 1973, perhaps prompted by Brecht and Grass, John Osborne published his *A Place Calling Itself Rome*, a 're-working' of Shakespeare's play which opens with Martius in bed with Virgilia, crying out in his sleep on Corioli and Aufidius. It brutalizes the play's invective with intense sexual nausea but allows Martius to be intelligibly exasperated by Roman democracy and to confront Aufidius with a sophisticated indictment of the Volscians (represented as urban fighters in paramilitary uniforms). Like John Dennis in 1720, Osborne omits the belly-fable.

There have been no major films of *Coriolanus*[2] but in 1963 the BBC included an abbreviated version in a series of nine one-hour plays of Shakespeare's Rome under the title *The Spread of the Eagle*, and Irish Television broadcast a production in 1972 with Frank Barry as Martius.

A complete account of *Coriolanus* in the theatre would attend

---

reflections later (*Bearbeitung*, p. 26). For fuller discussion of Brecht's version, see L. Lerner and L. Lob, '*Coriolanus*: Brecht and Shakespeare', *Shakespeare Newsletter*, XVII, 1959, p. 56; G. Bartolucci, 'Il Coriolano secondo Brecht', *Sipario* (Milan), no. 225, Jan. 1965, pp. 12–14; J. Kleinstück, 'Bertolt Brechts Bearbeitung von Shakespeare's *Coriolanus*', *Literaturwissenschaftlichen Jahrbuch der Görres-Gesellschaft*, Berlin, IX, 1968, pp. 319–32.

1. Published in London, 1966, with 'The Prehistory and Posthistory of the Tragedy of *Coriolanus* from Livy and Plutarch via Shakespeare down to Brecht and Myself', also a documentary report on the 17 June 1953 uprising, by Uta Gerhardt.

2. I judge from the filmography appended to Roger Manvell, *Shakespeare and the Film*, 1971.

to the intricate and often critically illuminating relationships between stage productions and the visual arts. Moelwyn Merchant has shown that eighteenth-century stagings of both Shakespeare's and Thomson's plays owe something to the imagination of Poussin.[1] Poussin stresses the tensions of the supplication scene, however, while Hayman and Casali, whose pictures also have their analogues in English theatre,[2] stress Martius' magnanimity in a tradition which looks back to Tiepolo.[3]

1. M. Merchant, *Shakespeare and the Artist*, 1959, ch. 11.

2. Hayman's drawing is reproduced in Merchant, *Shakespeare and the Artist*, plate 67, and discussed by Merchant in *S.Q.*, 9 Feb. 1958. Casali's painting is in Burton Constable Hall; it includes elements and properties relating it to other theatrical illustrations.

3. See A. Morassi, *A Complete Catalogue of the Paintings of G. B. Tiepolo*, 1962, plates 283 and 298. Morassi mistakenly describes the Würzburg *Coriolanus* as the *Family of Darius before Alexander*; the comparison of Coriolanus and Alexander, touched upon by Shakespeare, has a complex iconographical history.

THE TRAGEDY OF CORIOLANUS

DRAMATIS PERSONÆ

CAIUS MARTIUS, *afterwards Caius Martius Coriolanus.*
TITUS LARTIUS,⎫ *generals against the Volscians.*
COMINIUS,   ⎭
MENENIUS AGRIPPA, *friend to Coriolanus.*
SICINIUS VELUTUS,⎫ *tribunes of the people.*   5
JUNIUS BRUTUS,   ⎭
YOUNG MARTIUS, *son to Coriolanus.*
A Roman Herald.
NICANOR, *a Roman.*
TULLUS AUFIDIUS, *general of the Volscians.*   10
Lieutenant to Aufidius.
Conspirators with Aufidius.
ADRIAN, *a Volscian.*
A Citizen of Antium.
Two Volscian Guards.   15

VOLUMNIA, *mother to Coriolanus.*
VIRGILIA, *wife to Coriolanus.*
VALERIA, *friend to Virgilia.*
Gentlewoman attending on Virgilia.

*Roman and Volscian Senators, Patricians, Ædiles, Lictors, Soldiers,
Citizens, Messengers, Servants to Aufidius, and other Attendants.*

SCENE : *Rome and the neighbourhood; Corioles and the
neighbourhood; Antium.*

1. *Caius Martius Coriolanus*] Strictly there were four divisions of the Roman name, i.e. *praenomen*, applicable to the individual only; *nomen*, applicable to his 'gens'; *cognomen*, applicable to all members of the family within the 'gens'; and *agnomen*, an extra name commemorating a particular achievement. An example of the full name is, 'Publius Cornelius Scipio Africanus'; but in normal usage *cognomen* was often substituted for *agnomen*. Fully described, Caius Martius Coriolanus has *praenomen*, *nomen* and *agnomen* but no true *cognomen*. Shakespeare followed North (Appendix, p. 327) in treating the three names as Christian name, family name, and 'addition'. For convenience in the theatre he used 'Martius' for both intimate and public occasions. At a critical moment of the play, moreover, he apparently confused the order of names (see I. ix. 64 note, and Introduction, p. 41). North's spelling *Martius*, followed by

Shakespeare, has been retained throughout the present text. Its Latin meaning, 'pertaining to Mars', is appropriate in the play, even if the spelling in North (and in Holland's Livy) owed more to fashion than to deliberation.

2. *Titus Lartius*] For some anomalies in the spelling of this name and the character's presence in the play see Introduction, pp. 21–2. The form *Lartius* is correct.

5. *Sicinius Velutus*] Shakespeare takes over North's version of the name, given by Plutarch as *Sicinius Bellutus*.

9, 13. *Nicanor, Adrian*] For possible sources of these names, which do not occur in the 'Life of Coriolanus', see Introduction, p. 30.

10. *Tullus Aufidius*] The spelling is North's. F has *Auffidius* (in both compositors' stints) and occasionally *Auffidious* (B only).

THE TRAGEDY OF CORIOLANUS

ACT I

SCENE I

Enter a company of mutinous Citizens, with staves, clubs, and other weapons.

First Cit. Before we proceed any further, hear me speak.

All. Speak, speak.

First Cit. You are all resolved rather to die than to famish?

All. Resolved, resolved.   5

First Cit. First, you know Caius Martius is chief enemy to the people.

All. We know't, we know't.

First Cit. Let us kill him, and we'll have corn at our own price. Is't a verdict?   10

All. No more talking on't; let it be done. Away, away!

Second Cit. One word, good citizens.

First Cit. We are accounted poor citizens, the patricians good. What authority surfeits on would relieve us.   15

ACT I

Scene I

Act I Scene i] F (*Actus Primus. Scoena Prima.*)   6. First, you know] *Dyce;* First you know, *F.*   Martius] *F;* Marcius *Theobald.*   15. on] *F* (one), *F3.*

Scene i] located by Pope in 'A Street in Rome'. The citizens are presumably crossing the stage on the way to the Capitol (l. 47) when stayed by Menenius coming from it.

S.D.] This is unique among plays of the period in opening with a scene of public violence, but *Jack Straw* (1593) opens with an act of mutiny against a tax collector.

9–10. *corn . . . price*] Shakespeare anticipates the corn riots of North's account, which follow the war with the Volscians (see Appendix, p. 328).

10. *Is't a verdict?*] Is it an agreed judgement? The phrase is at once importunate and formally judicial.

11. *on't*] of it. A common usage.

15. *good*] wealthy, good for credit, with a play on 'virtuous'; cf. *Mer.V.*, I. iii. 12–17.

authority] i.e. those in authority, the ruling class; an early instance of this usage (see *O.E.D.*, s.v. 3).

If they would yield us but the superfluity while it
were wholesome, we might guess they relieved us
humanely; but they think we are too dear: the
leanness that afflicts us, the object of our misery, is
as an inventory to particularise their abundance;   20
our sufferance is a gain to them. Let us revenge
this with our pikes, ere we become rakes. For the
gods know, I speak this in hunger for bread, not in
thirst for revenge.

Second Cit. Would you proceed especially against Caius   25
Martius?

All. Against him first. He's a very dog to the commonalty.

Second Cit. Consider you what services he has done for
his country?   30

First Cit. Very well, and could be content to give him

27. *All.*] *F; First Cit.* | *Hudson, conj. Malone.*

on] F's *one* is a common rendering
of *on* in Shakespeare (see Introduction, p. 7).

16. *but*] merely. Wright, however,
thinks *but* qualifies *yield*, not *the
superfluity*, and paraphrases 'but yield
us'; the construction is grammatically
possible but does not accord well with
the argument about surfeit and
abundance.

17. *guess*] think, deduce; as often
in Shakespeare (e.g. *1H6*, II. i. 29).

18. *humanely*] out of fellow-feeling;
not then distinguished from 'human-
ly'.

they . . . dear] 'they think that the
charge of maintaining us is more
than we are worth' (Johnson). But
if the thought refers to what follows
it could mean, 'they set too high a
value on us'.

19. *object*] spectacle, object of
attention, as in *LLL.*, v. ii. 753,
'every varied object of his glance'.

20. *inventory . . . abundance*] i.e.
the means by which they itemize
their advantages. Cf. *Tw.N.*, I. v. 230.

21. *sufferance*] suffering; as often in
Shakespeare (e.g. *Meas.*, III. i. 81).

For a different use see below, III. i. 24.

22. *pikes*] pitchforks; not the 'steel
pikes' of v. vi. 150 (unless a pun is
intended).

rakes] i.e. as lean as rakes. For other
instances of the citizens' proverbs
see below, I. i. 204 and note.

27. All] Hudson's attribution to
the First Citizen (after Malone) is
supported by Sisson (*New Readings*)
and many others, but some collective
response seems appropriate. It is
likely that the first sentence is
spoken by all, and the second (*He's
. . . commonalty*) by one voice only.
Cf. l. 34 and note.

a very dog] i.e. ruthless, cruel; cf.
Gent., II. iii. 11, 'no more pity in him
than a dog'; *R3*, IV. iii. 6, 'flesh'd
villains, bloody dogs'; *2H4*, IV. v.
132–3, 'the wild dog / Shall flesh his
tooth in every innocent'. See also
below, III. iii. 120 and note.

27–8. *commonalty*] the common
people; as in *H8*, I. ii. 170, 'To gain
the love o'th'commonalty', Shakespeare's only other use. The word is
frequent in Holinshed and occurs in
North (Appendix, p. 350).

good report for't, but that he pays himself with
being proud.

Second Cit. Nay, but speak not maliciously.

First Cit. I say unto you, what he hath done famously,   35
he did it to that end: though soft-conscienced men
can be content to say it was for his country, he did it
to please his mother, and to be partly proud, which
he is, even to the altitude of his virtue.

Second Cit. What he cannot help in his nature, you   40
account a vice in him. You must in no way say he is
covetous.

First Cit. If I must not, I need not be barren of accusations. He hath faults, with surplus, to tire in
repetition.   *Shouts within.*   45
What shouts are these? The other side o'th'city is

---

34. *Second Cit.*] *Malone; All. | F.*   36. soft-conscienced] *Pope;* soft conscienc'd
F.   38. to please . . . proud] *F;* to please . . . partly to be proud *Hanmer;*
partly to please . . . to be proud *Capell, Wilson.*   partly] *F;* portly *conj. Staunton;* pertly *conj. Lettsom.*   46. these] *F;* those *F3.*

---

34. Second Cit.] Malone is here
preferred to F's *All.* Unlike the first
part of l. 27, this cannot be spoken
by the many. For the distinction
between the First and Second Citizens see below, I. i. 56 note.

35. *famously*] The citizens are
making Martius' 'fame' in the act of
talking about him. See Introduction,
p. 41.

36. *soft-conscienced*] soft-headed, lib-
eral-minded.

38. *to please . . . proud*] Capell's
recasting (*partly to please*) is supported
with the argument that the First
Citizen is consistently stressing Martius' pride; but so far from conceding anything to the Second
Citizen, the allusion to Martius'
mother intensifies the malice of the
judgement. See North, Appendix,
p. 317.

to be partly proud] i.e. partly to be
proud, to give himself reason to be
proud; for the adverbial construction
see Abbott 420.

39. *to . . . virtue*] i.e. he is as proud

as he is highly virtuous. Steevens
quotes *H8*, I. ii. 214, 'He's traitor to
th'height'. For the specific Roman
significance of 'virtue' (meaning
'valour') see Introduction, p. 40.

41–2. *no way . . . covetous*] For
Martius' disdain of spoils see below,
I. v. 4–8, I. ix. 37–40, and II. ii.
124–9; also North, Appendix, p. 325,
and Introduction, p. 50.

45. within] i.e. within the tiring-
house. The noise and the citizen's
location of it help to create in the
theatre the illusion of the city's
extent.

46. *The . . . city*] North tells of the
people meeting at 'the Holy Hill'
(Mons Sacer) where the tribunes
were appointed (see Appendix, p.
319, and I. i. 214 note); but this was
three miles outside the city, and
Shakespeare makes no specific reference to it. The topography of
Rome is sufficiently indicated by
fifteen allusions to the Capitol and
ten to the market-place, with Martius reporting trouble 'in these

risen: why stay we prating here? To th'Capitol!

All. Come, come.

First Cit. Soft, who comes here?

Enter MENENIUS AGRIPPA.

Second Cit. Worthy Menenius Agrippa, one that hath   50
always loved the people.

First Cit. He's one honest enough, would all the rest
were so!

Men. What work's, my countrymen, in hand? Where
go you

With bats and clubs? The matter? Speak, I pray you.   55

First Cit. Our business is not unknown to th'Senate;

54–5.] *As Theobald;* What . . . hand? / . . . matter / . . . you. / *F.*   56. *First*
Cit.] Capell (and throughout the scene); 2. Cit. / F.

several places of the city' (I. i. 184).
Wright suggests that Shakespeare
had London in mind and that 'the
Tower was to him the Capitol', in
support he cites *Caes.,* II. i. 110, where
the Capitol stands apparently in the
east. At a later stage of his narrative
North speaks of uproar 'on thother
side' of the city (Appendix, p. 346).

46, 47. *o'th', To th'*] For these and
other elisions in the text see Introduction, p. 4.

49. *Soft*] gently now, wait a moment; cf. *Tw.N.,* I. v. 277, 'not too
fast! Soft, soft!', and *Ham.,* III. i. 88.

50–1. *one . . . people*] For Menenius'
standing in the people's esteem see
North, Appendix, p. 319.

54.] Commentators remark the
propriety of the change to verse
with the entry of Menenius; the
citizen will be moved to verse at
l. 113 (see l. 119 note). The F
lineation here, as elsewhere in the
play when patricians and plebeians
talk together, is very insecure (see
Introduction, p. 14).

work's] either = *work is,* or *work*
has; a plural subject with a single
verb is common in Shakespeare.

55. *bats and clubs*] the weapons of
the London apprentices, often called
in to quieten an affray, and some-

times to start one. In *1H6,* I. iii. 83,
the Mayor of London threatens to
'call for clubs' to deal with a brawl,
and apprentices swear by their
cudgels and break heads with them
in *More,* II. i. and II. ii.

bats] cudgels, staffs; cf. *Compl.,* 64, 'So
slides he down upon his grained bat'.

56. First Cit.] Capell's reassignment is apt. Up to this point seven of
the First Citizen's eight contributions
to the dialogue (in F) have been
hostile to authority and to Martius,
while the Second Citizen's four
interventions have been sympathetic
or cautionary. Apparent consistency
of character requires that the critical
or watchful exchanges with Menenius
in the rest of the scene be offered by
the citizens' leader. Knight retains
the F assignment with the comment,
'The *first* Citizen is a hater of public
men—the *second,* of public *measures*;
the first would kill Coriolanus—the
second would repeal the laws relating to corn and usury'; he adds
that the 'low brawler' could not
argue so well with Menenius. The
First Citizen is not without wit,
however, and it is hard to imagine
him a mute audience to Menenius
and the Second Citizen.

not . . . Senate] Cf. North, 'The

they have had inkling this fortnight what we intend
to do, which now we'll show 'em in deeds. They
say poor suitors have strong breaths: they shall
know we have strong arms too.   60

Men. Why masters, my good friends, mine honest
    neighbours,
Will you undo yourselves?

First Cit. We cannot, sir, we are undone already.

Men. I tell you, friends, most charitable care
Have the patricians of you. For your wants,   65
Your suffering in this dearth, you may as well
Strike at the heaven with your staves, as lift them
Against the Roman state, whose course will on
The way it takes, cracking ten thousand curbs
Of more strong link asunder than can ever   70
Appear in your impediment. For the dearth,

57. intend] *F;* intended *Rowe².*   61–2.] *As Theobald;* Why . . . honest / . . .
your selues? / *F.*   65. you. For . . . wants,] *Johnson, Rowe subst.* (you: for);
you for . . . wants. *F;* you for . . . wants, *F3.*

Senate met many dayes in consultation about it: but in the end they
concluded nothing' (Appendix, p.
319).

  58–9. *They . . . breaths*] No equivalent saying has been found elsewhere;
it seems to be part of the created
proverbial wisdom of the play (see
I. i. 204 note). For the bad breath of
the populace cf. III. i. 65, III. iii. 121,
IV. vi. 99, and IV. vi. 131; instances
elsewhere in Shakespeare include
2H6, IV. vii. 10–11, and *Caes.,*
I. ii. 254. For an analogous quibble
on *strong* cf. *All's W.,* v. ii. 5–6, 'and
smell somewhat strong of her strong
displeasure'. King suggests a further
pun on *suitors* and 'souters' (*O.E.D.,*
souter, 'a type of workman of little
or no education'), but Shakespeare
does not use the word.

  65. *For your wants*] as for your
wants; the sense required by Johnson's punctuation, followed here.
F3's reading, virtually ending the
sentence at *this dearth,* makes plainer
sense and entails a slighter inter-

vention in the text. Johnson's version, however sustains the formidable
irony of Menenius' rebuke across
nine lines down to *help* ('as for your
suffering, you can do nothing about it
except pray').

  66. *dearth*] Cf. North, 'the extreme
dearth they had emong them'
(Appendix, p. 328).

  68. *will on*] will keep on; for the
construction see Abbott 405. The
omission of verbs of motion is still
heard in Ulster, e.g. 'I want out'
(Brooks).

  69. *curbs*] the literal sense, 'chains
attached to the bit of a horse's
bridle', stirs behind the figurative
sense of 'check, restraint', hence
cracking and *links*; but there may be a
further suggestion of arms linked to
form an obstructive phalanx.

  71. *your impediment*] obstruction of
your making. For similar battle
associations cf. *Oth.,* v. ii. 266–7, 'I
have made my way through more
impediments / Than twenty times
your stop', and *R3,* v. ii. 4.

The gods, not the patricians, make it, and
Your knees to them, not arms, must help. Alack,
You are transported by calamity
Thither where more attends you; and you slander   75
The helms o'th'state, who care for you like fathers,
When you curse them as enemies.

First Cit. Care for us? True indeed! They ne'er cared
for us yet. Suffer us to famish, and their store-
houses crammed with grain; make edicts for usury,   80
to support usurers; repeal daily any wholesome act
established against the rich, and provide more
piercing statutes daily, to chain up and restrain the
poor. If the wars eat us not up, they will; and
there's all the love they bear us.   85

78. indeed! They] *Theobald;* indeed, they *F.*

74. *transported*] carried along; carried away. The word is apt to the
people's fury and to their movement
through the streets.

calamity] Menenius attributes the
distress of the people to the disast-
rous circumstance of famine. Plutarch, on a later occasion, ascribes it
to neglect of agriculture in wartime
and reports that some thought it
'practised and procured' by the
nobility. (Appendix, p. 328.) The
rising in which Menenius intervened
was occasioned not by famine but
by 'the sore oppression of userers'
(Appendix, p. 318).

75. *Thither*] i.e. to the point of
mutiny.

76. *helms*] helmsmen, guides. A
figurative use of which *O.E.D.* gives
only this instance; but compare
2H6, I. iii. 98, where Margaret is
invited to 'steer the happy helm', and
3H6, v. iv. 1–38, where she imagines
the ship of state ravaged by storm
and 'will not from the helm'.

fathers] '*Patres*, i.e. "fathers", was
the title of the Senators of ancient
Rome; hence *patricians* = of noble
birth, noble, senatorial' (Verity).

78. *indeed! They*] Although Theo-

bald's punctuation is almost univ-
sally followed, Hudson retains F as
'more coherent and clear'. F could
mean 'As a matter of fact, they have
never cared for us'; but this slightly
strains the phrase *True indeed*, and
the indignant ironic effect of Theobald's version is more fitting. Commas
are elsewhere used in F where modern practice calls for exclamation
marks.

79–84. *Suffer . . . poor*] Shakespeare
continues to conflate Plutarch's accounts of two rebellions, see above
l. 74 note.

83. *piercing statutes*] severe laws; cf.
Meas., I. iii. 19, 'We have strict
statutes and most biting laws'. The
play restates the complaint reported
by Plutarch, that 'the Senate dyd
favour the riche against the people'
(Appendix, p. 318).

84. *wars eat us*] Cf. North, 'And
suche as had nothing left, their
bodies were layed holde of, and they
were made their bonde men, notwithstanding all the woundes and cuttes
they shewed, which they had receyved
in many battells, fighting for defence
of their countrie and common
wealth' (Appendix, p. 318).

Men. Either you must
    Confess yourselves wondrous malicious,
    Or be accus'd of folly. I shall tell you
    A pretty tale; it may be you have heard it,
    But since it serves my purpose, I will venture   90
    To stale't a little more.
First Cit. Well, I'll hear it, sir; yet you must not think
    to fob off our disgrace with a tale; but, and't please
    you, deliver.

91. stale't] *Theobald;* scale't *F, Steevens.*
thinke / . . . tale: / . . . deliver. *F.*

92–4.] *Prose, as Capell;* Well, / . . .

89. *pretty*] apt, nicely turned.
Furness quotes the *Fables of Bidpai,
The Morall Philosophie of Doni*, translated Thomas North, 1570 (ed.
Jacobs, p. 64): 'That noble Romaine
that fought and laboured to bring the
people and communaltie to love their
Magistrates and superiours, tolde
them a pretie tale . . . howe the
handes were angrie with the bodie.'
The tale itself is remote from the
play, but it is ended with the comment, 'With this pretie tale he made
the people sensibly to understand
what became them, and how they
should behave themselves to their
superiours.' The political attitudes
are as significant as the verbal
parallel, and might justify the
response of the citizen in ll. 92–4.

91. *stale't*] Theobald's emendation
gives the readiest sense and is graphically plausible. In support of it
Gifford enlists Massinger, *The Unnatural Combat*, IV. ii. 29–30, 'I'll not
stale the jest / By my relation'. The
reading is consistent with Shakespeare's several other uses of 'stale'
but none is quite parallel. Steevens
explains F *scale't* as 'disperse', and
paraphrases, 'Though some of you
have heard the story, I will spread it
yet wider, and impart it to the rest.'
Of his parallels the least unconvincing
is from Holinshed (1587), ii, p. 499,
'they would no longer abide, but
scaled and departed away', but his
interpretation severely strains sense,

syntax, and context, and is un-
supported by *O.E.D.*

Warburton glosses *scale't*, 'to weigh,
examine, and apply it', and compares II. iii. 247, 'Scaling his present
bearing with his past'. This is almost
acceptable: the tale is weighed
against the occasion, put in the
balance against the 'disgrace'; but it
is not confirmed by *a little more*,
where 'once again' might have been
apt. Warburton also quotes Fletcher,
The Maid in the Mill, 'What, scale
my invention beforehand?', but
Dyce's edition (IX, p. 259) emends
to 'stale' on appeal to Theobald's
emendation here.

Scale has also been taken as 'peel,
strip; to reveal the inner meaning',
but with little support.

92. *Well, I'll*] Possibly a misreading
and false correction of the copy's
We'll or *Wele*.

93. *fob off*] put off with a trick; a
'fob' was a cheat. There is no
occasion for this reaction in North's
Plutarch or in Livy.

disgrace] probably 'injury', as in
AYL., I. i. 133; but 'degrading mis-
fortune' is also possible, as in *Sonn.*,
XXIX. 1.

and't] The form *and* for 'an' = 'if'
has been retained throughout. The
form occurs both in Compositor B's
stint (as here) and in A's (II. i. 129);
it is not significantly more archaic
than 'an'.

94. *deliver*] carry on, out with it.

Men. There was a time, when all the body's members   95
  Rebell'd against the belly; thus accus'd it:
  That only like a gulf it did remain
  I'th'midst o'th'body, idle and unactive,
  Still cupboarding the viand, never bearing
  Like labour with the rest, where th'other instruments
  Did see, and hear, devise, instruct, walk, feel,   101
  And, mutually participate, did minister
  Unto the appetite and affection common

102. And, mutually] *Malone;* And mutually *F.*   103. appetite] *F4;* appetite; *F.*

95–6. *There . . . belly*] For the sources of the fable see Appendix, pp. 320, 369–70, and for its significance in the play, Introduction, p. 38.

95. *There . . . time*] Sidney's version in his *Apology for Poetrie* (1595) opens with the same words. See Introduction, p. 30.

97. *gulf*] whirlpool. Compare Camden, 'All the members of the body conspired against the stomacke, as against the swallowing gulfe of all their labors' (Appendix, p. 369), and Averell (c1ʳ) 'a bottomlesse whirlpoole of all gluttonie' (see Introduction, p. 29). For the symbolic properties of the whirlpool cf. *Ham.*, III. iii. 16–17, 'Like a gulf, doth draw / What's near it with it', and *R3*, III. vii. 128–9, 'the swallowing gulf / Of blind forgetfulness and dark oblivion'.

98. *unactive*] 'The only instance of this word (there is none of its modern equivalent *inactive*) in Shakespeare' (Case). For the prefixes *un* and *in* see Abbott 442.

99. *Still*] always, continually.

cupboarding] stowing away. Chambers comments on Shakespeare's readiness to make a verb out of a noun; see Introduction, p. 68. Averell (a3ᵛ) has 'the pattern of a gluttonous Pantrey'.

viand] food; elsewhere plural in Shakespeare. The word occurs in Averell, see Introduction, p. 30.

100. *where*] whereas, as often in Shakespeare. See Abbott 134.

100–2. *where . . . participate*] Camden's version has, 'for whereas the eies beheld, the eares heard, the handes labored, the feete traveled, the tongue spake, and all partes performed their functions' (Appendix, p. 369). North and Livy are less close. Camden is directly translating the Latin of John of Salisbury (*Policraticus*, VI, 24).

100. *instruments*] parts of the body having a special function, organs (*O.E.D.*, s.v. 4). Cf. *Wint.*, II. i. 153–4, 'As you feel doing thus; and see withal / The instruments that feel', and *Caes.*, II. i. 66–7, 'The Genius and the mortal instruments / Are then in council'.

101. *devise*] The most frequent sense in Shakespeare is 'contrive', but here it could equally be 'think, deliberate'.

102. *participate*] 'participant or participating' (Malone). For the construction Case compares *reverberate* for 'reverberating' in *Tw.N.*, I. v. 256. Shakespeare's *mutually participate* renders Camden's 'all parts performed their functions' (see note to ll. 100–2 above), but the word occurs in Averell, see Introduction, p. 30.

102–4. *minister . . . body*] North has 'carefully to satisfie the appetites and desiers of the bodie' (Appendix, p. 320).

103. *affection*] desire, inclination.

Of the whole body. The belly answer'd—
First Cit. Well, sir, what answer made the belly?   105
Men. Sir, I shall tell you. With a kind of smile,
   Which ne'er came from the lungs, but even thus—
   For look you, I may make the belly smile,
   As well as speak—it tauntingly replied
   To th'discontented members, the mutinous parts   110
   That envied his receipt; even so most fitly,
   As you malign our senators, for that
   They are not such as you.
First Cit.   Your belly's answer—what?
   The kingly crown'd head, the vigilant eye,
   The counsellor heart, the arm our soldier,   115

104. answer'd—] *Capell;* answer'd. *F.*   106. you. With] *Theobald subst.;* you
with *F.*   109. tauntingly] *F4;* taintingly *F;* tantingly *F2.*   113. answer—
what?] *Hanmer;* answer: What *F.*   114. kingly crown'd] *F;* kingly crowned
Pope; kingly-crowned *Theobald².*

106–7. *With . . . thus*] prompted by
North, 'the bellie . . . laughed at
their follie' (Appendix, p. 320).
The belly's disdainful smile is often
contrasted with Jacques's laugh in
AYL., II. vii. 30, 'My lungs began to
crow like chanticleer'. Menenius
enacts the smile (*thus*), perhaps with
his lips but more probably with his
belly, by belching, or by twisting his
garments or even his flesh. Chambers
sees the aside as 'really a bit of
literary criticism on Shakespeare's
part', a comment on North. But it is
more likely to be a theatrical joke.

109. *tauntingly*] Attempts to vindicate F's *taintingly* include Schmidt,
glossing 'to taint' as 'to express
scorn' and citing *Oth.,* II. i. 262, and
Herford who interprets as '*attaint-
ingly,* i.e. indicating (them in turn)';
neither is convincing. A minim error.

111. *his receipt*] what is received.
'His' is the usual neuter genitive
(Abbott 228). Deighton quotes *Lucr.,*
703, 'Drunken desire must vomit his
receipt'.

fitly] Wilson and Hibbard find this
'ironical'; but it may equally mean

that the belly's answer was as fittingly applied to the senate's malig-
ners as to the belly's.

113. First Cit.] 'Note how the
interruptions vivify the story' (Verity).
They also witness here to the intelligence of the citizens and to their
schooling in the received political
wisdom.

114. *kingly crown'd*] Both Pope's
metrical intervention in the text
and Theobald's hyphen are un-
necessary. E. E. Kellett, *Suggestions,*
1923, p. 29, quotes John of Salisbury,
'The King indeed holds the place of
head in the state, subject to none but
God' (*Policraticus,* v, p. 2).

115. *The counsellor heart*] 'The
heart was considered by Shakespeare
as the seat of understanding' (Malone). Case quotes *Sonn.,* CXIII, and
Ado, III. ii. 12, 'for what his heart
thinks, his tongue speaks'. Camden
tells how the body's members 'desired the advise of the Heart' and
were answered by 'Reason' (Appendix, p. 369). See below, l. 135 note.
For the link with Camden in relation
to the play's date, see Introduction,
p. 24.

Our steed the leg, the tongue our trumpeter,
With other muniments and petty helps
In this our fabric, if that they—
Men.   What then?
'Fore me, this fellow speaks! What then? What then?
First Cit. Should by the cormorant belly be restrain'd,   120
Who is the sink o'th'body—
Men.   Well, what then?
First Cit. The former agents, if they did complain,
What could the belly answer?
Men.   I will tell you,
If you'll bestow a small (of what you have little)
Patience awhile, you'st hear the belly's answer.   125
First Cit. Y'are long about it.
Men.   Note me this, good friend;
Your most grave belly was deliberate,
Not rash like his accusers, and thus answer'd:
'True is it, my incorporate friends,' quoth he,

118–19.] As *Capell;* In . . . they— / . . . speakes. / . . . then? / *F.*   125. you'st]
F; you'll *Rowe*³.   126. Y'are] *F;* You're *Capell;* Ye're *Delius.*   128. answer'd] *Rowe;* answered *F.*

117. *muniments*] The primary sense
is 'fortifications', but *O.E.D.* (s.v. 2b)
quotes this passage under, 'Things
with which a person or place is
provided: furnishings'; Wright glosses, 'supports, defences', which consorts with other military terms in the
account.

118. *fabric*] probably 'body', but
O.E.D., s.v. 3, cites a first example in
this sense from 1695. King finds a
pun on the military sense 'engine of
war', which would support *muniments* = fortifications.

119. *'Fore me*] either a substitute for
'Fore God (compare 'Upon my soul'),
or an abbreviation of 'God before
me'. Wright adduces the Blasphemy Act, but this is unlikely to be
relevant as *Fore me* and *Fore God*
occur close together in *All's W.,*
II. iii. 26, 43.

this . . . speaks!] Menenius responds
to the citizen's eloquent verse with ironic commendation of his rhetorical art.

120. *cormorant*] Elsewhere Shakespeare attributes the proverbial vora-
city of the cormorant to war (*Troil.,*
II. ii. 6), to vanity (*R2*, II. i. 38), and
to time (*LLL.,* I. i. 4).

124. *small*] 'A small quantity or
amount' (*O.E.D.*, s.v. B5).

125. *you'st*] Wright explains as a
provincial contraction of 'you shalt'
and quotes Marston, *Malcontent,*
v. iv. 36–7, 'Nay, if you'll do's no
good, / You'st do's no harm'; but
here and elsewhere in Marston the
form could contract 'you must', and
Menenius may mean either.

127. *Your . . . belly*] i.e. 'this belly
we're talking about'; cf. *Ant.,* II. vii.
26, 'Your serpent of Egypt is bred
now of your mud by the operation
of your sun; so is your crocodile'.

129. *incorporate*] united in one body.
The wit lies in the literal use of a
word that is usually (as elsewhere in
Shakespeare) figurative.

'That I receive the general food at first   130
Which you do live upon; and fit it is,
Because I am the store-house and the shop
Of the whole body. But, if you do remember,
I send it through the rivers of your blood
Even to the court, the heart, to th'seat o'th'brain;   135
And through the cranks and offices of man,
The strongest nerves and small inferior veins
From me receive that natural competency

135. brain;] *Theobald;* Braine, *F.*

134–9. *I send . . . they live*] Cf.
Holland's Livy, 'it digesteth and
distributeth by the veines into all
parts, that fresh and perfect blood
whereby we live, we like, and have
our full strength' (Bullough, p. 497).

134. *rivers . . . blood*] a metaphor
often related to spilled blood, as in
A Larum for London (M.S.R., l. 1572),
'This purple river, from this weeping
fount'. Applied to the idea in
Holland's Livy, however, it suggests
flowing (if not circulating) blood;
see Doran in *Shakespeare's England,*
I, p. 421).

135. *Even . . . brain*] Commentators
have differed about the progress of
the blood. The line could mean
either 'Even to the heart's court,
where the brain keeps its seat', or
'Even to the heart's court, and to the
throne of the brain'. Malone, in
support of the first version, gives
brain as 'reason' or 'understanding',
quoting Camden (as above, l. 115
note), and takes *seat* to be in apposition with *heart.* Maxwell (*N. & Q.,*
vol. 198, p. 329) takes *o'* (of) to be
the genitive of definition and *seat*
to mean 'throne', thus supporting
the second version. The difference
may be slight; for by the metaphor,
the understanding enthroned in the
brain keeps court in the council
chamber of the heart. The mysterious
relationship between brain and heart
often perplexes Shakespeare's language; tears are the 'brain's flow' in

Tim., v. iv. 76, the brain 'nourishes
our nerves' in *Ant.,* IV. viii. 21, and
elsewhere it 'beats' and 'seethes' while
the heart 'thinks'.

136. *cranks*] 'the meandrous ducts
of the human body' (Steevens).
O.E.D., s.v. I, quotes North's Plutarch (Life of Theseus), 'How he
might easily wind out of the turnings
and cranks of the Labyrinth'. Shakespeare uses only the verb elsewhere,
e.g. 'He cranks and crosses with a
thousand doubles' (*Ven.,* 682); but
Malone quotes an analogous metaphor from *Ham.,* I. v. 67, 'The
natural gates and alleys of the body',
which lends indirect support for
Verity's idea that *cranks* is closely
related to *offices.*

offices] 'The parts of a house or
buildings attached to a house,
specially devoted to household work
or service' (*O.E.D.,* s.v. 9). Verity
takes *cranks* to be the 'winding
passages' of the offices.

137. *nerves*] probably 'sinews', as
in *Cym.,* III. iii. 94–5, 'he sweats, /
Strains his young nerves'; but in
Mac., III. iv. 102–3, 'my firm nerves /
Shall never tremble', it has its
modern sense; and in *Ant.,* IV. viii. 21
it is ambiguous. In *Wounds of Civil
War* (M.S.R., ll. 952–3) nerves are
differentiated from sinews.

138. *competency*] means of life,
probably without the suggestion of
mere sufficiency.

Whereby they live. And though that all at once,
You, my good friends,'—this says the belly, mark me—
First Cit. Ay, sir; well, well.
Men.   'Though all at once cannot   141
See what I do deliver out to each,
Yet I can make my audit up, that all
From me do back receive the flour of all,
And leave me but the bran.' What say you to't?   145
First Cit. It was an answer. How apply you this?
Men. The senators of Rome are this good belly,
And you the mutinous members: for examine
Their counsels and their cares, digest things rightly
Touching the weal o'th'common, you shall find   150
No public benefit which you receive
But it proceeds or comes from them to you,
And no way from yourselves. What do you think,
You, the great toe of this assembly?
First Cit. I the great toe? Why the great toe?   155
Men. For that being one o'th'lowest, basest, poorest
Of this most wise rebellion, thou goest foremost:
Thou rascal, that art worst in blood to run,

140.] *As Cam.;* (You . . . Friends, . . . Belly) marke me. *F.*   144. flour] *Knight;*
Flowre *F;* flower *Capell.*   149. cares, digest] *Cam.;* cares; disgest *F;* care,
digest *Rowe.*

140. *You . . . friends*] It is possible
that F's punctuation is correct, and
that Menenius addresses these words
to his plebeian audience.

143. *audit*] i.e. balance-sheet prepared for audit; the argument reverts
to the trading metaphor of l. 132.

144. *flour*] few editors follow Capell
in retaining F's *flowre* as *flower*. As
Wilson observes, the two senses are
both spelled 'flower' in Johnson's
dictionary. It is hard altogether to
escape a pun; cf. I. vi. 32, 'Flower of
warriors', and North, 'flower of all
their force' (Appendix, p. 368).

149. *digest*] In III. i. 130 F's spelling
takes the modern form; both occur in
Compositor B's stint, but the inconsistency could be Shakespeare's.

158–9. *rascal . . . vantage*] 'Thou
that art a hound, or running dog of

the lowest breed, lead'st the pack,
when anything is to be gotten'
(Johnson). While *O.E.D.* (*rascal* A4)
gives 'The young, lean, or inferior
deer of a herd', it allows its application to other animals, including dogs;
Shakespeare has 'rascal dogs' in
Tim., v. i. 113, and cf. Barnes, *The
Divils Charter* (1607), Sig. K2ᵛ, 'a
raskall, coward, curre'. For the deer,
cf. *1H6*, IV. ii. 48–50, 'If we be
English deer, be then in blood; / Not
rascal-like to fall down with a
pinch, / But rather moody-mad, and
desperate stags', and *LLL.*, IV. ii. 3.
This explains one sense of *in blood*
('roused' even 'ferocious') and for the
rascal to lead, *worst in blood* would
have to mean 'most desperate' and
not 'poorest spirited' as some have
thought. Johnson may still be right

Lead'st first to win some vantage.
But make you ready your stiff bats and clubs;   160
Rome and her rats are at the point of battle;
The one side must have bale.

Enter CAIUS MARTIUS.

                              Hail, noble Martius.
Mar. Thanks. What's the matter, you dissenticus rogues
    That, rubbing the poor itch of your opinion,
    Make yourselves scabs?
First Cit.   We have ever your good word.
Mar. He that will give good words to thee, will flatter   166
    Beneath abhorring. What would you have, you curs,
    That like nor peace nor war? The one affrights you,
    The other makes you proud. He that trusts to you,
    Where he should find you lions, finds you hares;   170

162. bale] *Theobald;* baile *F.*

to take *blood* as 'breeding', and to see
the Citizen as leader of a scavenging
pack; the metaphor is not fully
realized and the ordinary sense of
rascal ('one of the common herd,
the rabble') remains dominant.

160. *stiff bats*] stout cudgels; see
above, l. 55 and note. Menenius
plays on *bats* and *battle.*

162. *bale*] Theobald's correction of
F *baile* is probably orthographic
merely; he gives other instances of
the spelling where sense requires
bale = sorrow, pain, misfortune; the
noun *bale* is not found elsewhere in
Shakespeare. The word 'bail' =
pledge is often used by Shakespeare,
but it strains the context here. Mason
takes *baile* to mean 'bane', citing
Rom., II. iii. 8 F, 'baleful weedes'.
Shakespeare and Menenius may well
be having it both ways.

noble] a significant word in the
play; it occurs 58 times, from this
first acclaim of Martius to the last
line. See Introduction, p. 68.

163. *Thanks*] Capell and others

comment on the monosyllabic, curtly
dismissive courtesy on which Martius
enters.

164–5. *rubbing . . . scabs*] i.e. the
citizens excite their superficial opinions into virulent states, and make
themselves loathsome. *Make yourselves scabs* is both 'give yourselves
scabs' and 'turn yourselves into
scabs'; cf. *Troil.,* II. i. 28, and *Ado,*
III. iii. 93. For the element of physical
revulsion in Martius' political attitudes see Introduction, p. 45 .Wilson
glosses *opinion* as 'self-conceit', but the
citizens are fully endowed with political opinions and Martius knows
this (see ll. 203–8, below).

168. *like . . . war*] i.e. are satisfied
with neither state (because frightened
in the one and rebellious in the other).

affrights you] See above, l. 84 and
note.

169. *proud*] Wilson gives 'high-
mettled', like 'high-spirited curs'.
Cf. above, l. 158, *worst in blood* and
note.

Where foxes, geese: you are no surer, no,
Than is the coal of fire upon the ice,
Or hailstone in the sun. Your virtue is,
To make him worthy whose offence subdues him,
And curse that justice did it. Who deserves greatness,
Deserves your hate; and your affections are   176
A sick man's appetite, who desires most that
Which would increase his evil. He that depends
Upon your favours, swims with fins of lead,
And hews down oaks with rushes. Hang ye! Trust ye?
With every minute you do change a mind,   181
And call him noble that was now your hate,
Him vile that was your garland. What's the matter,
That in these several places of the city,
You cry against the noble Senate, who   185
(Under the gods) keep you in awe, which else
Would feed on one another? What's their seeking?
Men. For corn at their own rates, whereof they say
        The city is well stor'd.

171. geese: you are] *Theobald subst.* (geese: You); Geese you are: *F, Rowe.*
183. vile] *F* (vilde), *F4.*

171. *geese: you are*] F's reading makes acceptable sense but is syntactically awkward. The compositor is unlikely to have misread his copy, but he might have misremembered or misconceived it, failing to recognize the continuing force of *finds you.*

173-5. *Your virtue . . . it*] i.e. you show your virtue, your characteristic quality, by honouring a man who has been properly punished for his crimes and by cursing justice for doing it.

176. *affections*] desires, propensities; see above, l. 103 and note, and below, II. iii. 229.

178. *evil*] in the obsolete sense, 'disease, malady' (*O.E.D.*, s.v. B7).

183. *vile*] F's *vilde* here and *vildly* in III. i. 10 are clearly the forms that stood in the copy (they occur respectively in the stints of Compositors B and A).

your garland] i.e. your hero; a

specifically Roman detail, cf. I. ix. 59 and *Ant.*, IV. xv. 64. Shakespeare also uses *garland* for 'crown', however, as in *2H4*, IV. v. 202. See below, I. iii. 14–15 note.

184. *several places*] North does not say there were riots in various parts of the city. See above, l. 46 note.

187. *Would . . . another*] For the occurrence of the same words in a similar context in *More* see Introduction, p. 37. F. P. Wilson (*Shakespeare Survey*, 1950, 3, p. 20) finds analogues in *Everyman* ('For now one would by envy another up eat') and *The Pride of Life* ('as fiscis in a pol / The gret eteit the smal'). See also Florio's Montaigne, II, xii, where Epicurus warns that we might 'endevour to destroy and devoure one another' (ed. Seccombe, p. 228).

188–9. *corn . . . stor'd*] Cf. North, 'Great store of corne brought to Rome' (Appendix, p. 334).

Mar.   Hang 'em! They say!
They'll sit by th'fire, and presume to know   190
What's done i'th'Capitol: who's like to rise,
Who thrives, and who declines; side factions, and give
  out
Conjectural marriages; making parties strong,
And feebling such as stand not in their liking
Below their cobbled shoes. They say there's grain
  enough?   195
Would the nobility lay aside their ruth,
And let me use my sword, I'd make a quarry
With thousands of these quarter'd slaves, as high
As I could pick my lance.
Men. Nay, these are almost thoroughly persuaded;   200
For though abundantly they lack discretion,
Yet are they passing cowardly. But I beseech you,
What says the other troop?
Mar.   They are dissolv'd. Hang 'em!

200. almost] *F;* all most *Collier.*

190. *They'll . . . fire*] Wilson compares North, 'the home-tarriers and housedoves that kept Rome still' (i.e. stayed in Rome). See Appendix, p. 330.

191–2. *who's . . . declines*] Verity compares *Lr.,* v. iii. 13–15, 'hear poor rogues / Talk of court news; and we'll talk with them too— / Who loses and who wins; who's in, who's out'. In both passages the cycles of power are turned to hearsay and gossip.

192. *side*] take sides with; or, possibly, 'assign factions', in anticipation of *making parties strong.* For the verb form see above, l. 99 note.

194. *feebling*] making feeble, as in *John,* v. ii. 146. For the verb form see above, l. 99 note. Case quotes Huloet's *Dictionarie,* enlarged by John Higgins, 1572, 'Feebled for lack of meat or made weak'.

195. *cobbled*] patched, roughly mended.

197. *quarry*] 'a heap of dead men';

but primarily, 'A heap made of the deer killed at a hunting' (*O.E.D.,* s.v. 2). Cf. *Mac.,* IV. iii. 206, where Ross refers to the slaughtered family of Macduff as 'the quarry of these murder'd deer'.

198. *quarter'd*] i.e. butchered, cut to pieces; as in *Caes.,* III. i. 268, 'Their infants quartered with the hands of war'.

199. *pick*] 'pitch, hurl' (*O.E.D.,* s.v. v.² 2, giving this example).

200. *persuaded*] prevailed upon, i.e. appeased.

202. *passing*] exceedingly, to a surpassing degree.

203. *the other troop*] i.e. those said by North to have met at the 'Holy Hill', but said in the play to be on the other side of the city (see above, l. 46 note).

204. *an-hungry*] Wright remarks that Martius is probably imitating a provincialism; it is not found elsewhere in Shakespeare, but is a variant of 'a-hungry' (cf. *Tw.N.,*

They said they were an-hungry, sigh'd forth proverbs—
That hunger broke stone walls; that dogs must eat; 205
That meat was made for mouths; that the gods sent not
Corn for the rich men only. With these shreds
They vented their complainings, which being answer'd
And a petition granted them, a strange one,
To break the heart of generosity   210
And make bold power look pale, they threw their caps
As they would hang them on the horns o'th'moon,
Shouting their emulation.

Men.   What is granted them?

213. Shouting] F (Shooting), *Pope;* Suiting *Rowe*[3].

II. iii. 119, *Wiv.*, I. i. 246, where Sir
Andrew and Slender use that word).

204–7. *proverbs . . . only*] Of the four
'proverbs' offered here, only the first
appears to have close parallels. (1)
Hart (*apud* Case) cites Dekker, *Old
Fortunatus* (1600), 'hunger is made of
Gun-powder, or Gun-powder of
hunger; for they both eat through
stone walls' (ed. Bowers, II. ii. 82);
Marston, *Antonio's Revenge* (1602),
'They say hunger breakes thorough
stone walles' (ed. Harvey-Wood,
v. ii. 2); and Jonson, *Eastward Hoe*
(1605), '"Hunger", they say, "breakes stone walls"' (ed. Herford and
Simpson, v. i. 25). Cf. also *Mirror for
Magistrates* ('Owen Glendower'), 229,
'Then hunger gnew, that doth the
stone wall brast', and Tilley, H 811.
(2) For *dogs must eat*, Furness quotes
Ray's *Collection of English Proverbs*,
'It's an ill dog that deserves not a
crust', and Case cites Matthew,
xv. 27. See also Tilley, D 533 and
D 487, '*Dignet canis pabula* 1580',
and Dekker, *Old Fortunatus*, II. ii. 73,
'a hungrie dog eates durtie puddings'.
(3) With *meat was made for mouths*
Case compares, 'All meats to be
eaten, and all maids to be wed'
(Heywood, *Proverbs*, II, ii, *Works*, ed.
Farmer, II, p. 55); cf. Tilley, M 828.
(4) The last of the 'proverbs' is more
of an emergent slogan, a response to
the political circumstances reported

by North. The citizens' wisdom in
the play is given considerable range,
force, and coherence.

207. *shreds*] Case compares *R3*,
I. iii. 337, 'old odd ends stol'n forth
of holy writ'.

208. *vented . . . complainings*] aired
their grievances; but with a play
upon senses connected with wind
and belly.

210. *To break . . . generosity*] 'That
is, to give the final blow to the
nobles' (Johnson); *generosity* = [those]
of noble birth (Lat. *generosus*).
Shakespeare uses *generous* in a related
sense elsewhere (e.g. *Oth.*, III. iii. 284,
Meas., IV. vi. 13, *LLL.*, v. ii. 621).
To break the heart may mean either 'to
break the spirit' or 'to end the life';
but elsewhere Shakespeare uses this
and analogous phrases only in intimate contexts (e.g. *John*, v. vii.
52–6, *Wint.*, III. ii. 170, and *Ham.*,
v. ii. 351). For Martius' fears about
authority in Rome, see North,
Appendix, pp. 334–5.

211. *threw their caps*] as often in this
play, cf. II. i. 104, 265, IV. vi. 131–2,
136; also *2H6*, IV. viii. 14, etc.

213. *Shouting their emulation*] either
'each of them striving to shout louder
than the rest' (Malone), or 'shouting
to express their emulous triumph'
(after Verity). It is possible that they
shout as they throw their caps—the
higher, the louder. For F's spelling,

Mar. Five tribunes to defend their vulgar wisdoms,
    Of their own choice. One's Junius Brutus,   215
    Sicinius Velutus, and I know not. 'Sdeath,
    The rabble should have first unroof'd the city
    Ere so prevail'd with me; it will in time
    Win upon power, and throw forth greater themes
    For insurrection's arguing.
Men.   This is strange.   220
Mar. Go get you home, you fragments!

Enter a Messenger hastily.

Mess. Where's Caius Martius?
Mar.   Here; what's the matter?
Mess. The news is, sir, the Volsces are in arms.
Mar. I am glad on't; then we shall ha' means to vent

217. unroof'd] *Theobald;* vnroos't *F.* throughout *F.*

223. Volsces] *Collier;* Volcies *or* Volces

cf. I. ix. 49, v. v. 4, and Introduction, p. 3.

214. *Five tribunes*] See North's and Holland's accounts, Appendix, p. 320, and Bullough, p. 500. Only two tribunes are named by North, and, as Verity observes, Shakespeare uses the omission to occasion Martius' dismissive *and I know not* in l. 216.

216. *'Sdeath*] God's death. Case compares *'Sblood* (*Oth.*, I. i. 4) and *'Swounds* (*Ham.*, II. ii. 571).

217. *unroof'd the city*] This allusion to the destruction of the fabric of the city anticipates III. i. 196, 202–5.

219. *Win upon power*] prevail over authority. For *win upon* = gain cf. *Ant.*, II. iv. 9, 'You'll win two days upon me'. Chambers has 'take advantage of the power already won to win more', and Wilson follows; this suggests an ellipsis of 'power upon power'.

219–20. *throw . . . arguing*] yield greater issues by which rebellion can justify itself. Deighton paraphrases *throw forth* as 'give birth to' and compares *Ant.*, III. vii. 79–80, 'the time's with labour, and throes forth /

Each minute some'. F's spelling does not differentiate, being *throwes* in the *Ant.* passage and in *Lucr.*, 1717, *Tp.*, II. i. 221, etc. The metaphor is not active in the present passage. For *theme* in relation to civil war cf. *Ant.*, II. ii. 48–9, 'their contestation / Was theme for you'; a *theme* was a topic of academic debate.

221. *Go get*] F's punctuation is retained; cf. 'go see', 'go sleep', and 'go and get'.

fragments] scraps of uneaten food, hence a general term of contempt. Cf. *Troil.*, v. i. 9, where Thersites is called a 'fragment' and retorts that Achilles is a 'full dish of fool'. Case compares 'remnant', addressed by Petruchio to his tailor in *Shr.*, IV. iii. 111.

224–5. *vent . . . superfluity*] suggested by Plutarch's account of the appeal to Rome from the Velitreans, whose city had been decimated by plague: 'by this occasion it was very mete in so great a scarsities of vittailes, to disburden Rome of a great number of cittizens: and by this meanes as well to take awaye this newe sedition, and

Our musty superfluity. See, our best elders.   225

Enter SICINIUS VELUTUS, JUNIUS BRUTUS; COMINIUS,
        TITUS LARTIUS, *with other Senators.*

First Sen. Martius, 'tis true, that you have lately told us,
        The Volsces are in arms.
Mar.   They have a leader,
        Tullus Aufidius, that will put you to't.
        I sin in envying his nobility;
        And were I anything but what I am,   230
        I would wish me only he.
Com.   You have fought together!
Mar. Were half to half the world by th'ears, and he
        Upon my party, I'd revolt to make

225. S.D. *Junius Brutus; Cominius*] *F4; Annius Brutus Cominisn* | *F.*
231. together!] together? *F*; together. *Capell.*

utterly to ryd it out of the cittie, as
also to cleare the same of many
mutinous and seditious persones,
being the superfluous ill humours that
grevously fedde this disease . . . and
they leavied out of all the rest that
remained in the cittie of Rome, a
great number to goe against the
Volsces, hoping by the meanes of
forreine warre, to pacifie their
sedition at home' (Appendix, p. 329).

vent] assimilates the meaning 'discharge, cast out' (like superfluous
humours from the body) to the
meaning 'vend, sell' (like marketing
musty corn). The idea of diverting
insurrection into foreign wars was
familiar to Shakespeare in his
history plays (e.g. *2H6*, IV. viii.
38–56, *2H4*, V. v. 107–8).

225. S.D.] Editors, following Malone, often change the order of entry
to give the senators priority. But F's
order may lend mocking point to
Martius' last words, and it precipitates a prompt confrontation with the
tribunes; decorum is at risk. The
first of two F misprints may suggest
that the direction was illegible but

does not justify other than local
emendation; the second is owed to a
turned ligature *us*.

226. *that*] = 'that which', as often
in Shakespeare. See Abbott 244.

lately told us] As Johnson notes, this
must refer to some earlier intelligence
or intimation. Shakespeare's invention attributes keen military judgement to Martius.

228. *Aufidius*] For F's spelling see
p. 93, note 10. He is not mentioned by
Plutarch until after Martius' banishment.

put you to't] put you to the test; cf.
Wint., I. ii. 16.

229. *sin in envying*] Cf. *1H4*,
I. i. 79.

231. *together!*] apparently one of
the instances in F where a query is
used for an exclamation mark (cf.
below, IV. v. 9 F, 'Pray go to the
doore?'). Had Cominius asked a
question Martius would presumably
have answered it; and see below,
l. 239.

232. *by th'ears*] at odds, fighting
(like animals); cf. Tilley E 23, and
All's W., I. ii. 1.

Only my wars with him. He is a lion
That I am proud to hunt.

First Sen.   Then, worthy Martius,   235
Attend upon Cominius to these wars.

Com. It is your former promise.

Mar.   Sir, it is,
And I am constant. Titus Lartius, thou
Shalt see me once more strike at Tullus' face.
What, art thou stiff? Standst out?

Lar.   No, Caius Martius,
I'll lean upon one crutch, and fight with t'other,   241
Ere stay behind this business.

Men.   Oh, true-bred!

First Sen. Your company to th'Capitol, where I know
Our greatest friends attend us.

Lar. [*To Cominius*]   Lead you on.
[*To Martius*] Follow Cominius, we must follow you,
Right worthy you priority.

Com.   Noble Martius.   246

First Sen. [*To the Citizens*] Hence to your homes, be gone!

Mar.   Nay, let them follow.

238. Lartius] *Rowe; Lucius | F.*   240, 244. *Lar.*] *Tit. | F.*   243, 247. *First Sen.*] *Rowe; Sen. | F.*   244, 245. *To Cominius, To Martius*] *Cam., conj. Malone; not in F.*   244–6.] *As Pope; prose in F.*   247. *To the Citizens*] *Rowe; not in F.*

238. *Lartius*] F's *Lucius* is probably a misreading; but for the spelling of *Lartius*, and for certain anomalies in the presentation of the character, see Introduction, p. 21.

240. *stiff*] Probably both the stiffness and the crutches of l. 241 are owed to wounds, not years. Other interpretations include 'obstinate' (Wright); 'stiff with age' (Case). There is no suggestion in Plutarch that Lartius was old; he is 'one of the valliantest men the Romaines had' and is represented as one of the most active (see Appendix, p. 321).

Standst out?] Keeping out of it? Cf. *Tw.N.*, III. iii. 35.

242. *true-bred*] i.e. bred to the wars; cf. *2H4*, v. iii. 65, 'A will not out'a; 'tis true bred'.

244–6. To Cominius . . . *priority*] Without the directions, the text leaves a first impression that *Lead you on* is addressed to the First Senator, and *Follow Cominius . . . priority* to Cominius. As this makes it hard to understand why Cominius should then address *Martius*, Theobald emended to *Lartius*! No emendation is needed, however, if Cominius (as consul) goes first after the senators, and Lartius yields second priority to Martius, with the acknowledgement of Cominius. Only the second of the editorial directions is essential, as the first may suggest unnecessarily that even Cominius hesitates to leave before Martius. Lartius' elliptical grammar in l. 246 is awkward but needs no emendation.

The Volsces have much corn: take these rats thither,
To gnaw their garners. Worshipful mutiners,
Your valour puts well forth: pray follow.   *Exeunt.*
    Citizens steal away. Sicinius and Brutus remain.
Sic. Was ever man so proud as is this Martius?   251
Bru. He has no equal.
Sic. When we were chosen tribunes for the people—
Bru. Mark'd you his lip and eyes?
Sic.   Nay, but his taunts.
Bru. Being mov'd, he will not spare to gird the gods.   255
Sic. Bemock the modest moon.
Bru. The present wars devour him! He is grown

253. people—] *F3;* people. *F.*   257. him!] *Hanmer;* him, *F.*

248. *rats*] Cf. above, l. 161. For the plenitude of corn among the Volscians see North, Appendix, p. 330.

249. *garners*] granaries; the only form of the word in Shakespeare (also in *Tp.*, IV. i. 111).

mutiners] The old form is retained because *mutineers* (as in *Tp.*, III. ii. 33) has a different metrical value.

250. *puts well forth*] promises well; for the full form of the metaphor cf. *3H6*, II. vi. 47–8, 'Who not contented that he lopp'd the branch / In hewing Rutland when his leaves put forth'.

250. S.D. Citizens . . . away] Wilson advances the direction to follow *garners*, as an indication that Martius' mockery, *Worshipful . . . forth*, is occasioned by the citizens' pusillanimity; but the F placing accommodates that interpretation as it stands.

254. *his lip*] Case remarks that drooping of the lips indicates contempt in *Wint.*, I. ii. 373–4, 'he . . . falling / A lip of much contempt, speeds from me', and in *Tw.N.*, III. i. 143. For the importance of physical gesture in the play see Introduction, p. 73.

Nay, but] i.e. 'never mind those, what about . . .'

255. *gird*] 'sneer or scoff at' (*O.E.D.*,

s.v. 4b); in current dialect form, usually with the preposition 'at'. Cf. *2H4*, I. ii. 6.

the gods] For Martius' hubristic emulation of the gods cf. III. iii. 68 and V. vi. 100.

256. *Bemock*] Shakespeare's only use of the word and the only instance from the period in *O.E.D.* *Tp.*, III. iii. 63, has *bemocked*.

modest moon] i.e. the chaste moon associated with Diana; perhaps with a suggestion that Martius mocks the moon for its reticence. Cf. V. iii. 64–7.

257–8. *The present . . . valiant*] a much disputed passage. Hanmer's reading (*him!*) yields the sense, 'May the present wars put an end to him! Being so valiant has made him too proud.' The vehemence of the imprecation and the political implication of *too proud* (i.e. dangerously proud, a menace to the state) make the version probable. F (*him,*) makes acceptable sense, 'The present wars are his consuming passion, making him too proud of being so valiant' (*too proud* meaning 'obsessively proud, too proud for his own good'); but this suggests a long-continuing process which is not likely in wars that are *present* (= just started), and it makes Brutus reflective rather than

Too proud to be so valiant.

Sic.   Such a nature,
Tickled with good success, disdains the shadow
Which he treads on at noon. But I do wonder   260
His insolence can brook to be commanded
Under Cominius!

Bru.   Fame, at the which he aims,
In whom already he's well grac'd, cannot
Better be held, nor more attain'd than by
A place below the first: for what miscarries   265
Shall be the general's fault, though he perform
To th'utmost of a man, and giddy censure
Will then cry out of Martius, 'Oh, if he
Had borne the business!'

258–62. Such . . . Cominius!] *As Pope; prose in F.*

assertive about Martius' nature.
For the idea of pride consuming
itself, Theobald compares *Troil.*,
II. iii. 165–7, and Steevens compares
2 H 4, IV. v. 164–5. Malone's punctuation (*him:*) retains F's ambiguity,
but F elsewhere has commas where
modern usage expects exclamation
marks (e.g. I. i. 78, I. v. 22).

258–60. *Such . . . noon*] Such a
man's nature, when things turn out
well for him, is excited to that
extremity of disdain he feels for the
shadow he treads beneath his feet
at noon. The expression is highly
elliptical. *Good success* is unlikely to be
tautological since *success* often means
'outcome', either good or bad,
although Shakespeare also used the
modern sense (as in II. ii. 44). For
tickled used about war excitement cf.
Troil., Prol., 20–2, 'Now expectation
tickling skittish spirits . . . sets all on
hazard'. Wilson observes that at
noon a man has 'no shadow' and
glosses, 'disdains the very ground he
walks on'; but in fact he dominates a
diminished shadow. Cf. Donne,
'First Anniversary' (1611), l. 145,
'We're scarse our Fathers shadowes
cast at Noone', and his 'Lecture upon
the Shadow'. King remarks that

noon here 'takes on the symbolic
sense "noon of fortune"; Martius
will later cast a more formidable
shadow'. The play does not characteristically invite that mode of metaphoric exegesis, however.

260–75. *But . . . merit not*] The
sources offer no direct occasion for
this subtle detraction, which is part
of the process of Martius' 'fame' and
serves the tribunes' political purposes.

261–2. *commanded Under*] under the
command of. For the nature of the
command see Introduction, p. 27.

263. *In whom*] i.e. in fame. Probably
a personification, with Martius well
graced in Fame's favours, as in
Troil., IV. v. 143–4, 'On whose
bright crest Fame with her loud'st
Oyes / Cries "This is he"'; in l. 262
which relates to *fame* in a more
abstract sense. But *whom* was often
used for *which* without any element of
personification, see Abbott 264.

267. *giddy censure*] fickle opinion.
Censure has its original sense of
'judgement', whether favourable or
not; cf. *Oth.*, II. iii. 184–5, 'your
name is great / In mouths of wisest
censure'. But the word is used in its
modern sense in v. vi. 141.

Sic.   Besides, if things go well,
Opinion, that so sticks on Martius, shall   270
Of his demerits rob Cominius.
Bru.   Come.
Half all Cominius' honours are to Martius,
Though Martius earn'd them not; and all his faults
To Martius shall be honours, though indeed
In aught he merit not.
Sic.   Let's hence, and hear   275
How the dispatch is made; and in what fashion,
More than his singularity, he goes
Upon this present action.
Bru.   Let's along.   *Exeunt.*

271–2.] *As Theobald;* Of . . . *Cominius.* | Come . . . *Martius* | F.

270. *Opinion*] 'Here used in the double sense of (a) reputation, honour, and (b) the public opinion that confers, or "sticks", it on him' (Wilson). Case compares *Meas.*, IV. i. 58–9, 'millions of false eyes / Are stuck upon thee'.

271. *demerits*] merits, as in *Oth.*, I. ii. 22–3, 'My demerits / May speak unbonneted to as proud a fortune'. Case quotes *Mac.*, IV. iii. 226, as Shakespeare's only use of the word in its modern sense. The two contrary senses were in general use.

Come] expressing encouragement rather than dissent, 'Come, you may go further'.

275. *aught*] anything.

276–8. *in what . . . action*] in what way, his personal qualities and attitudes apart, he is preparing the campaign now in hand. Opinions differ about the meaning of *singularity*; Steevens has 'singularity of disposition'; Case, 'usual peculiar bearing'; Whitelaw (after Johnson), 'own great self'; and Chambers, 'personal valour'. *O.E.D.*, s.v. II. 8a, 'individuality; distinctiveness', covers the first two interpretations; and II. 6, 'distinction . . . due to some superior quality', could accommodate the others. But the tribunes have just been discussing Martius' personal attributes, good and bad, and now go to find out more about the military.

[SCENE II]

Enter TULLUS AUFIDIUS *with Senators of Corioles.*

First Sen. So, your opinion is, Aufidius,
    That they of Rome are enter'd in our counsels,
    And know how we proceed.
Auf.   Is it not yours?
    What ever have been thought on in this state
    That could be brought to bodily act, ere Rome   5
    Had circumvention? 'Tis not four days gone
    Since I heard thence; these are the words—I think
    I have the letter here—yes, here it is:
    'They have press'd a power, but it is not known
    Whether for east or west. The dearth is great,   10

Scene II

SCENE II] *Rowe.*   4. have] *F; hath F2.*   on] *F* (one), *F3.*

Scene II] located by Rowe in 'Coriolus' and by later editors in the Senate House in Corioli. The scene may require a certain formality ('Take your commission', l. 26) but no ceremony is prescribed and the precise location seems unimportant.

S.D. Corioles] the usual spelling in F, which also has *Coriolus* (here), *Carioles,* and *Corialus.* See Introduction, p. 8.

4. *What ever have*] *What* is treated as a plural (= what things). Wright compares *H5,* II. ii. 74–6 F, 'Why what read you there, / That haue so cowarded and chac'd your blood / Out of apparence'. Wilson follows Theobald (*hath*) and postulates a compositor's slip.

on] For F's *one* see I. i. 15 note.

4–5. *thought . . . act*] The movement from thought to act was of continuing interest to Shakespeare in his tragedies; cf. *Caes.,* II. i. 63–5, *Mac.,* IV. i. 146–9.

6. *circumvention*] i.e. warning and opportunity to circumvent. Case

quotes Cotgrave, *French Dictionary* (1611), 'Circonvention: Circumvention, deceit, cousenage, an entrapping, beguiling, wylie compassing, or fetching over'. North says nothing about the superior military intelligence of the Romans at this point.

gone] ago, since.

9. *press'd a power*] For the conscription of the common people of Rome into campaign armies see North, Appendix, p. 318. For other uses of *press* or *impress* see *R2,* III. ii. 58, *1H4,* I. i. 21, and *Ham.,* I. i. 75.

10. *east or west*] Since the Volscian territory was south-west of Rome, this could mean 'against some other enemy or against us'. But as North gives little guidance about the geography of the area, it is more likely to mean east or west in Volscian territory; cf. Aufidius' designs on Rome at IV. v. 140–4. Antium was near the coast close to the modern Anzio; the location of Corioles was not known even in Pliny's time.

dearth] See above, I. i. 66 note.

The people mutinous; and it is rumour'd,
Cominius, Martius your old enemy
(Who is of Rome worse hated than of you)
And Titus Lartius, a most valiant Roman,
These three lead on this preparation   15
Whither 'tis bent: most likely 'tis for you.
Consider of it.'

First Sen.   Our army's in the field.
We never yet made doubt but Rome was ready
To answer us.

Auf.   Nor did you think it folly
To keep your great pretences veil'd, till when   20
They needs must show themselves, which in the
     hatching,
It seem'd, appear'd to Rome. By the discovery
We shall be shorten'd in our aim, which was
To take in many towns, ere, almost, Rome
Should know we were afoot.

Second Sen.   Noble Aufidius,   25
Take your commission, hie you to your bands;
Let us alone to guard Corioles.
If they set down before's, for the remove

27–8. Corioles. / If . . . before's, for] *Cam.*; *Corioles* / If . . . before's: for *F.*

13. *of Rome*] by Rome. For of = by,
see Abbott 170.
14. *Titus . . . Roman*] 'Titus
Lartius, a valliant Romaine' (North,
in margin; Appendix, p. 321).
15. *preparation*] prepared military
force; as in *Oth.*, I. iii. 14, 'The
Turkish preparation makes for Rhodes'.
19. *answer us*] meet our attack, as
in *John*, v. vii. 60.
20. *pretences*] designs (*O.E.D.*, s.v. 3).
Case compares *Mac.*, II. iii. 130, and
North, 'pretence and enterprise'
(Appendix, p. 367).
23. *We . . . aim*] We shall have to
lower our sights.
24–5. *To . . . afoot*] based on
North's account of the later Volscian
move against Rome, see North,
Appendix, p. 350.

24. *take in*] capture; cf. *Ant.*,
I. i. 23, 'Take in that kingdom and
enfranchise that'.
ere, almost] even before. For this
intensive use of *almost* Onions cites
John, IV. iii. 43, and Wilson, *Tp.*,
III. iii. 34. But *almost* is in brackets in
F, and Simpson (*Shakespearian Punctuation*, p. 89) treats it as 'a qualifying
expression or an afterthought', comparing *H5*, II. ii. 98 F, 'That (almost)
might'st haue coyn'd me into Golde'.
The intensive is only slightly more
probable here.
27. *Let us alone*] either 'Leave it to
us' (cf. *AYL.*, I. iii. 129), or 'Leave
us alone to' (cf. *John*, IV. i. 85). The
second sense is more common, the
first equally apt.
27–8. *Corioles . . . before's*] punctuated after F4 (Corioles:); F's pointing

Bring up your army; but I think you'll find
Th'have not prepar'd for us.
Auf.   Oh, doubt not that,   30
I speak from certainties. Nay more,
Some parcels of their power are forth already
And only hitherward. I leave your honours.
If we and Caius Martius chance to meet,
'Tis sworn between us, we shall ever strike   35
Till one can do no more.
All.   The gods assist you!
Auf. And keep your honours safe!
First Sen.   Farewell.
Second Sen.   Farewell.
All. Farewell.   *Exeunt.*

[SCENE III]

Enter VOLUMNIA *and* VIRGILIA, *mother and wife to* MARTIUS.
They set them down on two low stools and sew.

Vol. I pray you, daughter, sing, or express yourself in a
more comfortable sort. If my son were my husband
I should freelier rejoice in that absence wherein he
won honour, than in the embracements of his bed,

Scene III

SCENE III] *Rowe.*

makes good grammatical but inferior tactical sense.

28. *set down*] i.e. lay siege; as in
I. iii. 98, v. iii. 2, and *Mac.*, v. iv. 10.

remove] raising of the siege; elsewhere used by Shakespeare only in
siege-metaphors of love (*Ven.*, 423,
Rom., v. iii. 236).

32. *parcels*] portions, as often in
Shakespeare, but not elsewhere applied to military contingents.

Scene III

Scene III] Rowe locates the scene in
'Rome' merely, but most later
editors specify Caius Martius' House.
North reports that Martius took a

wife at his mother's desire and had
two children, 'and yet never left his
mothers house therefore' (Appendix,
p. 317). Shakespeare seems not to
assume otherwise (see II. i. 193).
Some have supposed an inner stage
to be used for this scene, but this
would needlessly confine it.

S.D.] a leisured, explanatory direction that could be written by
Shakespeare for the producer.

2. *comfortable sort*] cheerful manner
(*O.E.D.*, comfortable, II. 9). For the
Spartan nature of Volumnia's attitudes in the scene, see Introduction,
p. 47.

where he would show most love. When yet he was   5
but tender-bodied, and the only son of my womb;
when youth with comeliness plucked all gaze his
way; when for a day of kings' entreaties, a mother
should not sell him an hour from her beholding; I,
considering how honour would become such a per-   10
son—that it was no better than picture-like to hang
by th'wall, if renown made it not stir—was pleased
to let him seek danger where he was like to find
fame. To a cruel war I sent him, from whence he
returned, his brows bound with oak. I tell thee,   15
daughter, I sprang not more in joy at first hearing he
was a man-child, than now in first seeing he had
proved himself a man.

Vir. But had he died in the business, madam, how then?

Vol. Then his good report should have been my son, I   20
therein would have found issue. Hear me profess
sincerely: had I a dozen sons, each in my love alike,
and none less dear than thine and my good Martius,

7–8. *when . . . way*] Case compares *Wint.*, IV. iv. 365–6, 'were I the fairest youth / That ever made eye swerve', and *Sonn.*, v. 2.

9. *should*] = would. For Shakespeare's use of the conditional see Abbott 322.

10–11. *such a person*] i.e. so comely an appearance.

11–12. *it was . . . stir*] i.e. if such a person were not animated by love of renown, he would be no better than a picture hanging on a wall. Case compares *Ham.*, IV. v. 82–3, 'judgement, / Without the which we are pictures, or mere beasts'. As Wright says, 'to hang by the wall' in itself signified neglect (as in *Cym.*, III. iv. 50, and *Meas.*, I. ii. 160). Here it intensifies Volumnia's apparent scorn of pictures, mere appearances. For the idea that virtue must be active cf. *Troil.*, III. iii. 115–18, *Meas.*, I. i. 34–6.

13. *like*] = likely, as often in Shakespeare and other writers.

14–15. *cruel . . . oak*] referring to Martius' engagement in the war against the Latins under Tarquin, in which he was 'crowned with a garland of oken boughes' for saving the life of a Roman soldier; cf. II. ii. 92–8. Plutarch gives an account of the garland custom that does not quite justify Shakespeare's assumption that the award went to the best soldier in the field; see North, Appendix, p. 315. The expression *cruel war* also occurs in North, in the 'Comparison with Alcibiades' (*S.H.P.*, II, p. 228).

16–17. *I sprang . . . child*] Noble cites Luke, i. 44 (1585), 'For loe, assoone as the voyce of thy salvation sounded in mine ears, the babe sprang in my wombe for ioy'.

20. *Then . . . son*] in style, if not in source, a Laconian apophthegm, see Introduction, p. 68.

> I had rather had eleven die nobly for their country,
> than one voluptuously surfeit out of action.   25

Enter a Gentlewoman.

Gent. Madam, the Lady Valeria is come to visit you.
Vir. Beseech you give me leave to retire myself.
Vol. Indeed you shall not.
Methinks I hear hither your husband's drum;
See him pluck Aufidius down by th'hair,   30
As children from a bear, the Volsces shunning him.
Methinks I see him stamp thus, and call thus:
'Come on you cowards, you were got in fear
Though you were born in Rome.' His bloody brow
With his mail'd hand then wiping, forth he goes   35
Like to a harvest man that's task'd to mow
Or all, or lose his hire.
Vir. His bloody brow? O Jupiter, no blood!
Vol. Away you fool! it more becomes a man
Than gilt his trophy. The breasts of Hecuba   40

25. S.D. *a Gentlewoman*] *F; Gentlewoman* / Sisson.   30. Aufidius down] *F;*
down Aufidius *Var.* '73.   36. that's] *F2* (thats); that *F.*

25. S.D. a Gentlewoman] Wilson
glosses 'i.e. a waiting-gentlewoman'
noting that her superior rank would
indicate that Volumnia was a great
lady.

27. *retire myself*] For this reflexive
use of the verb cf. *R2*, IV. i. 96, and
Tp., V. i. 310; see Abbott 296.

29. *hither*] i.e. coming this way.
For this use of adverbs with a verb of
motion implied see Abbott 322.

30. *Aufidius down*] The aptness of
the rhythm to the action makes
metrical intervention inept.

31. *shunning*] seeking safety in
flight; for this obsolete sense of
'shun' see *O.E.D.*, s.v. 2, and cf.
below, I. vi. 44.

32. *stamp . . . call thus*] Volumnia
evidently mimics Martius.

33. *got*] begotten.

36–7. *Like . . . hire*] a poignant
glimpse of agricultural labour con-

ditions in Elizabethan England (see
Fripp, *Shakespeare, Man and Artist*,
II, p. 709), but North has much
generally to say about the miseries of
Roman workers (see Appendix, p.
318). For the harvest man on the
battlefield cf. *Troil.*, V. v. 24.

36. *task'd*] given the task, employed;
but often implying command, cf.
Oth., IV. i. 180, 'command his tasks',
and *Tp.*, I. ii. 192, 'to thy strong
bidding task Ariel'.

40. *Than . . . trophy*] than gilding
[becomes] the monument of his
triumph. Case quotes North's Plutarch, 'Life of Nicias' (1612), p. 541:
'There yet remaine monuments of his
consecrating unto the goddes: as the
image of Pallas in the castel of
Athens, the gilt being worn off'
(S.H.P., IV, p. 248). The gilding of
memorials was also an Elizabethan
practice, see *Mer.V.*, II. vii. 69, and

When she did suckle Hector, look'd not lovelier
Than Hector's forehead when it spit forth blood
At Grecian sword contemning. Tell Valeria
We are fit to bid her welcome.   *Exit Gentlewoman.*

Vir. Heavens bless my lord from fell Aufidius!   45
Vol. He'll beat Aufidius' head below his knee,
And tread upon his neck.

Enter VALERIA *with an Usher, and a Gentlewoman.*

Val. My ladies both, good day to you.
Vol. Sweet madam.
Vir. I am glad to see your ladyship.   50
Val. How do you both? You are manifest housekeepers.
What are you sewing here? A fine spot, in good
faith. How does your little son?

---

43. sword contemning.] *Leo, after Collier* (swords)*; sword. Contenning, | F;
swordes Contending: | F2, Theobald* (contending;)*; swords' contending. Capell;
sword, contemning. Ard¹.*   47. S.D. *a Gentlewoman*] F; *Gentlewoman | Sisson.*

the *trophy* could be the painted or
carved figure on a victory memorial
(see *O.E.D.*, s.v. I b).

43. *At . . . contemning*] i.e. Hector's
blood contemptuously spurned (spat
upon) the Grecian sword. Leo's
emendation, made after Collier but
anticipated by Seymour's conjecture
in 1805, has been accepted by most
modern editors. The italics of F's
Contenning show that Compositor B
took it for a Roman name, but no
probable name has been proposed;
the analogy with the servant *Cotus* in
IV. v. 3–4 shows that names were
sometimes casually assigned, but it is
not otherwise helpful. The Leo /
Collier reading is acceptable if it is
recognized that it is the spitting of the
blood that expresses contempt for the
Grecian swords, and that *at* relates
the forehead and the sword without
requiring the construction 'contemning at'. Collier's retention of F2
swords is needless as F2 was clearly
trying to make sense of *Contending*; the
same applies to Capell's *swords*.

Case, Wilson, and others put a comma
after *sword*, but this isolates *contemning* and relates it less actively to blood.
M. Charney, *Shakespeare's Roman Plays*,
1964, p. 239, would end at *sword*,
deleting *Contenning*. The minim error
nn for *mn* was easily made.

44. *fit*] 'ready, prepared; or, in the
ordinary sense, aimed at Virgilia,
who wished to avoid her visitor. Cf.
Ham., v. ii. 210.' (Case.)

47. *tread . . . neck*] words which
might be remembered at v. vi. 133.

47. S.D. Usher] Cf. II. i. 157, and
Ant., III. vi. 44–5, 'the wife of Antony /
Should have an army for an usher'.

51. *You . . . housekeepers*] Valeria
alludes both to their apparent
domesticity and to their readiness to
stay at home. Chambers compares
Cym., III. iii. 1, 'A goodly day not to
keep house'.

52. *A fine spot*] a finely worked
passage of embroidery; cf. *Oth.*,
III. iii. 439. Dowden (*apud* Case)
cites William Teril, *A Piece of Friar
Bacon's Brazen-head's Prophecie* (1604),

Vir. I thank your ladyship; well, good madam.

Vol. He had rather see the swords and hear a drum, than   55
look upon his schoolmaster.

Val. O'my word, the father's son! I'll swear 'tis a very
pretty boy. O'my troth, I looked upon him o'
Wednesday half an hour together: 'has such a confirmed countenance. I saw him run after a gilded   60
butterfly, and when he caught it, he let it go again,
and after it again, and over and over he comes, and
up again, catched it again; or whether his fall en-
raged him, or how 'twas, he did so set his teeth and
tear it. Oh, I warrant how he mammocked it!   65

Vol. One on's father's moods.

Val. Indeed, la, 'tis a noble child.

Vir. A crack, madam.

57, 58. O'my] *F* (A my).   58–9. o'Wednesday] *F* (a Wensday).

ll. 409–10: 'Now Sempsters few are
taught / The fine switch in their
spots.' See Introduction, p. 49.

55. *swords*] Case remarks that this
could mean 'soldiers'; the metonymy
occurs in *Lr.*, v. iii. 31–2, 'to be
tender-minded / Does not become a
sword.'

57–66. *father's . . . moods*] Cf. IV. vi.
94–6. A less grim allusion to the
tearing of butterflies occurs in
MND., III. i. 158.

59–60. *confirmed countenance*] determined look, as in *Ado.*, v. iv. 17.

60–1. *gilded butterfly*] Cf. *Lr.*, v. iii.
12–13, 'laugh / At gilded butterflies'.
Chambers tries to identify the type
(the Sulphur, Orange-tip, Clouded
Yellow, or one of the Fritillaries),
but Shakespeare's other uses of *gilded*
suggest light effects not wholly
dependent on local colour, e.g. the
'green and gilded snake' of *AYL.*,
IV. iii. 107, the 'gilded puddle' of
Ant., I. iv. 62, the newt in *Tim.*,
IV. iii. 181, and the fly of *Lr.*, IV. vi.
112. *MND.*, III. i. 158, has 'painted
butterflies'.

62. *over and over*] head over heels.

63. *catched*] a form used four times
by Shakespeare.

64. *set his teeth*] clenched them
tightly; as in *Ant.*, III. xiii. 181–2,
'but now I'll set my teeth, / And send
to darkness all that stop me'.

65. *mammocked*] tore into fragments
or shreds. *O.E.D.* gives this as the
earliest example; the noun 'mam-
mock' was more common and still
occurs in dialect.

66. *on's*] = of his, as often in
Shakespeare.

moods] furies, frenzies; cf. *Gent.*,
IV. i. 50–1, 'a gentleman / Who, in
my mood, I stabb'd unto the heart',
and *R 3*, I. ii. 242.

67. *la*] 'an exclamation formerly
used . . . to call attention to an
emphatic statement' (*O.E.D.*); there
are many examples in *Wiv.* (e.g.
I. i. 74, 282, 287, I. iv. 77) which may
suggest that its use was a modish
affectation.

noble] one of the play's more ironic
uses of the word; see Introduction,
p. 68.

68. *crack*] 'a lively lad; a "rogue"
(playfully), a wag. (Conjectured by
some to be short for crack-hemp,
crack-halter, crack-rope.)' (*O.E.D.*,
s.v. *sb.* III. 11.) Shakespeare uses it
only once elsewhere, also about a

Val. Come, lay aside your stitchery, I must have you
   play the idle huswife with me this afternoon.   70
Vir. No, good madam, I will not out of doors.
Val. Not out of doors?
Vol. She shall, she shall.
Vir. Indeed no, by your patience; I'll not over the
   threshold till my lord return from the wars.   75
Val. Fie, you confine yourself most unreasonably. Come,
   you must go visit the good lady that lies in.
Vir. I will wish her speedy strength, and visit her with
   my prayers; but I cannot go thither.
Vol. Why, I pray you?   80
Vir. 'Tis not to save labour, nor that I want love.
Val. You would be another Penelope; yet they say, all
   the yarn she spun in Ulysses' absence did but fill
   Ithaca full of moths. Come, I would your cambric
   were sensible as your finger, that you might leave   85
   pricking it for pity. Come, you shall go with us.
Vir. No, good madam, pardon me; indeed I will not forth.
Val. In truth, la, go with me, and I'll tell you excellent
   news of your husband.
Vir. Oh, good madam, there can be none yet.   90

71.] *As Pope;* No . . . Madam) / . . . doores. (*verse*) *F.*   81. *Vir.*] *F3; Vlug.* / *F.*
84. Ithaca] *F3; Athica* / *F.*

'moody' child, in *2H4*, III. ii. 30, 'I
see him break Scogin's head at the
court gate when a' was a crack not
thus high'. In both instances the
alleged playfulness is ironic, and
Middleton Murry and others are
probably right to take the word as a
deprecatory check to Volumnia ('the
little devil').

70. *play . . . huswife*] Case compares
a similar expression in *All's W.*,
II. ii. 54–5, 'I play the noble house-
wife with the time / To entertain it so
merrily with a fool'. Valeria is
perhaps returning to her word-play
of l. 51, and would make the good
housekeeper a 'lazy hussy'.

74. *by your patience*] by your leave.

76–7. *confine . . . lies in*] Since
lies in refers to an expectant mother,

King thinks *confine* may do so too,
making Volumnia's wit more telling.
O.E.D., however, gives no instance of
confine in this sense before 1774.

78. *speedy strength*] a quick recovery.

82–4. *Penelope . . . moths*] For the
witty levity towards classical story
Sherman compares *Tp.*, II. i. 75,
'Not since widow Dido's time'; cf.
also Rosalind's mockery of Troilus,
AYL., IV. i. 87. F's *Athica* is possibly a
misreading (see Introduction, p. 6)
but it could be, as King suggests, 'a
corruption of Ithaca by Attica'.

84. *cambric*] a fine linen, named
after Cambray in Flanders, where it
was first made.

85. *sensible*] sensitive.

leave] leave off, as often in Shakespeare.

Val. Verily I do not jest with you. There came news from
    him last night.

Vir. Indeed, madam?

Val. In earnest, it's true; I heard a senator speak it.
    Thus it is: the Volsces have an army forth, against   95
    whom Cominius the general is gone, with one part
    of our Roman power. Your lord and Titus Lartius
    are set down before their city Corioles; they nothing
    doubt prevailing, and to make it brief wars. This is
    true on mine honour, and so, I pray, go with us.   100

Vir. Give me excuse, good madam, I will obey you in
    everything hereafter.

Vol. Let her alone, lady; as she is now, she will but
    disease our better mirth.

Val. In troth, I think she would. Fare you well then.   105
    Come, good sweet lady. Prithee, Virgilia, turn thy
    solemness out o'door, and go along with us.

Vir. No, at a word, madam; indeed I must not. I wish
    you much mirth.

Val. Well then, farewell.   *Exeunt.* 110

[SCENE IV]

Enter MARTIUS, TITUS LARTIUS, *with drum and colours, with
Captains and Soldiers, as before the city Corioles. To them a
Messenger.*

Mar. Yonder comes news. A wager they have met.

98. Corioles] *Ard.*[1]; *Carioles* / *F;* Corioli *Pope.*   103–7.] *As Pope;* Let . . . now:
/ . . . mirth. / . . . would: / . . . Ladie, / . . . a doore, / . . . us. *(verse) F.*   103.
lady; . . . now,] *Cam.;* Ladie, . . . now: *F.*   110. Exeunt.] *F (Exeunt Ladies.).*

Scene IV

SCENE IV] *Rowe.*   1.] *As Pope;* Yonder . . . Newes / . . . met. *(verse) F.*

97. *power*] fighting force.

98. *set down*] Cf. I. ii. 28 and note.

99. *brief wars*] Case quotes Holland's Livy (1603), p. 337, 'The Tuscans spent the first daie in consulting whether they would make short warres of it by hot assaults, or temporize . . .'

104. *disease . . . mirth*] trouble our

good spirits (disease = dis-ease, *O.E.D.*, 1).

108. *at a word*] in a word, in short. Case quotes Sherwood, *English-French Dict.* (1632), 'At a word: En un mot'.

Scene IV

Scene IV] Most editors substantially follow Rowe's location 'The Walls of

Lar. My horse to yours, no.

Mar.   'Tis done.

Lar.   Agreed.

Mar. Say, has our general met the enemy?

Mess. They lie in view, but have not spoke as yet.

Lar. So, the good horse is mine.

Mar.   I'll buy him of you.   5

Lar. No, I'll nor sell nor give him: lend you him I will
    For half a hundred years. Summon the town.

Mar. How far off lie these armies?

Mess.   Within this mile and half.

Mar. Then shall we hear their 'larum, and they ours.
    Now Mars, I prithee make us quick in work,   10
    That we with smoking swords may march from hence
    To help our fielded friends. Come, blow thy blast.

*They sound a parley. Enter two Senators with others, on the
    walls of Corioles.*

Tullus Aufidius, is he within your walls?

6. nor sell] *F;* not sell *F2.*

Coriolus', but Capell has 'Trenches before Corioli' (see S.D. l. 29). The stage-gallery evidently served as the wall (S.D. l. 12) and the ladders called for in l. 22 may have assisted the illusion. The Volscian army emerges from the centre doors of the façade at l. 22 and retires into them at l. 42. It is not clear that the 'trenches' were simulated as the word is straight from North, but it is conceivable that the yard was used (cf. v. v headnote).

1–4. *met . . . spoke*] *met* = met in battle, and *spoke* = fought. Cf. *Ant.,* II. ii. 168, 'Would we had spoke together', and II. vi. 25, 'We'll speak with thee at sea'.

7. *Summon the town*] This may or may not be the trumpet-call described as a parley in l. 12 S.D. Martius appears to suspend Lartius' order until he is satisfied that the Roman armies are in touch. Theatrically, the

topography of the battle is established by distant trumpets and drums, much as is that of the rioting city by distant shouts.

8. *mile and half*] Steevens wished to omit *and half*, to save the metre and to accord with I. vi. 16, ''Tis not a mile', but the slight discrepancy is consistent with human judgement of the mobility and range of battle. As for the metre, alexandrines are not uncommon when a line is divided between two speakers.

9. *'larum*] i.e. *alarum*, a call to arms with drums or trumpets; here an element in the din of battle. The old form is traditionally retained in the modernized text in preference to 'alarm'.

12. *fielded*] probably 'in the field of battle' (as distinct from the siege encampment), or possibly 'already in the field'. Shakespeare does not use the word elsewhere.

First Sen. No, nor a man that fears you less than he;
　　That's lesser than a little.　　　　　　*Drum afar off.*
　　　　　　　　　　　　Hark, our drums　　　　　15
Are bringing forth our youth. We'll break our walls
Rather than they shall pound us up; our gates,
Which yet seem shut, we have but pinn'd with rushes;
They'll open of themselves. Hark you, far off!
　　　　　　　　　　　　　　　Alarum far off.
There is Aufidius. List what work he makes　　20
Amongst your cloven army.
Mar.　　　　　　　　Oh, they are at it!
Lar. Their noise be our instruction. Ladders ho!

Enter the Army of the Volsces.

Mar. They fear us not, but issue forth their city.
Now put your shields before your hearts, and fight
With hearts more proof than shields. Advance, brave
　　Titus.　　　　　　　　　　　　　25
They do disdain us much beyond our thoughts,

---

14. nor] *F;* but *Keightley.*　that] *F;* but *Johnson.*　less] *F;* more *Hudson.*
17. up; our] *F₄;* vp our *F.*　　25.] *As Pope;* With . . . Shields. / . . . *Titus,* / *F.*

14–15. *No . . . little*] 'The text, I am
confident, is right, our author almost
always entangling himself when he
uses *less* and *more*' (Malone). Johnson's *but fears* gives the sense.

16. *break our walls*] possibly 'break
out from our walls', as in 'break cover'
and 'break gaol'; but the ordinary
sense is acceptable.

17. *pound us up*] confine us, like
animals in a pound.

18. *pinn'd with rushes*] probably a
continuation of the pound metaphor.

21. *cloven*] proleptically, either
'being split, its ranks broken', or
'being cut to pieces'. Case prefers the
first, Wilson the second. There is no
analogous use elsewhere in Shakespeare. Case's version is better because it suggests a continuing process
and consorts with *amongst.*

22. *Their . . . instruction*] probably,

'Let their noise teach us to join
battle now'. Schmidt explains *instruction* as 'information' (i.e. 'Let us act
on the information about the course
of battle that the sounds give us'),
but Lartius speaks from indignant
impulse.

22. S.D.] Wilson thinks this
direction confusing to a reader,
'suggesting a sudden entry of the
"fielded" Volscian army'. The Volscians appear to sally out of the city
gates, which was probably a central
feature of the façade, see Introduction,
p. 72. Lartius may leave the stage
at this point, see below l. 47 S.D.
note.

25. *proof*] impenetrable (originally
because 'proved' or 'tested'); as in
Cym., v. v. 5, and *Ven.,* 626, 'His
brawny sides are better proof than
thy spear's point can enter'.

Which makes me sweat with wrath. Come on, my
    fellows:
He that retires, I'll take him for a Volsce,
And he shall feel mine edge.

Alarum. The Romans are beat back to their trenches.
Enter MARTIUS, *cursing.*

Mar. All the contagion of the south light on you,   30
    You shames of Rome! You herd of—boils and plagues
    Plaster you o'er, that you may be abhorr'd
    Farther than seen, and one infect another
    Against the wind a mile! You souls of geese,
    That bear the shapes of men, how have you run   35
    From slaves that apes would beat! Pluto and hell!
    All hurt behind, backs red, and faces pale
    With flight and agued fear! Mend and charge home,

29. S.D. *Martius, cursing*] F; *Martius.* | Rowe.   31. *of*—*boils*] *Johnson;* of Byles
F; of biles *Harrison.*

29. *edge*] Cf. v. vi. 112.

30–42. *All . . . trenches*] North tells
how after the Romans had been
driven 'backe againe into the trenches', Martius called them 'againe to
fight with a lowde voice'. The
detailed imprecations are Shakespeare's and help to reveal Martius'
obsession with physical revulsions
and energies. The common soldiers
are the common people at arms.

31. *herd of*—*boils*] Harrison is
alone among modern editors in not
substantially accepting Johnson's hia-
tus; he reads *herd of biles* and explains
that Martius 'when moved by strong
emotion becomes incoherent'.
Johnson, however, makes the in-
coherence more significant; Martius
passes convulsively from the herd to
the diseases he invokes to afflict it.
Ingleby (*apud* Furness) quotes *Tim.*,
III. vi. 98–9, 'Of man and beast the
infinite malady / Crust you quite
o'er'.

boils] Shakespeare elsewhere, as
here in F, uses only the forms *bile*

and *byle* (*Troil.*, II. i. 2, 4, *Lr.*, II. iv.
222).

32–4. *abhorr'd . . . mile*] i.e. they
may be smelt before they are seen,
and their infection carry a mile even
against the wind.

37. *All hurt behind*] Case quotes an
instance of the Greek (Theban) fear
of this disgrace from North, 'Life of
Pelopidas' (1595), p. 315: 'As
appeareth by the example of him,
that being striken down to the
ground, his enemie lifting up his
sworde to kill him, he prayed him he
would give him his deaths wound
before, least his friend that loved him,
seeing a wound on his backe should
be ashamed of him' (S.H.P., III,
p. 26). See also *Mac.*, v. viii. 46–8,
where young Siward is reported to
have his hurts 'on the front'. For
further possible traces in the play of
the same passage in the 'Life of
Pelopidas', see II. iii. 95 note.

38. *agued fear*] Cf. *R 2*, III. ii. 190,
'This ague fit of fear'.

Mend] probably, 'pull yourselves

Or, by the fires of heaven, I'll leave tne foe
And make my wars on you. Look to't. Come on;   40
If you'll stand fast, we'll beat them to their wives,
As they us to our trenches. Follow me!

Another alarum, and Martius follows them to [the] gates.

So, now the gates are ope. Now prove good seconds!
'Tis for the followers Fortune widens them,
Not for the fliers. Mark me, and do the like!   45

Enters the gates.

First Sol. Foolhardiness! not I.

Second Sol.   Nor I.   *[Martius] is shut in.*

First Sol. See, they have shut him in.   *Alarum continues.*

All.   To th'pot, I warrant him.

42. trenches. Follow me!] Dyce², conj. Lettsom; Trenches followes. F; trenches.
Follow's. Sisson.   42. S.D. alarum, and] F; alarum, the Volsces fly, and | Cam.
gates.] Dyce; gates, and is shut in. F.   45. S.D.] F₂; Enter the Gati. | F.   46.
[Martius] . . . in.] Dyce, after F 42 S.D.

together'; but Schmidt explains, 'do
better than before' (as in 'mend
your ways').

   charge home] This sense survives in
current phrases, e.g. 'strike home',
'press home', 'a home-thrust'.

   39. *fires of heaven*] the stars, as in
Ham., ii. ii. 115, 'Doubt thou the
stars are fire', and *Lr.*, iii. vii. 60,
'the stelled fires'; cf. *Mac.*, ii. i. 5.
Wilson glosses, 'sun, moon and stars',
which is also possible (Lear so
swears in *Lr.*, i. i. 108–10) but the
moon is only once associated with
fire by Shakespeare (*Tim.*, iv. iii.
436).

   39–40. *I'll leave . . . you*] Commentators have remarked the irony; but
Shakespeare's touch is light and
casual.

   41. *we'll . . . wives*] For soldiers
driven back to domesticity cf. *Ant.*,
iv. vii. 5, 9; viii. 19–20: 'we had
droven them home / With clouts
about their heads', 'We'll beat 'em
into bench-holes', 'We have beat
them to their beds'.

   42. *Follow me!*] F's reading can be
retained, taking *follows* as a plural
form with *they* as its subject, and
recognizing that the process is

continuing (i.e. 'As they are following
us to our trenches'). The syntax,
however, seems limp in the context,
and most editors have preferred to
end the speech with an exhortation.
Follow me! gets some support from
l. 45, *Mark me, and do the like!* On the
other hand *Follow em!* would be
more consistent with l. 44, and
could be prompted by North's
'followe them' (Appendix, p. 322).
Sisson's *Follow's* has the virtue of
being the minimal intervention, but it
reduces Martius' isolation. Wright
and Wilson omit *followes* on the
assumption that it is caught up by
the compositor from the S.D., but
that would be more probable if something resembling it stood in the copy.
The source passage is much concerned
with 'followers', see Appendix, p. 322.

   42. S.D. (F) *and is shut in*]
probably Shakespeare's direction for
the book-keeper anticipating the
sequence of action; the more specific
realizations at ll. 45 and 46 may be
either Shakespeare's or, conceivably,
the book-keeper's. See Introduction.
p. 5.

   44. *widens*] opens.

   47. *To th'pot*] i.e. the cooking-pot.

Enter TITUS LARTIUS.

Lar. What is become of Martius?
All.   Slain, sir, doubtless.
First Sol. Following the fliers at the very heels,
       With them he enters; who, upon the sudden,   50
       Clapp'd to their gates; he is himself alone,
       To answer all the city.
Lar.   Oh noble fellow!
       Who sensibly outdares his senseless sword,
       And when it bows, stand'st up. Thou art left, Martius:
       A carbuncle entire, as big as thou art,   55
       Were not so rich a jewel. Thou wast a soldier
       Even to Cato's wish, not fierce and terrible

51. Clapp'd to] *F (subst.)*; Clapp'd-to *Malone.*   54. stand'st] *F*; stands *Rowe.*
left] *F*; lost *Singer, Sisson, Wilson, conj. Collier*[1].   57. Cato's] *Theobald;*
Calues / F; Calvus *Rowe.*

Skeat (*apud* Furness) brings many
examples to support this interpretation, e.g. Udall's *Apophthegmes of
Erasmus* (1564), bk 1, Diogenes, § 108:
'by the said tyranne Dionisius, the
ryche and welthy of his subiectes
went daily to the potte and were
chopped up'. The soldiers believe
that Martius has been cut to pieces.
Wright explains the phrase as an
allusion to the melting-pot.

47. S.D.] Titus Lartius probably
leaves the stage at l. 22, for 'ladders',
or at l. 29, having been 'beat back'
with the other Romans.

50. *upon the sudden*] Shakespeare
sometimes preferred this stronger
form to 'suddenly' (cf. II. ii. 219);
here it is particularly apt.

51. *Clapp'd to*] Malone's *Clapp'd-to*
correctly renders the sense, but
emendation is needless.

himself alone] quite alone. Case
compares *John*, vi. 15.

52. *answer*] encounter.

53–4. *Who . . . stand'st up*] who,
though alive and sensitive, proves less
yielding than his inert sword, for it
bends, while he remains erect.

54. *left*] The obvious sense is 'left

alone in the city'; but the effect is
'left alone among men, without a
rival', anticipating the hyperbole
that follows. Sisson (*New Readings*),
supporting *lost*, argues that 'all
Lartius says indicates loss and not
desertion', and Wilson quotes *Oth.*,
v. ii. 148 and 349–51, observing
that both the 'entire and perfect
chrysolite' and the 'pearl richer than
all his tribe' are 'lost'. The misreading *left/lost* could easily occur in
secretary hand. Cf. the variants in
Ham., III. i. 99. Chambers, retaining
left, suggests 'Thou art Martius to the
last', adding that 'editors have
somewhat feebly proposed *lost* and
reft'.

55. *carbuncle*] any kind of red,
translucent, fiery stone. It is probably
the ruby and not the garnet that is
intended here (Wright).

entire] flawless.

57. *Cato's wish*] Theobald emended
F *Calues* on the prompting of North,
'For he was even such another, as
Cato would have a souldier and a
captaine to be' (Appendix, p. 322).
Rowe's *Calvus* has found few advo-
cates, but Monck Mason thought

Only in strokes, but with thy grim looks and
The thunder-like percussion of thy sounds
Thou mad'st thine enemies shake, as if the world   60
Were feverous and did tremble.

Enter MARTIUS, *bleeding, assaulted by the enemy.*

First Sol.   Look sir!
Lar.   Oh, 'tis Martius!
Let's fetch him off, or make remain alike.
                         They fight, and all enter the city.

[SCENE V]

Enter certain Romans, with spoils.

First Rom. This will I carry to Rome.
Second Rom. And I this.
Third Rom. A murrain on't! I took this for silver.   *Exeunt.*
                         Alarum continues still afar off.

Scene v

SCENE v] *Capell.*   3. *Exeunt.*] F; omitted Rowe.

Shakespeare invented an authority in order to escape the anachronism of naming Cato! For the significance of Cato's ideas to the play, see Introduction, p. 30.

60–1. *world . . . tremble*] The same metaphor is used of an earthquake in *Mac.*, II. iii. 59–60, 'the earth / Was feverous and did shake'.

61. S.D. Enter . . . bleeding] 'Shakespeare's spectacle—face, arms, and dress covered with blood—is so emphasised, so integral a part of the action, that it cannot be gainsaid' (Kirschbaum, 'Shakespeare's Stage Blood and its Critical Significance', *P.M.L.A.*, LXIV, 1949, p. 526). Cf. North, 'So the battell was marvelous bloudie about Martius' (Appendix, p. 324), and 'they sawe him at his first comming, all bloody, and in a swet'. The effect is sustained in

I. v. 14–18, I. vi. 21–2, I. viii. 9, I. ix. 47, I. ix. 67, 91, and II. ii. 108–11.

62. *fetch him off*] rescue him. King points out that this use antedates the first instance of the expression in *O.E.D.* (fetch 16, 1648).

make remain alike] make our stay with him, and share his fate. For *remain* as a noun = stay see *O.E.D.*, s.v. *sb.²*, and *Mac.*, IV. iii. 148.

Scene v

Scene v] Most editors substantially follow Capell's location, 'Within the Town, A Street'. If the Romans entered the façade doors at the end of the last scene, however, it would be apt to suppose some of them bearing their spoils out of the doors in this.

3. *murrain*] plague; strictly 'cattle plague' and Shakespeare's other uses are directly or indirectly related to

Enter MARTIUS *and* TITUS LARTIUS *with a Trumpet.*

Mar. See here these movers, that do prize their hours
　　　At a crack'd drachma! Cushions, leaden spoons,   5
　　　Irons of a doit, doublets that hangmen would
　　　Bury with those that wore them, these base slaves,
　　　Ere yet the fight be done, pack up. Down with them!

4. hours] *F*; honours *Rowe*[3].   5. drachma] *Singer;* Drachme *F.*   7. them,
these] *F4*; them. These *F.*

animals; cf. *Troil.*, II. i. 19, 'a red
murrain o' thy jade's tricks', *MND.*,
II. i. 97, 'the murrion flock', and *Tp.*,
III. ii. 75, 'A murrain on your
monster'.

S.D. Exeunt] The soldiers evidently
leave as Martius enters.

S.D. Trumpet] trumpeter (*O.E.D.*,
s.v. *sb.* 4); cf. *H5*, IV. ii. 61.

4. *See . . . movers*] 'Look at these
creatures!' Perhaps with a play on
'removers' as 'scavengers', and on
'fleers'; cf. *budger* at I. viii. 5, and
the budging of the common file,
I. vi. 43–4. The only other relevant use
by Shakespeare is *Ven.*, 368, 'O
fairest mover in this mortal round'.
Most commentators follow Schmidt,
who glosses *mover* as 'living, moving
creature', or Wright, who has 'an
active stirring fellow' used ironically;
but some follow Whitelaw with
'disturbers of the state' or 'agitators',
which gets no support from *O.E.D.*
and seems politically inept. For
North's comments on Martius and
the 'straggling' looters, see Appendix,
p. 323.

prize their hours] value their time
(Case). North reports that Martius
'cried out on them that it was no
time to looke after spoyle'. Rowe's
honours was adopted by Johnson, but
repudiated by Capell on the ground
that Martius would not use such a
word of such men, and by Steevens
on appeal to North; it has been
readopted by Wilson who claims
that Martius is preoccupied with the

soldiers' baseness, not with their
time-wasting, and adduces the same
misreading at *Rom.*, I. iii. 67–8, and
Tim., III. i. 56. In neither passage,
however, is there a comparably equal
choice of meanings; F makes ample
sense and is apt to source and context.

For a different understanding of
magnanimous indifference to spoil,
see *The Warres of Cyrus* (1594),
AI[v], 'It pleaseth me to see my
souldiers rich'.

5. *drachma*] a Greek silver coin.
Shakespeare found it named in
North's account of Caesar's will (cf.
Caes., III. ii. 243).

6. *Irons of a doit*] swords worth a
doit, which was 'a small Dutch
copper coin, value half a farthing'
(Case); also at IV. iv. 17, and IV. iv. 58.

doublets] The doublet was a closely
fitted coat which 'doubled' an outer
garment; it was made with or without sleeves. As Wilson points out,
Shakespeare's Caesar wears a doublet
(*Caes.*, I. ii. 265) and so does North's;
it does not therefore follow that
Elizabethan dress was always worn
in the theatre (see Introduction,
p. 74).

6–7. *hangmen . . . them*] The garments of his victim were the hang-
man's perquisite.

7–8. *them . . . pack up*] F's punctuation suggests that Martius puns on
pack up = quit, but Shakespeare does
not use the phrase in that sense
elsewhere.

And hark, what noise the general makes! To him!
There is the man of my soul's hate, Aufidius,   10
Piercing our Romans. Then, valiant Titus, take
Convenient numbers to make good the city,
Whilst I, with those that have the spirit, will haste
To help Cominius.

Lar.   Worthy sir, thou bleed'st;
Thy exercise hath been too violent   15
For a second course of fight.

Mar.   Sir, praise me not;
My work hath yet not warm'd me. Fare you well.
The blood I drop is rather physical
Than dangerous to me. To Aufidius thus
I will appear and fight.

Lar.   Now the fair goddess, Fortune,
Fall deep in love with thee, and her great charms   21
Misguide thy opposers' swords! Bold gentleman,
Prosperity be thy page!

Mar.   Thy friend no less
Than those she placeth highest! So farewell.

Lar. Thou worthiest Martius!   [*Exit Martius.*]   25
Go sound thy trumpet in the market-place;
Call thither all the officers o'th'town,
Where they shall know our mind. Away.   *Exeunt.*

19–20. Than . . . fight.] *As Capell; one line in F.*   22. swords! Bold gentleman,]
Johnson; swords, Bold Gentleman: *F.*   25. S.D.] *Capell; not in F.*   26. Go
sound] *F;* Go, sound *Theobald.*   27. o'th'] *F* (a'th').

9. *hark . . . makes*] This looks back
to I. iv. 9–20, and forward to I. vi.
5–6 and 16.

12. *make good*] hold against attack;
Wright quotes *Cym.*, v. iii. 19–23,
'He, with two striplings . . . Made
good the passage' (i.e. held the pass).

16. *second course*] O.E.D., course
I.5, 'charge, onset; a passage at arms,
bout, encounter'. Deighton relates it

to I. ix. 10–11, 'Yet cam'st thou to a
morsel of this feast, / Having fully
din'd before', and to *Mac.*, II. ii. 39;
but the immediate context will not
admit a feasting metaphor.

18. *physical*] therapeutic; cf. *Caes.*,
II. i. 261–3, 'Is Brutus sick, and is it
physical / To walk unbraced and
suck up the humours / Of the dank
morning?'

[SCENE VI]

Enter COMINIUS, *as it were in retire, with Soldiers.*

Com. Breathe you, my friends; well fought; we are come off
    Like Romans, neither foolish in our stands
    Nor cowardly in retire. Believe me, sirs,
    We shall be charg'd again. Whiles we have struck,
    By interims and conveying gusts we have heard   5
    The charges of our friends. The Roman gods
    Lead their successes as we wish our own,
    That both our powers, with smiling fronts encount'ring,
    May give you thankful sacrifice.

Enter a Messenger.

                      Thy news?
Mess. The citizens of Corioles have issued,   10

Scene VI

SCENE VI] *Capell.*   6. The Roman] *F;* Ye Roman *Hanmer.*   9. S.D. *a Messenger*] *F; Messenger | Sisson.*

Scene VI] Pope sets the scene in 'The Roman Camp', but Shakespeare merely specifies a point in the battlefield less than a mile from the 'trenches' of sc. iv, see below, l. 16.

1. *we are come off*] we have disengaged; not necessarily in retreat. Cf. *John*, v. v. 4–8, 'O bravely came we off . . . Last in the field, and almost lords of it!', and *H5*, III. vi. 74, 'who came off bravely'.

4. *Whiles . . . struck*] while we were fighting.

5–6. *By interims . . . friends*] Case compares *Caes.*, II. iv. 18–19, 'I heard a bustling rumour, like a fray, / And the wind brings it from the Capitol'. The formality and abstraction of Cominius' phrases (e.g. *conveying gusts*) assist the humanizing effect of *friends*. Cominius speaks in the tradition of Richmond before Bosworth and Henry at Agincourt; but here Martius' curtness is essential to victory.

6. *The . . . gods*] Hanmer's needless emendation *Ye . . . gods* was meant to consort with *give you* in l. 9. Wright observes that 'Shakespeare in other passages uses the definite article with the vocative in such a manner as to render the correction not absolutely certain'; he compares II. iii. 56, IV. i. 37, *Lr.*, I. i. 268, *Caes.*, v. iii. 99, and *Per.*, III. i. 1, 'The god of this great vast' (in which Q's *The* is often emended to *Thou*).

7. *Lead . . . own*] guide their fortunes, as we wish our own, to a happy outcome. See I. i. 259 note.

8. *fronts*] In relation to *powers* (i.e. armies) it is hard totally to exclude the military sense (cf. 'front of war' in *Ant.*, v. i. 44); but the dominant meaning is 'faces', as in *Ant.*, I. i. 6. Shakespeare nowhere uses the word to mean 'front ranks', but the impression here is of companion armies meeting with smiling faces.

10. *issued*] North says the Coriolans 'made a sally' upon the besieging Romans (see Appendix, p. 321).

And given to Lartius and to Martius battle.
I saw our party to their trenches driven,
And then I came away.

Com.   Though thou speak'st truth,
Methinks thou speak'st not well. How long is't since?

Mess. Above an hour, my lord.   15

Com. 'Tis not a mile; briefly we heard their drums.
How could'st thou in a mile confound an hour,
And bring thy news so late?

Mess.   Spies of the Volsces
Held me in chase, that I was forc'd to wheel
Three or four miles about; else had I, sir,   20
Half an hour since brought my report.

Enter MARTIUS.

Com.   Who's yonder,
That does appear as he were flay'd? O Gods,
He has the stamp of Martius, and I have
Beforetime seen him thus.

Mar.   Come I too late?

Com. The shepherd knows not thunder from a tabor,   25
More than I know the sound of Martius' tongue
From every meaner man.

Mar.   Come I too late?

13. speak'st] *Rowe;* speakest *F.*   16. briefly we] *F;* briefly, we *Theobald.*
24. Beforetime] *Hanmer (subst.);* Before time *F.*

13. *speak'st*] There seems no
sufficient reason for F's distinction
between *speakest* in this line and
speak'st in the text; but the inconsistency could be Shakespeare's,
and Gomme defends the extra-
metrical syllable as an expressive
slowing of the line.

16. *briefly*] a short time past; elsewhere in Shakespeare it refers to the
future.

17. *confound*] waste, as in *1 H 4,*
I. iii. 100, *Ant.,* I. i. 45.

19. *Held . . . chase*] The same
phrase occurs in *John,* I. i. 223,
Lucr., 1736, *Sonn.,* CXLIII. 5.

that] so that, as often in Shakespeare.

21–4. *Who's yonder . . . thus*]
Poisson (*S.Q.,* xv, 1964, p. 449)
cites Golding's Ovid, VI. 494,
'Nought else he was than one whole
wounde'. See above I. iv. 61 note.

23. *stamp*] impress, form, bearing.
From the mint.

24. *Beforetime*] formerly.

25. *tabor*] a small drum used by
dancers and revellers, as in V. iv. 51.
For the tabor as a symbol of gaiety
and peace cf. *Ado,* II. iii. 16.

27. *man*] For the construction,
where modern usage requires *man's,*

Com. Ay, if you come not in the blood of others,
       But mantled in your own.
Mar.   Oh! let me clip ye
       In arms as sound as when I woo'd; in heart   30
       As merry as when our nuptial day was done,
       And tapers burn'd to bedward.
Com.   Flower of warriors,
       How is't with Titus Lartius?
Mar. As with a man busied about decrees:
       Condemning some to death, and some to exile,   35
       Ransoming him, or pitying, threat'ning th'other;
       Holding Corioles in the name of Rome,
       Even like a fawning greyhound in the leash,
       To let him slip at will.
Com.   Where is that slave
       Which told me they had beat you to your trenches?   40
       Where is he? Call him hither.
Mar.   Let him alone,
       He did inform the truth; but for our gentlemen,
       The common file—a plague! tribunes for them!—

30. woo'd; in heart] *Theobald, conj. Thirlby;* woo'd in heart. *F.*   32–3. Flower
... Lartius?] *As Pope; one line in F.*   36. th'other] *F;* the other *Cam.*   43.
file—a plague! ... them!] *after Rowe;* file, (a plague—Tribunes for them) *F.*

Malone compares *Cym.*, IV. ii. 253–4
F, 'Thersites body is as good as
Ajax, / When neither are alive'.
   28–32. *Ay, if . . . bedward*] Cominius and Martius embrace on a
similar occasion in North (Appendix, p. 324), and cf. Aufidius'
embrace of Martius, IV. v. 107–19.
   29. *clip*] clasp. See IV. v. 110 note.
   30. *woo'd; in heart*] Theobald's
reading is almost certainly correct,
but F's *woo'd in heart* may chime
rhetorically with *clip ye in arms.*
Harrison retains F, but without
explanation; others follow Theobald
or read *woo'd, in heart.*
   36. *Ransoming . . . other*] releasing
one for ransom, sparing another for
pity, and threatening yet another.
   38–9. *greyhound . . . slip*] Wright
quotes the *Gentleman's Recreation* (1721),
p. 11, 'We let slip a Grey-Hound,

and cast off a hound. The string
wherewith we lead a Grey-Hound is
called a Lease; and for a Hound, a
Lyonne.' Shakespeare observes the
distinction here, but cf. *More*, II. iv.
143–4, 'And leade the maiestie of
lawe in liom, / to slipp him lyke a
hound', where *liom* (= Lyonne or
lien) is apt for a hound and *slipp him*
for a greyhound.
   42. *inform*] report.
   42–3. *gentlemen, The common file*]
gentlemen is used contemptuously,
with the *common file* in apposition.
Wright supposes Martius to distinguish between the gentlemen and
the rest, leaving his first thought
unfinished.
   43. *file*] strictly refers to the depth
of formation in an infantry line;
hence 'rank and file'; cf. *All's W.*,
IV. iii. 252, and below, II. i. 21–2 note.

The mouse ne'er shunn'd the cat as they did budge
From rascals worse than they.
Com.   But how prevail'd you?
Mar. Will the time serve to tell? I do not think.   46
     Where is the enemy? Are you lords o'th'field?
     If not, why cease you till you are so?
Com. Martius, we have at disadvantage fought,
     And did retire to win our purpose.   50
Mar. How lies their battle? Know you on which side
     They have plac'd their men of trust?
Com.   As I guess, Martius,
     Their bands i'th'vaward are the Antiates
     Of their best trust: o'er them Aufidius,
     Their very heart of hope.
Mar.   I do beseech you,   55
     By all the battles wherein we have fought,
     By th'blood we have shed together, by th'vows
     We have made to endure friends, that you directly
     Set me against Aufidius and his Antiates;

---

46. think.] F (thinke:); think—*Rowe*; think it. *Collier*².   49–50.] *As F;* Martius, / . . . did / . . . purpose. *Pope.*   53. Antiates] as *Pope;* Antients *F.*   57–9.] *As Pope;* By . . . together, / . . . made / . . . me / . . . *Antiats,* /F.   59. Antiates] F (*Antiats*), *Pope.*

---

44. *budge*] usually with a negative, in Shakespeare and elsewhere; here it evidently means 'flinch' or even 'fly'. Cf. above, I. v. 4 note.

46. *Will . . . tell?*] In the larger perspective of the play the time does so serve at v. vi. 113–15.

think] For the omission of *so* after *think* cf. *Meas.*, I. ii. 23, and see Abbott 64.

51. *battle*] i.e. battle formation.

53. *vaward*] Shakespeare uses only this form of *vanguard* (e.g. *1H6*, I. i. 132, *H5*, IV. iii. 130). The terms are equivalent, 'ward' being an early borrowing from Norman–French and 'guard' a later one from French proper.

Antiates] Compositor B's *Antients* makes sense ('ancients' is a common corruption of 'ensigns'), but Pope is clearly right. His spelling *Antiates* is consistent with v. vi. 80 and with North, but at l. 59 F has *Antiats*, which is graphically slightly closer to *Antients*; it is probable that Shakespeare was inconsistent and that in either spelling the word was trisyllabic.

55. *heart of hope*] Wright compares *Ant.*, IV. xii. 29, 'very heart of loss', *Tim.*, I. i. 277, 'very heart of kindness', and *1H4*, IV. i. 50, 'the soul of hope'.

56–9.] For the line-division here, see Introduction, p. 14.

59. *Set . . . Antiates*] 'Then prayed Martius, to be set directly against them [the Antiates]' (North, Appendix, p. 324).

And that you not delay the present, but,   60
Filling the air with swords advanc'd and darts,
We prove this very hour.

Com.   Though I could wish
You were conducted to a gentle bath,
And balms applied to you, yet dare I never
Deny your asking. Take your choice of those   65
That best can aid your action.

Mar.   Those are they
That most are willing. If any such be here—
As it were sin to doubt—that love this painting
Wherein you see me smear'd; if any fear
Lesser his person than an ill report;   70
If any think brave death outweighs bad life,
And that his country's dearer than himself;
Let him alone, or so many so minded,
Wave thus to express his disposition,
And follow Martius.   75

                They all shout and wave their swords.

60–1. but, . . . advanc'd] *Rowe;* (but . . . advanc'd) *F.*   70. Lesser] *F3;*
Lessen *F;* less for *Rowe.*   75 S.D. *swords* | *F.*

60. *not . . . present*] do not delay
now. For the transposed negative
see Abbott 305.

61. *swords advanc'd*] swords raised;
cf. II. i. 160, describing the advance
and decline of Martius' sword; also,
H5, v. ii. 345, *R3,* I. ii. 40.

62. *We prove*] put ourselves to
proof; try our fortune.

69. *fear*] (a) fear for, be concerned
about; (b) be afraid of.

70. *Lesser*] F3's reading is manifestly superior to F's *lessen.* Rowe's
less for gives the required sense but is a
needless emendation. A probable
minim error.

75. S.D.—76.] I have followed
Style and Tucker Brooke in supposing
that the soldiers variously shout the
words of l. 76. The response *O me
alone!* is invited by *Let him alone*
(l. 73), and *Make you a sword of me!*
by *Wave thus* (l. 74); both are cued
by the stage-direction, in a way

recognized by the present division of
the direction. Those who retain F's
assignment to Martius offer a wide
choice of exclamations and queries;
Sisson's version seems most satisfactory, suggesting that Martius is
responsive to the enthusiasm which
bears him aloft (raising him like a
sword) but not arrogantly so (the
effect of two exclamation marks).
Sisson's *O' me* is also attractive,
giving greater unity to the line; but
o' (= of) is usually rendered as *a'* in
F, and this would have to be one of
the exceptions (see Introduction,
p. 7). F's *Oh* may be a copy form (see
Introduction, p. 4) and therefore less
aptly interpreted as *O'* than *O* would
be. The producer who follows F must
find other words for the soldiers to
shout—perhaps the mere name of
Martius. In l. 76 *sword,* when assigned to the soldiers, is metonymic
for 'swordsman'.

All. O me alone! Make you a sword of me!
> *They take him up in their arms, and cast up their caps.*

Mar. If these shows be not outward, which of you
  But is four Volsces? None of you but is
  Able to bear against the great Aufidius
  A shield as hard as his. A certain number   80
  (Though thanks to all) must I select from all: the rest
  Shall bear the business in some other fight,
  As cause will be obey'd. Please you to march,
  And I shall quickly draw out my command,
  Which men are best inclin'd.

Com.   March on, my fellows:
  Make good this ostentation, and you shall   86
  Divide in all with us.   *Exeunt.*

76. *All.*] *Brooke (Soldiers), conj. Style* (ap. *Cam.²*)*; not in F.*   O me alone!
Make . . . me!] *This edn;* Oh me alone, make . . . me: *F;* O, me alone!
Make . . . me? *Cam.;* O! me alone? . . . me? *Ard.¹;* O' me alone? Make . . .
me? *Sisson.*   76. S.D. take . . . caps.] *Placed this edn; follows* 75 S.D. *swords / F.*
81–2.] *As Boswell;* (Though . . . all / . . . fight / F.   select from all] *F;* select
Hanmer.   83. As . . . obey'd] *F* ((As . . . obey'd)); rest (as . . . obey'd) shall
bear / The . . . fight: *conj. Rossiter.*   84. I shall] *Hudson, Wilson, conj. Capell;*
foure shall *F;* forth shall *Keightley.*

81–3.] Boswell's intervention makes an acceptable alexandrine of l. 81. Hanmer's omission of *from all* is based on the unwarranted assumption that Shakespeare is never superfluous or tautologous (see Honigmann, *Stability of Shakespeare's Text*, pp. 156–8). Rossiter's solution is elegant; the clause he transposes is inexplicably in parenthesis in F, and could be a marginal or interlineal MS. correction inserted into the wrong line by Compositor B.

83. *As . . . obey'd*] as occasion may demand.

84–5. *And I . . . inclin'd*] and I shall quickly select for my force whichever men are best disposed and suited. In supporting *I* for F's *foure*, Wilson notes that the *I* of Shakespeare's hand could be misread for the

numeral *4* (see e.g. Hand D, l. 95): this is the more probable as the compositor had just set *foure* in l. 78, possibly from a numeral. To the question 'why four?' there is only Wright's answer 'why not?'; for the indefinite use of 'four' to mean 'a few', Wright compares *Ham.*, II. ii. 159–60, 'Sometimes he walks four hours together, / Here in this lobby', but hyperbolic vagueness is not here to Martius' purpose. A *command* is a command-force.

86. *ostentation*] demonstration, show; not necessarily derogatory. Cf. *Ant.*, IV. vi. 52.

87. *Divide in all*] i.e. share the honour; cf. I. ix. 39–40. But Wilson gives 'share the booty', which is possible, if inconsistent with Martius' attitude to spoils.

[SCENE VII]

Titus Lartius, *having set a guard upon Corioles, going with drum and trumpet toward Cominius and Caius Martius, enters with a Lieutenant, other Soldiers, and a Scout.*

Lar. So, let the ports be guarded; keep your duties
     As I have set them down. If I do send, dispatch
     Those centuries to our aid; the rest will serve
     For a short holding: if we lose the field,
     We cannot keep the town.

Lieu.   Fear not our care, sir.   5
Lar. Hence; and shut your gates upon's.
     Our guider, come; to the Roman camp conduct us.

                                             Exeunt.

[SCENE VIII]

Alarum as in battle. Enter Martius *and* Aufidius *at several doors.*

Mar. I'll fight with none but thee, for I do hate thee
     Worse than a promise-breaker.
Auf.   We hate alike:
     Not Afric owns a serpent I abhor

Scene vii

Scene vii] *Capell.*

Scene viii

Scene viii] *Capell.*

Scene vii

Scene vii] Pope locates the scene in 'Corioli', Capell sets it at 'The gates of Corioli'. Both the opening direction and the dialogue attract attention to the gates which would have been 'forgotten' in the previous scene.

1. *ports*] gates.

3. *centuries*] companies of a hundred men under a centurion (Lat. *centuria*).

Scene viii

Scene viii] Editors variously adapt Pope's location, 'The Roman Camp', or Capell's, 'The Field of Battle between the Roman and Volscian Camps'. Shakespeare specifies only the stage locations, 'at several doors'. See Introduction, p. 72.

1–2. *hate . . . hate alike*] For North's account of the 'marvelous private hate' between Martius and Tullus see Appendix, p. 343.

3. *Afric . . . serpent*] For Africa as the country of serpents, Wright quotes Heywood, *Silver Age* (*Works*, ed. Shepherd, iii, 125–6), 'Fly into Affricke, from the mountaines there / Chuse me two venomous serpents'. The form *Afric* occurs four times in Shakespeare, *Africa* only once. For

More than thy fame and envy. Fix thy foot.

Mar. Let the first budger die the other's slave,   5
And the gods doom him after!

Auf.   If I fly, Martius,

Holloa me like a hare.

Mar.   Within these three hours, Tullus,
Alone I fought in your Corioles walls,
And made what work I pleas'd: 'tis not my blood
Wherein thou seest me mask'd. For thy revenge,   10
Wrench up thy power to th'highest.

Auf.   Wert thou the Hector
That was the whip of your bragg'd progeny,
Thou shouldst not 'scape me here.

Here they fight, and certain Volsces come in the aid of Aufidius.
Martius fights till they be driven in breathless.

6–7. If . . . hare] *As Theobald; one line in* F.   7. Holloa] F (hollow), *Cam.;* halloo
Theobald².

the story of the breeding of serpents
from the disembodied head of
Gorgon in Libya, Case cites Golding's
Ovid, *Met.,* IV. 756–63.

4. *fame and envy*] a disputed phrase.
The hendiadys 'envied fame' is
probably intended, but as Martius
confesses his envy of Tullus in I. i.
229, the radical sense should give
way to the ampler one, 'thy fame and
the envy it occasions'. Capell glosses
'thy envied fame', comparing 'death
and honour' = 'honourable death' in
Ant., IV. ii. 44. Malone gives *envy* as
'malice'. Steevens uses the radical
sense of *envy,* giving 'detested or
odious fame', with the further suggestion that *envy* may be intended as a
verb (i.e. 'I abhor and envy thy
fame').

5. *budger*] See I. vi. 44 and note.

7. *Holloa . . . hare*] Shakespeare
several times uses the hare as a
symbol of timidity (e.g. *Troil.,*
II. ii. 43–9, 'manhood and honour /
Should have hare-hearts, would they
but fat their thoughts / With this
cramm'd reason'). For the hunting of

the hare cf. *3H6,* II. v. 130, 'Having
the fearful flying hare in sight'.
Case quotes Golding's Ovid, *Met.,*
x. 621, 'she cheerd the hounds with
hallowing like a hunt', which might
support *hallow* for F's *hollow.* For
holloa cf. *TNK.,* II. ii. 52.

10. *mask'd*] Cf. the *mantled* bloody
figure of I. vi. 29.

12. *whip . . . progeny*] The Romans
(like the British) claimed descent
from the Trojans; Hector was
therefore of Martius' *bragg'd progeny*
and was the whip with which the
Trojans scourged the Greeks; *bragg'd*
= boastful, vaunting (*O.E.D.,* s.v. b).
For *progeny* = race cf. *1H6,* v. iv. 38,
'issued of a progeny of kings'. Elsewhere Shakespeare relates *whip* and
of comparably in *Tim.,* v. i. 59, 'all
the whips of heaven', and *Ham.,*
III. i. 70, 'the whips and scorns of
time'; the use is only slightly against
the grain of the language. Gomme
says 'the image may suggest alterna-
tively that Hector was the driving
force behind the Trojans, "whipping"
the rest into action', but this is
strained.

Officious, and not valiant, you have sham'd me
In your condemned seconds.   [*Exeunt.*]   15

[SCENE IX]

Flourish. Alarum. A retreat is sounded. Enter at one door, COMINIUS,
with the Romans; at another door, MARTIUS, *with his arm
in a scarf.*

Com. If I should tell thee o'er this thy day's work,
   Thou't not believe thy deeds; but I'll report it,
   Where senators shall mingle tears with smiles,
   Where great patricians shall attend, and shrug,
   I'th'end admire; where ladies shall be frighted,   5
   And, gladly quak'd, hear more; where the dull
      tribunes,
   That with the fusty plebeians hate thine honours,
   Shall say against their hearts, 'We thank the gods
   Our Rome hath such a soldier.'
   Yet cam'st thou to a morsel of this feast,   10
   Having fully din'd before.
   Enter TITUS LARTIUS, *with his Power, from the pursuit.*

15. condemned] *F;* contemned *conj. Johnson.*   S.D.] *Hanmer; not in F.*

Scene IX

SCENE IX] *Capell.*   2. Thou't] *F;* Thou'lt *F4;* Thou'ldst *Cam., after conj.
Capell* (Thou'dst).

15. *In . . . seconds*] with your
damned support. For *seconds* = supporters cf. I. iv. 43.

Scene IX

Scene IX] The entrance of Romans
from both sides of the stage expresses
their total command of the field.
The mention of a tent at the end of
the scene need not imply that a tent
structure was actually used but it
might have been.
   S.D. Flourish] usually sounded to
announce royalty, but six times used
by Shakespeare to herald a victorious
force (see E. W. Naylor, *Shakespeare
and Music* (1896), pp. 167–8).
   1–9. *If I . . . soldier*] With this
account of the processes of fame,

compare Henry V's prospective memories of St Crispin's day (*H5*, IV. iii.
41–67), and *Oth.*, I. iii. 127–66.
   2. *Thou't*] thou wilt. Corrections
to forms of 'thou shouldst' are
grammatical, not textual.
   4. *shrug*] another expressive gesture,
this time of incredulity.
   5. *admire*] wonder, marvel.
   6. *quak'd*] made to quake.
   dull] sullen.
   7. *fusty*] Cf. 'musty superfluity',
I. i. 225, and I. i. 58–9 note.
   plebeians] accented *plèbeians* (see
Abbott 492). Cominius' contempt
for tribunes and plebeians is as
active in private as Martius'.
   10. *morsel . . . feast*] i.e. morsel in
this feast; to Martius the feast was

Lar.   O general,
    Here is the steed, we the caparison:
    Hadst thou beheld—
Mar.   Pray now, no more. My mother,
    Who has a charter to extol her blood,
    When she does praise me, grieves me. I have done   15
    As you have done, that's what I can; induc'd
    As you have been, that's for my country.
    He that has but effected his good will
    Hath overta'en mine act.
Com.   You shall not be
    The grave of your deserving; Rome must know   20
    The value of her own. 'Twere a concealment
    Worse than a theft, no less than a traducement,
    To hide your doings, and to silence that
    Which, to the spire and top of praises vouch'd,
    Would seem but modest. Therefore I beseech you—   25
    In sign of what you are, not to reward
    What you have done—before our army hear me.
Mar. I have some wounds upon me, and they smart
    To hear themselves remember'd.

13-14. My mother . . . blood] *As Pope; one line in F.*   15-17.] *As Hanmer;* When . . . grieues me: | . . . can, | . . . Countrey: | *F.*   19-22. You . . . traducement] *As Pope;* You . . . deseruing, | . . . owne: | . . . Theft, | . . . Traducement, | *F.*   25-7. you— . . . done—] *F* (you, . . . done,).

only a morsel. Schmidt compares *All's W.*, v. iii. 1, 'We lost a jewel of her', where *of* = in.

12. *we the caparison*] North says that Cominius gave Martius 'a goodly horse with a capparison, and all furniture to him' (Appendix, p. 325); hence this metaphor, the episode below, ll. 60-2, and the wager opening I. iv.

13-22.] For the lineation of this passage see Introduction, p. 12.

14. *has a charter*] has a prerogative.

18-19. *He . . . act*] He who has simply carried out his resolution has accomplished more than I. Martius subtly betrays his pride in a super-human potential still imperfectly realized.

19-27.] Cf. North, 'There the Consul Cominius going up to his chayer of state, in the presence of the whole armie, gave thankes to the goddes for so great, glorious, and prosperous a victorie: then he spake to Martius, whose valliantnes he commended beyond the moone' (Appendix, p. 325).

22. *traducement*] censure, obloquy (Johnson's dictionary); Shakespeare's only use of the word.

23-5. *and . . . modest*] and to suppress (keep quiet about) accomplishments for which the very highest praises would seem inadequate.

26. *In sign . . . are*] i.e. as a token of recognition.

Com.   Should they not,
Well might they fester 'gainst ingratitude,   30
And tent themselves with death. Of all the horses—
Whereof we have ta'en good, and good store—of all
The treasure in this field achiev'd and city,
We render you the tenth; to be ta'en forth,
Before the common distribution, at   35
Your only choice.
Mar.   I thank you, general;
But cannot make my heart consent to take
A bribe to pay my sword: I do refuse it,
And stand upon my common part with those
That have beheld the doing.   40
    *A long flourish. They all cry, 'Martius! Martius!', cast up
        their caps and lances. Cominius and Lartius stand bare.*
May these same instruments, which you profane,
Never sound more! When drums and trumpets shall
I'th'field prove flatterers, let courts and cities be
Made all of false-fac'd soothing! When steel grows

31–2. horses— . . . store—of] *Alexander;* horses, . . . store of *F;* horses, . . . store, of *Rowe.*   35–6.] *As Theobald;* Before . . . distribution, / . . . choyse. *F.* 40. beheld] *F;* upheld *Capell.*   41. May] *Capell; Mar.* May *F.*   43–4. cities be / Made] *F;* cities / Be made *Theobald.*   44–50.] *As Theobald;* Made . . . soothing: / . . . Silke, / . . . Warres: / . . . wash'd / . . . Wretch, / . . . done, / . . . hyperbolicall, / *F.*

31. *tent . . . death*] make death their remedy; the *tent* was a roll of linen used for probing and for keeping green wounds clean and open. Cf. *Troil.*, II. ii. 14–17.

31–6. *Of all . . . choice*] Cf. North, 'So in the ende he willed Martius, he should choose out of all the horses they had taken of their enemies, and of all the goodes they had wonne (whereof there was great store) tenne of every sorte which he liked best, before any distribution should be made to other' (Appendix, p. 325).

32. *good, and good store*] good ones and plenty of them.

35. *distribution*] Retaining F's lineation, Harrison observes that *distribution* would be pronounced with five syllables.

40. *beheld the doing*] i.e. seen the action; Capell's emendation (*upheld*) is needless.

44–50.] F recognizes a natural pause after *soothing* and after *wars*, but Theobald's recasting is vindicated by the improved measure of ll. 49–50. See Introduction, p. 13.

44–6. *When steel . . . wars*] 'When steel grows as soft as the courtly sycophant's silk, let such a man receive ovations for his part in the wars!' This is the play's most disputed passage, and it may be that no solution is wholly satisfactory. I have followed the reading proposed by Hilda M. Hulme, *Explorations in Shakespeare's Language*, 1962, pp. 155–8, 205–6. She cites Rider's *Dictionarie* (1626), '*Ovator,* m. *trix* f. Hee or she that triumpheth', and paraphrases, 'Only when the man of steel grows soft should he be made "ovator" for what he has done in the wars'. She remarks that as the form *-ture* had begun to displace *-ter* in some words, the spelling *overture* might derive from MS. *ovater; overture* and *ovater* would have been similarly pronounced (see Kökeritz, p. 271). *O.E.D.* gives *ovator*, '*Rom. Hist.* One who receives an ovation', citing Morgan (1661), 'The Triumpher had a Lawrel crown, the Ovator one of Fir, being different in their pomp'. Unfortunately, there appears to be no use of the word antedating the play. North's full discussion of ovations in the 'Life of Marcellus' (S.H.P., III, pp. 87–9) has occasion to use it but does not. Of earlier editions of Rider's dictionary, the 1589 one does not include it, and the 1611 one offers it as a Latin word with the gloss, 'he that reioyceth'. Morgan's definition, however, would probably have won wide acceptance for *ovator* in this context had it been framed fifty years earlier, and Rider in 1626 must have had some precedent in mind. In a less precise sense, Martius is ovator both in this scene (see below, l. 59) and when he comes back to Rome (see II. i. head note). In the general tenor of the speech, however, it is not quite clear whether Martius is repudiating the role altogether or simply protesting against the attendant flattery. Commentators have found difficulty not only with the interpretation of *overture* but also with the ambiguous reference of *him*. If *overture* is retained, *him* may refer to *silk*, to *steel*, or to *parasite*. Taking it as referring to *parasite*, Sisson (*New Readings*) paraphrases, 'let the parasite be made the herald of war (instead of the soldier)'. It may be objected that no analogous use of *overture* for 'herald' has been adduced, and that the image of the herald sounding his trumpet as a prelude to war anticipates the sense

'musical prologue' which was not current until later in the seventeenth century. On the other hand, Martius is protesting at the *long flourish* sounded in his honour when the proper use of the trumpet is to summon to war (as at the opening of the action at I. iv. 12, where he gives order, 'Come, blow thy blast'); the radical sense of *overture* ('opening') can be aptly related therefore to the herald and his trumpet. The sense 'emissary' or 'bearer of an overture of war' would be a figurative transference of the use in *Tw.N.*, I. v. 25, 'I bring no overture of war'. Retaining *overture*, Tucker-Brooke takes *him* for a dative reference to *parasite* and paraphrases, 'When soldiers adopt the effeminate ways of courtiers let us recruit our armies among the latter class'. The proposed sense has no parallel in Shakespeare, however, and it diminishes the resonance as well as the obscurity of the word in its context. For other Shakespearean uses of *overture* see *All's W.*, IV. iii. 37, v. iii. 99, *Wint.*, II. i. 172, and *Lr.*, III. vii. 88. In an ampler perspective, Martius' *parasite* may be compared with the 'popinjay' at Holmedon (*1H4*, I. iii. 26–9), his city of *false-fac'd soothing* with the Angiers of *John*, II. i. 312–598, and his scorn of courtly ways with Hotspur's and the Bastard's.

Adopting Tyrwhitt's *coverture* (but retaining *him*) Wilson paraphrases, ' . . . let silk be used as armour', i.e. as a covering for the wars. But Shakespeare's other uses of *coverture* (*Ado*, III. i. 30, *3H6*, IV. ii. 13) do not refer to garments but to shelter afforded by trees or the night, and the emendation diverts attention from the parasite's role in war to his dress.

After reading *coverture*, Wright in his Addenda quotes Holland's Pliny, VII, 40, 'many times it falleth out that the day marked with a white stone for a good day, had in it the beginning and overture of some great

Soft as the parasite's silk, let him be made   45
An ovator for th'wars! No more, I say!
For that I have not wash'd my nose that bled,
Or foil'd some debile wretch, which without note
Here's many else have done, you shout me forth
In acclamations hyperbolical,   50
As if I lov'd my little should be dieted
In praises sauc'd with lies.

Com.   Too modest are you,
More cruel to your good report than grateful
To us that give you truly. By your patience,
If 'gainst yourself you be incens'd, we'll put you   55
(Like one that means his proper harm) in manacles,
Then reason safely with you. Therefore be it known,
As to us, to all the world, that Caius Martius

45–6. him . . . An ovator] *This edn, conj. Hulme;* him . . . an Ouerture *F;*
Hymns . . . overture *Warburton;* this . . . a coverture *conj. Tyrwhitt;* him . . . a
coverture *Steevens;* them . . . an overture *Knight;* him . . . an armature *Deighton.*
49. shout] *F* (shoot), *F4.*   52. praises sauc'd] *Hanmer;* prayses, sawc'st *F.*

misfortune and calamity'. This would
support the retention of *overture* in the
sense 'prologue'.

It is possible that consideration
should be given to the reading
orator for *overture;* cf. *All's W.,* v. iii.
249, 'He's a good drum, my lord, but
a naughty orator', where, as G. K.
Hunter observes, 'The connection
between *drum* and *orator* remains
mysterious'. In the present context
of drums and trumpets it is the
function of the orator (Cominius) to
acclaim the warrior's success. But
Martius appears to be protesting
more immediately against the shouted
popular acclaim than against the
oratory, and Shakespeare's uses of
orator elsewhere (e.g. *3H6,* III. ii. 188,
Caes., III. ii. 217) are attentive to skill
in pleading, not to hyperbolic
commendation.

47. *For that*] because; as at I. i. 112,
and III. iii. 93.

not] The force of the negative is
confined to *wash'd* and does not
extend to *foil'd.*

48. *foil'd*] overcome, overthrown;
cf. *Troil.,* I. iii. 372.

debile] feeble.

49. *shout me forth*] acclaim me, but
this way of putting it is characteristic
of the play's idiom (see Introduction,
p. 69).

51–2. *As if . . . lies*] 'As though I
were fond of having my poor merits
fed upon praises seasoned with
exaggeration' (Deighton). For *dieted*
cf. *Cym.,* III. iv. 179, and *Compl.,* 261;
for *sauc'd* cf. *Cym.,* IV. ii. 51; and for
the metaphor cf. *Wint.,* I. ii. 91–2,
'cram's with praise, and make's / As
fat as tame things'.

54. *give*] report. *O.E.D.,* s.v. 25,
offers this as the earliest instance; cf.
'give out' (e.g. *R3,* IV. ii. 58).

By your patience] by your leave (as
in I. iii. 74), but Wilson sees the
phrase and the passage as Cominius'
tactful reminder that Martius is
speaking to his general. Martius'
response to praise is embarrassed
and ungracious.

56. *Like . . . harm*] like one who
means to injure his own person.

Wears this war's garland: in token of the which,
My noble steed, known to the camp, I give him,   60
With all his trim belonging; and from this time,
For what he did before Corioles, call him,
With all th'applause and clamour of the host,
Martius Caius Coriolanus!
Bear th'addition nobly ever!   65
                   Flourish. Trumpets sound, and drums.
All. Martius Caius Coriolanus!
Cor.   I will go wash;
And when my face is fair, you shall perceive
Whether I blush or no: howbeit, I thank you.
I mean to stride your steed, and at all times
To undercrest your good addition,   70

64, 66. Martius Caius Coriolanus] F *subst.* (*Marcus*), Sisson; Caius Martius
Coriolanus *Rowe.*   64–5.] *As Johnson; one line in* F.   66. *All.*] Capell;
Omnes. | F.   *Cor.*] Steevens; *Mar.* | F. (*and to end of scene*).

59. *Wears . . . garland*] See note on
I. iii. 14–15, and above, ll. 44–6 note.
No garland is offered to Martius at
this point in North, but the play is
otherwise close to its source (see
Appendix, p. 325).

61. *trim belonging*] the trappings
that go with it (cf. *caparison*, l. 12).

64. *Martius Caius*] It is difficult to
exempt Shakespeare from responsibility for the sequence here, but most
editors have emended after Rowe.
North gives a full account of the
order and significance of the names
(see Appendix, p. 327), and the
correct form *Caius Martius* is used
thirteen times in the play. The form
Martius Caius occurs at II. i. 163 when
the herald formally welcomes Coriolanus to Rome, and at II. ii. 46 when
Menenius formally addresses the
senate. Finally, Volumnia comments
on the names in the order *Martius,
Caius,* and *Coriolanus* in II. i. 171–3.
The forms *Marcus Caius* and *Martius
Caius* occur only in the stint of
Compositor A (see Introduction,
p. 23), but as *Caius Martius* is also
his stint at l. 58 above, the fact has

little significance. Wilson suspects
editorial meddling with the copy,
both in the present passage and at
II. i. 163; but this cannot be postu-
lated of the order in Volumnia's
speech (II. i. 171–3), which must be
Shakespeare's. It follows that we
must assume that Shakespeare wrote
Martius Caius Coriolanus wherever all
three occur together, and reasons for
emending must be other than textual.
See Introduction, pp. 23, 41.

65. *th'addition*] title. Of the names,
North says, 'The third, was some
addition geven, either for some acte
or notable service . . . or els for some
speciall vertue' (see Appendix, p.
327). The word is equivalent to the
Latin *agnomen* and not, strictly, to
cognomen, which in most classical
prose is used for it, see p. 92, note 1.

66. *Cor.*] Most editors change
from Mar. to Cor. at this point, but F
keeps Mar. until the return to Rome
at II. i. 160.

70–1. *To undercrest . . . power*] 'to
bear the title as my crest, and
myself beneath it as becomingly as I

To th'fairness of my power.

Com.   So, to our tent;
Where, ere we do repose us, we will write
To Rome of our success. You, Titus Lartius,
Must to Corioles back: send us to Rome
The best, with whom we may articulate   75
For their own good and ours.

Lar.   I shall, my lord.

Cor. The gods begin to mock me: I, that now
Refus'd most princely gifts, am bound to beg
Of my lord general.

Com.   Take't, 'tis yours. What is't?

Cor. I sometime lay here in Corioles,   80
At a poor man's house: he us'd me kindly.
He cried to me. I saw him prisoner.
But then Aufidius was within my view,
And wrath o'erwhelm'd my pity. I request you
To give my poor host freedom.

Com.   Oh well begg'd!   85
Were he the butcher of my son, he should
Be free as is the wind. Deliver him, Titus.

Lar. Martius, his name?

Cor.   By Jupiter, forgot!
I am weary, yea, my memory is tired;
Have we no wine here?

Com.   Go we to our tent.   90
The blood upon your visage dries, 'tis time
It should be look'd to. Come.   *Exeunt.*

77–9.] *As Hanmer;* The . . . me: / . . . gifts, / . . . Generall. / *F.*   81. At] *F;*
And at *Hanmer, Wilson.*

can' (Case); *undercrest* appears to be a
coinage, and *O.E.D.* gives no other
instance; *addition* is used in the heraldic sense of 'honour added to a coat
of arms'.

75. *The best*] Cf. 'our best elders',
I. i. 225.

articulate] negotiate terms; literally,
draw up into articles, as in *1 H 4*,
v. i. 72.

78. *bound to*] probably 'obliged to';

but possibly 'about to' or 'going to',
as Case notes, citing *Lr.*, III. vii. 12.

80–9. *I sometime . . . tir'd*] In North,
Martius' host is a 'wealthie man' in
danger of being 'solde as a slave'
and his name is omitted but not
forgotten. The forgetfulness in Shakespeare's version is owed, not to an
affectation of magnanimity, but to
'the amnesia of an exhausted man'
(Case). One name is found in the
scene and another lost.

[SCENE X]

A flourish. Cornets. Enter TULLUS AUFIDIUS, *bloody, with
two or three Soldiers.*

Auf. The town is ta'en!
First Sol. 'Twill be deliver'd back on good condition.
Auf. Condition!
    I would I were a Roman, for I cannot,
    Being a Volsce, be that I am. Condition?   5
    What good condition can a treaty find
    I'th'part that is at mercy? Five times, Martius,
    I have fought with thee; so often hast thou beat me;
    And wouldst do so, I think, should we encounter
    As often as we eat. By th'elements,   10
    If e'er again I meet him beard to beard,
    He's mine, or I am his. Mine emulation
    Hath not that honour in't it had: for where
    I thought to crush him in an equal force,
    True sword to sword, I'll potch at him some way,   15
    Or wrath or craft may get him.
First Sol.   He's the devil.

Scene x

SCENE x] *Capell.*   2, 16, 29, 33. *First Sol.*] *Capell; Sol. | F.*   3. Condition!]
F (Condition?).

Scene x] located by Pope in the
Camp of the Volscians, but it is
enough that Aufidius is outside the
'town' and on his way to the 'cypress
grove' (l. 30); he should enter at one
door and leave by the other, or
otherwise cross the stage.

S.D. Cornets] Cowling (p. 54)
supposes the Volscian cornets in the
battle scenes to be distinguished from
the Roman trumpets, but also says
they were used in private theatres
where the din of trumpets would
have been unbearable. The cornet
was a kind of horn made of a tusk or
of wood covered in leather, quite
unlike its modern namesake. Cornets
'sound a flourish' in Marston's
Antonio and Mellida, I. i, and cf.

below, S.D.s II. i. 202, II. ii. 154, and
III. i. 1. For the suggestion that
Cornets was added by the prompter,
see Introduction, p. 5.

2–6. *'Twill . . . condition*] Shakespeare plays upon *condition*. It first
means 'terms', then 'the state of
being a Volscian', then 'quality' (as
at II. iii. 96 and *O.E.D.*, s.v. 10 c).
For the last, Case paraphrases,
'Condition indeed! What good quality will treaty-granters discover in
the side that is at their mercy?'

11. *beard to beard*] as in *Mac.*,
v. v. 6.

13. *where*] whereas, as in I. i. 100.
See Abbott 134.

15. *potch*] jab, poke.

16. *Or . . . or*] either . . . or. See

Auf. Bolder, though not so subtle. My valour's poison'd
    With only suff'ring stain by him: for him
    Shall fly out of itself. Nor sleep, nor sanctuary,
    Being naked, sick; nor fane, nor Capitol,   20
    The prayers of priests, nor times of sacrifice—
    Embarquements all of fury—shall lift up
    Their rotten privilege and custom 'gainst
    My hate to Martius. Where I find him, were it
    At home, upon my brother's guard, even there,   25
    Against the hospitable canon, would I
    Wash my fierce hand in's heart. Go you to th'city;
    Learn how 'tis held, and what they are that must
    Be hostages for Rome.
First Sol.   Will not you go?
Auf. I am attended at the cypress grove. I pray you—   30
    'Tis south the city mills—bring me word thither
    How the world goes, that to the pace of it
    I may spur on my journey.
First Sol.   I shall, sir.   [*Exeunt.*]

---

17. valour's] *F3* (*subst.*), valors *F;* valour *Pope.*   17–18. poison'd . . . him:] *F*
(poison'd, . . . him:); (poison'd . . . him) *Pope.*   21–2. sacrifice— . . . fury—]
F (Sacrifice: . . . Fury,).   33. *Exeunt.*] *Rowe; not in F.*

Abbott 136. The line epitomizes
Aufidius' attitude; some editors stress
the point by reading *way:* | *Or.*

17–19. *My valour's . . . itself*] For
stain = eclipse see, e.g., *R2*, III. iii. 66,
and *Sonn.*, XXXIII. 14, 'Suns of the
world may stain when heaven's sun
staineth'. The astronomical metaphor is perhaps sustained in *fly out of
itself* = 'fly out of its proper course, or
sphere'; but the more general sense
dominates, 'betray its own nature'.
Pope's emendation is elegant but
superfluous.

20. *fane*] temple; as again in *Cym.*,
IV. ii. 243.

22. *Embarquements*] impediments,
hindrances. Wright cites Cotgrave,
'Embarquement: an imbarking, taking ship . . . also an imbarguing'

(imbarguing = laying an embargo
upon).

25. *upon . . . guard*] enjoying my
brother's protection.

26. *the hospitable canon*] the law of
hospitality; a complex proleptic
irony, for Aufidius will both honour
the canon and outrage it in his dealings with Martius.

30. *attended*] waited for.

31. *south . . . mills*] Wright records
that 'in the year 1588 the Mayor and
Corporation of the City petitioned
the Queen that they might build
four corn mills on the river Thames
near the Bridge'. The mills were on
the south side and close to the Globe
theatre. Shakespeare's attention to
the imagined topography of Corioles
expresses the remoteness of Aufidius
from 'the world' (see Introduction,
p. 17).

ACT II

[SCENE I]

Enter MENENIUS *with the two Tribunes of the people,*
SICINIUS *and* BRUTUS.

Men. The augurer tells me we shall have news tonight.
Bru. Good or bad?
Men. Not according to the prayer of the people, for they
　　love not Martius.
Sic. Nature teaches beasts to know their friends.　　　　　5

ACT II

Scene I

ACT II] F (*Actus Secundus.*).　　　SCENE I] *Rowe.*　　1. augurer] *F2*; Agurer *F*;
Augur *Pope.*

Scene I] set by Rowe in 'Rome' and by Capell in 'Rome. A Publick Place'. The reception given to Coriolanus was in eighteenth-century adaptations aptly interpreted as an 'ovation' (see p. 79), which was described by the annalists as 'a lesser form of triumph', some saying that it celebrated a great victory but something less than the conquest of a country, and others supposing it appropriate to a peaceful victory, won by policy or eloquence (compare v. v). Bays were carried by the hero at a triumph and fir at an ovation, but Marcellus carried oak in his greatest triumph ('Life of Marcellus', S.H.P., III, p. 65). Both triumphs and ovations began outside the city (the triumph from the Campus Martius) and ended in the Capitol. The processional entry at l. 160 could be through the gates or towards the gates; in either case the procession moves towards the Capitol (l. 202). If Allardyce Nicoll is right about the use of the yard in v. v (see headnote),

it may also have been used here. In North's account there is no triumphal return to Rome, all the honours being conferred at Corioli only.

　1. *augurer*] '*Rom. Hist.* A religious official who interpreted omens derived from the flight, singing and feeding of birds, the appearance of the entrails of sacrificial victims etc., and advised upon the course of public business in accordance with them' (*O.E.D.*, augur). Cf. *Caes.*, II. i. 200 and II. ii. 37, where the *augurers*, reading 'apparent prodigies' and the entrails of a beast without a heart, discourage Caesar from going to the Capitol; the other uses are in *Ant.*, v. ii. 332, and IV. xii. 4 (where F has *auguries*, probably in error). The allusion here seems more casual. The form *augurer* was common, but Shakespeare uses *augur* in *Sonn.*, CVII. 6.

　5. *Nature . . . friends*] Noble cites Isaiah, i. 3 (1585), 'The oxe hath knowen his owner, and the asse his masters cribbe'.

151

Men. Pray you, who does the wolf love?

Sic. The lamb.

Men. Ay, to devour him, as the hungry plebeians would
the noble Martius.

Bru. He's a lamb indeed, that baes like a bear.   10

Men. He's a bear indeed, that lives like a lamb. You
two are old men: tell me one thing that I shall ask
you.

Both. Well, sir.

Men. In what enormity is Martius poor in, that you two   15
have not in abundance?

Bru. He's poor in no one fault, but stored with all.

Sic. Especially in pride.

Bru. And topping all others in boasting.

Men. This is strange now. Do you two know how you are   20
censured here in the city, I mean of us o'th'right-
hand file? Do you?

Both. Why, how are we censured?

Men. Because you talk of pride now—will you not be
angry?   25

Both. Well, well, sir, well.

Men. Why, 'tis no great matter; for a very little thief of
occasion will rob you of a great deal of patience.
Give your dispositions the reins, and be angry at
your pleasures; at the least, if you take it as a   30

17. with all] *F3;* withall *F.*   24. now—will] *F* (now, will).   30. pleasures;
. . . least] *F* (pleasures (at the least)).

10. *baes*] Brutus presumably mimics
the lamb's baa becoming the bear's
growl.

12. *old men*] implying that they
should therefore be wise enough to
answer the question.

15. *In . . . in*] What wickedness
impoverishes Martius, that you two
are not richly endowed with?
Shakespeare does not use *enormity*
elsewhere; for the repetition of *in* see
Abbott 407.

21. *censured*] judged; cf. *Ham.,* I. iii.
69, 'Take each man's censure, but
reserve thy judgement'.

21–2. *right-hand file*] 'A file in these
days consists of two men. In the
sixteenth century it numbered at
least ten . . . Again, the place of
honour to military men has always
been the right of the line, and accordingly a captain always drew up his
best and choicest men in the right-
hand files of his company.' (Fortescue,
Shakespeare's England, I. p. 114.)

27–8. *very . . . occasion*] i.e. that very
little thief, the slightest occasion.
For the construction Wilson compares 'city of London'.

pleasure to you in being so. You blame Martius for
being proud.

Bru. We do it not alone, sir.

Men. I know you can do very little alone, for your helps
are many, or else your actions would grow wondrous	35
single: your abilities are too infant-like for doing
much alone. You talk of pride. O that you could
turn your eyes toward the napes of your necks, and
make but an interior survey of your good selves. O
that you could!	40

Both. What then, sir?

Men. Why, then you should discover a brace of un-
meriting, proud, violent, testy magistrates (alias
fools) as any in Rome.

Sic. Menenius, you are known well enough too.	45

Men. I am known to be a humorous patrician, and one
that loves a cup of hot wine, with not a drop of
allaying Tiber in't; said to be something imperfect
in favouring the first complaint, hasty and tinder-

32. proud.] *F*; proud? *Capell.*

36. *single*] playing on the senses
'solitary' and 'feeble'; cf. *Mac.*,
I. iii. 139, 'Shakes so my single state
of man', and I. vi. 16, 'poor and
single business'.

38–9. *your eyes . . . selves*] 'With
allusion to the fable which says that
every man has a bag hanging before
him, in which he puts his neighbours'
faults, and another behind him in
which he puts his own' (Johnson).
The fable is in Phaedrus, IV. 10.
The allusion is dubious, however,
for, as Furness notes, an *interior
survey* calls for no exterior wallet; the
tribunes are invited to roll their eyes
and look within. Cf. *Ham.*, III. iv. 89,
'Thou turns't my eyes into my very
soul'.

43. *testy*] possibly in the root sense
'headstrong', from 'teste' = 'tête'
(see *O.E.D.*).

magistrates] Wilson notes that
Shakespeare's audience probably
equated the tribunes with London

Justices of the Peace, and compares
Shallow in *2H4*. Plutarch's *Moralia*
specifically states that the tribunes
were not magistrates (see Introduction,
p. 31), but they are described as such
by North (Appendix, p. 320).

46. *humorous*] whimsical; over-
susceptible to the flow of the body's
humours.

47–8. *hot wine . . . Tiber in't*]
probably alluding to mulled wine,
but it could be strong wine; cf.
Mer.V., II. ii. 170–2, 'Pray thee,
take pain / To allay with some cold
drops of modesty / Thy skipping
spirit'. Case quotes Horman, *Vulgaria*
(1530), 'It is a strong wine and
needeth to be allayed (Lat. dilven-
dum)'.

49. *favouring . . . complaint*] i.e.
giving premature judgement in favour of the first representation to
reach him.

49–50. *tinder-like*] quick to flare-up.

like upon too trivial motion; one that converses   50
more with the buttock of the night than with the
forehead of the morning. What I think, I utter, and
spend my malice in my breath. Meeting two such
wealsmen as you are—I cannot call you Lycurguses
—if the drink you give me touch my palate adversely,   55
I make a crooked face at it. I can say, your worships
have delivered the matter well, when I find the ass in

50. upon too] *Rowe*[3]; vppon, to *F.*
Theobald.

56. can] *F*; cannot *Capell*; can't

50. *too trivial motion*] too trifling
provocation (Case).

converses] is conversant, associates.

51. *buttock of the night*] Malone
compares Armado, *LLL.*, v. i. 75,
'in the posteriors of this day, which
the rude multitude call the afternoon'. It is doubtful, however, if a
pun on 'buttocks' is there intended;
O.E.D. does not support it.

53. *spend . . . breath*] expend my
malice in words.

54. *wealsmen*] men of the common
weal; the only use in Shakespeare
and the only instance in *O.E.D.*
King finds a complex pun on *wealsmen* and 'wellsmen', meaning 'people
who keep saying well', and 'people
who draw the water—not wine—of
their speech from a "well" and offer
it to Menenius who pulls a wry
face at it'. For the repetition of *well*,
see ll. 14, 26, 45, 65; Menenius'
well in l. 57 is therefore mockery and
not a hypocritical compliment (see
l. 57–8 note).
Lycurguses] F's aptly informal
spelling (*Licurgusses*) is usually regularized. King alleges an improbable pun on 'gushes', consonant with
the word-play on *well*. A life of
Lycurgus, the great Spartan legislator,
is included in North's Plutarch.
Wilson quotes North (S.H.P., I,
p. 113), 'Lycurgus . . . beganne to
devise how to alter the whole government of the common weale.' For

Shakespeare's interest in Lycurgus
see Introduction, p. 54.
56. *can*] F's reading is retained on
the assumption that Menenius is
being sarcastic, 'While I can say
you have spoken well when I find
you asinine, and while I must be
content to bear with those who find
you wise, yet I must say they are liars
who say you have honest, handsome
faces'. King's recognition of the pun
on *wealsmen* and 'wellsmen' explains
the sarcasm. Menenius can insinuate
a pause before *well* and speak the
word with a touch of mimicry; his
point coheres with the one about *the
ass* and the syllables (see next note).
Capell's emendation makes the
thought consistent with the previous
sentence; Schmidt (*apud* Furness)
thinks *I can say* equivalent to 'I dare
say', and supposes Menenius ready
to commend the tribunes when their
talk is not pure asininity. Theobald's
can't is a form not in use in Shakespeare's time.
57–8. *ass . . . syllables*] Within the
general sense ('Something asinine in
almost all you say') there may be a
more specific one. Verity compares
Ham., v. ii. 43, 'many suchlike as-es
of great charge', which suggests that
Menenius is mocking the tribunes'
forensic or opinionated use of 'as'
(see also *Tw.N.*, II. iii. 159); Beeching
thought the joke an allusion to Latin
grammar, and Sherman thought it 'a
pun on the last syllables of Sicinius
and Brutus'.

compound with the major part of your syllables.
And though I must be content to bear with those
that say you are reverend grave men, yet they lie   60
deadly that tell you have good faces. If you see this in
the map of my microcosm, follows it that I am
known well enough too? What harm can your bisson conspectuities glean out of this character, if I be
known well enough too?   65

Bru. Come, sir, come, we know you well enough.

Men. You know neither me, yourselves, nor any thing.
You are ambitious for poor knaves' caps and legs:
you wear out a good wholesome forenoon in hearing
a cause between an orange-wife and a faucet-seller,   70
and then rejourn the controversy of threepence to a
second day of audience. When you are hearing a
matter between party and party, if you chance to be

61. you] *F;* you, you *Pope.*   63–4. bisson] *Theobald;* beesome *F.*

59. *bear*] Whiter notices the association with *ass* and compares *Cym.,*
II. i. 51–2.

60. *grave*] worthy, dignified.

61. *deadly*] extremely, excessively
(*O.E.D.,* s.v. adv. 4).

tell] say, report, put it about; but it
is rarely used without the indirect
object (see *O.E.D.,* s.v.4) and Pope's
reading could be correct.

good faces] i.e. honest and handsome.

62. *map . . . microcosm*] i.e. my face,
index to the 'little world of man'.
Shakespeare does not use *microcosm*
elsewhere, but cf. *Sonn.,* LXVIII. 1,
'Thus is his cheek the map of days
outworn'.

63–4. *bisson conspectuities*] blind
sagacity, blear-eyed clearsightedness
(after Theobald). *Bisson* could mean
'blind' or, more rarely, 'purblind'; in
Ham., II. ii. 500, 'bisson rheum', it
seems to mean 'eye-blearing'. Wright
suggests F's *beesome* is a spelling or
dialect variant, and cites instances of
'bisom', 'bysom', and 'bysome'. *Conspectuities* is Shakespeare's coinage
from Lat. *conspectus.*

64. *character*] King notices the

consonance between the character-
writing in this scene and that which
was becoming popular when Hall's
Characters of Virtues and Vices was
published (1608).

68. *caps and legs*] bows and scrapes;
the doffing of caps and making of
legs. Cf. *Tim.,* III. vi. 108, *R2,*
III. iii. 175, *All's W.,* II. ii. 10, and
1H4, IV. iii. 68, 'The more and less
came in with cap and knee'.

69–72.] The tribunes have no such
judicial role in Plutarch; Shakespeare
again appears to have the English
magistrate in mind.

70 *orange-wife*] This use of *wife*
to mean 'woman' was still current,
even outside such forms as 'house-
wife' and 'fishwife'.

faucet-seller] pedlar of vent-pegs or
taps for wine-barrels. The 'faucet' or
peg was once distinguished from the
'spigot' into which it fitted; Case
cites Lyly, *Mother Bombie,* II. v. 29,
'to discerne a spigot from a faucet'.

71. *rejourn*] adjourn, postpone.
of threepence] about threepence.

73. *party*] party to a dispute;
litigant.

pinched with the colic, you make faces like mummers, set up the bloody flag against all patience, and,   75
in roaring for a chamber-pot, dismiss the controversy
bleeding, the more entangled by your hearing. All
the peace you make in their cause is calling both the
parties knaves. You are a pair of strange ones.

Bru. Come, come, you are well understood to be a per-   80
fecter giber for the table than a necessary bencher in
the Capitol.

Men. Our very priests must become mockers, if they shall
encounter such ridiculous subjects as you are. When
you speak best unto the purpose, it is not worth the   85
wagging of your beards; and your beards deserve
not so honourable a grave as to stuff a botcher's
cushion, or to be entombed in an ass's pack-saddle.
Yet you must be saying Martius is proud: who, in a
cheap estimation, is worth all your predecessors   90

84-5. When . . . purpose, it] *Rowe;* when . . . purpose. It *F;* when . . . purpose,
it *F4*.   86. beards;] *Rowe;* beards, *F*.

74-5. *faces like mummers*] alluding
to the grimaces of performers in
dumb-shows or country mummings.
Wright quotes Minsheu, *Spanish
Dictionary*: 'hazar Mómios, to make
mops and mows with the mouth, to
make visages and foolish faces'.
Menenius has his own gift for
mummery.

75. *bloody flag*] The red flag signified battle; cf. *H5*, I. ii. 101, 'Stand
for your own, unwind your bloody
flag'; and *Caes.*, v. i. 14, 'Their
bloody sign of battle is hung out',
where Shakespeare alludes to the
'arming scarlet coat' in North's
description of Brutus' 'signal of
battle' (Bullough, v, p. 119). Here,
the battle metaphor is grotesquely
conjoined with the importunities of
the colic.

77. *bleeding*] i.e. still raw and
unhealed.

80-1. *perfecter . . . bencher*] i.e.
more of a perfect giber than an
indispensable bencher.

81. *giber*] Cf. *Ham.*, v. i. 186,
'Where be your gibes now . . . that
were wont to set the table on a roar?'

bencher] 'one who officially sits on a
bench; a magistrate, judge, senator'
(*O.E.D.*). Shakespeare's only use of
the word.

84. *subjects*] objects, creatures
(Onions).

86-8. *beards . . . cushion*] Wright
compares Lyly's *Midas* (ed. Bond),
v. ii. 170, 'A dozen of beards, to
stuffe two dozen of cushions'; see
also *Midas*, III. ii. 127. Cf. *Ado.*,
III. ii. 40, 'the old ornament of his
cheek hath already stuff'd tennis-
balls'. A *botcher* was a patcher of
clothes, as in *Tw.N.*, I. v. 43, 'If he
mend, he is no longer dishonest; if
he cannot, let the botcher mend him.
Anything that's mended is but
patch'd.'

89-90. *in . . . estimation*] at the
lowest evaluation.

since Deucalion, though peradventure some of the
best of 'em were hereditary hangmen. God-den to
your worships. More of your conversation would
infect my brain, being the herdsmen of the beastly
plebeians. I will be bold to take my leave of you.   95
Brutus and Sicinius aside.

Enter VOLUMNIA, VIRGILIA, *and* VALERIA.

How now, my as fair as noble ladies—and the
moon, were she earthly, no nobler—whither do you
follow your eyes so fast?
Vol. Honourable Menenius, my boy Martius ap-
proaches; for the love of Juno, let's go.   100
Men. Ha? Martius coming home?
Vol. Ay, worthy Menenius, and with most prosperous
approbation.
Men. Take my cap, Jupiter, and I thank thee. Hoo!
Martius coming home?   105
Vir., Val. Nay, 'tis true.
Vol. Look, here's a letter from him; the state hath
another, his wife another; and I think there's one at
home for you.

96–7. my ... nobler—] *F* ((my ... Noble) Ladyes, and ... Earthly, no Nobler:)
106. *Vir., Val.*] *Capell; 2. Ladies | F; Vol.Vir. | Dyce*[1].

91. *since Deucalion*] i.e. since the
deluge. The story of Deucalion (the
Greek counterpart of Noah) was
probably known to Shakespeare in
the version of Golding's Ovid (*Met.*
I); cf. *Wint.*, IV. iv. 423. It is a
patrician wit that lays such stress on
ancestry.

92. *God-den*] good even; abbreviated from 'God give you good even';
also at IV. vi. 20, as *good den.*

93. *conversation*] probably 'society'
(*O.E.D.*, s.v. 5).

93–4. *your ... being*] The pro-
nominal adjective *your* implies the
pronoun in the next clause ('you
being'). See Abbott 379.

96–7. *the moon*] i.e. Diana; cf. v. iii.
65 and I. i. 256.

97–8. *whither . . . fast*] For a
comparable expression of eager gaze
and movement, Case cites *Oth.*,
II. i. 36–8, 'Let's to the seaside . . . to
throw out our eyes for brave Othello'.

102–3. *with . . . approbation*] either
'with success and acclaim', cf. *Troil.*,
I. iii. 59, 'the applause and approbation'; or 'with proof of success', cf.
Wint., II. i. 177–8, 'nought for
approbation / But only seeing'.

104. *Take . . . Jupiter*] Menenius
flings his cap to Jupiter, the god of
heaven and air. Cf. I. i. 211, IV. vi.
132, 136, and *Ant.*, II. vii. 132, 'Hoo!
says 'a. There's my cap.'

Men. I will make my very house reel tonight. A letter   110
    for me?

Vir. Yes, certain, there's a letter for you; I saw't.

Men. A letter for me! It gives me an estate of seven
    years' health; in which time I will make a lip at
    the physician. The most sovereign prescription in   115
    Galen is but empiricutic, and, to this preservative,
    of no better report than a horse-drench. Is he not
    wounded? He was wont to come home wounded.

Vir. Oh no, no, no.

Vol. Oh, he is wounded; I thank the gods for't.   120

Men. So do I too, if it be not too much. Brings a victory
    in his pocket? The wounds become him.

Vol. On's brows: Menenius, he comes the third time
    home with the oaken garland.

Men. Has he disciplined Aufidius soundly?   125

Vol. Titus Lartius writes, they fought together, but
    Aufidius got off.

Men. And 'twas time for him too, I'll warrant him that:
    and he had stayed by him, I would not have been so

116. empiricutic] *Malone (subst.)*; Emperickqutique *F.*   122. pocket? The] *F*;
pocket, the *Hanmer.*   123. brows: Menenius,] *F*; brows, Menenius; *Theobald.*

112. *certain*] The adjective is
similarly used as adverb in *Mer.V.*,
II. vi. 29.

113. *gives . . . estate*] endows me
with (Wilson). The legal sense of
estate occurs elsewhere in Shakespeare (e.g. *Mer.V.*, I. i. 43), but so
does the sense 'state or condition'
which is also apt.

114. *make a lip*] curl the lip, sneer;
cf. *Wint.*, I. ii. 372–3, 'falling / A lip
of much contempt'.

116. *Galen*] Although Galen lived
in the second century A.D., his
authority was still respected in
Shakespeare's time. Technically an
anachronism, the allusion nevertheless mediates aptly between the
Jacobean audience and the classical
past.

empiricutic] a nonce-word coined
from 'empiric' by analogy with
'pharmaceutic'; *O.E.D.* gives no

further instance. 'Empiric' and 'empi-
rical' signified the experimental, hit
and miss, methods of physicians
unlearned in Hippocrates and Galen,
hence 'quackery'. F's spelling is
closer to the usual Elizabethan form
'empirique'.

117. *horse-drench*] draught of horse
medicine.

121. *a*] for *ha = he*; a frequent form
in Shakespeare and elsewhere, not
confined to dialect and provincial use.

122. *pocket? . . . him*] Volumnia
appears directly to answer Menenius'
question—Martius brings victory not
in his pocket but *On's brows*. Wilson,
however, supports Hanmer's reading
with the claim that Menenius is
expressing a qualification about the
value of Martius' wounds.

124. *oaken garland*] See I. iii. 14–15
note and I. ix. 59.

'fidiussed for all the chests in Corioles and the gold   130
that's in them. Is the senate possessed of this?

Vol. Good ladies, let's go. Yes, yes, yes. The senate has
letters from the general, wherein he gives my son the
whole name of the war: he hath in this action out-
done his former deeds doubly.   135

Val. In troth, there's wondrous things spoke of him.

Men. Wondrous! Ay, I warrant you, and not without
his true purchasing.

Vir. The gods grant them true.

Vol. True? pow, waw!   140

Men. True? I'll be sworn they are true. Where is he
wounded? [*To the Tribunes*] God save your good
worships! Martius is coming home: he has more
cause to be proud. [*To Volumnia*] Where is he
wounded?   145

Vol. I'th'shoulder, and i'th'left arm: there will be
large cicatrices to show the people when he shall
stand for his place. He received in the repulse of
Tarquin seven hurts i'th'body.

Men. One i'th'neck, and two i'th'thigh—there's nine   150
that I know.

Vol. He had, before this last expedition, twenty-five
wounds upon him.

130. 'fidiussed] *F* (fiddious'd).   140. waw] *F; wow Capell.*   142. S.D.]
Theobald; not in F.   144. S.D.] *This ed., after Rossiter; not in F.*

130. *'fidiussed*] F's form of the name
is *Auffidius*, and here the spelling
fiddious'd suggests that Shakespeare did
not intend the further pun 'fidi-used'.

131. *possessed*] informed, as in
Mer.V., I. iii. 59.

134. *name*] credit, glory; but the
attributes of honour are closely
related to the conferring of the name
Coriolanus upon Martius.

138. *his . . . purchasing*] his truly
earning it.

140. *pow, waw*] Variants of this
expression, cited by Case, include
'Pew wew', 'baw waw', and 'bow
wow'.

147. *cicatrices*] scars.

148. *stand . . . place*] i.e. for the

consulship; *stand* is probably meant
literally, but the figurative sense
'offer oneself as a candidate' was
available.

148–9. *repulse of Tarquin*] Cf. II. ii.
88. For North's account of Martius'
part in the battle of Lake Regillus
(*c.* 496 B.C.), see Appendix, p. 315.

150. *nine*] The discrepant arithmetic is convincingly explained by
supposing Menenius to conclude
aloud an enumeration made to himself; but Case sees the neck and thigh
wounds as distinct from the body
wounds, and supposes Shakespeare
or Menenius to have hastily claimed
nine instead of ten.

Men. Now it's twenty-seven: every gash was an enemy's
  grave.   *A shout and flourish.* 155
  Hark, the trumpets!
Vol. These are the ushers of Martius: before him he
  carries noise, and behind him he leaves tears:
  Death, that dark spirit, in's nervy arm doth lie,
  Which, being advanc'd, declines, and then men die. 160

 A Sennet. Trumpets sound. Enter COMINIUS *the General, and*
 TITUS LARTIUS: *between them* CORIOLANUS, *crowned with an*
  oaken garland; with Captains and Soldiers, and a Herald.

Her. Know, Rome, that all alone Martius did fight
  Within Corioles gates: where he hath won,
  With fame, a name to Martius Caius. These
  In honour follows Coriolanus.
  Welcome to Rome, renowned Coriolanus! *Sound flourish.*
All. Welcome to Rome, renowned Coriolanus!   166

155. S.D.] *Follows* trumpets! *in F.* 157–8.] *Prose, as Pope;* These . . . *Martius:*
/ . . . Noyse; / . . . Teares: / *F.* 163–4.] *As Capell;* With . . . *Caius:* / . . .
Coriolanus. / *F.* 163. Martius Caius] *F, Sisson;* Caius Martius *Rowe.* 164.
Coriolanus] *Steevens; Martius Caius Coriolanus* / *F.* 165. S.D.] *F (Sound.
Flourish.).*

159. *nervy*] sinewy, muscular; but
see I. i. 137 note. Death energizes
Martius' sword-arm.

160. *advanc'd*] raised; cf. I. vi. 61
and note.

declines] descends; cf. *Ham.,* II.
ii. 471–3, 'his sword, / Which was
declining on the milky head / Of
reverend Priam'.

160. S.D. Sennet] While a sennet
differed from a flourish (ll. 155, 165),
it is not known what order of notes
was sounded for each. It accompanied, rather than announced, a
ceremonial entrance (see J. S.
Manifold, *Music in English Drama*
(1956), pp. 28–30).

S.D. *Cominius* the General] This
may indicate military uniform, as
distinct from the consular robes
appropriate at II. ii. 36 S.D. But see
Introduction, p. 6.

S.D. *Lartius*] Lartius was left at
Corioles at I. ix. 75 and is apparently
still there at II. ii. 38. His presence
here, although mute, is needed for
the spectacle of 'three / That Rome
should dote on' (ll. 185–6). The
oversight would scarcely be noticed
in the theatre. F's spelling *Latius*
also occurs in North's Plutarch
(1595, p. 238); for its possible bearing
on the composition of the play, see
Introduction p. 21.

163. *to*] in addition to.
Martius Caius] See I. ix. 64 note.

164. *follows Coriolanus*] Steevens's
emendation is generally adopted on
the assumption that the compositor
repeated the line above; this would
confirm that the order *Martius Caius*
stood in the copy.

Cor. No more of this; it does offend my heart.
  Pray now, no more.
Com.   Look, sir, your mother.
Cor.   Oh!
  You have, I know, petition'd all the gods
  For my prosperity.   *Kneels.*
Vol.   Nay, my good soldier, up;   170
  My gentle Martius, worthy Caius, and
  By deed-achieving honour newly nam'd—
  What is it?—Coriolanus, must I call thee?
  But oh, thy wife—
Cor.   My gracious silence, hail!
  Wouldst thou have laugh'd had I come coffin'd home,
  That weep'st to see me triumph? Ah, my dear,   176
  Such eyes the widows in Corioles wear,
  And mothers that lack sons.
Men.   Now the gods crown thee!
Cor. And live you yet? [*To Valeria*] O my sweet lady,
    pardon.

167–70. No . . . prosperity.] *As Pope; prose in F.*   171–2.] *As Theobald;* My
. . . *Caius,* | . . . nam'd, | *F.*   173. it? . . . must] *F* (it (*Coriolanus*) must).
177. wear]*F2;* were*F.*   179.*Cor.*]*Theobald; Com.* |*F.*   S.D.] *Theobald; not in F.*

172. *deed-achieving honour*] honour
which is achieved by deeds (Schmidt).
For the gerundive construction Schmidt compares *Lucr.*, 998, 'an un-
recalling crime', and *Ant.*, III. xiii. 77,
'his all-obeying breath'.

174. *My . . . silence*] Case quotes
North's Plutarch, 'Life of Numa'
(1595, p. 72): 'He much frequented
the Muses in the woddes. For he
would say he had the most part of
his revelations of the Muses and he
taught the Romans to reverence one
of them above all the rest, who was
called *Tacita*, as ye would say *Lady
Silence*.' (S.H.P., I, p. 176.) For the
frequent occurrence of abstract for
concrete in the play see Introduction,
p. 68, and for the significance of
silence, p. 60.

177–8.] It is characteristic of the
play that lines of this harsh import
can be spoken with solicitude and

tenderness. Jan Kott calls them
'suddenly objective, recalling those
who have been defeated' and compares Brecht's songs (*Shakespeare our
Contemporary*, 1965, p. 155).

179. Cor.] Only Harrison, among
recent editors, retains F's attribution
to Cominius. As Theobald recognized, the bantering question (cf.
Ado, I. i. 101) is addressed to Menenius, and the rest almost certainly to
Valeria. Gordon, however, suggests
that Martius 'asks his wife to forgive
him for jesting at her tears'. Murry
reassigns *And . . . yet* to Virgilia, with
Coriolanus responding *O . . . pardon*.
The effect is perhaps excessively
poignant, significantly modifying the
apparent temper of the play; but it is
not easily justified on textual grounds,
although Shakespeare's elaborate
Capital *C* could sometimes be read as
V. The S.H. *Cor.* occurs three times in

Vol. I know not where to turn: O welcome home!   180
    And welcome, general; and y'are welcome all.
Men. A hundred thousand welcomes. I could weep,
    And I could laugh, I am light and heavy. Welcome!
    A curse begnaw at very root on's heart,
    That is not glad to see thee! You are three   185
    That Rome should dote on: yet, by the faith of men,
    We have some old crabtrees here at home that will not
    Be grafted to your relish. Yet welcome, warriors!
    We call a nettle but a nettle, and
    The faults of fools but folly.
Com.   Ever right.   190
Cor. Menenius, ever, ever.
Her. Give way there, and go on.
Cor. [*To Volumnia and Virgilia*]   Your hand, and yours!
    Ere in our own house I do shade my head,
    The good patricians must be visited,

180–1.] *As Pope;* I . . . turne. / . . . Generall, / . . . all. *F.*   182–90.] *As Pope;*
A . . . Welcomes: / . . . laugh, / . . . welcome: / . . . heart, / . . . thee. / . . . on: /
. . . haue / . . . home, / . . . Rallish. / . . . Warriors: / . . . Nettle; / . . . folly. / *F.*
184. begnaw at] *Craig;* begin at *F;* begnaw the *Wilson.*   185. You] *F2;*
Yon *F.*   191. Menenius, ever] *F;* Menenius ever *Alexander.*   192. S.D.]
Cam.; not in F.

this column of F (with *Corio.* and
Coriol. also three); it is likely that the
transition from *Mar.* to *Cor.* made the
slip or misreading *Com.* easier.

    184. *begnaw*] Craig's emendation is
supported by *R3,* I. iii. 222, 'The
worm of conscience still begnaw thy
soul!', and *Tim.,* IV. iii. 48, 'The
canker gnaw thy heart'. The misreading *begnaw/beginne* is a possible
minim error and the slip is likely to
be owed to the habit and expectation
prompted by the first three letters.
F's reading makes sense but is scarcely cogent; it may suggest an infection spreading from the root.
    root on's heart] Case compares *Ant.,*
v. ii. 105, 'grief that smites my very
heart at root', and Chaucer, *Romaunt
of the Rose,* 1026, 'Me thinketh in myn
herte rote'.
    182–8.] For the line-division here
see Introduction, p. 13.

    187–8. *crabtrees . . . relish*] Cf. *2H6,*
III. ii. 213–14, 'noble stock / Was
graft with crab-tree slip'. 'Crabbed'
and 'crabby' were in general use to
express meanness, perversity, and
sourness of temper, from the gnarled
form of the crabstick and from the
taste of the crab-apple. Shakespeare
shared the Elizabethan awareness
of the social and political implications
of grafting; here the tribunes are of an
unserviceable stock.

    190. *faults . . . folly*] Noble com-
pares Proverbs, xiv. 24 (Geneva),
'the follie of fooles is foolishnesse',
and (Authorized), 'the foolishness of
fools is folly'.

    191. *Menenius, ever*] When F's
comma is omitted the meaning is
'always the same Menenius', but this
is a less precise response to *Ever right*
than the F text yields.

From whom I have receiv'd not only greetings,   195
But with them change of honours.

Vol.   I have liv'd
To see inherited my very wishes,
And the buildings of my fancy: only
There's one thing wanting, which I doubt not but
Our Rome will cast upon thee.

Cor.   Know, good mother,
I had rather be their servant in my way   201
Than sway with them in theirs.

Com.   On, to the Capitol.

Flourish. Cornets. Exeunt in state, as before.

BRUTUS *and* SICINIUS *come forward.*

Bru. All tongues speak of him, and the bleared sights
Are spectacled to see him. Your prattling nurse
Into a rapture lets her baby cry   205
While she chats him. The kitchen malkin pins

196. change] *F;* charge *Theobald.*   198–200.] *As Malone;* And . . . Fancie: /
. . . wanting, / . . . Rome / . . . thee. *F.*   202. S.D. *Brutus . . . forward.*] *Theo-*
bald; Enter Brutus and Scicinius. / *F.*   205. rapture] *F;* rupture *Hudson*[2].
206. malkin] *F (Malkin); ;* Maukin *Rowe.*

196. *change of honours*] probably
'fresh honours', as in 'change of
clothes'; cf. *Shr.*, IV. iii. 57, 'double
change of brav'ry'. It may, however,
be another allusion to Martius'
change of name.

197–8. *To see . . . fancy*] i.e. to
possess what I had dreamed of
possessing; cf. *Rom.*, I. ii. 28–30,
'Even such delight / Among fresh
female buds shall you this night /
Inherit at my house'; and *Lr.*, IV. ii.
85, 'All the building in my fancy'.

200. *cast upon*] as in *Tp.*, I. ii. 75,
'The government I cast upon my
brother'.

202. *sway*] bear sway, rule.

202. S.D. Cornets] See I. i. I S.D.
note. For the suggestion that *Cornets*
was added by the prompter see
Introduction, p. 5.

203–19.] Verity compares Pom-
pey's reception in Rome, *Caes.*, I. i.
38–52.

204. *spectacled*] 'Spectacles are said
to have been invented in the 13th
century by an Italian monk' (Verity).

Your] the familiar use, 'this nurse
I am telling you about'; cf. I. i. 127
and V. iv. 12.

205. *rapture*] paroxysm, fit. *O.E.D.*
(s.v. 5c) offers this as one of two
examples, and finds the sense 'rare
(now dialect)'. Steevens adduced an
apt parallel from '*The Hospital of
London's Follies*, 1602', 'Your darling
will weep itself into a rapture, if
you take not good heed'; but the
reference has never been traced and
may be spurious (see Furness, p. 205).
Hudson's *rupture* has received but
modest textual and medical support;
it is at best needless.

206. *chats him*] chats about him.
This is the only instance of the
transitive form in *O.E.D.* (s.v. chat
v.[1] 4).

malkin] slut, wench; diminutive of

Her richest lockram 'bout her reechy neck,
Clamb'ring the walls to eye him; stalls, bulks, windows,
Are smother'd up, leads fill'd and ridges hors'd
With variable complexions, all agreeing   210
In earnestness to see him. Seld-shown flamens
Do press among the popular throngs, and puff
To win a vulgar station. Our veil'd dames
Commit the war of white and damask in
Their nicely gauded cheeks, to th'wanton spoil   215
Of Phoebus' burning kisses. Such a pother,

208–9.] *As Pope;* Clambring . . . him: / . . . vp, / . . . hors'd / *F.*   214–15.] *As Pope;* Commit . . . Damaske / . . . spoyle / *F.*   215. gauded] *F* (gawded); guarded *Wilson, conj. Lettsom.*

Matilda or Maud (cf. Mald, Maldkin); F's italics treat the word as a proper name, and so does Rowe's *Maukin.*

207. *lockram*] a linen fabric, made in various qualities and named after the Breton village where it was first made (from *O.E.D.*).

reechy] dirty, greasy; presumably from kitchen smoke.

208–9.] For an explanation of F's line-divisions see Introduction, p. 15.

208. *stalls*] benches set before shops displaying goods for sale (*O.E.D.*, stall *sb.*[1] 6).

bulks] frameworks projecting from the front of a shop, stalls (*O.E.D.*, bulk *sb.*[2]).

209. *leads*] roofs (often of lead, particularly in flat areas).

209–10. *ridges . . . complexions*] i.e. people of all sorts astride the roof-ridges. *O.E.D.* gives only this instance of *horse* meaning 'bestride' (s.v. *v.* 7); cf. *Wint.*, i. ii. 288, 'horsing foot on foot'.

210. *complexions*] natures, types; strictly the four complexions of the humours: sanguine, phlegmatic, melancholy, and choleric.

211. *Seld-shown flamens*] priests who rarely show themselves. The exotic phrase is made familiar by conjunction with *puff. Seld* for 'seldom' was common, e.g. Marlowe, *Jew of*

Malta, i. i. 28, 'seld-seen costly stones', and *Troil.*, iv. v. 150. For *flamen* Case quotes North's Plutarch, 'Life of Numa' (1595, p. 71), 'His second act was, that he did adde to the two priests of *Iupiter* and *Mars*, a third in the honour of *Romulus*, who was called *Flamen Quirinalis*' (S.H.P., I, p. 173). Cf. *Tim.*, iv. iii. 154–5, 'hoar the flamen, / That scolds against the quality of flesh'.

213. *a vulgar station*] a place to stand with the common people. For a similar play on *station* cf. iv. v. 32.

veil'd] i.e. usually veiled.

214–16. *Commit . . . kisses*] i.e. expose their carefully made-up cheeks to the risk of sun-burn. Wilson, reading *guarded*, explains 'carefully protected by "sun-expelling masks"' (see *Gent.*, iv. iv. 149). The war of white and red was a lyrical commonplace; cf. *Lucr.*, 71–2, 'This silent war of lilies and of roses . . . in her fair face's field'.

216. *pother*] uproar, commotion. Retaining F's *poother*, Case claims it as a dialect form. Wright compares F's *pudder* and Q1 *powther* in *Lr.*, III. ii. 50. *O.E.D.* admits all three variants and adds *puther*. It is likely enough that *poother* stood in the copy, but *pother* is a current form and apt for a modernized text.

As if that whatsoever god who leads him
Were slily crept into his human powers,
And gave him graceful posture.
Sic.   On the sudden,
I warrant him consul.
Bru.   Then our office may,   220
During his power, go sleep.
Sic. He cannot temp'rately transport his honours
From where he should begin and end, but will
Lose those he hath won.
Bru.   In that there's comfort.
Sic.   Doubt not
The commoners, for whom we stand, but they   225
Upon their ancient malice will forget
With the least cause these his new honours; which
That he will give them make I as little question
As he is proud to do't.
Bru.   I heard him swear,
Were he to stand for consul, never would he   230
Appear i'th'market-place, nor on him put
The napless vesture of humility;

219-21. On . . . sleep.] *As Pope;* On . . . Consull. / . . . sleepe. *F.*   224. not]
Knight; not, *F.*   227-8.] *As Pope;* With . . . Honors, / . . . question, / *F.*
232. napless] *F* (Naples), *Rowe.*

217-19. *As if . . . posture*] 'As if that
god who leads him, whatsoever god
he be . . . ' (Johnson). The phrase
graceful posture has the force of
'divine form'; Malone compares
Sonn., XXVI. 9-10, and *Ant.*, IV. viii.
24-6, 'he hath fought today / As if a
god in hate of mankind had /
Destroy'd in such a shape'.

222-3. *He cannot . . . end*] He cannot
carry his honours equably from their
beginning to their proper end, but
will lose those he has won (before
they are consolidated). Cf. IV. vii.
36-7, 'he could not / Carry his
honours even'. For the construction
Malone compares *Cymb.*, III. ii. 61-3,
'and for the gap / That we shall make
in time from our hence-going / And
our return, to excuse'.

226. *Upon*] on the ground of,
owing to.

227-8. *which That*] i.e. the which
cause.

228-9. *make . . . do't*] I doubt as
little as the measure of his pride
warrants.

232. *napless vesture*] threadbare
garment. F's *Naples* is not italicized
and probably renders *naples* in the
copy. North speaks of the 'poore
gowne' and 'meane apparell' of the
petitioner, misunderstanding a passage in Amyot referring to 'une robe
simple . . . sans saye dessous';
according to Plutarch the candidate
for office wore only a toga, without a
tunic underneath it. See II. iii. 114
note.

Nor showing (as the manner is) his wounds
To th'people, beg their stinking breaths.

Sic.   'Tis right.

Bru. It was his word. Oh, he would miss it rather   235
Than carry it but by the suit of the gentry to him
And the desire of the nobles.

Sic.   I wish no better
Than have him hold that purpose, and to put it
In execution.

Bru.   'Tis most like he will.

Sic. It shall be to him then, as our good wills,   240
A sure destruction.

Bru.   So it must fall out
To him; or our authority's for an end;
We must suggest the people in what hatred
He still hath held them: that to's power he would
Have made them mules, silenc'd their pleaders, and
Dispropertied their freedoms; holding them,   246

235–6.] *As Steevens;* It was . . . word: / . . . carry it, / *F.*   236. gentry to him]
F; gentry *Pope.*   237. of the] *F;* o'th' *Pope.*   237–9. I wish . . . will.] *As
Pope; prose in F.*   240–1. It . . . destruction.] *As Rowe; prose in F.*   242. him,
. . . authority's . . . end;] *Hibbard (subst.)* him, . . . Authorities, . . . end. *F;* him,
. . . authority's at an end *conj. Thirlby (apud. Furness);* him, . . . authorities.
For . . . end, *Pope.*   245–6.] *As Pope;* Haue . . . Pleaders, / . . . them, / *F.*

234–41.] For the lineation problems here see Introduction, p. 12.

235–7. *he would . . . nobles*] i.e. he
would miss the office rather than go
through with the ritual, were it not
for the pleas of the patricians.

240. *as our good wills*] as our interest
would have it (Case).

242. *authority's . . . end*] i.e. it is
bound to come to an end; Hibbard
compares *Ant.,* v. ii. 192–3, 'the
bright day is done, / And we are for
the dark'. Thirlby's *authority's* is
acceptable as F twice uses the
singular form *authoritie* (III. i. 23, 206)
and *authority* only once (I. i. 15), and
on five other occasions in this text
appears to omit the apostrophe from
's = *is* (e.g. I. x. 17, 'my valors
poison'd' and III. i. 188, 'Confusions

neere'). Omitting the comma after
him, F's pointing can be encouraged
to mean 'for an end of either him or
our authorities', but the effect is
clumsy; also Brutus at III. i. 206
speaks of *our authoritie* and does not
use the plural. Pope's punctuation
relates *For an end* to what follows,
and it could mean 'in conclusion, to
cut the matter short' (*O.E.D.,* end,
sb. 16b). Wilson follows Pope but
glosses 'to this end', which is improbable since the end stated is not
desired. Thirlby's further intervention *at an end* is inept.

243. *suggest*] prompt, insinuate to.

244. *still*] always.

246. *Dispropertied*] dispossessed them
of. *O.E.D.* gives only this instance;
but cf. *John,* v. ii. 79, 'I am too high
born to be propertied', where

In human action and capacity,
Of no more soul nor fitness for the world
Than camels in their war, who have their provand
Only for bearing burthens, and sore blows   250
For sinking under them.

Sic.   This (as you say) suggested
At some time when his soaring insolence
Shall touch the people—which time shall not want,
If he be put upon't, and that's as easy
As to set dogs on sheep—will be his fire   255
To kindle their dry stubble; and their blaze
Shall darken him for ever.

---

249. their] *F;* the *Hanmer.*   253. touch] *Hanmer;* teach *F;* reach *Theobald*
255. his] *F;* the *Pope;* as *Capell.*

---

propertied = be in another's possession. Case cites *Ant.,* v. ii. 83–4, 'His voice was propertied / As all the tuned spheres', where it means 'having certain properties or qualities'; he therefore renders *dispropertied* as 'took away the qualities or essentials of their liberties'. The *John* usage seems more relevant.

249. *camels . . . war*] Case quotes Holland's Pliny, VIII, p. 18: 'In thise parts from whence they [camels] come they serve all to carry packs like labouring horses, and are put to service also in the warres'.

their war] Wilson and others follow Hanmer's *the war*; but as Chambers says, *their* attributes the war to the patricians. Since the stress falls so consistently on *him* and *he*, however, *their* does remain intrusive, and it is quite possible that the compositor anticipated *their provand*.

provand] food, provisions, provender; especially the food provided for an army (*O.E.D.*).

251. *suggested*] insinuated.

253. *touch*] kindle (Gomme). The word anticipates the metaphor in ll. 255–6; cf. *H5*, III. Prol. 32–3, 'the nimble gunner / With linstock now the devilish cannon touches'.

Also following Hanmer, Wilson glosses, 'touch to the quick', which is common in Shakespeare and fits the context. Retaining F's *teach*, Malone explains, 'instruct the people in their duty to their rulers', and some compare I. i. 166–87. *Teach* could be retained also to mean, 'teach the people his true nature (and therefore inflame them to revolt)'. The misreading is an easy one, however, and *touch* is both more imaginative and more precise. Theobald's *reach* has the effect of setting the people at a remote distance from Coriolanus; it has found little support.

254. *put upon't*] provoked to it.

255. *his fire*] i.e. the fire kindled by Coriolanus' insolence. But Wilson follows Pope, attributing the kindling to the 'suggestions' of the Tribunes.

255–6. *fire . . . stubble*] Noble compares Isaiah, v. 24–5 (Geneva): 'Therefore as the flame of fire devoureth the stubble, and as the chaffe is consumed of the flame . . . Therefore is the wrath of the Lord kindled against his people.'

257. *darken*] obscure, eclipse (Verity).

Enter a Messenger.

Bru.   What's the matter?

Mess. You are sent for to the Capitol. 'Tis thought
That Martius shall be consul.
I have seen the dumb men throng to see him, and   260
The blind to hear him speak. Matrons flung gloves,
Ladies and maids their scarfs and handkerchers,
Upon him as he pass'd; the nobles bended
As to Jove's statue, and the commons made
A shower and thunder with their caps and shouts: 265
I never saw the like.

Bru.   Let's to the Capitol,
And carry with us ears and eyes for th'time,
But hearts for the event.

Sic.   Have with you.   *Exeunt.*

[SCENE II]

Enter two Officers, to lay cushions, as it were in the Capitol.

First Off. Come, come, they are almost here. How many
stand for consulships?

258–61.] *As Dyce;* You . . . Capitoll: / . . . Consull: / . . . him, / . . . Gloues, / *F.*

Scene II

Scene II] *Capell.*

260–6.] There is no equivalent
passage in North, and Shakespeare is
again mediating between London
and Rome; as Malone remarks,
gloves, scarfs, and handkerchiefs
were common tournament favours.
Suggestions of deification may owe
something to a distant recollection of
Christ at Galilee (Matthew, xv. 30).

267. *th'time*] i.e. the present time.

268. *event*] outcome.

Have with you] both 'let's go' and
'I'm with you'; cf. *Oth.*, I. ii. 53,
and Nashe's title, *Have with you to
Saffron Walden.*

Scene II

Scene II] Editors follow Shakespeare's S.D. and locate in 'The

Capitol'. Shakespeare assumed that
the 'Capitol' was the citadel, and
seat of the senate. Strictly it was the
temple of Jupiter on the south peak
of the *Mons Capitolinus*, while the
citadel or *Arx* was on the north peak.
Historically, the senate most often
assembled at the *Cura Hostilia* near
the Forum. (After Verity.)

S.D. to lay cushions] Cf. III. i. 100,
and IV. vii. 43, where the cushion is
the symbol of administrative office.
The practice is not exclusively
Roman; cushions are provided in the
court at Elsinore (*Ham.*, v. ii. 217
S.D.) and for the sexton in *Ado*,
IV. ii. 2. We may suppose large
cushions, serving as seats; compare

Second Off. Three, they say; but 'tis thought of everyone
    Coriolanus will carry it.

First Off. That's a brave fellow; but he's vengeance   5
    proud, and loves not the common people.

Second Off. 'Faith, there hath been many great men that
    have flattered the people, who ne'er loved them; and
    there be many that they have loved, they know
    not wherefore: so that if they love they know not   10
    why, they hate upon no better a ground. Therefore,
    for Coriolanus neither to care whether they love or
    hate him manifests the true knowledge he has in
    their disposition, and out of his noble carelessness
    lets them plainly see't.   15

First Off. If he did not care whether he had their love
    or no, he waved indifferently 'twixt doing them
    neither good nor harm; but he seeks their hate with
    greater devotion than they can render it him, and
    leaves nothing undone that may fully discover him   20
    their opposite. Now to seem to affect the malice
    and displeasure of the people is as bad as that which
    he dislikes, to flatter them for their love.

Second Off. He hath deserved worthily of his country;

7. hath] *F;* have *F4.*

the wool-sack in the House of
Lords, and see J. E. Neale, *The
Elizabethan House of Commons,* 1949,
frontispiece.

5. *vengeance*] exceedingly, intensely
(*O.E.D.*, s.v. 5); cf. 'with a vengeance'.

8. *who . . . them*] *who* refers to
people, and *them* to *great men.*

9. *they*] the people.

14. *out of*] owing to, as in *Ham.,*
II. ii. 597 (Case).

noble carelessness] a trenchant but
ambiguous phrase, touching on the
one hand his *sprezzatura,* becoming
to a nobleman, and on the other his
culpable contempt of common life.

15. *lets*] For the omission of the
nominative see Abbott 399.

17. *he waved*] he would have
wavered (Case). For *wave* = waver,
see *O.E.D.*, s.v. *v.* 2. For this use of
the subjunctive in a form identical
with the indicative see Abbott 361.

18. *neither*] Two constructions are
confused, 'he waved indifferently
'twixt good and harm' and 'doing
them neither good nor harm'
(Wright).

21. *opposite*] adversary; cf. *Tw.N.,*
III. iv. 254, *Ham.,* v. ii. 62.

21–3. *seem to . . . love*] For the
judgement see North's similar remarks in his 'Comparison of Alcibiades and Coriolanus', S.H.P., II,
p. 226. As Case says, it is just
possible that *seems to* here means
'think fit to' (see *O.E.D.*, s.v. 9 b).

21. *affect*] aim at, desire.

and his ascent is not by such easy degrees as those   25
who, having been supple and courteous to the
people, bonneted, without any further deed to have
them at all into their estimation and report; but he
hath so planted his honours in their eyes and his
actions in their hearts, that for their tongues to be   30
silent and not confess so much were a kind of ingrateful injury. To report otherwise were a malice
that, giving itself the lie, would pluck reproof and
rebuke from every ear that heard it.

First Off. No more of him; he's a worthy man: make   35
way, they are coming.

*A Sennet. Enter the Patricians, and the Tribunes of the People,
Lictors before them;* CORIOLANUS, MENENIUS, COMINIUS *the
Consul.* SICINIUS *and* BRUTUS *take their places by themselves;*
CORIOLANUS *stands.*

Men. Having determin'd of the Volsces, and
    To send for Titus Lartius, it remains,

25. ascent] *F* (assent), *F2.*   27. people, bonneted,] *F;* people bonnetted,
Hanmer; people, unbonnetted *conj. Johnson.*   37–8.] *As Pope;* Hauing . . .
Volces, / . . . remaines, / *F.*

25. *degrees*] steps (used, for example,
of the rungs of a ladder); cf. *Caes.*,
II. i. 21–7.

    as those] i.e. as the ascent of those.

    27. *bonneted*] took off their bonnets;
the traditional interpretation, following Malone. *O.E.D.* gives only this
instance of the usage, but it is closely
analogous to *O.E.D.*, cap *v.*[1] 5, 'to
take off the cap in token of respect',
and 'capping' in this sense is still in
use at the old universities. Cotgrave
(1611) gives, '*Bonneter,* to put off his
cap unto', and in *Oth.*, I. ii. 23–5,
'unbonneted' apparently means 'with
bonnets on': 'my demerits [= merits]
/ May speak unbonneted to as proud
a fortune / As this that I have
reach'd'. Gomme, however, explains
Othello's *unbonneted* as 'unadorned,
fully revealed', and therefore takes

bonneted here to be intended in its
obvious sense; the Second Officer
then means, 'after a show of humility,
put their bonnets on again and did
nothing more'.

    28. *estimation*] esteem.
    report] repute, fame.

    36. S.D. Sennet] See II. i. 160 note.
    Lictors] attendants upon Roman
magistrates who bore the *fasces*
before them and executed their
sentences. According to Plutarch,
tribunes were not attended by
lictors; see Introduction, p. 31.

    Coriolanus stands] For the sugges-
tion that this was added by the
prompter see Introduction, p. 5.

    37. *of*] concerning.

    38. *Titus Lartius*] See I. ix. 75 and
II. i. 160 note.

As the main point of this our after-meeting,
To gratify his noble service that   40
Hath thus stood for his country. Therefore, please you,
Most reverend and grave elders, to desire
The present consul, and last general
In our well-found successes, to report
A little of that worthy work perform'd   45
By Martius Caius Coriolanus, whom
We met here, both to thank and to remember,
With honours like himself.   [*Coriolanus sits.*]
First Sen.   Speak, good Cominius.
Leave nothing out for length, and make us think
Rather our state's defective for requital   50
Than we to stretch it out. [*To the Tribunes*] Masters
    o'th'people,
We do request your kindest ears, and after
Your loving motion toward the common body,

40–1.] *As Pope; To . . . hath* / *. . . you,* / *F.*   46. Martius Caius] *F, Sisson;*
Caius Martius *Rowe.*   48. S.D.] *Neilson; not in F.*   50. state's] *F4, states F.*
51. S.D.] *Cam.; not in F.*

40. *gratify*] reward, requite.

noble] here unambiguously related to his service of his country. See Introduction, p. 68.

44. *well-found*] i.e. found to be good, of approved report. Other interpretations include, 'fortunately met with' (Wright); 'found to be as great as they were reported' (Schmidt). Onions supports Wright, but for the same phrase in *All's W.*, II. i. 101 ('In what he did profess, well found') glosses 'well equipped or furnished (as a ship, &c., with stores)'. The *All's W.*, context, however, also admits the sense 'found to be good'.

47. *met*] i.e. are met with.

47–8. *remember . . . himself*] commemorate and reward with becoming honours.

49. *for length*] for fear of going on too long.

49–51. *think . . . out*] rather think the state of Rome lacking in resources for requital, than suppose us lacking the will to strain them to the uttermost. I take *it* to refer to the state's requital, and not singly to either *state* or *requital; defective* refers to both *state* and *we.*

52–4. *and after . . . here*] and in accordance with your solicitous disposition towards the common people to render to them what happens here. For *after* in this sense cf. *Ant.*, IV. xv. 87, 'after the high Roman fashion' and *Tp.*, II. ii. 71, 'after the wisest'; and for *yield* = report cf. *Ant.*, II. v. 28. Some read *after,* / *Your,* however, and understand 'afterwards'.

53. *common body*] Cf. *Ant.*, I. iv. 44–7, 'This common body, / Like to a vagabond flag upon the stream, / Goes to and back, lackeying the varying tide, / To rot itself with motion'.

To yield what passes here.

Sic.   We are convented
Upon a pleasing treaty, and have hearts   55
Inclinable to honour and advance
The theme of our assembly.

Bru.   Which the rather
We shall be bless'd to do, if he remember
A kinder value of the people than
He hath hereto priz'd them at.

Men.   That's off, that's off!
I would you rather had been silent. Please you   61
To hear Cominius speak?

Bru.   Most willingly;
But yet my caution was more pertinent
Than the rebuke you give it.

Men.   He loves your people,
But tie him not to be their bedfellow.   65
Worthy Cominius, speak.

                        Coriolanus rises, and offers to go away.
                        Nay, keep your place.

First Sen. Sit, Coriolanus: never shame to hear
What you have nobly done.

Cor.   Your honours' pardon:
I had rather have my wounds to heal again
Than hear say how I got them.

Bru.   Sir, I hope   70
My words disbench'd you not?

Cor.   No, sir; yet oft,
When blows have made me stay, I fled from words.

54–66.] *As Pope; prose in F.*   67. *First Sen.*] *Rowe; Senat. | F.*

54. *convented*] convened, summoned;
cf. *Meas.*, v. i. 157, and *H8*, v. i. 52.
Shakespeare does not use the form
'convened'.

55. *treaty*] proposal requiring discussion and approval, matter to be
treated of; cf. *John*, II. i. 480, and
O.E.D., s.v. 2.

58. *bless'd to do*] happy to do,
blessed in doing; cf. *John*, III. i. 251.

58–9. *remember . . . people*] keep in

mind a more generous estimate of the
people's value.

60. *off*] beside the point, imperti-
nent; hence Brutus' claim to be
'pertinent' in l. 63.

64. *your people*] Menenius' tone is
open to a choice of interpretations—
'the people you care about' or 'those
people of yours'.

71. *disbench'd*] the only instance of
the word in its general sense given in
O.E.D.; it was in legal use in the
nineteenth century.

You sooth'd not, therefore hurt not: but your people,
I love them as they weigh—
Men.   Pray now, sit down.
Cor. I had rather have one scratch my head i'th'sun   75
When the alarum were struck, than idly sit
To hear my nothings monster'd.   *Exit Coriolanus.*
Men.   Masters of the people,
Your multiplying spawn how can he flatter—
That's thousand to one good one—when you now see
He had rather venture all his limbs for honour   80
Than one on's ears to hear it? Proceed, Cominius.
Com. I shall lack voice: the deeds of Coriolanus
Should not be utter'd feebly. It is held
That valour is the chiefest virtue and
Most dignifies the haver: if it be,   85
The man I speak of cannot in the world
Be singly counter-pois'd. At sixteen years,
When Tarquin made a head for Rome, he fought
Beyond the mark of others; our then dictator,

74. weigh—] *F;* weigh. *Hammer.*   78–9. flatter— . . . one—] *Capell;* flatter? . . . one, *F.*   81. one on's] *F3;* on ones *F.*   it?] *Capell;* it. *F.*   84–5.] *As F2;* That . . . Vertue, / . . . be, / *F.*

73. *sooth'd*] flattered; cf. I. ix. 44.
74. *as they weigh*] i.e. as lightly as they weigh, as little as they are worth. The editorial punctuation assumes that the particular thought is complete but that Coriolanus meant to say more.
76. *alarum*] battle summons with drum and trumpets; cf. I. iv. 9 note, and *R3,* IV. iv. 148.
77. *monster'd*] made unnatural marvels of; *O.E.D.* gives this as the only early instance of the sense 'exhibit as a monster', and cites only *Lr.,* I. i. 220, for another use of the verb; later instances appear to derive from Shakespeare. The phrase 'nothings monster'd' provides a sardonic comment on the processes of fame.
78. *multiplying spawn*] 'The lower classes of Romans were known as *proletarii,* good only to breed children

(*proles*)' (Chambers). There is no equivalent elsewhere in Shakespeare to this biological revulsion and observation. *Spawn* is used only here; for *multiplying* ominously used, cf. *Mac.,* I. ii. 11, and *Tim.,* IV. i. 34.
81. *one on's*] For F's *on ones* see Introduction, p. 7.
84. *valour . . . virtue*] For the source in North see Appendix, p. 314, and for the sovereignty of valour as a Roman virtue see Introduction, pp. 40–1.
87. *singly counter-pois'd*] matched once by anyone.
sixteen years] North has 'being but a stripling', see Appendix, p. 315.
88. *made a head for*] gathered an army against.
89. *mark*] reach, aim; from archery. Cf. *Ant.,* III. vi. 87.
our then dictator] North alludes to a dictator but does not name him

Whom with all praise I point at, saw him fight,   90
When with his Amazonian chin he drove
The bristled lips before him; he bestrid
An o'erpress'd Roman, and i'th'consul's view
Slew three opposers; Tarquin's self he met
And struck him on his knee. In that day's feats,   95
When he might act the woman in the scene,
He prov'd best man i'th'field, and for his meed
Was brow-bound with the oak. His pupil age
Man-enter'd thus, he waxed like a sea,
And in the brunt of seventeen battles since   100
He lurch'd all swords of the garland. For this last,

91. chin] *F* (Shinne), *F3*.   92. bristled] *F* (brizled), *Rowe*.   101. of the] *F*; o'th' *F2*.

(Appendix, p. 315); it was probably Aulus Posthumus Regillensis.

90. *Whom . . . at*] 'A reminiscence of the common phrase in Latin speeches, *quem honoris causa nomino*' (Chambers).

91. *Amazonian*] beardless, like the Amazons; Queen Margaret is called an 'Amazonian trull' in *3H6*, I. iv. 114.

chin] F's spelling *Shinne* records what was a Stratford and Warwickshire form at the time (H. M. Hulme, *Explorations in Shakespeare's Language*, 1962, p. 317).

92–3. *bestrid . . . Roman*] Cf. North, 'a Romaine souldier being throwen to the ground even hard by him, Martius straight bestrid him, and slue the enemie with his owne handes that had before overthrowen the Romaine' (Appendix, p. 315). The episode is mistranslated; Plutarch originally told of Martius 'standing before' the overwhelmed Roman. Cf. *1H4*, v. i. 120, 'Hal, if thou see me down in the battle, and bestride me, so; 'tis a point of friendship'.

95. *struck . . . knee*] This episode is not in North; for a comparable one cf. *1H6*, IV. vii. 5–6, 'When he perceived me shrink and on my knee /

His bloody sword he brandish'd over me'.

96. *might act*] i.e. was of an age to act (with unbroken voice); cf. *Ant.*, v. ii. 219, 'Some squeaking Cleopatra boy my greatness'.

97. *meed*] reward.

98. *the oak*] See I. iii. 14–15 note.

98–9. *His pupil . . . thus*] i.e. having entered like a man the age when he might fittingly have been a pupil; or, possibly, 'initiated into manhood while still in his minority' (after Wright). 'Pupillage' meant 'minority', but Shakespeare seems here to have in mind an apprenticeship to war; *pupil age* also occurs in *1H4*, II. iv. 91, 'the pupil-age of this present twelve o'clock at midnight', a way of saying the night is young.

100. *brunt*] shock, violence.

seventeen] the number of years of battle in North (Appendix, p. 332).

101. *lurch'd . . . garland*] robbed all other contenders of the garland. *O.E.D.* (lurch *v.*[1] 2 *trans.*) has, 'To get the start of (a person) so as to prevent him from obtaining a fair share of food, profit, etc. Later, to defraud, cheat, rob', giving both this passage and Jonson's allusion to it, 'You have lurch'd your friends of the better halfe of the garland'. Malone

Before and in Corioles, let me say
I cannot speak him home. He stopp'd the fliers,
And by his rare example made the coward
Turn terror into sport; as weeds before   105
A vessel under sail, so men obey'd
And fell below his stem: his sword, death's stamp,
Where it did mark, it took; from face to foot
He was a thing of blood, whose every motion
Was tim'd with dying cries: alone he enter'd   110
The mortal gate of th'city, which he painted

105. weeds] *F;* waves *Rowe.*   108. took; from . . . foot] *Steevens, conj. Tyrwhitt;*
tooke from . . . foot: *F.*

adduced the gaming sense, 'to win a
maiden set at cards etc.', but *O.E.D.*
(s.v. *sb.*¹) shows that this derives
from French *lourche,* and relates the
present use to a derivation from
'lurk' = 'to lie in ambush'. For
Jonson's allusion and the dating of
the play, see Introduction, p. 24.

103. *speak . . . home*] say all that
needs saying, bring it home to you;
cf. *Tp.,* v. i. 70–1, 'I will pay thy
graces / Home both in word and
deed'.

105. *weeds*] Rowe's *waves* is an
interesting vulgarization, followed
by many eighteenth-century editors.
For other images of irresistible motion cf. I. iii. 36 and *Troil.,* v. v. 24–5,
'And there the strawy Greeks, ripe
for his edge, / Fall down before him
like the mower's swath'. For weeds
and water cf. *Ant.,* I. iv. 45.

108. *too : . . . foot*] It is possible that
F's punctuation is correct; Hibbard
compares *Mac.,* I. ii. 22, 'Till he
unseam'd him from the nave to
th'chaps'; and Sherman pleads for
takes = infects, citing *Ham.,* I. i.
162–3, 'The nights are wholesome,
then no planets strike, / No fairy
takes, nor witch hath power to
charm'. It is hard, however, to
see *death's stamp* as a tearing movement from head to foot, or to see the
sword as marking with a plague-spot
and an infection spreading instantly

from head to foot. Tyrwhitt's punctuation makes a die-casting or sealing
metaphor predominate: the sword
impresses the stamp of death on
whatever it marks, with *took* meaning
'registered its impression'. The pla-
gue-metaphor, however, may still be
latent here, to be more fully realized
in the lines that follow; swords and
infection are closely associated in
Tim., IV. iii. 108–15. The rhythm of
Tyrwhitt's pointing might be preferred to F, because it offers a single
commanding movement relating
from head to foot to *dying cries.* For
Martius as *a thing of blood* see I. iv. 61
note.

110. *tim'd . . . cries*] 'The cries of
the slaughter'd regularly followed
his motion, as music and a dancer
accompany each other' (Johnson).

111. *mortal gate*] i.e. fatal to enter,
promising death to Coriolanus; also
the gate he made fatal to others.

111–12. *painted . . . destiny*] i.e.
stained with the blood that was
inescapably destined to flow. For
painting and blood cf. I. vi. 68,
3H6, I. iv. 12, and *Troil.,* I. i. 90;
for an analogous figure of war cf.
Tit., III. i. 169–70, 'And rear'd aloft
the bloody battleaxe, / Writing
destruction on the enemy's castle'.
Wright compares the painting of
houses with a red cross in time of
plague, and the association seems at

With shunless destiny, aidless came off,
And with a sudden reinforcement struck
Corioles like a planet. Now all's his;
When by and by the din of war gan pierce   115
His ready sense, then straight his doubled spirit
Requicken'd what in flesh was fatigate,
And to the battle came he, where he did
Run reeking o'er the lives of men, as if
'Twere a perpetual spoil; and till we call'd   120
Both field and city ours, he never stood
To ease his breast with panting.

Men.   Worthy man.

119–20.] *F2;* Runne . . . 'twere / . . . call'd /*F.*

least subliminally present (see notes
to ll. 108 and 113–14).

112. *came off*] See I. vi. 1–2 note.

113–14. *struck . . . planet*] alluding
to the malignant influence of a
planet in a hostile aspect; cf. *Oth.*,
II. iii. 174, and *Tim.*, IV. iii. 108–10,
'Be as a planetary plague, when
Jove / Will o'er some high-vic'd
city hang his poison / In the sick
air'. For planets 'striking' cf. *Tit.*,
II. iv. 14, 'some planet strike me
down'; Case compares Jonson, *Every
Man In* (1616), IV. vii. 141, 'by
Heaven! sure I was struck with a
planet thence, for I had no power to
touch my weapon'; the usage survives in 'moonstruck'. See also
the Hamlet passage quoted above,
l. 108 note. Hibbard remarks that
'the planet here involved is un-
dubitably Mars', but none of the
parallel uses appears to be specific.
Chambers wonders if 'Shakespeare
has not also before him the visual
image of a building physically struck,
not by a planet but by a thunder-
bolt'; Shakespeare nowhere uses the
word in this sense, however, and
'planet-struck' had the force of
'blasted' (see *O.E.D.*, s.v.), quite
strong enough for the context.

116. *doubled*] of redoubled strength.

117. *fatigate*] fatigued. The verb
'fatigate' was current until the
eighteenth century and the participle
'fatigated' occurs in Fielding (see
O.E.D., s.v.). The participle form
here is direct from the Latin past
participle (see Abbott 342), and was
common in Shakespeare's time.

119. *reeking*] reeking with blood,
referring to the fume or 'smoke' of
blood, as in *Caes.*, III. i. 159, 'your
purpled hands do reek and smoke'.

120. *spoil*] Wright and others
interpret as a hunting term and
compare *Caes.*, III. i. 206–7, 'here thy
hunters stand, / Sign'd in thy spoil'.
But Caesar's *spoil* is compared with
the skin of the hart that the hunter
bears about his neck, and it cannot
be claimed from this evidence that
spoil in the present passage means
'slaughter, massacre, esp. of deer'
(Wilson). The perspectives of metaphor require the dominant military
meaning ('spoliation, havoc') but
admit a hunting strain, from *run
reeking* to *ease his breast with panting*.
Spoil for Coriolanus is intimately
related to delight in slaughter, and
spoils has an ironically different force
when Cominius resumes at l. 124.

First Sen. He cannot but with measure fit the honours
        Which we devise him.
Com.   Our spoils he kick'd at,   125
        And look'd upon things precious as they were
        The common muck of the world. He covets less
        Than misery itself would give, rewards
        His deeds with doing them, and is content
        To spend the time to end it.
Men.   He's right noble.
        Let him be call'd for.
First Sen.   Call Coriolanus.   130
Off. He doth appear.

Enter CORIOLANUS.

Men. The senate, Coriolanus, are well pleas'd
        To make thee consul.
Cor.   I do owe them still
        My life and services.
Men.   It then remains
        That you do speak to the people.
Cor.   I do beseech you,   135
        Let me o'erleap that custom; for I cannot
        Put on the gown, stand naked, and entreat them

123, 130. *First Sen.*] Rowe; *Senat. | F.*   123–4. He . . . him] *As Rowe; prose in
F.*   127–8.] *As Pope;* Then Miserie . . . deeds / . . . content. / *F.*   129–30.
He's . . . for] *As Pope; one line in F.*   132–5. The senate . . . people] *As Rowe*[3]*;
prose in F.*

123. *with measure*] i.e. with becoming stature and distinction; cf.
'measure up to'.

125–9. *look'd . . . end it*] Carter
(*Shakespeare and Holy Scripture*, 1905,
p. 458) compares Philippians, iii. 7
(Geneva), 'But the things that were
vantage to me, the same I counted
losse . . . and do judge them to
be dongue'; and iii. 13, 'Brethren, I
count not myselfe that I have attained
to it, but one thing I doe; I forget
that which is behinde, and endeavour myselfe unto that which is
before. And folow hard toward the
marke for the prize of the high

calling'. The parallel illuminates
analogies between Roman and Christian asceticism.

128–9. *and . . . end it*] and is content
that the time [well] spent be an end
in itself.

133. *still*] always.

135. *speak . . . people*] Shakespeare
follows North (see Appendix, p. 331).
Warburton objected that in historical fact the custom was not introduced until a hundred years after
Coriolanus' banishment; but the
historical truth is obscure.

137. *naked*] i.e. naked beneath the
outward gown (not in the frequent

For my wounds' sake to give their suffrage. Please you
That I may pass this doing.

Sic.   Sir, the people
Must have their voices; neither will they bate   140
One jot of ceremony.

Men.   Put them not to't.
Pray you go fit you to the custom and
Take to you, as your predecessors have,
Your honour with your form.

Cor.   It is a part
That I shall blush in acting, and might well   145
Be taken from the people.

Bru. [*To Sicinius*]   Mark you that.

Cor. To brag unto them, thus I did, and thus,
Show them th'unaching scars which I should hide,
As if I had receiv'd them for the hire
Of their breath only!

Men.   Do not stand upon't.   150
We recommend to you, tribunes of the people,
Our purpose to them; and to our noble consul

138–43.] *As Capell;* For . . . suffrage: / . . . doing. / . . . Voyces, / . . . Ceremonie. / . . . too't: / . . . Costume, / . . . haue, / *F.*   138. suffrage] *F* (suffer-
age), *F4.*   144–6. It . . . people.] *As Pope;* It . . . acting, / . . . People. / *F.*
146. S.D.] *Craig; not in F.*   that.] *F;* that? *Rowe.*   147. thus . . . thus,] *F*
(thus . . . thus); thus . . . thus; *Cam.;* 'Thus . . . thus!' *Alexander.*

sense, 'unarmed'). Furness (after
Wright) quotes Holland's *Morals of
Plutarch,* 1603, p. 867: 'To the end,
therefore, that such scarres might be
better exposed to their sight whom
they met or talked withall, they went
in this maner downe to the place of
election, without inward coates in
their plaine gownes. Or haply,
because they would seem by this
nuditie and nakedness of theirs, in
humilitie to debase themselves, the
sooner thereby to curry favor, and
win the good grace of the commons.'
  139. *pass*] let pass.
  140. *voices*] votes.
  141. *Put . . . to't*] i.e. do not put
them to the test, drive them too hard;
cf. I. i. 228. Otherwise it may simply
refer back to Sicinius' last words

and mean 'do not press them to
abate one jot of ceremony'.
  144. *your form*] the formality
appropriate to your position.
  146. *Mark you that.*] There is no
need for the importunate tone of
Rowe's punctuation; Coriolanus is
behaving exactly as the tribunes
predicted.
  150. *breath*] often used by Shakespeare in relation to the spoken word
(e.g. *Ham.,* III. iv. 197, *Troil.,* IV. i. 75)
but with special relevance and
persistence in this play (e.g. II. i. 53,
III. iii. 120, IV. v. 116, V. ii. 46).
  stand upon't] make a stand about it,
insist upon it; cf. *Caes.,* III. i. 101.
  151. *recommend*] commit.
  152. *purpose to them*] i.e. intentions
towards the people.

Wish we all joy and honour.

Senators. To Coriolanus come all joy and honour!

　　　Flourish cornets. Then Exeunt. Sicinius and Brutus remain.

Bru. You see how he intends to use the people.　　　155

Sic. May they perceive's intent! He will require them
　　　As if he did contemn what he requested
　　　Should be in them to give.

Bru.　　　　　　　　　　　Come, we'll inform them
　　　Of our proceedings here; on th'market-place
　　　I know they do attend us.　　　　　[*Exeunt.*]　　160

[SCENE III]

Enter seven or eight Citizens.

First Cit. Once, if he do require our voices, we ought not
　　　to deny him.

Second Cit. We may, sir, if we will.

Third Cit. We have power in ourselves to do it, but it is
　　　a power that we have no power to do. For, if he　　　5
　　　show us his wounds and tell us his deeds, we are to
　　　put our tongues into those wounds and speak for
　　　them. So if he tell us his noble deeds, we must also

154. *Senators*] Dyce; *Senat.* | *F*; *Sic.* | *Rowe*². 　　　154. S.D. *Sicinius ... remain*]
Manet Sicinius and Brutus | *F*; *Manent ... Brutus* | *F2*. 　　　159. here; on] *Theobald*
(subst); heere on *F*. 　　　160. S.D.] *Rowe*; not in *F*.

Scene III

SCENE III] *Capell.* 　　1. Once,] *Theobald*; Once *F*.

156. *require them*] i.e. ask for their
voices. For this use of *require* cf. *H8*,
II. iv. 144.

157–8. *As if ... give*] as if he were
contemptuous [of the fact] that what
he requested should be in their
power to give.

159. *here; on*] As Theobald observes, this punctuation is necessary
because the events just enacted are
located in the Capitol not in the
market-place (see II. i. 266).

Scene III

Scene III] located by Pope in 'The
Forum' and by Knight in 'The

Market Place'; 'Forum' is not used
anywhere by Shakespeare, nor by
North at this point (see II. ii. 159,
and Appendix, p. 331).

1. *Once*] once for all. F's punctuation leaves the impression that
Coriolanus had only to ask once.

5. *power ... power to do*] i.e. it is a
legal prerogative that we are not
morally free to exercise.

7. *tongues ... wounds*] Cf. *Caes.*,
III. ii. 229 and III. i. 260–1, and
R3, I. ii. 55–6. Hulme (*Explorations in
Shakespeare's Language*) cites Nicolas
Udall's *Apophthegms of Erasmus* (1542),
pp. 234–5.

tell him our noble acceptance of them. Ingratitude
is monstrous, and for the multitude to be in-   10
grateful, were to make a monster of the multitude;
of the which we being members, should bring ourselves to be monstrous members.

First Cit. And to make us no better thought of, a little
help will serve: for once we stood up about the   15
corn, he himself stuck not to call us the many-
headed multitude.

Third Cit. We have been called so of many; not that
our heads are some brown, some black, some
abram, some bald, but that our wits are so diversely   20
coloured; and truly I think, if all our wits were to
issue out of one skull, they would fly east, west,
north, south, and their consent of one direct way
should be at once to all the points o'th'compass.

Second Cit. Think you so? Which way do you judge my   25
wit would fly?

Third Cit. Nay, your wit will not so soon out as another
man's will; 'tis strongly wedged up in a blockhead:

15. once] *F;* once when *Rowe.*   28. wedged] *F2;* wadg'd *F.*

9. *noble acceptance*] a nice appropriation of the word *noble* to plebeian
use, for common gratitude shows
generosity of spirit.

9–10. *Ingratitude is monstrous*] Cf.
Troil., III. iii. 147, *Lr.,* I. v. 37.
Shakespeare confers a proverbial
strength upon the thought, but there
is no record of such a proverb.

14–15. *to make . . . serve*] i.e. the
patricians will need little prompting
to think us no better than monsters.

15. *once*] The relative is apparently
omitted (see Abbott 244); Rowe's
once when supplies it.

16. *stuck not*] did not hesitate; cf.
2H4, I. ii. 21, *H8,* II. ii. 124, and
Sonn., x. 6. The expression was not
confined to colloquial use.

16–17. *many-headed multitude*] Cf.
III. i. 92, IV. i. 1, and *2H4,* Prol., 18.
Wilson notes that Elyot in *Governour,*

bk I. ii, calls Athenian democracy 'a
monstre with many heades', and
Plato uses the many-headed beast to
express the instabilities of human
nature in *Republic,* IX, 588. For other
parallels see IV. i. 1 note; also Tilley,
M 1308.

20. *abram*] a colloquial variant of
'auburn' (the reading of F4) originally denoting a light yellow, but its
association with the form 'abrun'
gradually yielded the modern meaning 'golden brown'. Here the context
requires blondes.

23–4. *consent . . . compass*] Their
agreement to go in one direction
would be to go in all directions.

28. *wedged*] Harrison retains F's
wadg'd and so does Gomme, finding
the word 'expressive'. It may be
accidentally so, however, as *O.E.D.*
offers no early instances. It could
mean 'coagulated in a lump'.

but if it were at liberty, 'twould, sure, southward.

Second Cit. Why that way?   30

Third Cit. To lose itself in a fog, where, being three parts
    melted away with rotten dews, the fourth would
    return for conscience' sake, to help to get thee a
    wife.

Second Cit. You are never without your tricks; you may,   35
    you may.

Third Cit. Are you all resolved to give your voices?
    But that's no matter, the greater part carries it. I
    say, if he would incline to the people, there was
    never a worthier man.   40

Enter CORIOLANUS *in a gown of humility, with* MENENIUS.

Here he comes, and in the gown of humility: mark
his behaviour. We are not to stay all together, but
to come by him where he stands, by ones, by twos
and by threes. He's to make his requests by particulars, wherein every one of us has a single honour,   45
in giving him our own voices with our own tongues:
therefore follow me, and I'll direct you how you
shall go by him.

All. Content, content.   [*Exeunt Citizens.*]

Men. O sir, you are not right. Have you not known   50
    The worthiest men have done't?

38–9. it. I say, if] *Theobald;* it, I say. If *F.*   42. all together] *F3;* altogether *F.*
49. S.D.] *Capell;* not in *F.*

29–31. *southward . . . fog*] Cf. I. iv.
30 and note.

32. *rotten*] unwholesome, promoting
rot; cf. III. iii. 121, *Tim,* IV. iii. 2,
Tp., II. i. 45, *Lucr.,* 778.

33–4. *for conscience' . . . wife*]
'Presumably to look after the poor
creature' (Wilson). This seems the
best explanation. Those who find a
satirical glance at marriage ('a man
needs little wit to choose a wife', or
'only quarter-wits wed') fail to
explain *conscience;* while Brower's

conjecture, 'because of the bastards
he has fathered', diverts attention
from the second citizen's slow
stupidity.

35–6. *you may, you may*] go on, go
on, have your joke; cf. *Troil.,* III. i.
102.

38. *the greater . . . it*] the majority
decides.

39. *incline to*] side with; cf. *Lr.,*
III. iii. 15.

44–5. *by particulars*] i.e. to each of
us, one by one.

Cor.   What must I say?—
'I pray, sir,'—Plague upon't! I cannot bring
My tongue to such a pace. 'Look, sir, my wounds!
I got them in my country's service, when
Some certain of your brethren roar'd and ran   55
From th'noise of our own drums.'
Men.   O me, the gods!
You must not speak of that; you must desire them
To think upon you.
Cor.   Think upon me? Hang 'em!
I would they would forget me, like the virtues
Which our divines lose by 'em.
Men.   You'll mar all.   60
I'll leave you. Pray you, speak to 'em, I pray you,
In wholesome manner.   *Exit.*

Enter three of the Citizens.

51–2. What . . . bring] *As Pope;* What . . . Sir? / . . . bring / *F.*   say?—'I
pray, sir,'] *Theobald;* say, I pray Sir? *F.*   56–8. O me . . . you] *As Pope;* Oh
me . . . that, / . . . you / *F.*   62. S.D.] *F; Enter two of the Citizens / Rowe; Re-
enter Second and Third Citizens / Wilson; Re-enter two of the Citizens [following clean],
Re-enter a third Citizen [following brace] / Cam.*

53. *to . . . pace*] alluding to the
trained, measured gait of a horse.
Cf. *Ant.*, II. ii. 66–8, *Ado*, III. iv. 83,
All's W., IV. v. 60, and, for the
curbing of the soldier's tongue,
R 2, I. i. 54–5.

58. *think upon*] think solicitously
about, remember. Beeching compares Jonah, i. 6 (Authorized), 'If
so be that God will think upon us,
that we perish not', and finds a
touch of epigram in Coriolanus' *I
would they would forget me.* Wilson
recalls North, 'to remember them at
the daye of election' (Appendix,
p. 331), and *Mac.*, II. iii. 19, 'I pray
you remember the porter', adding
that 'this beggar business' is not to be
found in Plutarch. Cf. also *Ant.*,
I. v. 27, and below, l. 186.

59–60. *like . . . by 'em*] as they forget
the virtuous precepts lost upon them
by our divines.

62. *wholesome*] Menenius intends

the figurative sense, 'salutary', but
Coriolanus takes it more literally and
relates it to cleanliness.

62. S.D. three . . . Citizens] There
is an awkwardness in F, as Coriolanus observes only a *brace* of citizens
(l. 63) and begs only two voices
(l. 80). Rowe reduces the citizens to
two, reassigning the third's speeches
to the first; Wilson gives the first
citizen's contribution (l. 75) to the
third. Both entail discontinuity, for
Rowe eliminates the third citizen
from an encounter that the later
'third citizen' reports (see ll. 77 and
164), and Wilson allows the first
citizen no place in the canvassing
and no occasion for his comments at
ll. 154 and 159. Because it is likely
that Shakespeare's intentions were
never fully clarified, I have retained
F's text. The problem of playing may
be overcome by allowing the first
and second citizens to enter together,

Cor.   Bid them wash their faces,
   And keep their teeth clean. So, here comes a brace.
   You know the cause, sir, of my standing here?
Third Cit. We do, sir; tell us what hath brought you to't.   65
Cor. Mine own desert.
Second Cit. Your own desert?
Cor. Ay, but not mine own desire.
Third Cit. How, not your own desire?
Cor. No, sir, 'twas never my desire yet to trouble the   70
   poor with begging.
Third Cit. You must think, if we give you anything, we
   hope to gain by you.
Cor. Well then, I pray, your price o'th'consulship?
First Cit. The price is, to ask it kindly.   75
Cor. Kindly, sir, I pray let me ha't. I have wounds to
   show you, which shall be yours in private. Your
   good voice, sir. What say you?
Second Cit. You shall ha't, worthy sir.
Cor. A match, sir. There's in all two worthy voices   80
   begged. I have your alms: adieu!
Third Cit. But this is something odd.
Second Cit. And 'twere to give again—but 'tis no matter.
                          Exeunt [the three Citizens].

67. desert?] *Rowe;* desert. *F.*   68. but not] *Cam.;* but *F;* not *F3.*
76. Kindly, sir,] *F4;* Kindly sir, *F;* Kindly, Sir? *Johnson.*   83. S.D. *the . . .*
Citizens] Cam. ; not in F.

with the third at a distance; the third
joins the group and speaks first
because the others are daunted by
Coriolanus' question; at the end of
the episode two voices are manifestly won but the third (l. 82)
remains aloof. It is possible that l. 79
should be assigned jointly to *First
and Second Cits.*, an emendation that
would postulate only one oversight
on the part of the compositor; more
elaborate interventions must assume
either confusion on Shakespeare's
part or some editorial meddling in
the printing shop. For further discussion of the roles of the citizens
see below ll. 83, 87, 154, 164–71
notes.

67. *desert?*] The editorial question-
mark (generally adopted) expresses
eagerness, not incredulity; without it,
the citizen's response is inert.

68. *but not*] In adopting the more
emphatic of the possible emendations,
I have supposed the compositor (B)
slightly more likely to omit *not* than to
misread *not* as *but.*

75.] Shakespeare finds an epi-
grammatic terseness in a live mode
of common speech.

80. *A match*] Done! Cf. *Shr.*, v. ii.
74, 'A match! 'tis done'; *match* is a
bargain or contract.

83. S.D.] It is possible that the third
citizen here withdraws and observes;
see below ll. 164–71 note.

Enter two other Citizens.

Cor. Pray you now, if it may stand with the tune of your
voices that I may be consul, I have here the custo-   85
mary gown.

Fourth Cit. You have deserved nobly of your country,
and you have not deserved nobly.

Cor. Your enigma?

Fourth Cit. You have been a scourge to her enemies, you   90
have been a rod to her friends; you have not indeed
loved the common people.

Cor. You should account me the more virtuous, that I
have not been common in my love. I will, sir, flatter
my sworn brother the people, to earn a dearer   95
estimation of them; 'tis a condition they account
gentle; and since the wisdom of their choice is rather
to have my hat than my heart, I will practise the

---

85. voices] *Cam.;* voices, *F.*   87, 90, 105. *Fourth Cit.] Cam.;* 1. *F;* 3 *Cit. Malone.*
89. enigma?] *Rowe;* Ænigma. *F.*

---

84. *stand with*] accord with, as in
AYL., II. iv. 86.

87. Fourth Cit.] F's numbering of
the citizens here begins again,
unrelated to the dispositions of
ll. 1–40 and 65–83. Malone's attribution to the third citizen was a
consequence of his admitting only
two at l. 63, but some case could be
made for it on grounds of character-
continuity.

90–1. *scourge . . . rod*] Noble cites
Psalms, lxxxix. 32 (1585), 'I will
visit their offences with the rod, and
their sin with scourges'.

94. *common . . . love*] facile and vulgar in my affections; cf. *Sonn.,*
LXIX, 14.

95. *sworn brother*] perhaps from the
'fratres jurati' of medieval chivalry,
knights bound by oath to share each
other's fortunes; cf. *AYL.,* v. iv. 96,
R2, v. i. 20, *H5,* II. i. 11. As a classical
instance Case cites North's Plutarch,
'Life of Pelopidas' (1579), ed. 1612,
p. 295, 'such as loved heartily
together, became sworne brethren,

one to another, upon Iolaus tomb'
(S.H.P., III, pp. 26–7). Flattery
offends against the spirit of such a
bond, which in the Plutarch passage
is formed between members of the
holy band of Cadmea, instituted to
resist the Spartans. See I. iv. 37 note.

95–6. *dearer . . . them*] higher place
in their esteem (Case).

96–7. *'tis . . . gentle*] either 'they
believe flattery an attribute of the
nobility', or 'they account the
condition of the flatterer a noble one'.
The first implies that they have come
to expect flattery from the nobility,
the second that they think highly of
the flatterer; it is hard to exclude
either implication. Case compares
H5, v. ii. 283, 'my condition is not
smooth . . . having neither the voice
nor the heart of flattery about me'.

98. *hat*] Here, and at l. 165, most
eighteenth-century editors followed
Pope in reading *cap* to soften the
anachronism; see T. J. B. Spencer,
Shakespeare Survey, 10, 1957, p. 28.

insinuating nod, and be off to them most counter-
feitly; that is, sir, I will counterfeit the bewitchment 100
of some popular man, and give it bountiful to the
desirers. Therefore, beseech you, I may be consul.
Fifth Cit. We hope to find you our friend, and therefore
give you our voices heartily.
Fourth Cit. You have received many wounds for your 105
country.
Cor. I will not seal your knowledge with showing them.
I will make much of your voices, and so trouble
you no farther.
Both. The gods give you joy, sir, heartily.   110
                                    [*Exeunt the two Citizens.*]
Cor. Most sweet voices!
Better it is to die, better to starve,
Than crave the hire which first we do deserve.
Why in this wolvish toge should I stand here,

103. *Fifth Cit.*] *Cam.*; 2. *F.*   110. S.D.] *After Rowe; not in F.*   113. hire] *F2;*
higher *F.*   114. wolvish toge] *after Malone* (woolvish toge), *conj. Steevens;*
Wooluish tongue *F;* woolvish gowne *F2;* woolless togue *Collier²;* Foolish toge
Leo; woolyish toge *conj. Wilson.*

99. *be off*] i.e. doff my hat. Cf. *R2*,
I. iv. 31, *Oth.*, I. i. 10, etc.
100–1. *bewitchment . . . man*] i.e.
the spells of the demagogue; for
popular = designed to gain the
favour of the people, see *O.E.D.*,
s.v. 5a. *Popular man* may also mean
'man of the people', however, for
Coriolanus probably has the tribunes
in mind not Menenius.
101. *bountiful*] bountifully. For the
use of adjectives as adverbs see
Abbott 1.
102. *desirers*] not elsewhere used by
Shakespeare.
107. *seal*] authenticate, confirm;
cf. III. i. 141.
111–23.] The sententious rhymes
of this passage disengage it a little
from the flux of the action; their
movement, however, does not confine each thought to a couplet, and
the effect is consonant both with
declaring a public attitude and with
betraying intimate reflection.

112. *starve*] F's *sterve* makes the
rhyme with *deserve* more evident to
the eye, but in fact both would then
have been pronounced as the modern *starve* (see Kökeritz, p. 250).
113. *hire . . . deserve*] reward already
merited. Malone took F's 'higher' to
be evidence of auditory error from
dictation, but it is a probable short-
term memory slip on the part of
Compositor B.
114. *wolvish toge*] i.e. the 'napless
vesture of humility' (II. i. 232) worn
by Coriolanus as the fabled wolf
wears sheep's clothing. F's *tongue* is
probably a mistaking of *toge* in the
copy for *tōge*, the same error occurring
in *Oth.*, I. i. 25, where F has 'Tongued
Consuls' for 'toged consuls'. *Toge*
was a common English form of the
word *toga*. F2's wild emendation
gowne is the term used by North (see
Appendix, p. 331). Some editors
have been reluctant to accept
wolvish because the garb should be

To beg of Hob and Dick that does appear   115
Their needless vouches? Custom calls me to't.
What custom wills, in all things should we do't,
The dust on antique time would lie unswept
And mountainous error be too highly heap'd
For truth to o'erpeer. Rather than fool it so,   120
Let the high office and the honour go
To one that would do thus. I am half through,
The one part suffer'd, the other will I do.

Enter three Citizens more.

Here come moe voices.
Your voices! For your voices I have fought,   125
Watch'd for your voices; for your voices, bear
Of wounds two dozen odd; battles thrice six
I have seen and heard of; for your voices have
Done many things, some less, some more: your voices!
Indeed I would be consul.   130

---

115. does] *F*; do *F4*.   117. wills, ... things] *Pope*; wills ... things, *F*.
124. moe] *F*; more *F3*.   125, 129. voices!] *F* (Voyces?).   128–30.] *After*
Pope; I ... Voyces, / ... more: / ... Consull. / *F*.

---

the sheep's; but it is the wolf's
property and symbolizes his treacherous nature.

115. *Hob ... appear*] i.e. any Tom,
Dick, or Harry that turns up. *Hob*
(a familiar form of Rob, from Robin
or Robert) and *Dick* were both in use
as common nouns to mean 'clown,
vulgar fellow' (cf. *LLL.*, v. ii. 464,
for *Dick*). The collective expression
has sufficient singleness of effect to
justify F's *does*, and the apparent
inconsistency with *Their* in the next
line.

116. *needless vouches*] superfluous
warrants. The senate have made him
consul (II. ii. 133) and he finds the
people's suffrage (II. ii. 138) *needless*.
For *vouches* cf. *Meas.*, II. iv. 156, and
Oth., II. i. 145.

118. *antique time*] i.e. ancient
traditions.

124. *moe*] 'more in number, while
more referred to degree' (Case, citing
Numbers, xxii. 15 (Authorized),
'And Balak sent yet againe Princes,
moe, and more honourable than
they'). *O.E.D.* does not support Case,
but *moe* is used by North in the sense
he alleges (see Appendix, p. 326). See
also IV. ii. 21 note.

125–30. *Your voices ... consul*] For
the 'mockery' in Coriolanus' manner
see the citizen's mimicry of it in
ll. 165–71.

127. *thrice six*] Cf. II. ii. 100.

128. *and heard of*] a piece of rhetorical teasing, like *some less, some*
more, in the next line; but commentators have found an allusion to
the noise of battle, evidence of
Coriolanus' diffidence, or an elliptical rendering of 'made heard-of,
made famous'.

Sixth Cit. He has done nobly, and cannot go without any
    honest man's voice.
Seventh Cit. Therefore let him be consul. The gods give
    him joy, and make him good friend to the people!
All. Amen, amen. God save thee, noble consul!   135
                    [Exeunt the three Citizens.]
Cor. Worthy voices!

      Enter MENENIUS, *with* BRUTUS *and* SICINIUS.

Men. You have stood your limitation, and the tribunes
    Endue you with the people's voice; remains
    That, in th'official marks invested, you
    Anon do meet the senate.
Cor.   Is this done?   140
Sic. The custom of request you have discharg'd.
    The people do admit you, and are summon'd
    To meet anon upon your approbation.
Cor. Where? At the senate-house?
Sic.   There, Coriolanus.
Cor. May I change these garments?
Sic.   You may, sir.   145
Cor. That I'll straight do; and knowing myself again,
    Repair to th'senate-house.
Men. I'll keep you company. Will you along?
Bru. We stay here for the people.
Sic.   Fare you well.
                Exeunt Coriolanus and Menenius.
    He has it now; and by his looks, methinks   150
    'Tis warm at's heart.
Bru.   With a proud heart he wore
    His humble weeds. Will you dismiss the people?

131. *Sixth Cit.*] *Cam.;* 1. *Cit.* / *F.*   133. *Seventh Cit.*] *Cam.;* 2. *Cit.* / *F.*   135.
S.D.] *After Rowe; not in F.*   137–9.] *As Pope;* You . . . Limitation: / . . .
Voyce, / . . . inuested, / *F.*   151–2. With . . . people?] *As Pope;* With . . .
Weeds: / . . . People? / *F.*

    137. *limitation*] allotted time
(*O.E.D.*, s.v. 2b, giving only this
instance).

    138. *remains*] For the common, and
correct, omission of 'it' see Abbott
404.

    139. *official marks*] insignia of office.

    143. *anon*] immediately.

    upon your approbation] to approve or
ratify your election; cf. l. 207, 'He's
not confirm'd'.

Enter the Plebeians.

Sic. How now, my masters, have you chose this man?
First Cit. He has our voices, sir.
Bru. We pray the gods he may deserve your loves.   155
Second Cit. Amen, sir. To my poor unworthy notice,
    He mock'd us when he begg'd our voices.
Third Cit.   Certainly,
    He flouted us downright.
First Cit. No, 'tis his kind of speech; he did not mock us.
Second Cit. Not one amongst us, save yourself, but says   160
    He us'd us scornfully: he should have show'd us
    His marks of merit, wounds receiv'd for's country.
Sic. Why, so he did, I am sure.
All.   No, no; no man saw 'em.
Third Cit. He said he had wounds which he could show
        in private;
    And with his hat, thus waving it in scorn,   165
    'I would be consul,' says he; 'aged custom,
    But by your voices, will not so permit me:
    Your voices therefore.' When we granted that,
    Here was, 'I thank you for your voices, thank you;
    Your most sweet voices: now you have left your
        voices,   170
    I have no further with you.' Was not this mockery?

157–8. Certainly . . . downright.] *As Capell; one line in F.*   164.] *As Pope;*
Hee . . . Wounds, / . . . priuate: / *F.*

152. S.D. Plebeians] Shakespeare
several times uses 'plebeians' when
thinking of the citizens as a political
faction; see Introduction, p. 20.

154. First Cit.] F's numbering of
the citizens in this part of the scene is
retained here and by all editors. Its
correspondence with the numbering
at ll. 1–40 and 65–83 remains
uncertain.

164.] For the lineation see Introduction, p. 10.

164–71.] The third citizen's mimicry is composed of Shakespeare's
recollections of ll. 77 (the wounds
to be shown in private), 98 (the hat

waved in scorn), 85–6, 116 (the
glances at custom), 111 and 124–30
(the repetitious patter about voices).
Convention does not require the third
citizen to be present on all these
occasions, particularly as the allusions to 'custom' occur in soliloquy,
but it would encourage a performance
in which he kept watch on the
canvassing after participating himself; a 'third citizen', perhaps the
same one, is given powers of direction
in l. 47. In production the third
citizen here is often played by the
first citizen, the 'great toe', of I. i. 155.

165. *hat*] See above, l. 98 note.

Sic. Why either were you ignorant to see't,
Or, seeing it, of such childish friendliness
To yield your voices?

Bru.   Could you not have told him
As you were lesson'd: when he had no power,   175
But was a petty servant to the state,
He was your enemy, ever spake against
Your liberties and the charters that you bear
I'th'body of the weal; and now arriving
A place of potency and sway o'th'state,   180
If he should still malignantly remain
Fast foe to th'plebeii, your voices might
Be curses to yourselves? You should have said
That, as his worthy deeds did claim no less
Than what he stood for, so his gracious nature   185
Would think upon you for your voices, and
Translate his malice towards you into love,
Standing your friendly lord.

Sic.   Thus to have said,
As you were fore-advis'd, had touch'd his spirit
And tried his inclination: from him pluck'd   190
Either his gracious promise, which you might

---

175. lesson'd:] *F;* lesson'd? *Hanmer.*   183. yourselves?] *Cam.;* your selues. *F.*
186-7.] *F2;* Would . . . Voyces, / . . . Loue, / *F.*

---

175. *lesson'd*] Plutarch offers no
evidence for the systematic schooling
of the plebeians in political art, but
both he and Livy offer ample
instances of the tactical skill of the
tribunes.

179. *weal*] commonwealth, state;
as in *1H6,* I. i. 177. Cf. I. i. 150 and
II. i. 54.

arriving] reaching. For the omission
of 'at' cf. *Caes.,* I. ii. 110, 'ere we
could arrive the point propos'd'; see
Abbott 198.

180. *sway o'th'state*] state authority.

182. *plebeii*] 'Elsewhere "plebeians"; but here thought of as an
estate of the realm' (Wilson); this
suggests a class exercising political

power (compare 'common people'
and 'commons').

186. *Would*] i.e. should, ought to,
see Abbott 323.

think upon you] think solicitously of
you; cf. l. 58 and note.

188. *Standing . . . lord*] i.e. acting
and speaking on the people's behalf.
For the idiom cf. *2H4,* IV. iii. 81,
where Falstaff asks Prince John
'stand my good lord, pray, in your
good report'. The phrase remains
apt for the election (cf. 'stand for
consul', II. i. 230).

189. *touch'd*] put to the test, like
gold by the touchstone; cf. *Tim.,*
III. iii. 6, and *John,* III. i. 100–1,
'Resembling majesty, which, being
touch'd and tried, / Proves valueless'.

As cause had call'd you up, have held him to;
Or else it would have gall'd his surly nature
Which easily endures not article
Tying him to aught; so putting him to rage,   195
You should have ta'en th'advantage of his choler,
And pass'd him unelected.

Bru.   Did you perceive
He did solicit you in free contempt
When he did need your loves; and do you think
That his contempt shall not be bruising to you   200
When he hath power to crush? Why, had your bodies
No heart among you? Or had you tongues to cry
Against the rectorship of judgement?

Sic.   Have you,
Ere now, denied the asker, and now again,
Of him that did not ask but mock, bestow   205
Your sued-for tongues?

Third Cit. He's not confirm'd: we may deny him yet.

Second Cit. And will deny him!
I'll have five hundred voices of that sound.

First Cit. I twice five hundred, and their friends to piece 'em.

Bru. Get you hence instantly, and tell those friends   211
They have chose a consul that will from them take
Their liberties, make them of no more voice
Than dogs that are as often beat for barking

---

195. aught;] *Theobald²*; ought, *F.*   203–6. Have . . . tongues?] *As Pope;*
Haue . . . asker; / . . . mock, / . . . Tongues? / *F.*   205. Of] *F* (of); on
Theobald.   210. I twice] *F*; I, twice *F4*; Ay, twice *Rowe.*

192. *As cause . . . up*] i.e. as occasion
demanded, cf. i. vi. 83.

194. *article*] stipulation, condition;
cf. *articulate*, i. ix. 75.

195. *aught;*] Theobald's punctuation prevents *so . . . rage* from becoming consequential to *article . . .
aught;* F leaves this possibility con-
fusingly open. *Ought* (F) was a
common variant of *aught.*

198. *free*] frank, open. For the
reciprocal use cf. iii. i. 129, 'frank
donation'.

202. *heart*] spirit, implying both
wit and courage. The expression is

characteristic of the play's idiom,
cf. i. i. 135 note, and iii. i. 255.

202–3. *to cry . . . judgement*] to rebel
against the sovereignty of reason.
Cf. i. i. 185, 'cry against the noble
Senate'; *rectorship* is not elsewhere
used by Shakespeare.

205. *Of him*] For other examples of
of for *on*, see Abbott 175.

206. *sued-for*] Some have had
difficulty in reconciling *sued-for* with
did not ask; but it is the failure to ask
properly that makes the suit a
mockery; cf. l. 220.

210. *piece 'em*] join to them.

As therefore kept to do so.

Sic.   Let them assemble;   215
And, on a safer judgement, all revoke
Your ignorant election. Enforce his pride
And his old hate unto you. Besides, forget not
With what contempt he wore the humble weed,
How in his suit he scorn'd you; but your loves,   220
Thinking upon his services, took from you
Th'apprehension of his present portance,
Which most gibingly, ungravely, he did fashion
After the inveterate hate he bears you.

Bru.   Lay
A fault on us, your tribunes: that we labour'd,   225
No impediment between, but that you must
Cast your election on him.

Sic.   Say you chose him
More after our commandment than as guided
By your own true affections; and that your minds
Pre-occupied with what you rather must do,   230
Than what you should, made you against the grain
To voice him consul. Lay the fault on us.

Bru. Ay, spare us not. Say we read lectures to you,
How youngly he began to serve his country,   234
How long continued, and what stock he springs of—
The noble house o'th'Martians: from whence came

215–17. Let . . . pride] *As Theobald;* Let . . . Iudgement, / . . . Pride, / *F.*
223. most gibingly] *F;* gibingly *Pope;* gibing most *Hudson, conj. Lettsom.*
224–30. Lay . . . do,] *As Capell;* Lay . . . Tribunes, / . . . between) / . . . him. /
. . . commandment, / . . . that / . . . do, / *F.*

215. *therefore*] for that purpose.

216. *safer*] sounder.

217. *Enforce*] emphasize; as in *Ant.*, II. ii. 103.

219–23. *weed . . . suit . . . services . . . fashion*] Shakespeare puns on *weed* and *suit;* also, as Whiter (p. 76) observes, *services* and *fashion* are associated; cf. *Lr.*, IV. i. 6–7, *H5*, IV. iii. 115–19.

221–2. *took . . . portance*] prevented you from taking notice of his bearing and demeanour at the time; for *portance* cf. *Oth.*, I. iii. 139.

223. *most gibingly*] There is no reason to suppose that the extra-metric *most* was added by the compositor.

225–7. *labour'd . . . him*] were at pains to urge that nothing was to prevent you from voting for him.

231. *against the grain*] The earliest use of the phrase recorded in *O.E.D.* (grain *sb.*¹ 16) is dated 1650. Cf. IV. v. 109 note.

236–43.] a rendering of the opening sentences of North's account, see Appendix, p. 313. As Verity says, Shakespeare's fidelity to his source

That Ancus Martius, Numa's daughter's son,
Who after great Hostilius here was king;
Of the same house Publius and Quintus were,
That our best water brought by conduits hither;   240
[And Censorinus that was so surnam'd]
And nobly named so, twice being censor,
Was his great ancestor.

Sic.   One thus descended,
That hath beside well in his person wrought,
To be set high in place, we did commend   245
To your remembrances; but you have found,
Scaling his present bearing with his past,
That he's your fixed enemy, and revoke
Your sudden approbation.

Bru.   Say you ne'er had done't—
Harp on that still—but by our putting on;   250
And presently, when you have drawn your number,
Repair to th'Capitol.

241–3. [And . . . ancestor] *Delius;* And Nobly nam'd, so twice being Censor, /
Was his great Ancestor *F;* And Censorinus, darling of the people / (And nobly
nam'd so for twice being censor) / Was . . . ancestor *Pope;* And Censorinus,
named so by the people, / And nobly named so, twice being Censor, / Was . . .
ancestor *Leo;* and Censorinus, nobly named so, / Twice being by the people
chosen censor, / Was . . . ancestor *Globe;* And Censorinus nobly named so, /
Twice being censor, was his great ancestor *Sisson.*

led him into historical inaccuracies:
Ancus Martius was traditionally
fourth king of Rome (642–617 B.C.),
Numa Pompilius, the second (715–
673 B.C.), and Tullus Hostilius, the
third (673–642 B.C.); Quintus Martius Rex commanded the building
of the Aqua Marcia in 144 B.C., and
Caius Marcius Rutilus received the
title Censorinus in 265 B.C. when he
was made censor for the second time.
Shakespeare, by giving Brutus Plutarch's prelude at this point of the
play, allows us to recognize the element of patrician propaganda in the
'lecture' about the 'noble house o'th'-
Martians'.

241.] North reads, 'Censorinus
also came of that familie, that was so
surnamed, bicause the people had
chosen him Censor twise'. Editors
have variously supplied the words
manifestly missing from F. If we
assume that the compositor missed a
whole line, then Delius's solution,
followed by most editors, is satisfactory; the compositor (A) might
be supposed to have skipped the
first of two lines beginning *And.*
Sisson's solution is the minimal
intervention in the text but it yields
a metrically infelicitous line at the
end of Brutus' speech and an isolated
half-line at the start of Sicinius'.

247. *Scaling*] weighing; cf. *Meas.,*
III. i. 245.

249. *sudden*] hasty.

250. *our putting on*] our putting
you up to it.

251. *drawn your number*] gathered
your supporters.

All.   We will so: almost all
      Repent in their election.   *Exeunt Plebeians.*
Bru.   Let them go on;
      This mutiny were better put in hazard
      Than stay, past doubt, for greater.   255
      If, as his nature is, he fall in rage
      With their refusal, both observe and answer
      The vantage of his anger.
Sic.   To th'Capitol, come:
      We will be there before the stream o'th'people;
      And this shall seem, as partly 'tis, their own,   260
      Which we have goaded onward.   *Exeunt.*

252–3. We . . . election.] *As Hanmer; one line in F.*

253. *in*] For other examples of *in* for *of* see Abbott 162.

255. *Than . . . greater*] than wait for the greater mutiny that would undoubtedly come later.

257–8. *answer . . . anger*] take advantage of his anger. Case compares *Ant.*, IV. i. 9–10, 'Make boot of his distraction. Never anger / Made good guard for itself'. For a comparable use of *answer* cf. *All's W.*, I. i. 145, 'Off with't while 'tis vendible; answer the time of request'.

259. *stream o'th'people*] Cf. *H8*, IV. i. 63.

ACT III

[SCENE I]

Cornets. Enter CORIOLANUS, MENENIUS, *all the Gentry.*
COMINIUS, TITUS LARTIUS, *and other Senators.*

Cor. Tullus Aufidius then had made new head?
Lar. He had, my lord; and that it was which caus'd
    Our swifter composition.
Cor. So then the Volsces stand but as at first,
    Ready when time shall prompt them to make road   5
    Upon's again.
Com.   They are worn, lord consul, so,
    That we shall hardly in our ages see
    Their banners wave again.
Cor.   Saw you Aufidius?
Lar. On safeguard he came to me, and did curse
    Against the Volsces for they had so vilely   10
    Yielded the town: he is retir'd to Antium.
Cor. Spoke he of me?

ACT III
Scene I

ACT III] *Actus Tertius.* / F. SCENE I] *Rowe.*

Scene I] located by Rowe in 'Rome';
others specify 'a street'. The 'great
pompe' with which Martius came to
the market-place is given by North
as a reason for the people's hostility
(see Appendix, p. 332). The procession
here is on its way to the market-place
and meets the tribunes on their way
back.

    S.D. all the Gentry] i.e. the
patricians; see Introduction, p. 21.
E. C. Pettet (*Shakespeare Survey*, 3,
1950, p. 38) remarks the transposition of the Roman class-system
into contemporary terms; cf. II. i. 236,
III. i. 143.

    1. *made new head*] raised a fresh force,
cf. II. ii. 88.

1. head?] *Rowe;* head. *F.*

    3. *Our . . . composition*] our coming
to terms sooner than expected. The
short line can be rectified only at the
expense of other lines.

    5. *road*] inroad, raid.

    6. *worn*] exhausted.

    lord consul] Cominius' ironically
premature use of the title is an apt
preface to his false prediction about
Volscian power.

    7. *ages*] lifetimes.

    9. *On safeguard*] under safe-conduct.

    10. *for*] because; as often in
Shakespeare.

    11. *is retir'd*] For the use of *is*
with certain intransitive verbs see
Abbott 295.

Lar.   He did, my lord.
Cor.   How? What?
Lar. How often he had met you, sword to sword;
        That of all things upon the earth he hated
        Your person most; that he would pawn his fortunes   15
        To hopeless restitution, so he might
        Be call'd your vanquisher.
Cor.   At Antium lives he?
Lar. At Antium.
Cor. I wish I had a cause to seek him there,
        To oppose his hatred fully. Welcome home.   20

                Enter SICINIUS *and* BRUTUS.

        Behold, these are the tribunes of the people,
        The tongues o'th'common mouth. I do despise them:
        For they do prank them in authority,
        Against all noble sufferance.
Sic.   Pass no further.
Cor. Ha! what is that?   25
Bru. It will be dangerous to go on. No further.
Cor. What makes this change?
Men.   The matter?
Com. Hath he not pass'd the noble and the common?
Bru. Cominius, no.
Cor.   Have I had children's voices?
First Sen. Tribunes, give way: he shall to th'market-place.
Bru. The people are incens'd against him.

30. *First Sen.*] *Capell; Senat. | F.*

16. *To hopeless restitution*] i.e. hope-
lessly beyond recovery.
  19–20. *I wish . . . fully*] The irony of
these lines, which have been prepared as a climax to this phase of the
scene, has often been remarked.

  23. *prank them*] dress themselves up;
cf. *Meas.*, II. ii. 118, 'Dress'd in a
little brief authority', and for a less
contemptuous use of *prank* cf. *Tw.N.*,
II. iv. 85.

  24. *Against . . . sufferance*] beyond all

that nobility can endure. The word
noble is now appropriated to class use.

  28. *noble . . . common*] the nobility
and the common people; for other
uses of the singular form cf. *2H4*,
IV. iii. 53, 'believe not the word of the
noble', and above, I. i. 150.

  29. *children's voices*] Case compares
Caes., III. i. 38–9, 'turn pre-ordinance
and first decree | Into the law of
children'.

Sic.   Stop,   31
    Or all will fall in broil.
Cor.   Are these your herd?
    Must these have voices, that can yield them now
    And straight disclaim their tongues? What are your
       offices?
    You being their mouths, why rule you not their teeth?
    Have you not set them on?
Men.   Be calm, be calm.   36
Cor. It is a purpos'd thing, and grows by plot,
    To curb the will of the nobility:
    Suffer't, and live with such as cannot rule,
    Nor ever will be rul'd.
Bru.   Call't not a plot.   40
    The people cry you mock'd them; and of late,
    When corn was given them gratis, you repin'd,
    Scandal'd the suppliants for the people, call'd them
    Time-pleasers, flatterers, foes to nobleness.
Cor. Why, this was known before.
Bru.   Not to them all.   45
Cor. Have you inform'd them sithence?
Bru.   How! I inform them!

31–2. Stop . . . broil.] *As Pope; one line in F.*   40. rul'd] *Pope;* ruled *F.*
43. suppliants for] *F4;* Suppliants: for *F.*   46. How! . . . them!] *Pope;* How?
. . . them? *F.*

32. *herd*] Cf. I. iv. 31, II. i. 94.
34. *straight*] immediately.
35–6. *mouths . . . on?*] A grim joke
about the function of mouths and
teeth in the body politic is transposed
into a covert allusion to dogs;
Warburton thought the metaphor to
be 'from setting a bull-dog or mastiff
upon anyone', and Wilson associates
it with bear-baiting.

37. *purpos'd thing*] put-up job.
42. *gratis*] In North's account, corn
is distributed free on a later occasion
(see Appendix, p. 334). Cf. I. i.
187–9 where Coriolanus objects to corn
being distributed 'at their own rates'.

43. *Scandal'd*] slandered, as in
Caes., I. ii. 76.

44. *Time-pleasers . . . nobleness*] Cf.
North, 'Martius . . . called them
people pleasers, and traitours to the
nobilitie' (Appendix, p. 334). For
time-pleaser (= time-server, an expression not found in Shakespeare) cf.
Tw.N., II. iii. 138, and *Ham.* (Q1),
l. 1234, 'time-pleasing tongs'.

46. *sithence*] a common Elizabethan
form of 'since'; used also in *All's W.*,
I. iii. 110.
inform] The word was apt to give
offence. Wilson compares *Ven.*, 655,
'This sour informer, this bate-breeding
spy', and *Sonn.*, cxxv. 13, 'thou sub-
orn'd informer!'

Com. You are like to do such business.
Bru.   Not unlike
     Each way to better yours.
Cor. Why then should I be consul? By yond clouds,
     Let me deserve so ill as you, and make me   50
     Your fellow tribune.
Sic.   You show too much of that
     For which the people stir. If you will pass
     To where you are bound, you must inquire your way,
     Which you are out of, with a gentler spirit,
     Or never be so noble as a consul,   55
     Nor yoke with him for tribune.
Men.   Let's be calm.
Com. The people are abus'd; set on. This palt'ring
     Becomes not Rome; nor has Coriolanus
     Deserv'd this so dishonour'd rub, laid falsely
     I'th'plain way of his merit.
Cor.   Tell me of corn!   60
     This was my speech, and I will speak't again.

47. *Com.*] *F; Coriolanus | Theobald.*   47–8. Not . . . yours.] *As Johnson; one line
in F.*   57. abus'd; set on.] *F* (abus'd: set on,)*; abus'd.—Set on;—*Theobald;*
abused. Set on! *Chambers.*   60–1. Tell . . . again.] *As Pope;* Tell . . .
speech, / . . . againe.

47. *Com.*] Following Theobald's
reading, Wilson repeats the argument
that there is little to choose graphically between the abbreviated forms
Com. and *Cor.*; Compositor A,
however, retains the apparently
Shakespearean spelling *Scicin.* in
S.H. 24, 32, and 51, and may be
following the copy in his S.H.s
Corio. and *Com.*, between which
confusion is less probable. I agree
with Knight (*apud* Furness) that 'the
interruption of Cominius gives spirit
and variety to the scene'; and it
anticipates the more sustained intervention of ll. 57–60. Brutus' reply
could be addressed to the patricians
jointly. Cominius' words are pro-
vocative, but not outrageously so,
and we need not attribute to Shakespeare too mechanical and superficial a consistency; Cominius' temper is between Menenius' and

Coriolanus'. For Cominius' attitude
to the tribunes and people, see I. ix.
6–7.

47–8. *Not . . . yours*] not unlikely,
in any case, to do better than you.
Brutus is comparing fitnesses to rule.

53. *To . . . bound*] i.e. to the market-
place and to the consulship.

54–5. *gentler . . . noble*] Sicinius
plays ironically upon senses connecting quality of spirit with 'the quality'.

57. *abus'd*] deceived, imposed upon;
as in *Ado*, v. ii. 84.

set on] Cf. above, l. 36.

palt'ring] equivocating, playing fast
and loose (see *O.E.D.*, s.v. 2); cf.
Mac., v. viii. 20, and, for 'fast and
loose', *Ant.*, IV. xii. 28.

59. *dishonour'd rub*] dishonourable
obstruction; the tribunes are seen as
cheating at bowls, treacherously
fouling the *plain way* that Coriolanus'
course should by merit take. For

Men. Not now, not now.
First Sen.   Not in this heat, sir, now.
Cor. Now as I live, I will. My nobler friends,
　　I crave their pardons.
　　For the mutable, rank-scented meinie, let them   65
　　Regard me as I do not flatter, and
　　Therein behold themselves. I say again,
　　In soothing them, we nourish 'gainst our senate
　　The cockle of rebellion, insolence, sedition,
　　Which we ourselves have plough'd for, sow'd and
　　　　scatter'd,   70
　　By mingling them with us, the honour'd number
　　Who lack not virtue, no, nor power, but that
　　Which they have given to beggars.
Men.   Well, no more.
First Sen. No more words, we beseech you.
Cor.   How? no more!
　　As for my country I have shed my blood,   75
　　Not fearing outward force, so shall my lungs
　　Coin words till their decay, against those measles

62, 74. *First Sen.*] *Capell; Senat. | F.*   63–7.] *As Capell; Now . . . will. | . . .*
pardons: | . . . Meynie, | . . . flatter, | . . . againe, | *F.*   65. meinie] *F*
(Meynie); many *F4, Cam.*

dishonour'd = 'dishonourable' see
Abbott 374.
　65. *mutable*] not used elsewhere by
Shakespeare. Case compares *2H4*
Ind., 19, 'The still-discordant wav'-
ring multitude'.
　meinie] multitude, crew; in *Lr.*, II.
iv. 34, it means household retainers,
and is closer to the Lat. *mansionem*
(see *O.E.D.*, meinie). F4's *many* is a
confusion, not a correction or
modernization, occasioned by F's
spelling *Meynie*.
　65–7. *let . . . themselves*] as I am no
flatterer, let them look to me, as to a
mirror, for an image of their true
condition.
　68. *soothing*] flattering. Cf. I. ix. 44
and II. ii. 73.
　68–70. *nourish . . . scatter'd*] Cf.
North, 'Moreover he sayed they
nourrished against them selves, the

naughty seede and cockle, of insolencie and sedition, which had bene
sowed and scattered abroade emongest the people' (Appendix, p. 334).
　69. *cockle*] Shakespeare follows
North in treating cockle as a noxious
weed infesting cornfields; it may
therefore be here confused with
darnel (see *Lr.*, IV. iv. 5) and not
refer to what is now known as corn-
cockle. Cf. *LLL.*, IV. iii. 379, 'Sow'd
cockle reap'd no corn', and Job,
xxxi. 40. Wilson compares the
parable of the wheat and the tares
(Matthew, xiii. 24–30) which has
cockle (for 'tares') in the Rheims
version. Noble cites Hosea, x. 13.
　71. *honour'd*] honourable. See l. 59
note.
　72. *virtue*] For the specialized senses
of the word see II. ii. 84 and note.
　77. *measles*] either (a) in the

    Which we disdain should tetter us, yet sought
    The very way to catch them.
Bru.   You speak o'th'people
    As if you were a god to punish, not   80
    A man of their infirmity.
Sic.   'Twere well
    We let the people know't.
Men.   What, what? His choler?
Cor. Choler!
    Were I as patient as the midnight sleep,
    By Jove, 'twould be my mind!
Sic.   It is a mind   85
    That shall remain a poison where it is,
    Not poison any further.
Cor.   Shall remain!
    Hear you this Triton of the minnows? Mark you

79–84. You . . . sleep,] *As Capell;* You . . . God, / . . . Infirmity. / . . . know't. / . . . His Choller? / . . . sleep, *F.*   85–7. It . . . further.] *As Pope;* It . . . poison / . . . further, *F.*

modern sense, from M.E. *maseles* = spots, or (b) lepers, from O.E. *misel*, O.F. *mesel*, Lat. *misellus*. The two words were often confused, and the diseases further confounded with small-pox. *Mesel* (leper) was often transferred and extended to include any victim of a foul infection. Steevens cites *The London Prodigal*, II. iv. 73, 'what, doe you thinke, chil be abaffelled up and downe the towne for a messell and a scoundrel?' In the present passage *coin words . . . against* may refer either to the abuse of lepers or to the weaving of spells against infection; *disdain . . . tetter us* could refer either to the disease or its carriers; and *catch them* must refer to the disease and its marks.

   78. *tetter*] infect with tetters or skin eruptions. For the connection with leprosy cf. *Ham.*, I. v. 71–3, 'And a most instant tetter bark'd about, / Most lazar-like, with vile and loathsome crust, / All my smooth body'.

   sought] apparently a subjunctive

form, following an implied 'as if' before *against*.

   81. *man . . . infirmity*] Chambers compares Hebrews, iv. 15, Wilson, Acts, xiv. 15, and Noble, Romans, vi. 19.

   82. *choler*] See North, Appendix, p. 333.

   84. *patient*] quiet in mind, free of all turbulent humours.

   86–9. *shall . . . absolute 'shall'*] Shakespeare is here attending to a grammatical distinction between 'will' and 'shall' that elsewhere he usually ignores; see Abbott 316, 317.

   88. *Triton . . . minnows*] Lord of the small fry. Martius' taunt has oddly provoked the commentators: Rushton thought *shall* a play upon the 'shell' (i.e. the conch or 'wreathed horn') that Triton was supposed to blow at the approach of Neptune; and Furness (following Delius) hazards an alliterative allusion from *Triton of the minnows* to 'Tribune of the many'.

His absolute 'shall'?

Com.   'Twas from the canon.

Cor.   'Shall!'

O good but most unwise patricians: why,   90
You grave but reckless senators, have you thus
Given Hydra here to choose an officer,
That with his peremptory 'shall', being but
The horn and noise o'th'monster's, wants not spirit
To say he'll turn your current in a ditch   95
And make your channel his? If he have power,

89. canon] *Rowe;* Cannon *F.*   89–90. 'Shall!' . . . why,] *As Pope; one line in F.*
90. good] *Theobald;* God! *F.*   91. reckless] *F* (wreaklesse), *Hanmer.*   92.
here] *F;* leave *Collier².*   94. monster's] *F* (monsters), *Delius.*

89. '*Twas from the canon*] Commentators have generally supported
Johnson's rendering, 'Was contrary
to the established rule; it was a form
of speech to which he has no right'.
Mason, however, takes the phrase in
the opposite sense, 'according to the
rule', in allusion to the 'absolute veto
of the Tribunes'. Either is possible
within Shakespeare's non-specific interpretation of the Roman constitution, but Cominius is more likely to be
slighting the tribunes than formally
conceding their authority. The metrically natural stress on *from* would
tend to confirm Johnson's reading.

90. *good*] Harrison alone among
modern editors retains F's *God!*
Theobald is largely vindicated by the
antitheses in the next line (*good . . .
unwise, grave . . . reckless*). As Gomme
says, the *More* MS. (Hand C) has
several times the form *god;* Compositor B might readily have misread
good as *god* after the exclamatory *O*.

91. *reckless*] F's spelling also occurs
in *Meas.*, IV. ii. 136 F, 'carelesse,
wreaklesse, and fearlesse', and in
3H6, v. vi. 7. There is therefore no
need to invite the rare word *wreakless*
('unpunished, unavenged') into the
context.

92. *Given*] permitted, given leave to.
There is no need for Collier's emendation of *here* to *leave.*

Hydra] probably a not very specific
allusion to the serpent of the Lernaean marsh, killed by Hercules; it
had nine heads and could grow two
where one was struck off. Cf. *1H4*,
v. iv. 25, 'Another king! They grow
like Hydra's heads'; also *Oth.*, II. iii.
295, *2H4*, IV. ii. 38, and *H5*, I. i. 35.
Case notes that a Hydra with fifty
heads guards the judgement hall of
Rhadamanthus in *Aeneid*, VI. 576–7.
See also II. iii. 16–17, IV. i. 1 and l. 130
below.

94. *horn and noise*] a hendiadys for
'noisy horn'. Another alleged pun
on the Triton's shell and the Tribune's shall (see above, l. 88 note).

o'th'monster's] F has *monsters*, but
there is precedent for imputing the
double genitive to Shakespeare.
Wright cites *Cym.*, II. iii. 143–4, 'a
revenue / Of any king's in Europe',
R2, III. iv. 70.

95–6. *turn . . . his*] i.e. divert your
power and resources to his own ends.
The metaphor is apparently from
farm irrigation, but it may have been
prompted by association with Triton's power over water. G. B.
Harrison finds here an allusion to
Hugh Middleton's scheme (started
on 20 Feb. 1609) to bring clean
water into London by channels
from streams in Hertfordshire; see
Introduction, p. 25.

Then vail your ignorance; if none, awake
Your dangerous lenity. If you are learn'd
Be not as common fools; if you are not,
Let them have cushions by you. You are plebeians   100
If they be senators; and they are no less
When, both your voices blended, the great'st taste
Most palates theirs. They choose their magistrate,
And such a one as he, who puts his 'shall',
His popular 'shall', against a graver bench   105
Than ever frown'd in Greece. By Jove himself,
It makes the consuls base; and my soul aches
To know, when two authorities are up,
Neither supreme, how soon confusion

97–100. Then . . . ignorance . . . Let . . . you] *F; Let . . . you . . . Then . . . ignorance Hanmer.*

97. *vail your ignorance*] abase your ignorant selves in submission; cf. *Shr.*, v. ii. 176–7, 'Then vail your stomachs, for it is no boot, / And place your hands below your husband's foot'. The patricians are *ignorant* because they conceded power in ignorance of the consequences. Hanmer's transposition of clauses is attractive but entails the accommodating emendation of *he* to *they* (l. 96), which assumes that the compositor was both careless enough to misinterpret the order of clauses and vigilant enough to cover the tracks of his error; to accept the reading it would be necessary to postulate ambiguously corrected foul-papers.

97–8. *awake . . . lenity*] i.e. rouse yourselves from this dangerous acquiescence; cf. North, 'the lenitie that was favored, was a beginning of disobedience' (Appendix, p. 319). For *lenity* in its more precise sense ('mildness') cf. *3H6*, ii. ii. 9–10, 'this too much lenity / And harmful pity must be laid aside'.

98. *learn'd*] i.e. in the arts of government.

100. *Let . . . by you*] let them sit with you on the senate. Cf. ii. ii. 1 S.D., and iv. vii. 43.

102–3. *great'st . . . theirs*] i.e. the people's taste will better relish the popular ingredient in the blend of voices, and the patricians will always be over-ruled. Many, however, follow Malone in finding that the blend of voices will always taste more strongly of the people. The metaphor is probably not quite stabilized between the two possibilities; but *palate* = relish is used elsewhere by Shakespeare (*Ant.*, v. ii. 7, *Troil.*, iv. i. 61), while there is no other recorded instance of its meaning 'savours of'. *O.E.D.* gives only the senses 'relish' and 'season'.

105. *popular*] of the people, plebeian; cf. ii. i. 212, ii. iii. 101.

105–6. *graver . . . Greece*] See below, ll. 112–15 and note.

108. *up*] roused to the exertion of their power.

109. *confusion*] several times used by Shakespeare to denote cataclysm and chaos; cf. *2H6*, v. ii. 31, *John*, iv. iii. 152.

May enter 'twixt the gap of both, and take   110
The one by th'other.

Com.   Well, on to th'market place.

Cor. Whoever gave that counsel, to give forth
The corn o'th'storehouse gratis, as 'twas us'd
Sometime in Greece—

Men.   Well, well, no more of that.

Cor. Though there the people had more absolute power—
I say they nourish'd disobedience, fed   116
The ruin of the state.

Bru.   Why shall the people give
One that speaks thus their voice?

Cor.   I'll give my reasons
More worthier than their voices. They know the corn
Was not our recompense, resting well assur'd   120
They ne'er did service for't; being press'd to the war,
Even when the navel of the state was touch'd,
They would not thread the gates: this kind of service

116–17. I . . . state.] *As Pope; one line in F.*   117. Why shall] *F;* Why, shall *Capell.*

110–11. *'twixt . . . th'other*] i.e. confusion will overthrow one authority by means of the other. The political insight is clear, but the metaphors contributing to it are not explicitly realized. The *gap* suggests the vulnerability of a city wall or a dam (cf. *Mac.*, II. iii. 112–13, 'like a breach in nature / For ruin's wasteful entrance'), while *take . . . th'other* suggests dogs set at each other's throats (cf. *Oth.*, v. ii. 358). For images of internecine destruction cf. *Troil.*, I. iii. 121–4, *Lr.*, IV. ii. 49–50, and *More* (D), 80–7.

112–15. *Whoever . . . power*] In North, Coriolanus denounces those who think 'corne should be geven out to the common people *gratis*, as they used to doe in citties of Græce, where the people had more absolute power' (Appendix, p. 334).

116–17. *nourish'd . . . state*] Cf. North, 'only nourishe their disobedience, which would break out in the ende, to the utter ruine and

overthrowe of the whole state' (Appendix, pp. 334–5). For the lineation see Introduction, p. 11.

119–29. *They know . . . donation*] closely dependent on North's version of Coriolanus' 'oration against the insolencie of the people' (Appendix, p. 334).

120. *recompense*] i.e. payment for services rendered.

121–3. *press'd . . . gates*] Shakespeare insinuates the body-politic metaphor (*navel of the state*) into North's account of Coriolanus' charge against the people. For other versions of the people's exposure to war, see Appendix, pp. 318 and 328, and above, I. i. 84 note.

121. *press'd*] impressed, conscripted.

122. *navel . . . touch'd*] i.e. when its very survival was threatened.

123. *thread*] Cf. *R2*, v. v. 16–17, 'It is as hard to come as for a camel / To thread the postern of a small needle's eye'.

Did not deserve corn gratis. Being i'th'war,
Their mutinies and revolts, wherein they show'd   125
Most valour, spoke not for them. Th'accusation
Which they have often made against the senate,
All cause unborn, could never be the native
Of our so frank donation. Well, what then?
How shall this bosom multiplied digest   130
The senate's courtesy? Let deeds express
What's like to be their words, 'We did request it,
We are the greater poll, and in true fear
They gave us our demands.' Thus we debase
The nature of our seats, and make the rabble   135
Call our cares fears; which will in time
Break ope the locks o'th'senate, and bring in
The crows to peck the eagles.

128. native] *F*; motive *Ard.*[1], conj. *Johnson.*   130. bosom multiplied] *F*; bisson multitude *Dyce*, after *Collier*[2] (beson-multitude); bissom multitude *Singer*: beesom multitude *Kittredge.*

128. *All cause unborn*] for which no cause existed.

native] origin (*O.E.D.*, 5.v. *a.* 3b, 'original, parent'); the choice of word is prompted by *unborn.* There is, however, no recorded use of the noun to mean 'origin', although *native* = native land, occurs in Chapman's *Odyssey*, ix. 66 (cited *O.E.D.*, s.v. *sb.* 7). Johnson's conjecture *motive* is graphically plausible, but it lacks the metaphoric energy of *native.*

129. *frank donation*] free gift. For the reciprocal use of *free* = frank see II. iii. 198.

130. *bosom multiplied*] The figure here sustains the *hydra* of l. 92 above, and anticipates the *beast with many heads* of IV. i. 1–2. The emendation *bisson multitude* and its variants become graphically plausible when it is recalled that at II. i. 63–4 F reads *beesome* (= bisson, purblind). But Shakespeare uses *bosom* in related contexts elsewhere: in *Lr.*, v. iii. 50, the people are called 'the common bosom', and in *2H4*, I. iii. 94–100, they are called collectively a 'beastly feeder', 'common dog', and said to

'disgorge' their 'glutton bosom of the royal Richard'.

digest] assimilate, take in; hence 'understand'. Commentators have been embarrassed by the attribution of digestive powers to the bosom. Since in *2H4* the bosom is said to 'disgorge' (see last note) it may be allowed to digest; but Case objects that rejected food only passes through the breast, 'which may therefore disgorge but not digest'. Gordon compares *Mac.*, v. iii. 44–5, 'Cleanse the stuff'd bosom of that perilous stuff / Which weighs upon the heart'.

131–2. *deeds . . . words*] This formulation appears to anticipate the 'deeds' of ll. 137–8 after the 'words' of 132–4; otherwise *deeds* and *words* invite transposition.

133. *poll*] number of heads.

true fear] very fear.

136. *cares*] solicitous measures.

137. *Break . . . senate*] This fear has no precise occasion in North.

138. *crows . . . eagles*] Shakespeare, as King noticed, puns upon *crows* = crow-bars (for the breaking of locks); cf. *Err.*, III. i. 80–4, 'Well, I'll

Men.   Come, enough.
Bru. Enough, with over-measure.
Cor.   No, take more!
What may be sworn by, both divine and human,   140
Seal what I end withal! This double worship,
Where one part does disdain with cause, the other
Insult without all reason: where gentry, title, wisdom,
Cannot conclude but by the yea and no
Of general ignorance, it must omit   145
Real necessities, and give way the while
To unstable slightness. Purpose so barr'd, it follows
Nothing is done to purpose. Therefore beseech you—
You that will be less fearful than discreet,
That love the fundamental part of state   150
More than you doubt the change on't; that prefer
A noble life before a long, and wish

---

142. Where one] *Rowe;* Whereon *F.*   145. ignorance,] *F;* ignorance,—*Capell.*

---

break in; go borrow me a crow . . . A crow without feather? . . . If a crow help us in, sirrah, we'll pluck a crow together . . . Go get thee gone; fetch me an iron crow.' For the outrage upon the natural order cf. *Mac.*, II. iv. 12–13, 'A falcon, tow'ring in her pride of place, / Was by a mousing owl hawk'd at and kill'd', and for another allusion to the created hierarchy cf. IV. vii. 33–5, 'he'll be to Rome / As is the osprey to the fish, who takes it / By sovereignty of nature'. The eagle was specifically a symbol of Roman power.

141. *double worship*] i.e. the 'two authorities' of l. 108.

142. *Where one*] F's *Whereon* could be owed to Shakespeare's spelling *on* for *one* (as at I. i. 15 etc.).

143. *without all*] beyond all; cf. *Mac.*, III. ii. 11–12, 'Things without all remedy / Should be without regard'.

144. *conclude*] reach decisions.

145. *general*] common, popular.
it] i.e. *This double worship.*
omit] neglect, disregard.

146–7. *give . . . slightness*] yield to irresolute trifling (Case).

147–8. *Purpose . . . purpose*] Purposeful deliberation being thus obstructed, nothing is done to any effect.

149. *will . . . discreet*] wish to be less cowardly than discerning.

150–1. *love . . . change on't*] 'you who do not so much fear the danger of violent measures, as wish the good to which they are necessary, the preservation of the original constitution of our government' (Johnson). Johnson clarifies the main argument without attending to its infelicitous ambiguity. The difficult phrase, *you doubt the change on't*, probably means 'fear the consequences of any change in the recently agreed laws of state (which concede power to the tribunes)'; but it may mean 'question the need for any change in the fundamental laws of the state (which vest power in the patricians)'.

152. *noble . . . long*] a Laconian sentiment vindicated by the play (see Introduction, p. 68).

To jump a body with a dangerous physic
That's sure of death without it—at once pluck out
The multitudinous tongue: let them not lick   155
The sweet which is their poison. Your dishonour
Mangles true judgement, and bereaves the state
Of that integrity which should becom't,
Not having the power to do the good it would
For th'ill which doth control't.

Bru.   'Has said enough.   160
Sic. 'Has spoken like a traitor, and shall answer
    As traitors do.
Cor.   Thou wretch, despite o'erwhelm thee!
What should the people do with these bald tribunes?
On whom depending, their obedience fails
To th'greater bench. In a rebellion,   165
When what's not meet, but what must be, was law,
Then were they chosen. In a better hour,
Let what is meet be said it must be meet,
And throw their power i'th'dust.
Bru. Manifest treason!

---

165. bench. In a rebellion,] *Pope;* Bench, in a Rebellion: *F.*

---

153. *jump*] risk, hazard; cf. *Mac.*, I. vii. 7, *Cym.*, v. iv. 182, *Ant.*, III. viii. 6. Steevens cites Holland's Pliny (1601), xxv. v, 'If we look for good success in our cure by ministring of Ellebore, in any wise wee must take heed and be carefull how wee give it in close weather, and upon a dark and cloudie day; for certainly it putteth the patient to a jumpe or great hazard.'

155. *multitudinous tongue*] Cf. *Hydra* and his *officer* in l. 92. The *tongue* is the tribunes' voice in the government; they are the tongue of the multitude.

155–6. *lick . . . poison*] taste of the power that will be their undoing. Steevens compares *Meas.*, I. ii. 123, 'Like rats that ravin down their proper bane'.

156–8. *Your dishonour . . . becom't*] Your dishonourable yielding of power

has cruelly impaired the judgement of the state and deprived it of its proper unity and function.

159–60.] Cf. Romans, vii. 19.

160. *control*] overpower, overmaster (Onions); cf. *Tp.*, I. ii. 373–4, 'His art is of such pow'r, / It would control my dam's god, Setebos'.

161. *answer*] take the consequences; cf. *R3*, IV. ii. 97.

162. *despite*] contempt.

163. *bald*] literally and metaphorically, 'barren, meanly endowed'. Wright quotes Cotgrave, '*Chauve d'esprit.* Bauld spirited: that hath as little wit in as he hath haire on his head'.

166. *not meet . . . must be*] not right and fitting but imposed by force and circumstance.

168. *Let . . . be meet*] Let what is right be declared necessary.

Sic.   This a consul? No!   170
Bru. The ædiles, ho!

Enter an Ædile.

Let him be apprehended.
Sic. Go call the people;   [*Exit Ædile.*]
                    in whose name myself
        Attach thee as a traitorous innovator,
        A foe to th'public weal. Obey I charge thee,
        And follow to thine answer.
Cor.   Hence, old goat!   175
All Patricians. We'll surety him.
Com.   Aged sir, hands off.
Cor. Hence rotten thing! or I shall shake thy bones
        Out of thy garments.
Sic.   Help, ye citizens!

Enter a rabble of Plebeians with the Ædiles.

Men. On both sides more respect.
Sic. Here's he that would take from you all your power.
Bru. Seize him, ædiles!   181
All Pleb. Down with him! Down with him!

---

171. S.D.] *Follows 170 in F.*   172. Exit Ædile.] *Collier; Exit Brutus. | Capell;*
not in F.   176. All Patricians.] *All. | F.*   Aged] *Rowe;* Ag'd *F.*   182, 191,
197, 200, 227. All Pleb.] *Ard.¹; All. | F; Citizens | Capell.*

171. *ædiles*] 'The *Ædiles Plebeii* (as
distinguished from the *Ædiles Curules*,
of later origin) were instituted at the
same time as the tribunes, and
probably at first merely as their
assistants or executive officers' (Case).
Shakespeare slightly telescopes events
reported in North (see Appendix,
p. 336).
    173. *Attach*] arrest.
    innovator] revolutionary, rebel; cf.
1 H 4, v. i. 76–8, 'fickle changelings
and poor discontents, / Which gape
and rub the elbow at the news / Of
hurlyburly innovation'.

175. *answer*] trial, or perhaps
'punishment'.
    old goat] Sicinius may be bearded
like a goat or smell like one. Furness
quotes ii. i. 85–6, 'the wagging of
your beards', and Case compares
l. 177, 'Hence, rotten thing'.

177. *rotten thing*] For a fuller realiz-
ation of the idea cf. *John*, ii. i.
455–7, 'Here's a stay / That shakes
the rotten carcase of old Death /
Out of his rags!' (Steevens.)

178. S.D. rabble of Plebeians] See
Introduction, p. 20.

Second Sen. Weapons, weapons, weapons!

         They all bustle about Coriolanus.

All. Tribunes! Patricians! Citizens! What ho!

  Sicinius! Brutus! Coriolanus! Citizens!   185

  Peace, peace, peace! Stay! Hold! Peace!

Men. What is about to be? I am out of breath;

  Confusion's near, I cannot speak. You, tribunes

  To th'people! Coriolanus, patience!

  Speak, good Sicinius!

Sic.   Hear me, people. Peace! 190

All Pleb. Let's hear our tribune. Peace! Speak, speak, speak!

Sic. You are at point to lose your liberties:

  Martius would have all from you, Martius

  Whom late you have nam'd for consul.

Men.   Fie, fie, fie!

  This is the way to kindle, not to quench. 195

First Sen. To unbuild the city and to lay all flat.

Sic. What is the city but the people?

All Pleb.   True,

  The people are the city.

Bru. By the consent of all we were establish'd

  The people's magistrates.

All Pleb.   You so remain. 200

Men. And so are like to do.

---

183. *Second Sen.*] *F* (*2. Sen.*); *Senators, & c.* | *Cam.*; *A Senator* | *Sisson*; *Two Senators* | *conj. Rossiter.* 183. S.D. *Coriolanus.*] *F*; *Coriolanus, crying* | *Cam.* 184. *All.*] *Cam.*; *not in F.* 186. Peace] *Cam.*; *All.* Peace *F*; *Patricians.* Peace *Alexander.* 189–90. To ... Sicinius!] *As Capell; one line in F.* 194–5. Fie ... quench.] *As Pope; prose in F.* 196. *First Sen.*] *Capell; Sena.* | *F.* 199–200. By ... magistrates.] *As Pope; prose in F.*

188. *Confusion*] See above, l. 109 note.

188–9. *You . . . people*] It is possible that Menenius is asking the tribunes to speak to the people, and that a comma after *tribunes* would better express his intention. There have been many editorial interventions to assist Menenius to recover his breath.

192. *at point to*] on the point of.

197. *What . . . people?*] 'In this passage Shakespeare probably refers to the maxim: Civitas et urbs in hoc differunt, quod incolae dicuntur civitas, urbs vero complectitur aedificia (Mirror, cap. 2, sect. 18, Brit. fol. 87, Col Litt. 109 b). A city and town differ in this, that the inhabitants are called the city, but the town comprises the building' (Rushton, *Shakespeare's Legal Maxims*, edn II, p. 53, *apud* Furness). Sicinius would appear to apply the maxim perversely, claiming that the plebeians only are the people and the city.

Com. That is the way to lay the city flat,
       To bring the roof to the foundation,
       And bury all which yet distinctly ranges
       In heaps and piles of ruin.
Sic.   This deserves death.   205
Bru. Or let us stand to our authority
       Or let us lose it: we do here pronounce,
       Upon the part o'th'people, in whose power
       We were elected theirs, Martius is worthy
       Of present death.
Sic.   Therefore lay hold of him.   210
       Bear him to th'rock Tarpeian, and from thence
       Into destruction cast him.
Bru.   Ædiles, seize him!
All Pleb. Yield, Martius, yield!
Men.   Hear me one word.
       Beseech you, tribunes, hear me but a word.
Æd. Peace, peace!   215
Men. Be that you seem, truly your country's friend,
       And temp'rately proceed to what you would
       Thus violently redress.
Bru.   Sir, those cold ways,
       That seem like prudent helps, are very poisonous
       Where the disease is violent. Lay hands upon him,   220
       And bear him to the rock.

                          Coriolanus draws his sword.

202. *Com.*] *F; Coriolanus | Pope.*   213–14. Hear . . . a word.] *As Johnson; prose in F.*

204. *all . . . ranges*] alluding to the buildings and streets of Rome, but perhaps also to the social order of which the architecture is an expression; cf. I. i. 217. For *distinctly,* see below, IV. iii. 45, and *Tp.,* I. ii. 199–201, 'on the topmast, / The yards and bowsprit would I flame distinctly, / Then meet and join'; and for *ranges* cf. *Ant.,* I. i. 33–4, 'the wide arch / Of the rang'd empire fall!'

205. *This*] i.e. Coriolanus' move to abolish the tribunate. Pope supposed

it to mean Cominius' last speech, which he therefore ascribed to Coriolanus.

206. *Or*] either.

211. *Bear . . . Tarpeian*] Cf. North, where Sicinius pronounces death upon Coriolanus, 'Then presently he commanded the Ædiles to apprehend him, and carie him straight to the rocke Tarpeian, and to cast him hedlong downe the same' (Appendix, p. 338). The cliff on the Capitoline was regularly used for the execution of criminals and traitors.

Cor.   No, I'll die here.
There's some among you have beheld me fighting:
Come, try upon yourselves what you have seen me!
Men. Down with that sword! Tribunes, withdraw awhile.
Bru. Lay hands upon him.
Men.   Help Martius, help!   225
You that be noble, help him, young and old!
All Pleb. Down with him, down with him!

> *In this mutiny, the Tribunes, the Ædiles, and the People*
> *are beat in [and] Exeunt.*

Men. Go, get you to your house: be gone, away!
All will be naught else.
Second Sen.   Get you gone.
Cor.   Stand fast.
We have as many friends as enemies.   230
Men. Shall it be put to that?
First Sen.   The gods forbid.
I prithee, noble friend, home to thy house:

225–6. Help . . . old!] *After Hanmer; prose in F.*   227. S.D. *Exeunt.] F (follow-
ing him).*   228. your] *Rowe;* our *F.*   229. *Cor.] Warburton; Com. | F, Sisson.*
229–30. Stand . . . enemies.] *As Capell; one line in F.*

225. *Help . . . help*] Menenius is
calling on the patricians to help
Martius; but some editors have
supposed him to be crying for
Martius' help, and have punctuated
accordingly. See North, Appendix,
p. 338.

227. S.D.] as F. The plebeians
'exeunt' as they are beaten 'in' to the
tiring house and off the stage.

228. *your house*] Confusion of *our*
and *your* occurs commonly in F, and
Rowe's emendation is plausible.
There is no suggestion elsewhere in
the play that Menenius and Coriolanus share a house. See I. iii. 1
S.D. note.

229. *naught*] lost, ruined, brought
to naught; cf. *Ant.,* III. x. 1. There is
also an allusion to 'be naught'
meaning 'make yourself scarce', with
a glance at l. 228 *be gone, away!*

Menenius puts the stress on *All* (see
Whiter, p. 10).

Cor.] Warburton's emendation of
F's *Com.* is the more plausible in
relation to the confusion of assignments in ll. 235, 236, and 238 below.
The generally accepted editorial
version makes Coriolanus eager to
fight while Menenius, the Senator,
and Cominius plead with him to go
home. Sisson (*New Readings*) argues
for F that Cominius is more a soldier
than a politician, and his attitude lies
between the rashness of Coriolanus
and the discretion of the senators;
Coriolanus, he claims, would not have
considered the balance of forces as
Cominius does here. Attributed to
Coriolanus, however, the speech
gives a firm focus to the lines which
follow, and it is perfectly consistent
with the appeals for support that he
has made in ll. 149–56. The misreading *Com.* for *Cor.* is plausible.

Leave us to cure this cause.

Men.   For 'tis a sore upon us
You cannot tent yourself: be gone, beseech you.

Com. Come, sir, along with us.   235

Cor. I would they were barbarians—as they are,
        Though in Rome litter'd; not Romans—as they are
            not,
        Though calv'd i'th'porch o'th'Capitol.

Men.   Be gone!
Put not your worthy rage into your tongue.
One time will owe another.

Cor.   On fair ground   240
I could beat forty of them.

Men.   I could myself
Take up a brace o'th'best of them; yea, the two
        tribunes.

Com. But now 'tis odds beyond arithmetic;

---

233. upon us] *F* (upon us,); *omitted Pope.*   235. *Com.*] *F2; Corio.* | *F.*   236.
Cor.] *Steevens, conj. Tyrwhitt; Men.* | *F.*   238. *Men.*] *Steevens, conj. Tyrwhitt; not
in F.*   238–9. Be gone! . . . tongue.] *As Capell; one line in F.*   240–2. On . . .
tribunes.] *Capell; prose in F.*   242. best of them] *F;* best *Capell.*

---

233. *cause*] disease; cf. *All's W.*,
II. i. 109–10, 'touch'd / With that
malignant cause'; from a late Latin
use of *causa* (see *O.E.D.*, s.v. 12).

upon us] omitted by Pope who
resisted Shakespeare's alexandrines.
Menenius attributes the *sore* (=
wound) to the patricians generally.

234. *tent*] treat (specifically, with a
roll of linen to keep a wound open);
cf. I. ix. 31 and note.

235–40. S.H.s] F's manifestly
erroneous assignment of l. 235 to
Corio. evidently precipitated the careless conflation of ll. 236–40 (*I would
. . . another*) into one speech, and its
misassignment to Menenius. Wilson
attributes the error to 'crowding' in
the MS., and Gomme supposes that
the compositor is trying to save
space; the passage occurs at the
bottom of the first column, towards
the end of Compositor A's stint, on
bb2ᵛ. Nothing about crowding in the

copy, however, can be inferred from
crowding on the printed page, and
the stint continues for another half-
column, leaving scope for a lineation
adjustment which would have admitted the correct speech-heading.
It is better to suppose the compositor
negligent than to claim that in order
to save space he deliberately made the
text implausible.

237–8. *litter'd . . . calv'd*] i.e. like
swine and bullocks (Wilson).

240. *One . . . another*] i.e. one
occasion will be compensated by
another; cf. *Tw.N.*, v. i. 362, 'the
whirligig of time brings in his
revenges'.

241. *forty*] often used of an indefinite large number; e.g. *Wiv.*, I. i. 179.

242. *Take up*] take on; cf. *2H4*,
I. iii. 73.

243. *beyond arithmetic*] beyond calcu-
lation.

And manhood is call'd foolery when it stands
Against a falling fabric. Will you hence   245
Before the tag return? Whose rage doth rend
Like interrupted waters, and o'erbear
What they are us'd to bear.

Men.   Pray you be gone.
I'll try whether my old wit be in request
With those that have but little: this must be patch'd
With cloth of any colour.

Com.   Nay, come away.   251

Exeunt Coriolanus and Cominius, [and others].

Pat. This man has marr'd his fortune.

Men. His nature is too noble for the world:
He would not flatter Neptune for his trident,
Or Jove for's power to thunder. His heart's his mouth:
What his breast forges, that his tongue must vent;   256
And being angry, does forget that ever
He heard the name of death.   *A noise within.*
Here's goodly work!

Pat.   I would they were abed!

251. S.D. *and others*] Capell.   252. *Pat.*] F (*Patri.*); *First Pat.* / Capell (1.P.).
259. *Pat.*] F (*Patri.*); 1.P. *Capell*; 2 Pat. / Malone.

244–5. *And . . . fabric*] Cf. IV. vi.
104–6.

244. *manhood*] manliness, courage.

foolery] foolhardiness, folly; Shakespeare seems not to use this sense
elsewhere.

244–5. *stands Against*] stands its
ground in face of (Gomme).

246. *tag*] rabble; cf. *Caes.*, I. ii. 258,
'the tag-rag people'.

246–8. *whose rage . . . bear*] i.e. the
waters carry away the banks that
usually constrain them; cf. *Gent.*,
II. vii. 25–6, 'The current that with
gentle murmur glides, / Thou
know'st, being stopp'd, impatiently
doth rage'. The metaphor is a
recurring one in Shakespeare (cf.
e.g. *MND.*, II. i. 90–3, *Ham.*, IV. v.
96–7) and helps to establish his
claim to the Hand D additions to
Sir Thomas More; cf. *More*, II. iv.
54–5, 'Whiles they ar ore the banck

of their obedyence, / Thus will they
bere downe all things'. For a full
discussion of the motif see R. W.
Chambers, in *Shakespeare's Hand in
Sir Thomas More*, ed. A. W. Pollard,
pp. 159 ff.

249. *whether*] often contracted in
speech to 'wh'er' (see Abbott 466).

251. *Nay . . . away*] apparently
addressed to a reluctant Coriolanus.

253. *too . . . world*] Menenius intends
a political truth, related to the
impatience colloquially expressed in
ll. 260–1; but in Shakespeare's play
it has tragic significance.

255–8. *His heart's . . . death*] For the
physical compulsions of Coriolanus'
disposition see Introduction, p. 46.
Noble compares Ecclesiasticus, xxi.
26, 'The heart of fooles is in their
mouth; but the mouth of the wise is
in his heart'.

256. *vent*] utter.

Men. I would they were in Tiber! What the vengeance,
    Could he not speak 'em fair?

      Enter BRUTUS *and* SICINIUS *with the rabble again.*

Sic.   Where is this viper   261
    That would depopulate the city and
    Be every man himself?
Men.   You worthy tribunes—
Sic. He shall be thrown down the Tarpeian rock
    With rigorous hands: he hath resisted law,   265
    And therefore law shall scorn him further trial
    Than the severity of the public power,
    Which he so sets at naught.
First Cit.   He shall well know
    The noble tribunes are the people's mouths
    And we their hands.
All Pleb.   He shall, sure on't.
Men.   Sir, sir!   270
Sic. Peace!
Men. Do not cry havoc where you should but hunt
    With modest warrant.

260–3. I . . . himself?] *As Pope;* I . . . Tyber. / . . . faire? / . . . Viper, / . . . himself / *F.*   263. tribunes—] *Rowe;* Tribunes. *F.*   268–70. He shall . . . hands.] *As Johnson;* He . . . are / . . . hands. / *F.*   270, 278. *All Pleb.*] *F* (*All.*). 273–6. Sir . . . faults.] *As Pope;* Sir . . . holpe / . . . rescue? / . . . know / . . . Faults. / *F.*   273. comes't] *Capell;* com'st *F.*

260. *What the vengeance*] phrase used to strengthen interrogations (*O.E.D.*, vengeance 3, giving this example); not elsewhere in Shakespeare. Cf. 'What the hell!'

261. *viper*] Vipers were believed to eat their way at birth through the parental bowels (see Pliny, *Nat. Hist.*, x. 82); hence the general implication of treachery, cf. l. 284 below. Cf. also *1H6*, III. i. 72, and *2H6*, III. i. 343–4, 'I fear me you but warm the starved snake, / Who, cherish'd in your breasts, will sting your hearts'; this last refers to Aesop's fable in which the frozen snake bites the breast that warms it.

269. *noble tribunes*] The phrase reverses the earlier class-appropriation of *noble*, l. 24.

272. *cry havoc*] originally the signal to plunder (O.F. *crier havot*), given by the king. Shakespeare associates it with the hunt; cf. *John*, II. i. 357, *Caes.*, III. i. 274, 'Cry "Havoc!" and let slip the dogs of war', and *Ham.*, v. ii. 356, 'This quarry cries on havoc'. There is, however, no independent evidence of its use in sport.

273. *modest warrant*] perhaps 'restricted licence', setting limits on the kill.

Sic.   Sir, how comes't that you
    Have holp to make this rescue?
Men.   Hear me speak!
    As I do know the consul's worthiness,   275
    So can I name his faults.
Sic.   Consul! What consul?
Men. The consul Coriolanus.
Bru.   He consul!
All Pleb. No, no, no, no, no.
Men. If, by the tribunes' leave, and yours, good people,
    I may be heard, I would crave a word or two,   280
    The which shall turn you to no further harm
    Than so much loss of time.
Sic.   Speak briefly then:
    For we are peremptory to dispatch
    This viperous traitor. To eject him hence
    Were but our danger, and to keep him here   285
    Our certain death. Therefore it is decreed
    He dies tonight.
Men.   Now the good gods forbid
    That our renowned Rome, whose gratitude
    Towards her deserved children is enroll'd

279.] *As Pope;* If . . . leaue, / . . . people, / *F.*   285. cur] *Theobald;* one *F.*

274. *nolp*] abbreviation of 'holpen', the old strong past participle: see Abbott 343.

rescue] in the technical sense, 'the forcible taking of a person or goods out of legal custody' (*O.E.D.*, s.v. *sb.* 2); cf. *2 H 4*, II. i. 53, where Fang cries, 'A rescue! a rescue!', as Falstaff calls on Bardolph to help him resist arrest.

281. *turn you to*] bring about for you. See *O.E.D.*, turn 43 b.

283. *peremptory*] resolutely determined, as in *John*, II. i. 454; or, possibly, as in Roman law, 'finally decided' (*O.E.D.*, s.v. 1). Cf. l. 286, *it is decreed.*

284. *eject*] not elsewhere used by Shakespeare.

285. *our danger*] Theobald's *our*

makes a better foil to *Our . . . death,* and F's *one* is an easy minim misreading. If *one* is retained it might mean 'one kind of danger, as distinct from another kind—death'. It is less likely to mean 'one all-pervading constant souroe of danger' (Wright's version).

289. *deserved*] deserving. For Shakespeare's general disposition to convert one part of speech to another see Abbott 22; for his confounding of participle-forms, Abbott 372 ff. But opinions differ about the nature of the present licence; Malone compares 'delighted' for 'delighting' in *Oth.*, I. iii. 289, and Wright 'dishonour'd' for 'dishonourable' in l. 59 above; but Whitelaw glosses 'children that *have* deserved well'. Smithers (*Shakespeare Survey*, 23, p. 34) remarks that

In Jove's own book, like an unnatural dam   290
Should now eat up her own!

Sic. He's a disease that must be cut away.

Men. Oh, he's a limb that has but a disease:
Mortal, to cut it off; to cure it, easy.
What has he done to Rome that's worthy death?   295
Killing our enemies, the blood he hath lost
(Which I dare vouch, is more than that he hath
By many an ounce) he dropp'd it for his country;
And what is left, to lose it by his country
Were to us all that do't and suffer it   300
A brand to th'end o'th'world.

Sic.   This is clean kam.

Bru. Merely awry. When he did love his country,
It honour'd him.

Sic.   The service of the foot,

293. disease:] *Rowe (subst.)*; Disease *F.*   302–3. When . . . him.] *As Pope; one*
line in F.   303. *Sic.* The] *Hanmer, conj. Warburton; Menen.* The *F;* The *conj.*
Lettsom.

deserving occurs in *Othello*, III. iii. 279, and supposes *deserved* to be coined as its equivalent.

290. *Jove's own book*] Gordon suggests 'the rolls and registers of the Capitol, which was Jove's temple', citing *Caes.*, III. ii. 37–8, 'The question of his death is enroll'd in the Capitol'. Others, less convincingly, have explained it as a Roman counterpart of the 'book of remembrance' in Malachi, iii. 16, or the similar book in Exodus, xxxii. 32 (Wright), or of the book of life in Revelations, xx. 12, 15, and *R2*, I. iii. 202 (Deighton).

unnatural dam] Case quotes Holland's Pliny, VIII, 53, 'That a sow should eat her own pigs is no prodigious wonder.'

294. *Mortal*] fatal; cf. *Oth.*, V. ii. 208, 'Thy match was mortal to him'. Cf. V. iii. 189.

301. *clean kam*] quite crooked, absolutely perverse. For *clean* = quite cf., e.g., *2H4*, I. ii. 91, 'though not clean past your youth'. 'Kam' or, more correctly, 'cam', is from Welsh,

meaning 'crooked, awry'.

302. *Merely awry*] absolutely wide of the mark. Brutus' phrase echoes Sicinius'.

303. Sic.] Hanmer's assignment of the speech to Sicinius is wholly consistent with what has gone before, and it is only necessary to assume that one word was misread or misremembered by Compositor B. Lettsom's conjecture, continuing Brutus' words, postulates an inexplicable intrusion into the copy text by the compositor. If F's attribution to Menenius is retained, the speech becomes a perverse and sardonic retort to his own point about the diseased limb (l. 293)—not to cut away a gangrened limb is indeed 'mortal'. Capell claims that the argument would have served Menenius' purpose had he been allowed to finish it, but does not say how. Malone explains that Menenius is about to ask, 'Is this just?', but to that question the answer could be 'Yes!' Furness thinks Brutus' *We'll*

Being once gangren'd, is not then respected
For what before it was.

Bru.   We'll hear no more: 305
Pursue him to his house, and pluck him thence,
Lest his infection, being of catching nature,
Spread further.

Men.   One word more, one word.
This tiger-footed rage, when it shall find
The harm of unscann'd swiftness will, too late,   310
Tie leaden pounds to's heels. Proceed by process,
Lest parties, as he is belov'd, break out
And sack great Rome with Romans.

Bru.   If it were so!

Sic. What do ye talk?
Have we not had a taste of his obedience?   315
Our ædiles smote? ourselves resisted? Come.

Men. Consider this: he has been bred i'th'wars
Since a could draw a sword, and is ill school'd
In bolted language; meal and bran together

305. Bru.] F; Sic. | conj. Lettsom.   313. so!] F (so?); so—F3.

hear no more 'could hardly be addressed to his fellow tribune', but the words are not meant to cut Sicinius short but to forestall Menenius' reply; *We* refers to Brutus, Sicinius, and the plebs. R. R. Simpson, *Shakespeare and Medicine*, 1959, p. 202, discusses the medical context (and accepts the assignment to Sicinius).

307–8. *infection . . . further*] Gangrene is not strictly 'of catching nature' but it does 'spread further' within the affected body. Brutus (and Shakespeare) extends the disease metaphor to other possibilities, or, more probably, thinks of the 'body politic'.

309. *tiger-footed*] Case cites several instances of the tiger's reputed swiftness, including Holland's Pliny, VIII. 18, 'This beast (the Tyger) is most dreadful for incomparable swiftness, and most of all seen it is in the taking of her young'. He adds that *tiger-footed rage* may be a re-collection of Pliny's, 'for very anger she rageth on the shore and the sands'.

310. *unscann'd*] may be used actively (cf. *deserved* in l. 289) to mean 'unobservant'; more probably it means 'unconsidered'. The word is not used elsewhere, but for *scan* = consider cf. *Oth.*, III. iii. 249. Case compares *MND.*, I. i. 237, 'unheedy haste'.

311 *Tie . . . heels*] apparently a form of hobbling; but the syntax seems to require rage to constrain its own fury, and the metaphor cannot be made fully explicit. Wilson compares *Wint.*, IV. iv. 667, 'with his clog at heels'.

to's] to its.

by process] i.e. by process of law; cf. ll. 320–31.

312. *parties*] factions.

314. *What*] why (*O.E.D.*, s.v. A III *adv.* 19).

319. *bolted*] refined, sifted (anticipating *meal and bran*). For the connec-

He throws without distinction. Give me leave,   320
I'll go to him, and undertake to bring him
Where he shall answer by a lawful form—
In peace—to his utmost peril.
First Sen.   Noble tribunes,
It is the humane way. The other course
Will prove too bloody, and the end of it   325
Unknown to the beginning.
Sic.   Noble Menenius,
Be you then as the people's officer.
Masters, lay down your weapons.
Bru.   Go not home.
Sic. Meet on the market-place: we'll attend you there,
Where, if you bring not Martius, we'll proceed   330
In our first way.
Men.   I'll bring him to you.
[*To the Senators*] Let me desire your company. He
    must come,
Or what is worst will follow.
First Sen.   Pray you, let's to him.
                                        Exeunt.

---

321. bring him] *Pope;* bring him in peace, *F.*   323. In peace—] *F* ((In
peace)).   326-7. Noble . . . officer] *As Pope;* one line in *F.*   332. S.D.]
Hanmer; not in F.   333. First Sen.] *Rowe; Sena. / F.*   333. S.D. Exeunt.]
Exeunt Omnes / F.

tion with sophistications of language
Whiter cites *Comus*, 756, 'I hate when
vice can *bolt* her arguments', adding
that in his day disputations in law
'are still called *boultings*'.

321. *bring him*] F's *bring him in
peace* may be Compositor B's anticipation of l. 323; but the words *in peace*
could be Shakespeare's, with their
repetition (in parenthesis in F)
meant for emphasis. Gomme's reading, *bring him in*, is forceful but
needless, and it yields an excrescent
syllable.

322–3. *answer . . . peril*] i.e. stand
lawful trial even at the peril of his
life.

323. *Noble tribunes*] Cf. l. 269;
from the Senator, however, the phrase
seems a concession to the tribunes'
power, but it is a part of the appeal
to their 'humane' natures.

324. *humane*] properly human; not
differentiated from 'human' in Shakespeare's time, either in spelling or
pronunciation (the accent was on the
second syllable); cf. I. i. 18 'humanely'.

324-5. *course . . . bloody*] Cf. *Caes.*,
II. i. 162, 'Our course will seem too
bloody'.

329. *attend*] await.

[SCENE II]

Enter CORIOLANUS *with Nobles.*

Cor. Let them pull all about mine ears, present me
Death on the wheel, or at wild horses' heels,
Or pile ten hills on the Tarpeian rock,
That the precipitation might down stretch
Below the beam of sight: yet will I still   5
Be thus to them.

Enter VOLUMNIA.

Pat.   You do the nobler.
Cor. I muse my mother
Does not approve me further, who was wont

Scene II

SCENE II] *Capell.*
6. S.D.] *Placed as F; following* war (*l.13*) *Dyce after Collier².*   *Pat.*] *Capell:*
Noble | F; 1. Pat. | Malone.

Scene II] Most editors follow Pope
and locate in 'The House of Coriolanus'. Since Jacobean interiors often
employed the same architectural
conventions as the exterior façades,
the transition from public to domestic
setting would be easy (see also I. iii.
headnote).

S.D. Nobles] Shakespeare, like
North, uses the term co-extensively
with 'Patricians'; see Introduction,
p. 20.

2. *Death . . . heels*] Malone notes
that neither punishment was known
in Rome, but he and Case adduce
evidence to show that breaking upon
a wheel was a punishment known in
Shakespeare's time in England and
France, and that certain assassins in
the Netherlands and France were
torn to pieces by wild horses. Case
cites Dekker, *Old Fortunatus* (1600),
v. ii. 238–9, 'Thou shalt be torturd
on a wheele to death, / Thou with
wild horses shalt be quartered'. For a

sustained account of torture upon the
wheel see the closing pages of Nashe,
The Unfortunate Traveller (1594), where
Cutwolf the cobbler of Verona is
cruelly punished at Bologna.

4. *precipitation*] 'steepness of descent; precipitousness. *rare*' (*O.E.D.*,
s.v. I b, giving this as the only early
instance). Cf. III. iii. 102, where the
word occurs in its more usual sense.

5. *Below . . . sight*] i.e. beyond
reach of the eye; *beam of sight* = eye-
beam. Cf. North, 'as if the Senate
should hedlong cast downe the people
into a most bottomles pyt' (Appendix,
p. 330).

6. S.D.] Volumnia apparently
approaches in the course of Coriolanus' speech.

Pat.] F's *Noble* masks the possible
continuity between the speaker here
and at III. i. 259; see Introduction,
p. 20.

7. *muse*] wonder.

8. *further*] to a greater degree.

To call them woollen vassals, things created
To buy and sell with groats, to show bare heads   10
In congregations, to yawn, be still, and wonder,
When one but of my ordinance stood up
To speak of peace or war. I talk of you.
Why did you wish me milder? Would you have me
False to my nature? Rather say I play   15
The man I am.

Vol.   O sir, sir, sir.
I would have had you put your power well on
Before you had worn it out.

Cor.   Let go.

Vol. You might have been enough the man you are,
With striving less to be so: lesser had been   20
The thwartings of your dispositions, if
You had not show'd them how ye were dispos'd,

---

18. Let go] *F*; Let's go *F4*; Why, let it go *Hanmer*; Let't go *conj. Wilson*.
21. thwartings] *Theobald*; things *F*; things that thwart your *Rowe*; taxings
Sisson; crossings *Hibbard*; things that cross *conj. Wright*.

---

9. *woollen vassals*] slaves clad in coarse wool; cf. II. iii. 114, 'this woolvish toge', and *MND.*, III. i. 68, 'hempen homespuns'.

10. *groats*] English fourpenny pieces.

10–11. *show . . . congregations*] probably referring to the humble demeanour of gatherings assembled at the Capitol; cf. *Ado*, III. ii. 111, and III. iii. 145, 'at the temple . . . before the whole congregation'; elsewhere Shakespeare uses the word only once, metaphorically, in *Ham.*, II. ii. 299.

12. *ordinance*] 'rank, order (in the state)' (*O.E.D.*, s.v. 11, giving only this instance); elsewhere in Shakespeare the word is associated with divine edict or order, and it may here mean 'authority', as in *Lr.*, IV. i. 69.

18. *Let go*] Have done! No more of that! Cf., *John*, III. iii. 33, 'I had a thing to say—but let it go', which

has a slightly different effect ('never mind!').

21. *thwartings*] Schmidt retained F's *things* and explained it as an allusion to the plebeians, but the sense so yielded is clumsy and improbable. Theobald's *thwartings* does not occur elsewhere as a noun in Shakespeare, but it is rhetorically potent and could be misread. (Wilson aptly suggests a copy spelling 'thwarthings', with the compositor's eye skipping from 'th' to 'th'). Wright's conjecture and Hibbard's reading are defended as anticipations of *cross you* in l. 23. But the neatness of the repetition (chiming with *dispositions . . . dispos'd*) diminishes the impact of the lines, which owes much to the exploitation of two words expressing frustration. Sisson finds *taxings* more plausible graphically and the sense (public criticisms) more apt; but *dispositions* (inclinations, purposes) are more cogently thwarted than taxed.

Ere they lack'd power to cross you.
Cor.   Let them hang.
Vol. Ay, and burn too.

Enter MENENIUS *with the Senators.*

Men. Come, come, you have been too rough, something
    too rough.   25
    You must return and mend it.
First Sen.   There's no remedy,
    Unless by not so doing, our good city
    Cleave in the midst, and perish.
Vol.   Pray be counsell'd;
    I have a heart as little apt as yours,
    But yet a brain that leads my use of anger   30
    To better vantage.
Men.   Well said, noble woman.
    Before he should thus stoop to th'herd, but that
    The violent fit o'th'time craves it as physic
    For the whole state, I would put mine armour on,
    Which I can scarcely bear.
Cor.   What must I do?   35
Men. Return to th'tribunes.

25–6.] *As Pope; prose in F.*   26. *First Sen.*] *Capell; Sen.* | *F.*   29. as little apt]
F; as little soft conj. Singer; of mettle apt *conj. Staunion.*   32. herd] *Theobald;*
heart *F.*

23. *Ere . . . you*] i.e. before they
confirmed Coriolanus as consul.

24. *Ay . . . too*] As Wright observes,
this could be an aside; but it seems
unlikely. Volumnia, speaks at once
from her unapt heart (l. 29) and to
tactical effect, leading her 'use of
anger / To better vantage' (ll. 30–1).
Her arrogance, here and elsewhere,
has no warrant in North.

29. *apt*] yielding, compliant; cf.
Oth., II. iii. 309, *Caes.*, v. iii. 68, and
Ven., 354, 'As apt as new-fall'n snow
takes any dint'.

32. *herd*] Theobald's reading is the
more probable since F's usual spelling

of 'herd' was 'heard' (e.g. *Mer.V.*,
v. i. 71). Schmidt keeps *heart* and
treats the phrase as an emphatic one
comparable to *2H4*, II. iv. 9, 'It
ang'red him to the heart'; but *heart*
is infelicitously related to Volumnia's different use of it in l. 29.

33. *fit*] probably 'fever' but possibly
'paroxysm of lunacy'; Shakespeare
uses the word in both senses, the
second being rare elsewhere. Cf.
Caes., I. ii. 119–21, 'He had a fever
when he was in Spain, / And when
the fit was on him I did mark / How
he did shake' (cf. I. iv. 60 above),
and *Tit.*, IV. i. 17, 'Unless some fit
or frenzy do possess her'.

Cor.   Well, what then? what then?
Men. Repent what you have spoke.
Cor. For them? I cannot do it to the gods,
       Must I then do't to them?
Vol.   You are too absolute.
       Though therein you can never be too noble,   40
       But when extremities speak. I have heard you say,
       Honour and policy, like unsever'd friends,
       I'th'war do grow together: grant that, and tell me,
       In peace what each of them by th'other lose
       That they combine not there.
Cor.   Tush, tush!
Men.   A good demand.
Vol. If it be honour in your wars to seem   46
       The same you are not, which, for your best ends
       You adopt your policy, how is it less or worse
       That it shall hold companionship in peace
       With honour, as in war, since that to both   50
       It stands in like request?
Cor.   Why force you this?

---

38. them?] *F3;* them, *F.*

39. *absolute*] positive; hence inflexible, uncompromising; cf. III. i. 89.
40–1. *therein . . . speak*] i.e. you
cannot be too uncompromisingly
noble except in situations of extreme
crisis. The terse syntax masks the
anomalies of Volumnia's position.
Hibbard, however, reads a stop after
noble, and a comma after *speak*, thus
relating *extremities* to the conditions
under which honour and policy are
said to meet; but it is more probable
that they should keep constant company in war. There is no precise analogue in North for the views that
Volumnia attributes to Coriolanus,
and they are allowed no scope in the
play, but in the 'Comparison of
Coriolanus with Alcibiades' it is said
that 'both of them in their charge
were alike hardy and valiant for
their persons, as also wise and

politick in the wars'. For policy in
war cf. *1H6*, III. ii. 2. Volumnia
appears to misjudge the nature of her
son's nobility.

42. *unsever'd*] inseparable. Wright
compares 'unvalued' for 'invaluable'
in *R3*, I. iv. 27.

46–51. *If . . . request*] i.e. if it is
honourable in war to use dissimula-
tion as a policy to achieve your ends,
why should it be otherwise in peace-
time, since in peace and war alike,
honour and policy are equally
necessary? The perplexities of syntax
arise from the three uses of *it* in
ll. 48, 49, and 51; the first is un-
attached, the second refers back to
policy, and the third refers back to
companionship.

51. *force*] enforce, urge; cf. *H8*,
III. ii. 2.

Vol. Because that now it lies you on to speak
    To th'people; not by your own instruction,
    Nor by th'matter which your heart prompts you,
    But with such words that are but roted in   55
    Your tongue, though but bastards and syllables
    Of no allowance to your bosom's truth.
    Now, this no more dishonours you at all,
    Than to take in a town with gentle words
    Which else would put you to your fortune and   60
    The hazard of much blood.
    I would dissemble with my nature where
    My fortunes and my friends at stake requir'd
    I should do so in honour. I am in this
    Your wife, your son, these senators, the nobles;   65

52–6.] *As Malone;* Because, that / . . . people: / . . . matter / . . . words / . . . Tongue; / . . . Syllables. / *F.*   52. you on] *F;* on you *Pope.*   55. roted] *Malone;* roated *F;* rooted *Johnson.*   65. son, these] *Theobald;* Sonne: These *F.* nobles;] *Capell;* Nobles, *F.*

52. *lies you on*] it is incumbent on you. For the placing of the preposition Wilson compares *R 2*, II. iii. 138, 'It stands your Grace upon to do him right'. Cf. *R 3*, IV. ii. 60, and *Ham.*, v. ii. 63.

52–6.] F's lineation is more than usually indefensible in this passage. It yields one inexplicably short line, three awkwardly extended pentameters, and two octosyllabics. The variations have no expressive appropriateness. See Introduction, p. 15.

53. *not . . . instruction*] not according to your own precepts and convictions. Volumnia distinguishes *instruction* from the promptings of the heart. Coriolanus must obey neither if the 'policy' is to work. Cf. III. i. 255–8 note, and below, ll. 100–1.

55–6. *roted . . . tongue*] i.e. that the tongue has got by rote. Johnson's *rooted* yields an acceptable metaphor and consorts naturally with *in*; but *roted* is the more precise word, and *in* may be due, as Case says, to 'preoccupation with place'. Without alleging a pun, it is possible also to

recognize the pressure of one word upon the other, with some contact of sound, usage, and sense. No earlier use of *roted* is recorded, but Shakespeare makes several uses of *rote*, e.g. *Rom.*, II. iii. 88, 'Thy love did read by rote that could not spell'.

56–7. *bastards . . . allowance*] i.e. illegitimate words that truth would not acknowledge.

59. *take in*] capture; cf. I. ii. 24.

62–4. *I would . . . honour*] I would pretend to be other than I am, if, because my fortunes and friends were at risk, honour so required it.

64. *I am in this*] Retaining F's punctuation, the meaning is, 'In this, I speak for your wife . . .' Many, however, follow Johnson in placing a comma after *this* and inviting the stress to fall on *I*; the meaning then becomes, 'I am involved in this, and so is your wife . . .' Either interpretation is admissible, since all at risk can be assumed to speak with one voice; but the first may be preferred since it entails no intervention in the text.

And you will rather show our general louts
How you can frown, than spend a fawn upon 'em
For the inheritance of their loves and safeguard
Of what that want might ruin.

Men.   Noble lady!
Come, go with us; speak fair; you may salve so   70
Not what is dangerous present, but the loss
Of what is past.

Vol.   I prithee now, my son,
Go to them, with this bonnet in thy hand,
And thus far having stretch'd it—here be with them—
Thy knee bussing the stones—for in such business   75

69. lady!] *Rowe;* Lady, *F.*   74. —here . . . them—] *F* ((here . . . them)).

66. *general louts*] the vulgar clowns of our community (Case).

68. *inheritance*] acquisition.

68–9. *safeguard . . . ruin*] protection of that which might be ruined for lack of such fawning.

71. *Not . . . but*] not only . . . but also; cf. III. iii. 97.

72, 89, 98, 107. *prithee*] King remarks that Volumnia's repetition of *prithee* is 'one of the effects that in this scene detract from her dignity'; but there is no necessary indignity in pleading, the dishonour is an attribute of Volumnia's code (see l. 124).

72–86. *I prithee . . . person*] The expressiveness of this speech owes much to gesture and mimicry, and its difficulties cannot be resolved by attention merely to its syntax and argument.

73. *bonnet*] cap or hat; cf. *R2*, I. iv. 31. Shakespeare's Roman conspirators unclassically pluck their hats about their ears in *Caes.*, II. i. 73. See Introduction, p. 74.

74. *stretch'd it*] i.e. reached forward in obeisance. Or possibly, 'having gone so far to meet them'.

here . . . them] go along with them; or, possibly, 'go all the way with them' (see last note). Editorial paraphrases include, 'adopt this action' (Staunton), 'get hold of them'

(Beeching), 'humour them thus much' (Verity), 'go thus far with them' (Gordon), 'get at them this way' (Case), 'comply with their wish' (Hibbard), and 'do what they want' (Gomme). After enlisting a number of parallels to show that the phrase 'varies in meaning according to circumstance', Case observes that in Shakespeare it always indicates that the speaker is conscious of making a good move against another, or that he fears to be caught at a disadvantage himself (cf. *Lr.*, IV. vi. 145, *AYL.*, v. ii. 27, and *Wint.*, I. ii. 217). In Brome's *Joviall Crew* (1641), first cited by Staunton, a beggar pretending to be a cripple says of his patron, 'here I was with him' (II. i, *Works*, 1873, III, p. 380), meaning perhaps, 'at this point I took him in'. It is possible, after all, to take Volumnia's phrase quite literally, 'at this point come right up to them', but an idiom seems more probable. Brooks suggests 'match yourself with them', in a double sense—'do what they want' and 'act against them'.

75. *bussing*] kissing. Case claims that it was not then a vulgar word, citing *John*, III. iv. 35, 'And buss thee as thy wife'. But Wright quotes *Troil.*, IV. v. 220, 'Yond towers,

Action is eloquence, and the eyes of th'ignorant
More learned than the ears—waving thy head,
Which often, thus, correcting thy stout heart,
Now humble as the ripest mulberry
That will not hold the handling; or say to them,   80
Thou art their soldier, and being bred in broils,
Hast not the soft way which, thou dost confess,

---

78. Which] *F;* And *Capell;* With *conj. Johnson;* While *conj. Staunton.*   often,
thus,] *F* (often thus).   80. or] *F; omitted Hanmer.*

---

whose wanton tops do buss the
clouds', to illustrate the association
with 'coarseness or wantonness'. A
suggestion of vulgar abasement is
apt in the context. King notes the
ironical play of *bussing* and *businesse*
(F).

76–7. *Action . . . ears*] Case compares Bacon, 'Of Boldnesse' (*Essays*,
1625, no. 12): 'Question was asked of
*Demosthenes: What was the Chiefe Part
of an Oratour?* He answered, *Action;*
what next? *Action;* what next again?
Action. He said it, that knew it best;
. . . A strange thing . . . But the reason
is plaine. There is in Humane
Nature, generally, more of the Foole
then of the Wise'. The story is also
told by Erasmus. See Introduction,
p. 47.

77. *waving*] Cf. *Ham.*, II. i. 93, 'And
thrice his head thus waving up and
down'. But Volumnia may be bowing
in all directions.

78. *Which . . . thus*] *Which* in *F*
refers to *head* and requires that the
demonstrative gesture which follows
(*thus*) should be made with the head
and should take the place of a verb in
the sentence. If Johnson's *With* or
Staunton's *While* are accepted, the
gesture could be with the hands. If
Volumnia is kneeling (which seems
likely) and *waving* (i.e. bowing) her
head remorsefully, she may at this
point hide her face slowly and
gently in one hand while resting the
other on her heart (cf. the expression
of shame, *pudet*, illustrated from

Bulwer in Bertram Joseph, *Elizabethan Acting*, 1964, p. 50); the whole
body would then convey the vulnerability suggested by the *ripest mulberry* in l. 79.

stout] proud (German, *stolz*); cf.
Tw.N., II. v. 151, and North's
marginal note, 'Coriolanus stowtnes
in defence of him selfe' (Appendix,
p. 338).

79. *humble . . . mulberry*] For the
mulberry as a symbol of a yielding
disposition Case cites Erasmus, *Ad-
ages*, under Proclivitas, 'Maturior
moro'. Some have mistakenly attempted to read *humble* as a verb.
The point is that ripe mulberries are
too soft to take hold of without
crushing. For the 'soft phrase of
peace' and the warrior cf. *Oth.*,
I. iii. 82. Fripp (II, p. 709) observes
that many mulberries were planted
early in 1608 in the hope of cultivating the silk-worm, but the culture of
silk-worms had been a concern for
some years (e.g. T. Moffett, *Silk-
worms*, 1599). For the alleged bearing
on the date of the play see Introduction, p. 25.

80. *hold*] bear, stand up to; as in
Ham., v. i. 161, and *Tim.*, I. ii. 148,
where Apemantus says of the ladies
of Athens that the worst 'would not
hold taking'.

or say] The *or* is apparently not
exclusive but equivalent to 'or
again'.

81–4. *Thou . . . loves*] Cf. III. i.
317–20.

Were fit for thee to use, as they to claim,
In asking their good loves; but thou wilt frame
Thyself, forsooth, hereafter theirs, so far   85
As thou hast power and person.
Men.   This but done,
Even as she speaks, why, their hearts were yours:
For they have pardons, being ask'd, as free
As words to little purpose.
Vol.   Prithee now,
Go, and be rul'd; although I know thou hadst rather
Follow thine enemy in a fiery gulf   91
Than flatter him in a bower.

Enter COMINIUS.

                                   Here is Cominius.
Com. I have been i'th'market place; and, sir, 'tis fit
You make strong party, or defend yourself
By calmness or by absence. All's in anger.   95
Men. Only fair speech.
Com.   I think 'twill serve, if he
Can thereto frame his spirit.
Vol.   He must, and will:
Prithee now, say you will, and go about it.
Cor. Must I go show them my unbarb'd sconce? Must I

92.] *As Capell; two lines in F, dividing* Bower. | .   96–7. I . . . spirit] *As Rowe³;
prose in F.*   99. unbarb'd] *F;* unbarbed *Rowe.*   99–100] Must . . . sconce?
Must I / With my] *Capell;* Must . . . Sconce? / Must I with my *F;* Must . . .
sconce? / Must my *Pope;* Must . . . sconce? / With my *Wilson.*

85–6. *so far . . . person*] to the full
extent of thy personal authority.

88. *free*] i.e. 'generous, freely
offered' in relation to *pardons*, and
'ready, gratuitous' in relation to
words. For Menenius' judgement of
the citizens see Introduction, p. 55.

91. *fiery gulf*] an abyss full of flame
(*O.E.D.,* gulf, 4, citing this passage).
'Gulf' in Shakespeare usually means
whirlpool, however; and the image
is undeveloped and phantasmagoric,
not specific enough to be related to
volcanic action (as in *O.E.D.*),

to hell-fire (see III. iii. 68) or to
burning cities.

92. *bower*] either 'leafy covert',
as elsewhere in Shakespeare (e.g.
1H4, III. i. 209), or 'boudoir, a lady's
private apartment', which seems
more probable; cf. *R3,* I. i. 12,
where 'Grim-visag'd war . . . capers
nimbly in a lady's chamber'.

99. *Must I . . . Must I*] For the
repetition cf. *R2,* IV. i. 228.

unbarb'd sconce] unprotected, un-
covered head; *unbarbed* is not used
elsewhere by Shakespeare and *barbed*

With my base tongue give to my noble heart   100
A lie that it must bear? Well, I will do't:
Yet were there but this single plot to lose,
This mould of Martius, they to dust should grind it
And throw't against the wind. To th'market-place!
You have put me now to such a part which never   105
I shall discharge to th'life.

Com.   Come, come, we'll prompt you.

Vol. I prithee now, sweet son, as thou hast said
My praises made thee first a soldier, so,
To have my praise for this, perform a part
Thou hast not done before.

Cor.   Well, I must do't.   110
Away my disposition, and possess me
Some harlot's spirit! My throat of war be turn'd,
Which choired with my drum, into a pipe

---

101. bear? Well,] *Pope;* beare well? *F.*   102. plot to lose,] *Theobald;* Plot, to loose *F.*   113. choired] *F* (quier'd); quiered *Cam.*

is twice used for the armour of horses (e.g. *R3*, I. i. 10). *O.E.D.* (unbarbed *ppl. a.*²) gives 'unarmed, not caparisoned' citing this example. *Sconce* (Lat. *abscondo*, conceal) may mean a fort (*H5*, III. vi. 71), a helmet (*Err.*, II. ii. 37), and, hence, a head (*Ham.*, v. i. 99). The phrase is therefore a very military rendering of 'bare head'. Stevens proposed 'unshaven head', observing that Roman suppliants had to present themselves in a neglected state.

100. *noble*] i.e. patrician. Coriolanus' social and moral judgements are at this point indistinguishable.

102. *single plot*] i.e. the piece of earth that is Martius. Cf. *Sonn.*, CXXXVII. 9.

103. *mould*] The dominant sense is probably 'earth regarded as the material of the human body' (*O.E.D.*, s.v. *sb.*¹ 4), recalling 'single plot' and anticipating 'dust'. But the sense 'form', as in *Wint.*, II. iii. 102, 'mould and frame', and *Ham.*, III. i. 153, 'the mould of form', is inescapably present. Cf. below, v. iii.

22–3, where Martius calls Volumnia 'the honour'd mould / Wherein this trunk was fram'd'.

105. *such . . . which*] For the construction cf. Abbott 278.

part] For the theatre metaphor cf. v. iii. 40–1.

106. *discharge*] perform; as in *MND.*, I. ii. 82, and IV. ii. 8, 'You have not a man in all Athens able to discharge Pyramus but he'.

112. *harlot's*] beggar's, vagabond's. There may be a contemptuous allusion to actors, as in *1H4*, II. iv. 385, 'these harlotry players'; but the sense 'prostitute' was used by Shakespeare several times (e.g. *Ham.*, III. i. 51).

113. *choired with*] made music with, harmonized with; cf. *Mer.V.*, v. i. 62. *O.E.D.* finds the past participle 'rare' and does not cite this passage.

pipe] i.e. the throat as instrument of a piping voice; cf. *AYL.*, II. vii. 162, and *Tw.N.*, I. iv. 31–2, 'thy small pipe / Is as the maiden's organ, shrill and sound'.

Small as an eunuch, or the virgin voice
That babies lull asleep! The smiles of knaves   115
Tent in my cheeks, and schoolboys' tears take up
The glasses of my sight! A beggar's tongue
Make motion through my lips, and my arm'd knees
Who bow'd but in my stirrup, bend like his
That hath receiv'd an alms! I will not do't,   120
Lest I surcease to honour mine own truth,
And by my body's action teach my mind
A most inherent baseness.

Vol.   At thy choice then:
To beg of thee it is my more dishonour
Than thou of them. Come all to ruin; let   125
Thy mother rather feel thy pride than fear
Thy dangerous stoutness, for I mock at death
With as big heart as thou. Do as thou list.

---

115. lull] *F;* lulls *Rowe.*   129. suck'st] *F;* suck'dst *Rowe*[3].

---

115. *lull*] The plural object, *babies,* has attracted the verb; the solecism is probably Shakespeare's, not the compositor's. Wright compares *Ham.,* I. ii. 36–7, 'More than the scope / Of these delated articles allow'.

115–20. *The smiles . . . alms*] For comment on the language of this passage see Introduction, p. 69.

116. *Tent . . . take up*] camp . . . occupy. Coriolanus is probably adapting the terms of siege warfare. For *Tent, O.E.D.* (*v.*[6] 1 b) has 'sojourn', quoting this instance. White, however, thought *tent in* an allusion to the tent-stitch, meaning 'catch or draw in'; this is just possible.

117. *glasses of my sight*] eyeballs. Used of tearful eyes in *R2,* I. iii. 208–9, 'even in the glasses of thine eyes / I see thy grieved heart', and *R2,* II. ii. 16–17, 'For sorrow's eye, glazed with blinding tears, / Divides one thing entire to many perspectives'.

121. *surcease*] cease; cf. *Rom.,* IV. i. 97, and *Lucr.,* 1766.

122–3. *body . . . baseness*] For the significance of this insight in the play as a whole see Introduction, p. 46.

123. *inherent*] 'cleaving fast . . . permanently indwelling' (*O.E.D.,* s.v. 2, quoting this instance); not elsewhere in Shakespeare.

126–7. *feel . . . stoutness*] Volumnia's predicament registers in difficulties of paraphrase. Johnson says, 'Perhaps she means, "Go, do thy worst; let me rather feel the utmost extremity that thy pride can bring upon me, than live thus in fear of thy dangerous obstinacy"'. Case objects that Johnson 'practically identifies "pride" with "stoutness", which more nearly corresponds with "valiantness", in line 129'. Volumnia does seem ready to suffer rather than merely to fear the *dangerous stoutness* that is a negative manifestation of Coriolanus' *pride,* and she attempts to distinguish *valiantness* from both. For *stoutness* = obstinacy see V. vi. 27 below, and for *stout* = proud, above, l. 78 and note. Cf. North,

Thy valiantness was mine, thou suck'st it from me,
But owe thy pride thyself.
Cor.   Pray be content.   130
Mother, I am going to the market-place:
Chide me no more. I'll mountebank their loves,
Cog their hearts from them, and come home belov'd
Of all the trades in Rome. Look, I am going.
Commend me to my wife. I'll return consul,   135
Or never trust to what my tongue can do
I'th'way of flattery further.
Vol.   Do your will.   *Exit.*
Com. Away! The tribunes do attend you: arm yourself
To answer mildly; for they are prepar'd
With accusations, as I hear, more strong   140
Than are upon you yet.
Cor. The word is 'mildly'. Pray you, let us go.
Let them accuse me by invention: I
Will answer in mine honour.
Men.   Ay, but mildly.
Cor. Well, mildly be it then. Mildly!   *Exeunt.*   145

137. S.D. *Exit*] *Exit Volumnia* / F.

Appendix, p. 333, 'stowte man of nature'; '*stowtnes*' (pp. 314, 337) is a rendering of Amyot's French, *force*.

130. *owe*] own (a common Shakespearean sense).

132. *mountebank*] the earliest instance of the verb cited in *O.E.D.* Case recalls Peregrine's description of Italian mountebanks in *Volpone*, II. ii. 5–6, 'quacksalvers, / Fellows that live by venting oil and drugs'. Cf. *Err.*, I. ii. 101, 'Disguised cheaters, prating mountebanks'.

133. *Cog*] wheedle, swindle; cf. *R 3*,

I. iii. 47–8, 'Because I cannot flatter and look fair, / Smile in men's faces, smooth, deceive, and cog'. The word is used about cheating at dice in *LLL.*, v. ii. 235; and Case argues its derivation from the cogs of a mill, the caster turning (cogging) the die with his finger.

142. *word*] pass-word, order of the day; cf. *Mer.V.*, III. v. 45, *Ham.*, I. v. 110, and *Caes*, v. v. 4, 'Slaying is the word'.

143. *accuse . . . invention*] invent accusations against me.

[SCENE III]

Enter SICINIUS *and* BRUTUS.

Bru. In this point charge him home, that he affects
Tyrannical power. If he evade us there,
Enforce him with his envy to the people,
And that the spoil got on the Antiates
Was ne'er distributed.

Enter an Ædile.

What, will he come?   5

Æd. He's coming.
Bru.   How accompanied?
Æd. With old Menenius, and those senators
That always favour'd him.
Sic.   Have you a catalogue
Of all the voices that we have procur'd,
Set down by th'poll?

Scene III

SCENE III] *Capell.*   5–6. Was . . . accompanied?] *F*; distributed. / . . .
accompanied? *Capell.*   5. S.D.] *As Capell; follows* come *in F.*   9–10. Of . . .
poll?] *As Pope; one line in F.*

Scene III] usually located in 'The
Forum' or the market-place. North
speaks of the people 'ronning to the
market place out of all partes of the
cittie' (Appendix, p. 336) but sets
some of the subsequent procedures in
the senate-house; Shakespeare keeps
all the judicial procedures wholly
public, with the voices of the populace instantly heard.

1. *charge . . . home*] press home your
charges; cf. I. iv. 38, II. ii. 103, IV. ii.
48.

3. *Enforce him*] urge against him.
envy to] malice against.

4–5. *spoil . . . distributed*] Cf.
North, 'And for the third, they charged him a newe, that he had not made
the common distribution of the
spoyle he had gotten in the invading
the territories of the Antiates'

(Appendix, p. 341). The play, of
course, does not support this charge
(see I. ix. 37–40, II. ii. 124–9).

9–11. *voices . . . tribes*] North
reports that the tribunes preferred
that 'the people would proceede to
geve their voyces by Tribes, and not
by hundreds: for by this meanes the
multitude of the poore needy people
. . . came to be of greater force
(bicause their voyces were numbred
by the polle) then the noble honest
cittizens' (Appendix, pp. 340–1). The
parenthetic allusion to 'voyces numbred by the polle' translates Amyot,
'a cause que les voix se contoyent
par teste', and has no equivalent in
the Greek. The tribes were territorial
districts of Rome (twenty to thirty-
five in number) and the centuries
were a hundred and ninety-three

Æd.   I have: 'tis ready.   10
Sic. Have you collected them by tribes?
Æd.   I have.
Sic. Assemble presently the people hither:
    And when they hear me say, 'It shall be so
    I'th'right and strength o'th'commons,' be it either
    For death, for fine, or banishment, then let them   15
    If I say fine, cry 'Fine', if death, cry 'Death',
    Insisting on the old prerogative
    And power i'th'truth o'th'cause.
Æd.   I shall inform them.
Bru. And when such time they have begun to cry,
    Let them not cease, but with a din confus'd   20
    Enforce the present execution
    Of what we chance to sentence.
Æd.   Very well.
Sic. Make them be strong, and ready for this hint
    When we shall hap to give't them.
Bru.   Go about it.
                                        [*Exit Ædile.*]
    Put him to choler straight; he hath been us'd   25
    Ever to conquer, and to have his worth

24. S.D.] *Pope; not in F.*

---

subdivisions of five classes discriminated by wealth, so arranged
that ninety-eight were in patricians'
control. Plutarch recognized that
voting by centuries yielded a patrician
majority while voting by tribes gave
'three voyces odde' banishing Coriolanus for life. In the play, the
voices . . . Set down by th'poll are
apparently the votes regist'ered by a
count of heads in the course of
determining the judgement of the
tribes. Wilson, however, relates them
to the cries in chorus organized in
ll. 15–16. That Shakespeare had
Elizabethan procedure in mind is
suggested by J. E. Neale's observation that 'lists compiled during
canvassing' came in useful 'for
marshalling the voters' (*Elizabethan*

House of Commons, 1949, p. 88). See
Introduction, p. 48.

12. *presently*] immediately.

17. *old prerogative*] probably, 'the
right and strength of the commons';
possibly, 'the ancient precedence of
the people's verdict'. Cf. North,
'More also, that it was not for
contempt of nobilitie or the Senate,
that they sought to have the
authoritie of justice in their handes,
as a preheminence and prerogative
of honour' (Appendix, p. 340).

18. *power . . . cause*] a demagogic
flourish, possibly meaning 'the power
that the truth of their cause gives
them'.

21. *Enforce . . . execution*] insist
upon the immediate carrying out.

26–7. *his . . . contradiction*] 'his

Of contradiction. Being once chaf'd, he cannot
Be rein'd again to temperance; then he speaks
What's in his heart, and that is there which looks
With us to break his neck.

Sic.   Well, here he comes.   30

Enter CORIOLANUS, MENENIUS, *and* COMINIUS, *with others.*

Men. Calmly, I do beseech you.

Cor. Ay, as an hostler, that for th'poorest piece
Will bear the knave by th'volume. Th'honour'd gods
Keep Rome in safety, and the chairs of justice
Supplied with worthy men, plant love among's,   35
Throng our large temples with the shows of peace
And not our streets with war.

30. S.D.] *As Dyce; follows* neck *in* F.   32. hostler] *F;* ostler *Hanmer.*   for
th'] *F2;* fourth *F.*   33.] *As Pope;* Will . . . Volume: / . . . Goddes / *F.*
35. among's] *Dyce;* amongs *F;* amongst you *F2;* amongst us *Var.* '73.
36. Throng] *Theobald;* Through *F.*

pennyworth of answering back (that
is, give as good as he gets)' (Hibbard).
But the phrase is much disputed.
Hibbard quotes Holland's Livy (Bullough, p. 501) where the people
complain that famine threatened
them 'unlesse the Tribunes be
delivered and yeelded prisoners hands
and foot bound to *C. Martius*, unlesse
he might have his penniworths of the
backe and shoulders of the commons
of Rome', but the parallel assists
more with *worth* than with *contradiction*. Capell and Malone also
retain *worth* as 'pennyworth', Malone
citing *Rom.*, IV. v. 4–5, 'You take
your pennyworths now. / Sleep for a
week'. Schmidt, however, takes *worth*
as 'worthiness, repute', attributed to
Coriolanus' way of carrying his
point by contradiction; Wilson, in
support, says that Coriolanus flourishes in opposition and quotes North
on Martius' conviction 'that to overcome allwayes, and to have the upper
hande in all matters, was a token of
magnanimitie' (Appendix, p. 333).

If Schmidt is right, Brutus alludes
ironically to Coriolanus' worthiness;
but as the construction is awkward
and the drift improbable, the meaner
version is more likely, 'enjoying his
fill of contumely and defiance'.

29. *looks*] looks likely, promises
(*O.E.D.*, s.v. 8 b, citing only this
passage).

30. *With us*] i.e. with our assistance.

32. *piece*] i.e. coin.

33. *Will . . . volume*] will put up
with being called knave any number
of times; cf. *R2*, I. iv. 18, 'volume of
farewells'.

34. *chairs of justice*] Case quotes
North's Plutarch, 'Life of Brutus'
(1595), p. 1057, 'His tribunal (or
chaire) where he gave audience
during the time he was Praetor'.
(S.H.P., VII, p. 114.)

36. *shows of peace*] probably the
spectacle and pageants appropriate
to peace, for which Shakespeare may
have had Elizabethan models in
mind; but possibly, everyday scenes
of piety and good order. For the

First Sen.   Amen, amen.
Men. A noble wish.

              Enter the Ædile with the Plebeians.

Sic. Draw near, ye people.
Æd. List to your tribunes. Audience! Peace, I say!   40
Cor. First, hear me speak!
Both Trib.   Well, say. Peace, ho!
Cor. Shall I be charg'd no further than this present?
    Must all determine here?
Sic.   I do demand,
    If you submit you to the people's voices,
    Allow their officers, and are content   45
    To suffer lawful censure for such faults
    As shall be prov'd upon you.
Cor.   I am content.
Men. Lo, citizens, he says he is content.
    The warlike service he has done, consider: think
    Upon the wounds his body bears, which show   50
    Like graves i'th'holy churchyard.
Cor.   Scratches with briers,
    Scars to move laughter only.
Men.   Consider further,
    That when he speaks not like a citizen,
    You find him like a soldier. Do not take

40.] *As Steevens;* List . . . Audience: / . . . say. / *F.*   51–2. Scratches . . .
only.] *As Capell;* Scratches . . . moue / . . . onely. *F.*

first use cf. *LLL.*, v. i. 95, 'some
delightful ostentation, or show, or
pageant, or antic, or firework'; and
for the general sense 'manifestations,
appearances' cf. *Ado*, IV. i. 39. See
Introduction, pp. 35–6.

40. *Audience!*] Attend!

42. *Shall . . . present*] Will no other
charges be brought against me on a
further occasion? Cf. North, Appendix, p. 340, where Coriolanus
submits to trial upon the charge of
tyranny, 'conditionally . . . that you
charge me with nothing els besides'.

43. *determine*] conclude, be decided.

45. *Allow*] acknowledge. For a
similar use of 'allowance' see III. ii. 57.

51. *graves . . . churchyard*] 'We are
left at liberty to think of the size, or
the number of the wounds, or of the
sanctity of the hero's person, in the
comparison' (Case). We may also
think of each scar as a memorial to
the enemy who inflicted it, cf. II. i.
154–5, 'every gash was an enemy's
grave' (where Menenius is also the
speaker). Cf. *MND.*, v. i. 369
'graves all gaping wide', and *2H4*,
II. iv. 188, 'ghastly, grievous, gaping
wounds'.

His rougher accents for malicious sounds,   55
But, as I say, such as become a soldier,
Rather than envy you.
Com.   Well, well, no more.
Cor. What is the matter,
That being pass'd for consul with full voice,
I am so dishonour'd that the very hour   60
You take it off again?
Sic.   Answer to us.
Cor. Say then: 'tis true, I ought so.
Sic. We charge you, that you have contriv'd to take
From Rome all season'd office, and to wind
Yourself into a power tyrannical;   65
For which you are a traitor to the people.
Cor. How! Traitor?
Men.   Nay, temperately: your promise!
Cor. The fires i'th'lowest hell fold in the people!
Call me their traitor! Thou injurious tribune!

---

55. accents] *Theobald;* Actions *F.*   68. hell fold] *Pope;* hell. Fould *F.*

---

55. *rougher*] probably 'rougher
than other men's', but possibly
distinguishing his rougher manner
from the milder one he is trying to
assume.

accents] Supporting Theobald's
reading, Sisson (*New Readings*) suggests that *accents* was misread by the
compositor as *accōns* (= *actions*).

57. *envy you*] show malice against
you, but perhaps with a suggestion of
grudging the people their power; cf.
ll. 95–6 below and l. 3 above.

64. *season'd*] 'established and settled
by time' (Johnson), a sense supported
by *O.E.D.* (s.v. 3 b). But Case,
following Schmidt, is probably right
to see an antithesis between *season'd*
office and *power tyrannical*, with
'season'd' meaning 'qualified, tempered'. Onions gives (a) matured,
(b) made palatable, and other
passages offer a similar ambiguity
(e.g. *Mer.V.*, v. i. 107–8), 'How many

things by season season'd are / To
their right praise and true perfection'.
The fact that the tribunate was an
innovation need not deter Sicinius
(or Shakespeare) from claiming the
virtues of maturity for the system in
which he plays a part.

wind] insinuate.

65. *power tyrannical*] North says
that the tribunes tried to prove that
all Martius' actions 'tended to
usurpe tyrannicall power over Rome'
(Appendix, p. 340).

67. *Traitor*] Shakespeare's featuring
of this word has no occasion in the
source, where Coriolanus is particularly provoked by the charge that
he failed to distribute the spoil from
the Antiates (Appendix, p. 341).

68. *hell fold*] F's punctuation is probably a careless misreading, not the expression of an emphatic pause.

69. *injurious*] calumniating, insulting (Onions).

Within thine eyes sat twenty thousand deaths,   70
In thy hands clutch'd as many millions, in
Thy lying tongue both numbers, I would say
'Thou liest' unto thee, with a voice as free
As I do pray the gods.
Sic.   Mark you this, people?
All Pleb. To th'rock, to th'rock with him.   75
Sic. Peace!
We need not put new matter to his charge.
What you have seen him do, and heard him speak,
Beating your officers, cursing yourselves,
Opposing laws with strokes, and here defying   80
Those whose great power must try him—even this,
So criminal and in such capital kind,
Deserves th'extremest death.
Bru.   But since he hath
Serv'd well for Rome—
Cor.   What do you prate of service?
Bru. I talk of that, that know it.
Cor.   You?   85
Men. Is this the promise that you made your mother?
Com. Know, I pray you—
Cor.   I'll know no further.
Let them pronounce the steep Tarpeian death,
Vagabond exile, flaying, pent to linger

70–1. deaths, ... clutch'd as] *Rowe;* deaths ... clutcht: as *F.*   71–2. millions, ... tongue] *Rowe;* Millions ... tongue, *F.*   72. numbers, I] *F* (numbers I).   75, 106, 119, 137, 142. *All Pleb.*] *F* (*All*.).   81–2. even ... kind,]
As Pope; one line in F.   83–4. But ... Rome—] *As Pope; one line in F.*

70. *Within*] introduces a subjunctive construction (= If within),
as Rowe's adjustments of F's punctuation make clear.

71. *clutch'd*] In Jonson's *Poetaster*,
Crispinus (Marston) is made to
cough up the word 'clutch' when
given a pill by Horace (v. iii. 555).
O.E.D. cites the relevant Marston
passage, *Antonio's Revenge* (1602),
Prol., 'The earth is cloucht / In the
dull leaden hand of snoring sleepe',
as the earliest occurrence in the sense
'hold tightly in the hand'. Shake-

speare's uses here and in *Mac.*, II. i.
34, were comparatively novel.

73. *free*] open, candid.

82. *So ... kind*] For the intensified
degree of capital desert cf. *Ham.*,
IV. vii. 7, 'So crimeful and so capital
in nature'.

85. *I talk ... know it*] Cf. IV. vii. 31,
where Aufidius remarks, 'The tribunes are no soldiers'. Brutus'
service is of the civic kind, unacknow-
ledged by Coriolanus.

89. *pent*] i.e. let me be pent (im-
prisoned).

But with a grain a day, I would not buy   90
Their mercy at the price of one fair word,
Nor check my courage for what they can give,
To have't with saying, 'Good morrow'.

Sic.   For that he has,
As much as in him lies, from time to time
Envied against the people, seeking means   95
To pluck away their power, as now at last
Given hostile strokes, and that not in the presence
Of dreaded justice, but on the ministers
That doth distribute it—in the name o'th'people,
And in the power of us the tribunes, we,   100
Ev'n from this instant, banish him our city,
In peril of precipitation
From off the rock Tarpeian, never more
To enter our Rome gates. I'th'people's name,
I say it shall be so.   105

All Pleb. It shall be so, it shall be so! Let him away!
He's banish'd, and it shall be so!

Com. Hear me, my masters, and my common friends!

Sic. He's sentenc'd: no more hearing.

Com.   Let me speak.
I have been consul, and can show for Rome   110
Her enemies' marks upon me. I do love
My country's good with a respect more tender,
More holy and profound, than mine own life,
My dear wife's estimate, her womb's increase
And treasure of my loins: then if I would   115
Speak that—

Sic.   We know your drift. Speak what?

99. doth] *F*; doe *F2*.   110. for] *Theobald*; from *F*.

92. *courage*] Collier found the vaunt inconsistent with Coriolanus' nobility and 'corrected' to *carriage*. Dyce glosses 'spirit, mettle' and compares *3H6*, II. ii. 57.

95. *Envied*] shown malice (by grudging power to the people); cf. l. 57 above.

97. *not*] not only; cf. III. ii. 71.

99. *doth*] The singular form is possibly owed to the attraction of *it*.

104. *Rome gates*] Shakespeare often used proper names as adjectives; cf. I. viii. 8, II. i. 162, and Abbott 22.

105. *it shall be so*] The phrase is offered by Sicinius in l. 13, transposed in ll. 104–5, and transformed into an imperative incantatory cry in l. 106.

114. *estimate*] repute, honour.

Bru. There's no more to be said but he is banish'd,
       As enemy to the people and his country.
       It shall be so!
All Pleb.   It shall be so, it shall be so!
Cor. You common cry of curs! whose breath I hate   120
       As reek o'th'rotten fens, whose loves I prize
       As the dead carcasses of unburied men
       That do corrupt my air: I banish you!
       And here remain with your uncertainty!
       Let every feeble rumour shake your hearts!   125
       Your enemies, with nodding of their plumes,
       Fan you into despair! Have the power still
       To banish your defenders, till at length

120. *cry*] pack; as in *MND.*, iv. i. 121–2, 'A cry more tuneable / Was never holla'd to, nor cheer'd with horn', and *Ham.*, iii. ii. 272, 'get me a fellowship in a cry of players'; also below, iv. vi. 148.

121. *rotten fens*] Cf. *Tp.*, ii. i. 45, 'As if it had lungs, and rotten ones . . . Or, as 'twere perfum'd by a fen'.

123. *I banish you*] Cf. *Tim.*, iii. v. 98–100, 'Banish me! / Banish your dotage! Banish usury / That makes the Senate ugly', *Lr.*, i. i. 181, and *R 2*, i. iii. 279–80. Malone compares Lyly, *Euphues* (ed. Bond, p. 314), 'When it was cast in Diogenes' teeth that the Sinopenetes had banished him Pontus, yea, said he, I them of Diogenes'. Bullough (p. 487) remarks that Martius at this point in Plutarch 'dyd outwardly shewe no manner of passion', and suggests that Shakespeare owed the anger to a passage in Florus comparing Coriolanus with Camillus; but the theatrical and political situations alike call for it.

127. *Fan . . . despair*] The nodding of helmet plumes suggests a fan, and the imagined situation prompts more violent associations. Cf. *Troil.*, v. iii. 41, 'fan and wind of your fair sword', *Mac.*, i. ii. 50–1, 'the Norweyan banners flout the sky / And

fan our people cold', and *Ant.*, i. i. 9–10, 'the bellows and the fan / To cool a gipsy's lust'. Cf. also iv. vi. 119–21, below.

127–31. *Have . . . foes*] Editors have had difficulty in deciding whether the passage is corrupt or elliptical. The dominant sense may be clarified by abbreviating and recasting: 'Have the power still to banish your defenders, till at length, making but reservation of yourselves, your ignorance deliver you as most abated captives'; *making but reservation of yourselves* then clearly means 'leaving none but yourselves unbanished'. The function of the omitted clauses is also explicable: *which finds not till it feels* is a comment on the nature of ignorance, which learns only from bitter experience (Cf. *Lr.*, iv. i. 68–9, 'the . . . man . . . that will not see / Because he does not feel'); and *Still your own foes* a comment on the people, who are always their own worst enemies. This interpretation (substantially Johnson's) assumes some infelicitous but not uncharacteristic ellipsis in the passage. The structure might be further clarified by setting brackets about *which . . . feels* and *Still . . . foes*, but I have left the punctuation as close to F as it can intelligibly be.

Your ignorance—which finds not till it feels,
Making but reservation of yourselves,   130
Still your own foes—deliver you as most
Abated captives to some nation
That won you without blows! Despising
For you the city, thus I turn my back.
There is a world elsewhere!   *Exeunt Coriolanus,*
      Cominius, [Menenius] with the other Senators and Patricians.
Æd. The people's enemy is gone, is gone!   136
All Pleb. Our enemy is banish'd! He is gone! Hoo! hoo!
                      They all shout, and throw up their caps.
Sic. Go see him out at gates, and follow him
As he hath follow'd you, with all despite.
Give him deserv'd vexation. Let a guard   140
Attend us through the city.
All Pleb. Come, come, let's see him out at gates! Come!
The gods preserve our noble tribunes! Come!   *Exeunt.*

129–31.—which . . . foes—] *F* ((which . . . Foes)).   130. but] *F;* not *Capell.*
131–2. as most . . . nation] *As Capell; one line in F.*   133–4. blows! Despising
. . . city,] *Capell;* blowes, despising . . . City. *F.*   135. S.D. *Senators . . . Patri-*
cians.] *Capell; with Cumalijs. | F.*   137. hoo! *F3;* oo *F.*   S.D.] *as Cam.;*
Immediately follows l. 135 S.D. in F.   139–40. despite. | Give] *Cam. (subst.);*
despight | Giue *F.*

132. *Abated*] beaten, subdued,
cast down (*O.E.D.*).

133–4. *blows . . . city*] Capell's
punctuation relates *Despising . . . city*
to what follows and attributes the
despite to Coriolanus. F attaches the
phrase to the previous sentence and
the despite to *some nation*. In view of
Coriolanus' disposition and values,
Capell's version is the more probable.

135 S.D. with the other] For F's

bizarre reading see Introduction,
p. 5.

140. *vexation*] affliction, torment.
Wright compares Matthew, xv. 22
(Authorized), 'My daughter is griev-
ously vexed with a devil', and *Tp.*,
iv. i. 5–6, 'All thy vexations / Were
but my trials of thy love'.

143. *The gods . . . tribunes!*] Cf.
iii. i. 269, 323, and iv. vi. 20, where
at their next appearance, the people
bless their tribunes.

ACT IV

[SCENE I]

Enter CORIOLANUS, VOLUMNIA, VIRGILIA, MENENIUS,
COMINIUS, *with the young Nobility of Rome.*

Cor. Come, leave your tears. A brief farewell! The beast
    With many heads butts me away. Nay, mother,
    Where is your ancient courage? You were us'd
    To say, extremities was the trier of spirits;

ACT IV

Scene I

ACT IV] *Actus Quartus.* / F.   SCENE I] *Rowe.*
4. extremities] *F;* Extreamity *F2.*   was] *F;* were *Malone.*

Scene I] Rowe locates the scene outside Rome, Pope at 'The Gates of Rome', and Theobald 'Before the Gates . . .' It seems likely that the party enters through the 'gates' in the façade and that all but a few intimates leave the same way. Martius, Volumnia, Virgilia, Menenius, and perhaps Cominius leave left or right-stage, with three returning in IV. ii, either from the same direction or through the 'gates'. If the yard was meant to be used (see v. v headnote) Martius could make his final exit that way, alone. It is possible that sounds of 'deserved vexation' (III. iii. 140) can still be heard from the 'Rome' of the tiring-house.

S.D. young Nobility] i.e. young patricians; see Introduction, p. 21.

1. *leave your tears*] North tells how Martius 'had taken his leave of his mother and wife, finding them weeping, and shreeking out for sorrowe, and had also comforted and persuaded them to be content with his chaunce' (Appendix, p. 342).

leave] leave off.

1–2. *beast . . . heads*] Cf. II. iii. 16–17, III. i. 92 and notes. For a classical source Steevens cites Horace, *Ep.*, I. i. 76, 'Bellua multorum es capitum', and as evidence of an Elizabethan commonplace Case cites *Jack Straw* (M.S.R., 188–9), 'The Multitude a Beast of many heads, / Of misconceiving and misconstruing minds'. For a full discussion of the theme see C. A. Patrides, 'The Beast with many Heads, Renaissance views on the Multitude', *S.Q.*, XVI, 1965, pp. 241–6.

3. *You were us'd*] For the construction see Abbott 295.

4. *extremities . . . spirits*] Cf. *Troil.*, I. iii. 20–1, 'But the protractive trials of great Jove / To find persistive constancy in men', and III. ii. 41 above.

was] Shakespeare was evidently embarrassed by the plural subject with a single predicate. See Abbott 333–7.

237

    That common chances common men could bear,   5
    That when the sea was calm all boats alike
    Show'd mastership in floating; fortune's blows,
    When most struck home, being gentle wounded,
      craves
    A noble cunning. You were us'd to load me
    With precepts that would make invincible   10
    The heart that conn'd them.
Vir. O heavens! O heavens!
Cor.   Nay, I prithee woman.
Vol. Now the red pestilence strike all trades in Rome,
    And occupations perish!
Cor.   What, what, what!
    I shall be lov'd when I am lack'd. Nay, mother,   15
    Resume that spirit when you were wont to say,
    If you had been the wife of Hercules,
    Six cf his labours you'd have done, and sav'd
    Your husband so much sweat. Cominius,
    Droop not: adieu. Farewell, my wife, my mother: 20
    I'll do well yet. Thou old and true Menenius,

---

5. chances common] *F4;* chances. Common *F.*

5–7. *common chances . . . floating*]
Cf. *Troil.,* I. iii. 33–7, 'In the reproof
of chance, / Lies the true proof of
men. The sea being smooth, / How
many shallow bauble boats dare
sail / Upon her patient breast,
making their way / With those of
nobler bulk!'

7–9. *fortune's . . . cunning*] When
fortune's blows are hardest, to be
noble when wounded by them
demands a nobleman's art and
understanding. This version (owing
much to Johnson) assumes that
being gentle wounded is the subject of
craves. If *blows* is taken as the subject,
being wounded becomes a conditional
clause ('if the wounded state is to be a
gentle one'). Johnson renders *gentle*
as 'calm', but in this play it is more
likely to be antithetic to *common,*
Onions includes this use of *cunning*
under 'knowledge', and offers different instances of the sense 'skill,
ability', but the context is best
served by a complex of both; the
modern sense of 'underhand craft' is
not admissible.

12. *O . . . heavens!*] Virgilia's words
serve to emphasize her silent presence.

13. *red pestilence*] probably typhus
fever, which causes red skin-erup-
tions; cf. *Tp.,* I. ii. 364, 'The red
plague rid you', and *Troil.,* II. i. 18,
'A red murrain o'thy jade's tricks'.

14. *occupations*] handicrafts, trades.

15. *lov'd . . . lack'd*] Cf. *Ant.,* I. iv.
43–4, 'And the ebb'd man, ne'er
lov'd till ne'er worth love, / Comes
dear'd by being lack'd', and *Ado,*
IV. i. 217–22. *O.E.D.* offers only
Shakespearean instances of *lack* meaning 'to perceive the absence of, to
miss'.

Thy tears are salter than a younger man's,
And venomous to thine eyes. My sometime general,
I have seen thee stern, and thou hast oft beheld
Heart-hard'ning spectacles; tell these sad women,   25
'Tis fond to wail inevitable strokes,
As 'tis to laugh at 'em. My mother, you wot well
My hazards still have been your solace; and
Believ't not lightly, though I go alone,
Like to a lonely dragon that his fen   30
Makes fear'd and talk'd of more than seen, your son
Will or exceed the common, or be caught
With cautelous baits and practice.

Vol.   My first son,

27. My] *F; omitted Pope, Wilson.*

22–3. *tears . . . eyes*] Shakespeare relates the salt of tears to gall in *Ham.*, I. ii. 154–5, 'Ere yet the salt of most unrighteous tears / Had left the flushing in her galled eyes'. Cf. *Troil.*, v. iii. 55, 'Their eyes o'ergalled with recourse of tears', and *Ham.*, IV. v. 151–2, 'tears seven times salt / Burn out the sense and virtue of mine eye!' For the idea that tears grow salter with age I can find no analogue, but Shakespeare may have had it in mind in *Lr.*, IV. viii. 46–8.

26–7. *'Tis fond . . . at 'em*] For other versions of this great commonplace cf. *Ant.*, III. vi. 84–5 and IV. xv. 51–5, *3H6*, v. iv. 1–2, 37–8, and *R2*, III. ii. 178–9. Among proverbs, cf. Tilley C 921, C 923, F 83.

26. *fond*] foolish.

27–8. *My mother . . . solace*] Cf. I. iii. 5–25.

27. *wot*] know, as often in Shakespeare and elsewhere.

28. *still*] always.

29. *Believ't not lightly*] Do not take this assurance lightly.

30. *dragon . . . fen*] Wright quotes Topsell's *History of Serpents* (1658), p. 105: 'Of the Indian Dragons there are also said to be two kindes, one of them fenny, and living in marishes . . . the other in the mount-

ains.' Spenser's Orgoglio (*Faerie Queene*, I. VII. xvi) keeps 'A monstrous beasty bred in filthy fen' that is compared with the Hydra of the Lernaean marsh. A specific allusion to the Hydra (applied to the plebeians at III. i. 92) would be inapposite here, where Shakespeare needs evocations of isolation, pathos, menace, rumour, and uncertainty. Noble cites Job, xxx. 29 (Geneva), 'I am a brother to the dragons, and a companion to the ostriches', also Isaiah, xxxiv. 11–13, xiii. 20–2. Cf. IV. vii. 23, v. iv. 13, and Introduction, p. 51.

32. *or . . . or*] either . . . or. But, as Wilson says, 'both futures await him'.

exceed the common] surpass common expectation. King suggests 'get the better of the common people', cf. I. i. 150 and III. i. 28; but this seems too specific an objective.

33. *cautelous*] deceitful, crafty.

practice] i.e. sharp practice, trickery.

first] Since Volumnia declares herself 'fond of no second brood' (v. iii. 162) and appears to have only one son, *first* probably means both 'firstborn' and 'pre-eminent', the simple literal truth turned to metaphorical acclaim.

Whither wilt thou go? Take good Cominius
With thee awhile; determine on some course   35
More than a wild exposture to each chance
That starts i'th'way before thee.

Vir.   O the gods!

Com. I'll follow thee a month, devise with thee
Where thou shalt rest, that thou mayst hear of us
And we of thee. So if the time thrust forth   40
A cause for thy repeal, we shall not send
O'er the vast world to seek a single man
And lose advantage, which doth ever cool
I'th'absence of the needer.

Cor.   Fare ye well.

Thou hast years upon thee, and thou art too full   45
Of the wars' surfeits to go rove with one
That's yet unbruis'd: bring me but out at gate.
Come, my sweet wife, my dearest mother, and
My friends of noble touch: when I am forth,
Bid me farewell, and smile. I pray you, come: 50

34. Whither wilt thou] *Capell;* Whether will thou *F;* Whither will you *F2.*
36. exposture] *F;* exposure *Rowe.*   37. *Vir.*] *Keightley; Cor. | F.*

35-7. *some . . . thee*] Wilson (after
Maxwell) compares *Wint.,* IV. iv.
557-60, 'A course more promising /
Than a wild dedication of yourselves /
To unpath'd waters, undream'd
shores, most certain / To miseries
enough'. North says Coriolanus 'could
revolve no waye, to take a profitable
or honorable course' (Appendix,
p. 343).

36. *exposture*] = exposure. *O.E.D.*
gives only this instance and assumes
it formed 'on the analogy of *posture,
composture,* etc.'

37. *starts*] starts up; cf. *thrust forth*
in l. 40.

Vir.] Keightley's assignment of
these words to Virgilia is supported
by the analogy with l. 12, allowing a
highly characteristic contribution to
the effect of the scene. It is just
conceivable that Coriolanus cries out
in apprehension or distress, or even
intends a dismissive blasphemy, but

either would be inconsistent with the
assumed role of 'lonely dragon'.

41. *cause*] occasion.

repeal] recall; cf. *Caes.,* III. i. 54.

43. *advantage*] i.e. the propitious
time; in one sense, the heat of the
moment, as in *Lr.,* I. i. 306, 'We
must do something, and i'th'heat'.

47. *bring . . . gate*] In North 'a
great number of Patricians' accompany Coriolanus to the gate, and
'three or foure' go with him to his
country house. For the omission of
the article see III. iii. 138 note, and
Abbott 143.

49. *noble touch*] For the touchstone
metaphor cf. II. iii. 189 above; also
1H4, IV. iv. 10, *R3,* IV. ii. 8, and
Tim., III. iii. 6, where Timon's
friends, 'have all been touch'd and
found base metal'. Coriolanus gives a
less magnanimous account of the
patricians at IV. v. 76-9.

> While I remain above the ground you shall
> Hear from me still, and never of me aught
> But what is like me formerly.

Men.   That's worthily
> As any ear can hear. Come, let's not weep.
> If I could shake off but one seven years   55
> From these old arms and legs, by the good gods
> I'd with thee every foot.

Cor.   Give me thy hand.
> Come.   *Exeunt.*

[SCENE II]

Enter the two Tribunes, SICINIUS *and* BRUTUS, *with the Ædile.*

Sic. Bid them all home; he's gone, and we'll no further.
> The nobility are vex'd, whom we see have sided
> In his behalf.

Bru.   Now we have shown our power,
> Let us seem humbler after it is done
> Than when it was a-doing.

Sic.   Bid them home.   5
> Say their great enemy is gone and they
> Stand in their ancient strength.

Bru.   Dismiss them home.
>   [*Exit Ædile.*]
> Here comes his mother.

Enter VOLUMNIA, VIRGILIA, *and* MENENIUS.

Sic.   Let's not meet her.

57–8. Give . . . Come.] *As Steevens; one line in F.*

Scene II

SCENE II] *Pope.*   5–8. Bid . . . mother.] *As Pope;* Bid . . . gone, / . . . strength.
/ . . . Mother. / *F.*   7. S.D.] *Capell.*

51–4. *shall Hear . . . hear*] another
crucial passage in Shakespeare's
analysis of Coriolanus' fame and
reputation (see Introduction, p. 41).
Case and others have wondered if
Coriolanus here has 'learned dissimu-
lation', but see below IV. iv. 12 note.

Scene II

Scene II] Most editors, following
Capell, locate the scene in a street
leading from the gate. If the tribunes
are dispersing a noisy crowd, and if
Volumnia, Virgilia, and Menenius
enter through the façade 'gates' the

Bru.   Why?

Sic. They say she's mad.

Bru. They have ta'en note of us: keep on your way.   10

Vol. Oh, y'are well met: the hoarded plague o'th'gods
Requite your love!

Men.   Peace, peace, be not so loud.

Vol. If that I could for weeping, you should hear—
Nay, and you shall hear some. [*To Brutus*] Will
you be gone?
[*To Sicinius*] You shall stay too.

Vir.   I would I had the power
To say so to my husband.

Sic.   Are you mankind?   16

Vol. Ay, fool; is that a shame? Note but this fool.
Was not a man my father? Hadst thou foxship
To banish him that struck more blows for Rome
Than thou hast spoken words?

11–12.] *As Capell;* Oh . . . met: / . . . loue. / *F.*   11. the hoarded] *Johnson;*
Th'hoorded *F.*   12. Requite] *F* (requit), *F3.*   14, 15. S.D.s] *Johnson; not
in F.*   15. You . . . too. *Vir.*] *Warburton; Vir.* You . . . too. *F.*   17. this
fool.] *F* (this Foole,); this, Fool, *Staunton.*

location is sufficiently established.

9. *mad*] furious; cf. Hotspur on the 'popinjay' who accosts him at Holmedon, *1 H 4*, i. iii. 53–4, 'for he made me mad / To see him shine so brisk'.

11. *hoarded plague*] as in *Lr.*, ii. iv. 160–1, 'All the stor'd vengeance of heaven fall / On her ingrateful top!'

15. *You . . . too*] I have followed Warburton and Middleton Murry in assigning these words to Volumnia, leaving Virgilia to speak aside. The peremptory *shall stay* is consistent with Volumnia's mood and it precisely anticipates her exasperation in ll. 22–3. See J. M. Murry, *Countries of the Mind*, 1st series, 1931, pp. 18–22, and below, ll. 26 and 28 notes. The misinterpretation of the alignment in copy is an easy error.

16. *mankind*] 'used maliciously by the first speaker, and taken perversely by the second' (Johnson).

Sicinius intends either 'furious, mad' (*O.E.D.*, s.v. *a.*[2]) or, more likely, 'masculine, virago-like' (*a.*[1] B 3), senses related to *mankeen* or *mankynde* (= savage; used of animals inclined to attack men). Volumnia responds, however, to the sense 'of humankind'. Cf. *Wint.*, ii. iii. 67, 'A mankind witch!'

17. *Note . . . fool*] F's pointing leaves it uncertain whether the phrase is addressed to onlookers or to Sicinius. If to the onlookers it means 'Just note this fool', and has the effect of setting Sicinius up for general mockery.

18. *foxship*] Verity remarks that the fox was the type of ingratitude as well as cunning, citing *Lr.*, iii. vi. 22, where Regan and Goneril are called 'she-foxes', and *Lr.*, iii. vii. 27, where 'Ingrateful fox!' is used of Gloucester. The term is also a retort to *mankind*.

Sic.   Oh blessed heavens!
Vol. Moe noble blows than ever thou wise words;   21
And for Rome's good. I'll tell thee what—yet go!
Nay, but thou shalt stay too: I would my son
Were in Arabia, and thy tribe before him,
His good sword in his hand.
Sic.   What then?
Vir.   What then!
Vol. He'd make an end of thy posterity,   26
Bastards and all.
Good man, the wounds that he does bear for Rome!
Men. Come, come, peace!
Sic. I would he had continued to his country   30
As he began, and not unknit himself
The noble knot he made.
Bru.   I would he had.

22. good.] *Capell;* good, *F.*   25–8. *Vir.* . . . Rome!] *This edn; Virg.* . . . posterity / *Volum.* . . . all. / . . . Rome! *F; Vol.* . . . then? / . . . posterity, / . . . all./
. . . Rome! *Hanmer; Vol.* . . . then? / . . . posterity, / . . . all. / . . . *Vir.* Rome!
conj. Murry.

21. *Moe*] more in number (as in
II. iii. 124, but cf. *more* in l. 19).

noble blows] another Laconian
phrase.

wise words] Volumnia speaks sar-
castically. If *moe* were equivalent to
more as in current use, the phrase
would be ambiguous (i.e. it could
mean Coriolanus' blows have been
nobler than Sicinius' words have
been wise).

22–3. *I'll . . . too*] It may be the
tribunes' readiness to be gone that
prompts Volumnia to recall them.
Some have supposed *thou . . . too* a
reference to Brutus, but the words
are for Sicinius still, and *too* is used to
intensify her imperative (= 'after
all').

23–5. *I would . . . hand*] Cf. *Mac.*,
III. iv. 104, 'dare me to the desert
with thy sword'; *R 2*, IV. i. 74, 'I dare
meet Surrey in a wilderness', and
Cym., I. i. 167–9, 'I would they were
in Afric both together; / Myself by

with a nceole, that I might prick /
The goerback'.

26.] I follow Hanmer and Murry
in assigning this line to Volumnia,
but differ from Murry in retaining
What then! (l. 25) as an aside for Virgilia. Since two speech-headings occur
in F at this point, it is likely that two
stood in the copy; but the alignment
may have been uncertain. See notes
on ll. 15 and 28.

28.] Murry's reassignment of this
line to Virgilia is less convincing
textually than the intervention at
l. 26. It entails the assumption that
Compositor B both misinterpreted
the assignments and inverted them.
Theatrically, it has much to recommend it; but the line remains within
Volumnia's range and true to her
values.

32. *noble knot*] 'The bond by which
he bound Rome to him' (Wright).
Allegiance and fidelity are the
common associations in Shakespeare;

Vol. 'I would he had!' 'Twas you incens'd the rabble:
　　Cats, that can judge as fitly of his worth
　　As I can of those mysteries which heaven   35
　　Will not have earth to know.
Bru.   Pray let's go.
Vol. Now, pray sir, get you gone.
　　You have done a brave deed. Ere you go, hear this:
　　As far as doth the Capitol exceed
　　The meanest house in Rome, so far my son—   40
　　This lady's husband here, this, do you see?—
　　Whom you have banish'd, does exceed you all.
Bru. Well, well, we'll leave you.
Sic.   Why stay we to be baited
　　With one that wants her wits?   *Exeunt Tribunes.*
Vol.   Take my prayers with you.
　　I would the gods had nothing else to do   45
　　But to confirm my curses! Could I meet 'em
　　But once a day, it would unclog my heart
　　Of what lies heavy to't.
Men.   You have told them home,
　　And, by my troth, you have cause. You'll sup with me?
Vol. Anger's my meat: I sup upon myself   50

36. let's] *F;* let us *Pope.*   40–1. son— . . . see?—] *F* (Sonne . . . (do you see)).

e.g. *1H6*, v. i. 16, 'surer bind this knot of amity'; *3H6*, III. iii. 55, 'nuptial knot'; *Troil.*, v. ii. 152–5, and *Rom.*, IV. ii. 24. Schmidt supposes a more general metaphor expressing Coriolanus' undoing of his own work, and cites *Wiv.*, III. ii. 63, 'he shall not knit a knot in his fortunes with the finger of my substance'.

34. *Cats*] Cf. *All's W.*, IV. iii. 221, 'I could endure anything before but a cat, and now he's a cat to me'; *MND.*, III. ii. 260, 'thou cat, thou burr; vile thing, let loose'; and *Mer. V.*, IV. i. 48, 'Some that are mad if they behold a cat'. The term expresses a general revulsion rather than contempt for a particular attribute (e.g. stealth).

35. *mysteries*] as in *Lr.*, v. iii. 16–17,

'And take upon's the mystery of things / As if we were God's spies'. Not elsewhere used by Shakespeare in this sense.

43. *baited*] harassed (like bears by dogs). Cf. *R3*, I. iii. 109, 'baited, scorn'd, and stormed at'.

44. *With*] by. As often, e.g. *Tp.*, II. ii. 100, 'I took him to be kill'd with a thunderstroke'.

47–8. *unclog . . . heavy to't*] The metaphor is from the practice of fettering animals or men with blocks of wood; *clog* occurs several times in Shakespeare, but this is his only use of *unclog* and the earliest instance in *O.E.D.*

48. *told them home*] Cf. I. iv. 38, II. ii. 103, and III. iii. 1; also *Ham.*, III. iii. 29, 'I warrant she'll tax him home', and the phrase 'home truths'.

And so shall starve with feeding. Come, let's go.
Leave this faint puling, and lament as I do,
In anger, Juno-like. Come, come, come!

Exeunt [*Volumnia and Virgilia*].

Men. Fie, fie, fie!   *Exit.*

[SCENE III]

Enter a Roman and a Volsce.

Rom. I know you well, sir, and you know me: your name
I think is Adrian.
Vols. It is so, sir; truly I have forgot you.
Rom. I am a Roman; and my services are, as you are,
against 'em. Know you me yet?   5
Vols. Nicanor? No?
Rom. The same, sir.
Vols. You had more beard when I last saw you, but
your favour is well appeared by your tongue.

---

52. faint puling] *Rowe;* faint-puling *F.*

Scene III

SCENE III] *Pope.*
9. appeared] *F* (appear'd); affear'd *Hanmer;* approv'd *Steevens, Wilson.*

---

51. *starve with feeding*] probably
'die from consuming my own resources'; but the more limited sense
'go hungry' was available.

52. *Leave*] cease, as in IV. i. I.

faint] faint-hearted, as in *Tim.*,
III. i. 53, 'a faint and milky heart'.

puling] whining; cf. *Gent.*, II. i. 23,
and *Rom.*, III. v. 184–5, 'a wretched
puling fool, / A whining mammet'.
Cotgrave gives '*Piauler* . . . to pule or
howle (as a younge whelpe)', and
also '*Piuler*. To pule, or cheepe like a
little chicken'.

53. *In anger, Juno-like*] Cf. Virgil
Aen., I. 4, 'saevae memorem Junonis
ob iram' (Case).

Scene III

Scene III] located by Rowe in
Antium, by Capell in 'Volscian
territories. A highway', but most

follow Malone, 'A Highway between
Rome and Antium'. We are told that
the place is 'a day's journey' from
Rome (l. 12) and hours at most
from the Volscian's 'home' (l. 39).
The encounter could be played
front-stage, with no significance
attached to the façade.

5. *'em*] i.e. the Romans. The speaker
is in the pay of the Volscians. Both
in the disposition of allegiances and
in the recognition-play, the scene
anticipates Coriolanus' encounter
with Aufidius. For the traitorous
associations of 'Nicanor', see Introduction, p. 30. Brecht saw the
scene as evidence of good-will between
the ordinary people of Rome and
Antium; see Introduction, p. 86,
and Brecht, *Stücke*, 11, pp. 331–2.

9. *favour . . . tongue*] i.e. your
identity is made apparent by your

What's the news in Rome? I have a note from the   10
Volscian state to find you out there; you have well
saved me a day's journey.

Rom. There hath been in Rome strange insurrections:
the people against the senators, patricians and
nobles.   15

Vols. Hath been! Is it ended then? Our state thinks
not so; they are in a most warlike preparation, and
hope to come upon them in the heat of their
division.

Rom. The main blaze of it is past, but a small thing   20
would make it flame again. For the nobles receive
so to heart the banishment of that worthy Coriolanus, that they are in a ripe aptness to take all
power from the people, and to pluck from them their
tribunes for ever. This lies glowing, I can tell you,   25
and is almost mature for the violent breaking out.

Vols. Coriolanus banished?

Rom. Banished, sir.

Vols. You will be welcome with this intelligence,
Nicanor.   30

Rom. The day serves well for them now. I have heard it
said, the fittest time to corrupt a man's wife is when
she's fallen out with her husband. Your noble
Tullus Aufidius will appear well in these wars, his

---

34. will] *F2;* well *F.*

speech. For *favour* = face, appearance, cf. *Oth.*, I. iii. 340, 'defeat thy
favour with an usurp'd beard!' No
precisely analogous use of *appeared* is
recorded elsewhere, but Abbott (296)
attempts to identify a reflexive use in
Ado, I. ii. 17, 'we will hold it as a
dream, till it appear itself', and
Cym., III. iv. 144. In support of his
conjecture *approv'd* (= confirmed)
Steevens cites *Ham.*, I. i. 29, 'He may
approve our eyes'.

10. *note*] note of instruction; cf.
Meas., IV. ii. 98, 'My lord hath sent
you this note; and by me this further
charge, that you swerve not from the
smallest article of it'.

13. *hath*] often used as a plural form;
but here it may be the singular,
preceding the plural subject (see
Abbott 335).

17. *preparation*] perhaps, as in I. ii.
15, 'army, assembled force'; cf.
l. 42 below.

23–4. *ripe . . . pluck*] 'An example of
image-drift. The fruit image in *ripe
aptnesse*, first used of the nobles, is
transferred to the tribunes in *plucke*'
(King).

25–6. *glowing . . . out*] Cf. 1 *H6*,
III. i. 190–1, where a similar metaphor
is applied to imminent civil war.

31. *them*] i.e. the Volscians.

great opposer, Coriolanus, being now in no request   35
of his country.

Vols. He cannot choose. I am most fortunate, thus
accidentally to encounter you. You have ended my
business, and I will merrily accompany you home.

Rom. I shall between this and supper tell you most   40
strange things from Rome, all tending to the good
of their adversaries. Have you an army ready, say
you?

Vols. A most royal one: the centurions and their charges
distinctly billeted, already in th'entertainment, and   45
to be on foot at an hour's warning.

Rom. I am joyful to hear of their readiness, and am the
man, I think, that shall set them in present action.
So, sir, heartily well met, and most glad of your
company.   50

Vols. You take my part from me, sir: I have the most
cause to be glad of yours.

Rom. Well, let us go together.   *Exeunt.*

[SCENE IV]

Enter CORIOLANUS *in mean apparel, disguised and muffled.*

Cor. A goodly city is this Antium. City,
'Tis I that made thy widows: many an heir
Of these fair edifices 'fore my wars

Scene IV

SCENE IV] *Capell.*

36. *of*] either possessive or = from,
as often (Case).

37. *He cannot choose*] He's bound to;
cf. *Wint.*, I. i. 24.

45. *distinctly*] separately, i.e. charge
by charge. The centurion's charge or
century probably consisted originally
of a hundred men.

billeted] enrolled (*O.E.D.*, s.v. *v.*¹,
giving this and other instances).

in th'entertainment] mobilized, on
the pay-roll; cf. *All's W.*, IV. i. 15.

48. *present*] immediate.

Scene IV

Scene IV] The scene locates itself,
and most follow Capell, Antium.
Before Aufidius' House' (see Introduction, p. 17). We are made
aware of the facade by the opening
line, and it is made to stand for the
house in l. 10. Martius could leave
by a door 'entering' the house, and
return through it early in the next
scene.

3. *'fore my wars*] in face of my
onslaughts; the phrase relates to

Have I heard groan, and drop. Then know me not;
Lest that thy wives with spits, and boys with stones,   5
In puny battle slay me.

Enter a Citizen.

Save you, sir.

Cit. And you.
Cor.   Direct me, if it be your will,
Where great Aufidius lies. Is he in Antium?
Cit. He is, and feasts the nobles of the state   9
At his house this night.
Cor.   Which is his house, beseech you?
Cit. This, here before you.
Cor.   Thank you, sir. Farewell.   *Exit Citizen.*
O world, thy slippery turns! Friends now fast sworn,
Whose double bosoms seems to wear one heart,

6. S.D.] *As Dyce; follows* sir *in F.*   7–10. *As Capell; prose in F.*   13. seems . . .
one] *F; seene . . . on F2; seem . . . one F4.*

what follows. Cf. below v. iv. 19,
2H4, Ind. 31, and *Troil.*, v. v. 24–5.
For *wars* = assaults see *O.E.D.*, s.v.
4 b. For the intimate appropriation
'my' *wars* cf. I. i. 233–4.

5. *wives*] probably 'women'. See
II. i. 70 note.

6. *Save you*] God save you.

8. *lies*] dwells.

12–26. *O world . . . service*] This
soliloquy may be regarded as serving
the same purpose as a passage in
North explaining the genesis of
Coriolanus' resolution to seek support
from the Volscians, 'So he remained
a fewe dayes in the countrie at his
houses, turmoyled with sundry sortes
and kynde of thoughtes, suche as the
fyer of his choller dyd sturre up. In
the ende, seeing he could revolve no
waye, to take a profitable or honorable course, but only was pricked
forward still to be revenged of the
Romaines: he thought to raise up
some great warres against them, by
their neerest neighbours. Whereupon,
he thought it his best waye, first to

stirre up the Volsces against them'
(Appendix, p. 343). The totality of
the metamorphosis and the bleak
economy of its expression contribute
much to the play's understanding of
processes of human change and
growth (see Introduction, p. 51).

12. *slippery turns*] treacherous
changes of fortune and circumstance;
cf. *Troil.*, III. iii. 82–7: 'places, riches,
and favour, / Prizes of accident, as
oft as merit; / Which when they fall,
as being slippery standers, / The love
that lean'd on them as slippery too, /
Doth one pluck down another, and
together / Die in the fall'. Coriolanus' large reflections on the instabilities of the world are designed,
as Verity observes, 'to diminish the
shock and unnaturalness of his own
defection'.

13–16. *double . . . Unseparable*] Cf.
MND., III. ii. 203–14, esp. 212, 'two
seeming bodies, but one heart'; and
AYL., I. iii. 69–72. Malone cites also
Painter, *Palace of Pleasure* (1575),
nov. 59: 'Besides the countrie of

Whose hours, whose bed, whose meal and exercise
Are still together, who twin, as 'twere, in love   15
Unseparable, shall within this hour,
On a dissension of a doit, break out
To bitterest enmity: so fellest foes,
Whose passions and whose plots have broke their sleep
To take the one the other, by some chance,   20
Some trick not worth an egg, shall grow dear friends
And interjoin their issues. So with me:
My birthplace hate I, and my love's upon
This enemy town. I'll enter: if he slay me
He does fair justice; if he give me way,   25
I'll do his country service.   *Exit.*

23. hate] *Capell;* haue *F.*

Perche, there were two Gentlemen, which from the tyme of theyr youthe lyved in sutche great and perfect amitie, as there was betwene them but one harte, one bed, one house, one table and one purse' (ed. Jacobs, II, p. 104).

16. *Unseparable*] not elsewhere in Shakespeare.

17. *dissension of a doit*] squabble about a trifle. See I. v. 6 and note.

19. *broke their sleep*] i.e. disturbed their sleep; cf. IV. v. 123–7 below. Shakespeare used both forms of the participle, *broke* and *broken.*

20. *take . . . other*] seize hold of one another. See III. i. 110–11 and note.

21. *trick . . . egg*] i.e. worthless trifle; cf. *Shr.,* IV. iii. 67, 'A knack, a toy, a trick, a baby's cap', and *Ham.,* IV. iv. 53, 'even for an egg-shell'. Coriolanus brings his reflections to an ignominious climax.

22. *interjoin their issues*] 'allow their children to intermarry' (Wright); 'unite their designs' (Chambers). Shakespeare may have had in mind the marriage pact sealed by 'commodity' in *John,* II. i. 423–598.

24. *enemy town*] Cf. North, 'and as Homer sayd of Ulysses, "So dyd he enter into the enemies towne"' (Appendix, p. 344).

25. *give me way*] afford me my free course (Brooks); cf. V. vi. 31–3.

[SCENE V]

Music plays. Enter a Servingman.

First Serv. Wine, wine, wine! What service is here! I
think our fellows are asleep.   [*Exit.*]

Enter another Servingman.

Second Serv. Where's Cotus? My master calls for him.
Cotus!   *Exit.*

Enter CORIOLANUS.

Cor. A goodly house: the feast smells well, but I   5
Appear not like a guest.

Enter the first Servingman.

First Serv. What would you have, friend? Whence are
you? Here's no place for you: pray, go to the
door!   *Exit.*
Cor. I have deserv'd no better entertainment   10
In being Coriolanus.

Scene v

SCENE v] *Capell.*   2. *Exit*] *Rowe.*   3. master] *F* (M.), *F4.*   5-6.] *As Pope;*
A . . . House: / . . . Guest. / *F.*   10-11.] *As Capell; prose in F.*

Scene v] Editors follow Rowe and
locate in 'A Hall in Aufidius's
House'. The music, played perhaps
in the gallery, and the calls for wine
establish the nature of the interior.
If Martius enters through a façade
door, the scene precisely reverses the
previous one. For the occasion in
North, where Coriolanus is described
as a muffled, majestic, and silent
figure at Tullus' hearth, see Appendix, p. 344, and Introduction, p. 18.

1. *What service*] As King observes,
there is a nice ironical recoil of
service upon the last line of the
previous scene—noticeable when the
playing is virtually continuous.

3. *Cotus*] the name, usually in the
form 'Cotys', of several Thracian
princes. For alleged sources, see
Introduction, p. 30.

8–9. *to the door*] i.e. out of the house
(*O.E.D.*, door 5).

Enter Second Servingman.

Second Serv. Whence are you sir? Has the porter his eyes
 in his head, that he gives entrance to such com-
 panions? Pray, get you out.
Cor. Away!   15
Second Serv. Away? Get you away!
Cor. Now th'art troublesome.
Second Serv. Are you so brave! I'll have you talked with
 anon.

Enter Third Servingman. The First meets him.

Third Serv. What fellow's this?   20
First Serv. A strange one as ever I looked on. I cannot
 get him out o'th'house. Prithee call my master to
 him.   *[Retires.]*
Third Serv. What have you to do here, fellow? Pray you,
 avoid the house.   25
Cor. Let me but stand; I will not hurt your hearth.
Third Serv. What are you?
Cor. A gentleman.
Third Serv. A marv'llous poor one.
Cor. True, so I am.   30
Third Serv. Pray you, poor gentleman, take up some
 other station. Here's no place for you; pray you,
 avoid. Come.
Cor. Follow your function, go, and batten on cold bits.
          Pushes him away from him.

---

11. S.D. *Servingman.*] F (*Servant.*).   23. S.D.] *Cam.; not in F.*

13–14. *companions*] often in Shakespeare and elsewhere a term of
contempt; e.g. *Wiv.*, III. v. 67, 'a
rabble of his companions'. Cf.
below, v. ii. 59.
 18. *brave*] insolent.
 23. S.D. Retires] The direction,
like that at l. 53, is prompted by the
need to admit the first two servingmen
to the dialogue at l. 149 when they talk
of the 'strange alteration' that they
have evidently witnessed.

25, 33. *avoid*] quit, clear out; as
often, e.g. *Err.*, IV. iii. 43, 'Satan,
avoid!'
 26. *hearth*] Cf. North, 'he got him
up straight to the chimney harthe'
(Appendix, p. 344).
 31–2. *gentleman . . . station*] puns on
station, 'standing-place' and 'status';
cf. II. i. 213.
 34. *Follow your function*] i.e. carry
out your servile role; cf. *Oth.*, IV. ii.
27, 'Some of your function, mistress'.

Third Serv. What, you will not? Prithee, tell my master   35
    what a strange guest he has here.
Second Serv. And I shall.   *Exit Second Servingman.*
Third Serv. Where dwell'st thou?
Cor. Under the canopy.
Third Serv. Under the canopy?   40
Cor. Ay.
Third Serv. Where's that?
Cor. I'th'city of kites and crows.
Third Serv. I'th'city of kites and crows? What an
    ass it is! Then thou dwell'st with daws too?   45
Cor. No, I serve not thy master.
Third Serv. How, sir! Do you meddle with my master?
Cor. Ay; 'tis an honester service than to meddle with thy
    mistress. Thou prat'st, and prat'st. Serve with thy
    trencher: hence! *Beats him away.* [*Exit Third Servingman.*]

Enter AUFIDIUS *with the* [*Second*] *Servingman.*

Auf. Where is this fellow?   51
Second Serv. Here sir; I'd have beaten him like a dog,
    but for disturbing the lords within.   [*Retires.*]
Auf. Whence com'st thou? What wouldst thou? thy name?

48–50.] *As F;* Ay . . . mistress. / . . . hence! *Capell.*   50. *Exit . . . Servingman.*]
Cam.; not in F.   53. S.D.] *Cam.; not in F.*

batten] gorge, grow fat; cf. *Ham.*,
III. iv. 66–7, 'Could you on this fair
mountain leave to feed, / And batten
on this moor'.

   cold bits] Cf. *Cym.*, II. iii. 114–15,
'One bred of arms and foster'd with
cold dishes, / With scraps o'th'court'.

   37. *And I shall*] so I will.

   39. *Under the canopy*] Coriolanus
plays upon the senses 'under the sky'
and 'royally enthroned'; for the
second, cf. *2H4*, III. i. 13, 'Under the
canopies of costly state'; and for the
first, *Ham.*, II. ii. 300, 'this most
excellent canopy the air . . . this
majestical roof fretted with golden
fire'. Case cites Nashe, *Christ's Teares
over Jerusalem* (ed. MacKerrow, II,

p. 121), 'Hath the vast azur'd
Canopy nothing above it?'

   43. *kites and crows*] associated with
the battlefield in *2H6*, v. ii. 11,
'prey for carrion kites and crows';
cf. also the desolate city of the
Vellitres in North (Appendix, p. 329).

   45. *daws*] noodles, dolts. The jack-
daw was thought to be a particularly
foolish bird. Coriolanus alludes to the
servants, not to Aufidius (as the third
servant supposes).

   47, 48. *meddle*] The servant means
'busy yourself about', and Coriolanus
puns on the sense 'have sexual inter-
course with' (see *O.E.D.*, s.v. 5, 7).

   54–74. *name . . . name remains*] The
repetition of *name* reaches an almost

Why speak'st not? Speak, man: what's thy name?

Cor. [*Unmuffling*]   If, Tullus,
Not yet thou know'st me, and, seeing me, dost not   56
Think me for the man I am, necessity
Commands me name myself.

Auf.   What is thy name?
                              [*Servants retire.*]

Cor. A name unmusical to the Volscians' ears,
And harsh in sound to thine.

Auf.   Say, what's thy name?
Thou hast a grim appearance, and thy face   61
Bears a command in't. Though thy tackle's torn,
Thou show'st a noble vessel. What's thy name?

Cor. Prepare thy brow to frown: know'st thou me yet?

Auf. I know thee not! Thy name?   65

Cor. My name is Caius Martius, who hath done
To thee particularly, and to all the Volsces,
Great hurt and mischief: thereto witness may
My surname, Coriolanus. The painful service,
The extreme dangers, and the drops of blood   70
Shed for my thankless country, are requited
But with that surname: a good memory
And witness of the malice and displeasure

---

55. S.D.] *Capell; not in F.*   55–8. If . . . myself.] *As Steevens; prose in F.*
58. S.D. *Servants retire.*] *Capell; not in F.*

incantatory intensity. For the general
importance of 'name' in the play see
Introduction, p. 41.

55. *Unmuffling*] Capell's direction
is prompted by North, 'Then Martius unmuffled him selfe', and the
speech that follows is very close to the
source (see Appendix, p. 344).

61–2. *face . . . in't*] Cf. North, 'yet
there appeared a certaine majestie
in his countenance' (Appendix, p.
344).

62–3. *tackle's . . . vessel*] The metaphor (not in North) may imply only a
splendid body raggedly dressed; but
Wilson sees *vessel* not only as a ship
representing the body but also as 'the
body as receptacle of the soul'

(*O.E.D.*, 3 b), and compares *All's W.*,
II. iii. 201–3 and *Cym.*, IV. ii. 320.
Cf. also *Per.*, IV. iv. 29–30, and
Tim., V. i. 198–210, 'throes / That
nature's fragile vessel doth sustain /
In life's uncertain voyage'. In
comparison with other Shakespearean
uses of the metaphor the *Coriolanus*
one is characteristically terse.

66–102.] a close rendering of
North, 'Coriolanus oration to Tullus
Aufidius' (Appendix, pp. 344–5).

70. *extreme*] accented on first
syllable.

72. *memory*] memorial, memento;
cf. North, 'a good memorie and
witnes' (Appendix, p. 345).

Which thou should'st bear me. Only that name
  remains.
The cruelty and envy of the people,   75
Permitted by our dastard nobles, who
Have all forsook me, hath devour'd the rest;
And suffer'd me by th'voice of slaves to be
Whoop'd out of Rome. Now this extremity
Hath brought me to thy hearth, not out of hope   80
(Mistake me not) to save my life: for if
I had fear'd death, of all the men i'th'world
I would have 'voided thee; but in mere spite
To be full quit of those my banishers,
Stand I before thee here. Then if thou hast   85
A heart of wreak in thee, that wilt revenge
Thine own particular wrongs, and stop those maims
Of shame seen through thy country, speed thee
  straight,
And make my misery serve thy turn: so use it
That my revengeful services may prove   90
As benefits to thee, for I will fight

---

79. Whoop'd] *F* (Hoop'd), *Hanmer*.   83. 'voided] *F* (voided), *Var. '78;*
avoided *Rowe*[2].   86. wilt] *F;* will *Hanmer*.

---

75. *envy*] malice.

76. *dastard nobles*] North has 'dastardly nobilitie'. The conspicuous change in Coriolanus' attitude towards the patricians registers in the source as well as the play. Cf. above IV. i. 49 and note.

79. *Whoop'd . . . Rome*] North says simply, 'banished by the people' (Appendix, p. 345). Both here and in III. iii. 140 the jeering is Shakespeare's innovation; for the charge of physical revulsion carried by *Whoop'd* (a hunting term—of. III. i. 272) see Introduction, p. 48.

83–4. *but . . . banishers*] Cf. North, 'but prickt forward with spite and desire I have to be revenged of them that thus have banished me' (Appendix, p. 345). The parallel suggests

that *be full quit of* means 'fully to settle accounts with, pay back'; cf. *R3*, v. iii. 262. Case, however, supposes Coriolanus ready to die and so be quit of (i.e. rid of) his banishers, if he cannot be revenged.

86. *wreak*] vengeance; cf. North, 'if thou hast any harte to be wrecked of the injuries thy enemies have done thee' (Appendix, p. 345).

87–8. *maims Of shame*] possibly referring to mutilations of Volscian territory, but more probably another instance of the state generally conceived as a vulnerable body; cf. v. iii. 102–3, 'tearing / His country's bowels out'. Coriolanus is weighing the pervasive humiliation and suffering (*seen through thy country*) with Aufidius' *particular wrongs*. There is no equivalent phrase in North.

Against my canker'd country with the spleen
Of all the under fiends. But if so be
Thou dar'st not this, and that to prove more fortunes
Th'art tir'd, then, in a word, I also am   95
Longer to live most weary, and present
My throat to thee and to thy ancient malice;
Which not to cut would show thee but a fool,
Since I have ever follow'd thee with hate,
Drawn tuns of blood out of thy country's breast,   100
And cannot live but to thy shame, unless
It be to do thee service.

Auf.   O Martius, Martius!
Each word thou hast spoke hath weeded from my heart
A root of ancient envy. If Jupiter
Should from yond cloud speak divine things   105
And say ''Tis true', I'd not believe them more
Than thee, all-noble Martius. Let me twine
Mine arms about that body, where against

92. *canker'd country*] The phrase implies general corruption and the immediate context does not support specific applications such as 'the canker of ingratitude' (Wright) or 'the canker of democracy' (Verity). Within the metaphoric field of the play it is likely that *canker'd* here refers to ulcerated or gangrenous growth, as in *John*, v. ii. 14, 'the inveterate canker of one wound', but the more common Shakespearean reference is to the canker-worm. There is no equivalent phrase in North's version.

92–3. *spleen . . . fiends*] The spleen was regarded as the seat of many kinds of intense feeling including, as here, martial ferocity; cf. *R3*, v. iii. 350, 'Inspire us with the spleer of fiery dragons', and *1H4*, v. ii. 19. Steevens thought *under fiends* were subordinate fiends, but Malone's 'infernal fiends' is more probable; cf. *1H6*, v. iii. 10–11, 'ye familiar spirits that are cull'd / Out of the powerful regions under earth'.

94. *prove more fortunes*] Cf. North, 'prove fortune any more' (Appendix, p. 345). For *prove* = try cf. *Cym.*, I. v. 38.

100. *tuns*] large casks.

101–2. *And . . . service*] Shakespeare introduces the idea that Aufidius would be shamed by Coriolanus' living on without doing him service. North has, 'And it were no wisedome in thee, to save the life of him, who hath bene heretofore thy mortall enemie, and whose service now can nothing helpe nor pleasure thee' (Appendix, p. 345).

102–36.] Aufidius' speech has only slight occasion in North (see Appendix, p. 345). He assumes in the play a magnanimous role that, as events take their course, he is unable to 'discharge to the life'.

104–6. *Jupiter . . . true*] 'The classical conception of thunder as an omen of assent from *Jupiter* "the thunderer" (*Tonans* or *Tonitrualis*)' (Ver ty). Cf. *Wint.*, III. i. 9–10, 'the ear-deaf'ning voice o'th'oracle, / Kin

My grained ash an hundred times hath broke,
And scarr'd the moon with splinters. Here I clip   110
The anvil of my sword, and do contest
As hotly and as nobly with thy love
As ever in ambitious strength I did
Contend against thy valour. Know thou first,
I lov'd the maid I married; never man   115
Sigh'd truer breath; but that I see thee here,
Thou noble thing, more dances my rapt heart
Than when I first my wedded mistress saw
Bestride my threshold. Why, thou Mars! I tell thee

---

110. scarr'd] *F;* scar'd *Rowe.*   clip] *F* (cleep), *Pope.*

---

to Jove's thunder'. Aufidius assists in
the creation of the 'god' Martius;
cf. l. 119.

109. *grained ash*] evidently a strong
ashen lance; but it is not clear whether
grained means 'long-grained', referring to the shaft, or 'pronged'
(*O.E.D.*, s.v. *ppl.a.*[3]), referring to the
head. The splintering of the lance,
however, asks that the stress be on
the quality of the shaft. The only other
relevant Shakespearean use is in
Compl., 64, 'So slides he down upon
his grained bat', which may refer to a
pitch-fork or merely to a countryman's staff. Lances, like swords,
would be an important element in
the play's spectacle.

110. *scarr'd*] F's reading is retained,
as a perfectly acceptable hyperbole.
Rowe's *scar'd*, however, may be a
modernization, not an emendation,
as the form *scarr'd = scared* occurs
elsewhere in F (*Wint.*, III. iii. 65 F),
together with *scarre* for *scare* (*Troil.*,
v. x. 21 F). Malone follows F but in
support of *scar'd* cites *R3*, v. iii. 341,
'Amaze the welkin with your broken
staves!' Delius compares *Wint.*, III.
iii. 89, 'now the ship boring the
moon with her mainmast', an effect
closer to *scarr'd*.

clip] embrace (O.E. *clyppan*); F's
cleep was a common form, but
Shakespeare also uses *clip* elsewhere

(e.g. I. vi. 29, also in Compositor B's
stint, and *Ant.*, v. ii. 356).

111. *anvil . . . sword*] Steevens
compares *Ham.*, II. ii. 483–6, 'And
never did the Cyclops' hammers
fall / On Mars's armour, forg'd for
proof eterne, / With lesse remorse
than Pyrrhus' bleeding sword / Now
falls on Priam'.

114. *first*] probably 'in the first
place', contributing to the hyperbole
of the claim that follows. But Staunton and others take it as 'first, or
noblest of men', and compare IV. i.
33, 'My first son'.

115–19. *I lov'd . . . threshold*] For the
mode of intimacy cf. I. vi. 28–32 and
note.

116. *Sigh'd . . . breath*] Malone
compares *Ven.*, 189, and *Two Noble
Kinsmen* (ed. Brooke, *Sh. Apoc.*),
v. i. 131.

117. *noble thing*] almost a perverse
phrase. Tullus means it colloquially,
but in the tragedy it anticipates IV.
vi. 91 and v. iv. 22.

dances] possibly 'causes to dance,
sets dancing' (*O.E.D.*, s.v. *v.* 6), but
this use would antedate others, and it
may be that *that* in l. 116 = because.

119. *Bestride*] step across (*O.E.D.*,
s.v. 4). Steevens remarks that Roman
brides were lifted across the threshold,
and cites Lucan, II, 39. Plutarch's
Moralia (trans. Holland, 1603, p. 852)

We have a power on foot; and I had purpose   120
Once more to hew thy target from thy brawn,
Or lose mine arm for't. Thou hast beat me out
Twelve several times, and I have nightly since
Dreamt of encounters 'twixt thyself and me—
We have been down together in my sleep,   125
Unbuckling helms, fisting each other's throat—
And wak'd half dead with nothing. Worthy Martius,
Had we no other quarrel else to Rome, but that
Thou art thence banish'd, we would muster all
From twelve to seventy, and pouring war   130
Into the bowels of ungrateful Rome,
Like a bold flood o'erbear't. O come, go in,
And take our friendly senators by'th'hands
Who now are here, taking their leaves of me
Who am prepar'd against your territories,   135
Though not for Rome itself.

Cor.   You bless me, gods!

Auf. Therefore, most absolute sir, if thou wilt have
The leading of thine own revenges, take

---

128. other] *F; omitted F3.*   132. o'erbear't] *White, conj. Jackson;* o're-beate
F; o'er-bear *Rowe.*

---

asks why the Romans 'would not
permit the new wedded bride to pass
of herselfe over the doore-sill or
threshold'; see Introduction, p. 31.

121. *target*] a light shield or buckler,
worn on the arm (hence *brawn* in this
line); cf. North, 'they were put in
battell raye, and ready to take their
targettes on their armes' (Appendix,
p. 323).

122. *out*] outright.

123. *several*] separate.

125. *down together*] fighting on the
ground; cf. *H5*, iv. vii. 150, 'when
Alençon and myself were down
together, I pluck'd this glove from
his helm'.

131. *bowels*] The metaphor could
be fairly inert, as in *R3*, v. ii. 3–4,
'Thus far into the bowels of the land /
Have we marched on without impedi-

ment'; but in this play it suggests
physical purgation by violence. Cf.
v. iii. 102–3, 'tearing / His country's
bowels out', and *1H6*, iii. i. 72–3,
'Civil dissension is a viperous worm /
That gnaws the bowels of the
commonwealth'.

132. *o'erbear't*] White's reading is
grammatically apter than Rowe's
o'erbear, but either may be preferred
to F's *o're-beate,* a form that does not
occur elsewhere; Compositor B could
have misread or misremembered.
For other instances of overbearing
flood-water cf. iii. i. 246–8 and note,
Oth., i. iii. 56, *Per.,* v. i. 191–2, and
MND., ii. i. 91–2. For *o'erborne* used
of invaded territory see below, iv. vi.
79, and for flood and military violence together cf. *Cym.,* v. iii. 47–8.

137. *absolute*] perfect, consummate.

Th'one half of my commission, and set down
As best thou art experienc'd, since thou know'st   140
Thy country's strength and weakness, thine own ways:
Whether to knock against the gates of Rome,
Or rudely visit them in parts remote,
To fright them, ere destroy. But come in.
Let me commend thee first to those that shall   145
Say yea to thy desires. A thousand welcomes!
And more a friend than e'er an enemy—
Yet, Martius, that was much! Your hand: most
        welcome!   *Exeunt* [*Coriolanus and Aufidius*].

        [*The two Servingmen come forward.*]

First Serv. Here's a strange alteration!

Second Serv. By my hand, I had thought to have   150
        strucken him with a cudgel; and yet my mind
        gave me his clothes made a false report of
        him.

First Serv. What an arm he has! He turned me about
        with his finger and his thumb, as one would set up   155
        a top.

Second Serv. Nay, I knew by his face that there was
        something in him. He had, sir, a kind of face,
        methought—I cannot tell how to term it.

First Serv. He had so, looking as it were—would I   160
        were hanged, but I thought there was more in him
        than I could think.

139–41. down . . . weakness,] *As F;* down— . . . weakness—*Cam.*   148. S.D.
Coriolanus . . . Aufidius] *Capell; not in F.*   *The . . . forward.*] *Cam.; Enter two
of the Seruingmen. | F.*   149. *First Serv.*] *F* (1) *(also 2 and 3, throughout scene).*

139. *commission*] apparently referring both to his warrant and to the
force under his command.

set down] probably 'determine', as
in *Cym.*, I. iv. 159 (*O.E.D.*, set 143 g),
related (as the Cambridge punctuation brings out) to *thine own ways*. It
may, however, refer to the disposing
of the army, as at v. iii. 2, where it
means 'encamp' (*O.E.D.*, 143 a).

The syntactical uncertainty of F's
punctuation is probably Shakespeare's.

150. *By my hand*] Cf. Parolles in
All's W., III. vi. 63, 'By the hand of a
soldier I will undertake it'.

152. *gave me*] warned me, made me
suspicious; cf. *H8*, v. iii. 109.

155. *set up*] i.e. set spinning.

Second Serv. So did I, I'll be sworn. He is simply the
     rarest man i'th'world.
First Serv. I think he is: but a greater soldier than he,   165
     you wot on.
Second Serv. Who? my master?
First Serv. Nay, it's no matter for that.
Second Serv. Worth six on him.
First Serv. Nay, not so neither: but I take him to be the   170
     greater soldier.
Second Serv. Faith, look you, one cannot tell how to say
     that: for the defence of a town our general is
     excellent.
First Serv. Ay, and for an assault too.   175

Enter the Third Servingman.

Third Serv. O slaves, I can tell you news, news you
     rascals.
First and Second Serv. What, what, what? Let's partake.
Third Serv. I would not be a Roman of all nations; I had
     as lief be a condemned man.   180
First and Second Serv. Wherefore? Wherefore?

165–6. he, you wot on] *This edn.;* he, / You wot one *F;* he you wot on *Dyce.*
178, 181. *First . . . Serv.*] *F (Both.).*   180. lief] *F4* (lieve); liue *F.*

163–75. *He is . . . assault too*] The
ambiguities of this exchange are
largely owed to the tentativeness of
the servants as they sound out each
other's reactions, and they should
not be wholly eliminated by editorial
meddling and fussing. Yet it is possible, as Gomme says, that Shakespeare 'allowed the servants' defective
syntax to get the better of him'.

165–6. *but . . . on*] The text retains
F's punctuation with Dyce's *on* for
one. The *but* appears to qualify the
praise of Coriolanus, but only the
slight pause after *he* saves the first
servant from claiming that Coriolanus
is the greater soldier. Reading *one*
in a modernized text has the effect
of committing the speaker to Aufidius.

As Shakespeare did not differentiate
on and *one* in his spelling (cf. I. i. 15,
I. ii. 4, II. ii. 81, III. i. 142) and as
they were pronounced alike, it *is*
apt that the equivocation be pre-
served. As Case says, 'you wot on' is
an expression to avoid imprudent
reference (cf. *Gent.,* IV. iv. 25).

169. *Worth . . . him*] Some, from
what has gone before, have taken
him to refer to Coriolanus; others,
from what follows, take the reference for Aufidius. There is comedy
in allowing the apparently vehement
commitment to be non-committal.

170. *him*] Again, this may refer to
Aufidius, but the reply seems to
make the opposite assumption.

180. *lief*] gladly, willingly.

Third Serv. Why, here's he that was wont to thwack our
  general, Caius Martius.
First Serv. Why do you say 'thwack our general'?
Third Serv. I do not say 'thwack our general'; but he   185
  was always good enough for him.
Second Serv. Come, we are fellows and friends: he was
  ever too hard for him; I have heard him say so
  himself.
First Serv. He was too hard for him directly, to say the   190
  truth on't: before Corioles he scotched him and
  notched him like a carbonado.
Second Serv. And he had been cannibally given, he might
  have broiled and eaten him too.
First Serv. But more of thy news.   195
Third Serv. Why, he is so made on here within as if he
  were son and heir to Mars; set at upper end o'th'
  table; no question asked him by any of the senators
  but they stand bald before him. Our general himself
  makes a mistress of him, sanctifies himself with's   200

191. on't:] *Pope;* on't *F.*   194. broiled] *Pope;* boyld *F.*

187. *Come . . . friends*] an invitation
to speak openly after the riddling
obliquities that have gone before.

190. *directly*] probably 'in direct
encounter, face to face', as in I. vi. 58,
and as suggested by the placing of the
comma. But the more usual Shakespearean meaning is 'without eva-
sion', which may be intended here;
cf. *1H4*, II. iii. 83, *Cym.*, I. iv. 153,
Oth., II. i. 216. Wright compares
simply in l. 163. Cf. the play with
'directly' where the plebs accost
Cinna the poet in *Caes.*, III. iii. 9–22.

192. *carbonado*] 'A piece of fish,
flesh or fowl, scored across and
grilled or broiled upon the coals'
O.E.D.).

194. *broiled*] Pope's emendation of
F's *boyld*. It is easier to attribute the
slip to the compositor than to Shakespeare; the culinary knowledge allowed to the first servant is aptly
sustained by the second.

196. *so made on*] made so much of.
197. *upper end*] i.e. next to Aufidius.
North says of Aufidius, 'he feasted
him for that time, and entertained
him in the honorablest manner he
could' (Appendix, p. 346).

198–9. *no question . . . bald*] i.e. no
senator would ask him a question
without first removing his hat. As
evidence that Elizabethan gentlemen
wore their hats at dinner, Wilson
enlists the National Portrait Gallery's
'Masque of the Wedding of Sir
Henry Unton in 1580'. *O.E.D.* gives
only this instance of *bald* meaning
'bareheaded' (s.v. 4 d), and it may
therefore mean, as Wilson supposes,
'showing their bald heads'. For the
inauthentic Roman hats cf. III. ii.
73 note.

200–1. *sanctifies . . . hand*] 'considers
the touch of his hand as holy; clasps
it with the same reverence as a lover
would clasp the hand of his mistress'

hand, and turns up the white o'th'eye to his
discourse. But the bottom of the news is, our general
is cut i'th'middle, and but one half of what he was
yesterday; for the other has half, by the entreaty
and grant of the whole table. He'll go, he says,   205
and sowl the porter of Rome gates by th'ears.
He will mow all down before him, and leave his
passage polled.

Second Serv. And he's as like to do't as any man I can
imagine.   210

Third Serv. Do't? He will do't: for look you, sir, he
has as many friends as enemies; which friends, sir,
as it were, durst not, look you sir, show themselves,
as we term it, his friends, whilst he's in directitude.

First Serv. Directitude! What's that?   215

Third Serv. But when they shall see, sir, his crest up
again, and the man in blood, they will out of their
burrows, like conies after rain, and revel all with
him.

First Serv. But when goes this forward?   220

Third Serv. Tomorrow, today, presently; you shall

---

206. sowl] *Rowe (subst.)*; sole *F*.   214, 215. directitude] *F*; discreditude *conj.*
Malone; dejectitude *Wilson, conj. Collier*[2].

(Malone). Cf. *Rom.*, I. v. 93, 'palm to
palm is holy palmers' kiss', and
AYL., III. iv. 12.

201. *turns . . . eye*] expressing pious
adoration.

202. *bottom . . . news*] i.e. what it
comes down to; cf. *1H4*, IV. i. 50,
'The very bottom and the soul of
hope'.

203. *cut i'th'middle*] i.e. like a joint
of meat (King).

206. *sowl*] seize roughly, drag.

208. *polled*] lopped, cleared.

214. *directitude*] Malone thought it
unlikely that Shakespeare would
make the third servant talk total
nonsense and suggested *discreditude*
as a word 'with some resemblance to
sense'. Wilson on similar grounds
supports Collier's *dejectitude*, citing
Lr., IV. i. 3, and *Per.*, II. ii. 46. Either,

however, would be intelligible to
the first servant and would make his
bewilderment unconvincing; either
could be the impressive word sought
after; and no emendation is defen-
sible in view of the repetition being of
a kind to alert the compositor.

216. *his crest up*] Cf. *1H4*, I. i. 98–9,
'bristle up / The crest of youth', and
John, IV. iii. 148–9, 'Now for the
bare-pick'd bone of majesty / Doth
dogged war bristle his angry crest'.

217. *in blood*] in full vigour and cry
(a hunting term, cf. I. i. 158–9 and
note).

221–32.] In Helene Weigel's production of Brecht's version, these
lines are characteristically reassigned
to two drunken Volscian officers.
See Introduction, p. 87.

221. *presently*] now.

have the drum struck up this afternoon. 'Tis as it
were a parcel of their feast, and to be executed ere
they wipe their lips.

Second Serv. Why, then we shall have a stirring world   225
again. This peace is nothing but to rust iron,
increase tailors, and breed ballad-makers.

First Serv. Let me have war, say I. It exceeds peace as
far as day does night: it's sprightly walking, audible,
and full of vent. Peace is a very apoplexy, lethargy;   230
mulled, deaf, sleepy, insensible; a getter of more
bastard children than war's a destroyer of men.

Second Serv. 'Tis so, and as wars, in some sort, may be
said to be a ravisher, so it cannot be denied but
peace is a great maker of cuckolds.   235

First Serv. Ay, and it makes men hate one another.

229. sprightly walking] *F, Sisson;* sprightly, waking *Pope.*   231. sleepy] *F3;*
sleepe *F.*   232. war's] *Rowe²;* warres *F.*   233. wars] *F;* war *Rowe³.*

223. *parcel*] part.

229–30. *sprightly . . . vent*] a much
disputed passage, but there is little
doubt that the metaphor makes war a
hunting hound (cf. *Caes.*, III. i. 274,
'let slip the dogs of war') and that
emendation is needless. As Sisson
says (following Baynes and others),
'*vent* is "scent", and *audible* refers to
the hound's cry upon scent'. *O.E.D.*
gives vent (*sb.²* 13 a) as 'The scent
given off by a hunted animal', and
cites Turberville, *Venerie,* 61, 'When
my Hounde doth streyne upon good
vent'. It is just possible, however,
that *audible* is here used in the rare
sense 'able to hear' (*O.E.D.*, s.v. 2).
Other interpretations of *full of vent*
include 'full of rumour' (Johnson),
'efficacious to clear the country of its
surplus population' (Craig), 'full of
utterance' (Case), and 'effervescent
or full of scent' (Wright). Craig's
otherwise surprising version receives
some support from I. i. 224, while
Wright claims a point-by-point
antithesis 'in inverted order' between
the terms of this sentence and those
of the next (see below, l. 231 note).

230. *apoplexy, lethargy*] Cf. *2H4,*
I. ii. 105, 'This apoplexy, as I take it,
is a kind of lethargy, an't please your
lordship'.

231. *mulled*] *O.E.D.* (mull *v.²*)
offers this as an instance of the rare
sense 'dull, stupefy' and cites also
Cotton's *Poems,* 1689, p. 96, 'Till ale
which crowns all such pretences, /
Mull'd them again into their senses'.
As Case says, however, both contexts would suggest the sense 'soften-
ed, rendered mild', which is an
O.E.D. conjecture for the original
meaning (from Dutch *mul,* soft).
Wright thinks that mulled wine is
here metaphorically contrasted with
the lively, effervescent wine of war
('full of vent').

232. *war's*] The apostrophe and
the single form are preferred here
because the speaker uses *war* in
l. 228. F's plural form would otherwise be acceptable, and many retain
it, keeping consonance with l. 233
where *wars* = the wars, and governs
a singular construction (i.e. is *a
ravisher*); see *O.E.D.*, s.v. I c.

Third Serv. Reason: because they then less need one
    another. The wars for my money. I hope to see
    Romans as cheap as Volscians. They are rising,
    they are rising.   240
First and Second Serv. In, in, in, in!   *Exeunt.*

[SCENE VI]

Enter the two Tribunes, SICINIUS *and* BRUTUS.

Sic. We hear not of him, neither need we fear him;
    His remedies are tame i'th'present peace
    And quietness of the people, which before
    Were in wild hurry. Here do we make his friends
    Blush that the world goes well; who rather had,   5
    Though they themselves did suffer by't, behold
    Dissentious numbers pest'ring streets, than see
    Our tradesmen singing in their shops and going
    About their functions friendly.
Bru. We stood to't in good time.

Enter MENENIUS.

                    Is this Menenius?   10

241. *First . . . Serv.*] F (*Both.*).

Scene VI

SCENE VI] *Pope.*   2. tame i'th'] *Theobald;* tame, the *F;* ta'en the *conj. Johnson;* tame. The *White.*   4. hurry. Here] *F;* hurry, here *White.*   10. S.D.]
Follows friendly (*l. 9*) *in* F.

Scene vi] usually set in 'Rome. A
public Place', following Rowe and
Theobald. Sicinius' opening speech
makes it clear that a busy market-
place would best suit the scene (see
Introduction, p. 73).

2–5. *tame . . . well*] Sisson (*New
Readings*) defends F on the ground
that *His remedies* means 'remedies
against Coriolanus, antidotes to Coriolanus', and *tame* means characterized
by peace and quiet. But this strains
the more usual meaning of *tame* as
found elsewhere in Shakespeare, and
as distinguished from *wild* in l. 4; it is
also at odds with the thought of the
previous line, which suggests a men-

ace disarmed and rendered powerless.
The quiet of the city leaves no occasion for those who hoped Coriolanus
would prove a necessary remedy to
recover the peace of Rome. Theobald's intervention is slightly less
unsatisfactory than the repunctuating
of l. 4 together with the deletion of
we, and it is not graphically implausible.

7. *pest'ring*] obstructing, crowding.
8–9. *singing . . . friendly*] Sicinius is
setting Shakespeare's scene, see headnote.

9. *functions*] occupations.
10. *stood to't*] were resolute on the
issue.

Sic. 'Tis he, 'tis he. Oh, he is grown most kind
    Of late. Hail, sir!
Men.   Hail to you both!
Sic. Your Coriolanus is not much miss'd
    But with his friends: the commonwealth doth stand,
    And so would do, were he more angry at it.   15
Men. All's well, and might have been much better if
    He could have temporiz'd.
Sic.   Where is he, hear you?
Men. Nay, I hear nothing. His mother and his wife
    Hear nothing from him.

Enter three or four Citizens.

All. The gods preserve you both!
Sic.   Good den, our neighbours.
Bru. Good den to you all, good den to you all.   21
First Cit. Ourselves, our wives, and children, on our knees
    Are bound to pray for you both.
Sic.   Live, and thrive!
Bru. Farewell, kind neighbours. We wish'd Coriolanus
    Had lov'd you as we did.
All.   Now the gods keep you!   25
Both Trib. Farewell, farewell.   *Exeunt Citizens.*
Sic. This is a happier and more comely time
    Than when those fellows ran about the streets
    Crying confusion.
Bru.   Caius Martius was
    A worthy officer i'th'war, but insolent,   30
    O'ercome with pride, ambitious past all thinking,

11–12. 'Tis . . . late] *As Capell; one line in F.*   13–17. Your . . . temporiz'd]
After Capell (Coriolanus, sir)*; prose in F.*   18–19. His mother . . . him] *As
Capell; one line in F.*   20, 21. Good den] *Collier;* Gooden *F;* Good e'en *F4.*
22. First Cit.] *F* (1).   24–5. We . . . did] *As Hanmer; one line in F.*   31. ambitious . . . thinking,] *F4;* ambitious, . . . thinking *F.*

18, 19. *hear nothing*] Cf. iv. i. 50–3.   plague! death! confusion!' Cf. *1H4,*
20. *Good den*] Cf. ii. i. 92 and note.   v. i. 82, *2H6,* v. ii. 31, and above
29. *Crying confusion*] perhaps literally   iii. i. 109; also 'cry havoc', *Caes.,*
so, as in *Lr.,* ii. iv. 93, 'Vengeance!   iii. i. 274.

Self-loving.
Sic.   And affecting one sole throne,
Without assistance.
Men.   I think not so.
Sic. We should by this, to all our lamentation,
If he had gone forth consul, found it so.   35
Bru. The gods have well prevented it, and Rome
Sits safe and still without him.

Enter an Ædile.

Æd.   Worthy tribunes,
There is a slave whom we have put in prison,
Reports the Volsces with two several powers
Are enter'd in the Roman territories,   40
And with the deepest malice of the war,
Destroy what lies before 'em.
Men.   'Tis Aufidius,
Who, hearing of our Martius' banishment,
Thrusts forth his horns again into the world,
Which were inshell'd when Martius stood for Rome,
And durst not once peep out.
Sic.   Come, what talk you   46
Of Martius?
Bru. Go see this rumourer whipp'd. It cannot be

32. Self-loving.] *F;* Self-loving,—*Capell.*   32-3. And ... assistance] *As Theo-*
bald; one line in F.   33. assistance] *F* (assistace), *Rowe;* assistants *Hanmer.*
34. lamentation] *F2;* lamention *F.*   35. found] *F;* have found *conj. Malone.*

32-3. *affecting . . . assistance*] In
North, Coriolanus is formally charged
with seeking 'to take the soveraine
authoritie out of the peoples handes'
(Appendix, p. 337), but the form of
words here shadows the emergence of
Caesar.

34-5. *should . . . found*] Abbott (415)
describes the elliptical omission of
'have' here as 'anomalous'.

41. *deepest malice*] as *R 2,* I. i. 155,
'Deep malice makes too deep in-
cision'.

44-6. *Thrusts . . . peep out*] Case

compares Nashe, *Pasquil's Apologie*
(ed. McKerrow, I, p. 131), 'I
wonder how these seelie snayles,
creeping but yesterdaie out of shoppes
and Grammer-schooles, dare thrust
out theyr feeble hornes, against so
tough and mighty adversaries.' The
hero of the interlude *Thersites* (1537)
does battle with a snail until it draws
in its horns (Dodsley, ed. Hazlitt,
I, p. 413).

46. *what*] i.e. what for? why?

48. *rumourer whipp'd*] For the beating of bearers of bad news cf. *R 3,*

The Volsces dare break with us.

Men.   Cannot be?
We have record that very well it can,   50
And three examples of the like hath been
Within my age. But reason with the fellow
Before you punish him, where he heard this,
Lest you shall chance to whip your information,
And beat the messenger who bids beware   55
Of what is to be dreaded.

Sic.   Tell not me.
I know this cannot be.

Bru.   Not possible.

Enter a Messenger.

Mess. The nobles in great earnestness are going
         All to the senate-house. Some news is coming
         That turns their countenances.

Sic.   'Tis this slave—   60
Go whip him 'fore the people's eyes—his raising,
Nothing but his report.

Mess.   Yes, worthy sir,
The slave's report is seconded; and more,
More fearful, is deliver'd.

Sic.   What more fearful?

Mess. It is spoke freely out of many mouths,   65
         How probable I do not know, that Martius,
         Join'd with Aufidius, leads a power 'gainst Rome,

---

51. hath] *F;* have *F4.*   56–7. Tell . . . be] *As Pope; one line in F.*
59. coming] *F;* come *Rowe;* come in *Malone.*

IV. iv. 510, and *Ant.*, II. v. 61. It is a
sign of authority demoralized and
frustrated; cf. *Mac.*, v. iii. 11.

50. *record*] accented on second
syllable; cf. *Ham.*, I. v. 99.

51. *hath*] 'An example of the
surviving plurals in -*th*, very common
in the words *hath* and *doth* especially'
(Case).

52. *reason*] converse, talk; cf.
Mer.V., II. viii. 27, *R3*, II. iii. 39.

59. *coming*] i.e. is in the process of
coming in by instalments. No emendation is needed, but it is nevertheless possible that -*ing* was caught
from *going* in the previous line.

60. *turns*] possibly 'turns pale';
cf. *Ham.*, II. ii. 512 and 547, where
Polonius observes that the player
has 'turn'd his colour, and has
tears in's eyes', and Hamlet speaks
of his 'visage wann'd'.

61. *raising*] i.e. rumour-raising.

And vows revenge as spacious as between
The young'st and oldest thing.
Sic.   This is most likely!
Bru. Rais'd only that the weaker sort may wish   70
Good Martius home again.
Sic.   The very trick on't.
Men. This is unlikely:
He and Aufidius can no more atone
Than violent'st contrariety.

Enter [a Second] Messenger.

Second Mess. You are sent for to the senate.   75
A fearful army, led by Caius Martius,
Associated with Aufidius, rages
Upon our territories, and have already
O'erborne their way, consum'd with fire, and took
What lay before them.   80

Enter COMINIUS.

Com. O, you have made good work.
Men.   What news? What news?
Com. You have holp to ravish your own daughters, and
To melt the city leads upon your pates,
To see your wives dishonour'd to your noses—
Men. What's the news? What's the news?   85

---

74. contrariety] *F;* contrarieties *Hanmer, Wilson.*   74. S.D. *a Second*] *Cam.*
84. noses—] *Capell;* Noses. *F.*

68. *as spacious as between*] wide
enough to include.

69. *young'st . . . thing*] The obvious
meaning—the youngest to the oldest
—is questioned by Chambers, who
glosses, 'as from the creation to
today', referring to the infinite
extent of Coriolanus' revenge.

73. *atone*] in the radical sense,
'make one', hence 'agree, be reconciled'; cf. *AYL.,* v. iv. 104.

74. *contrariety*] The singular form

is the more expressive because the
more abstract (cf. 'mere oppug-
nancy', *Troil.,* i. iii. 111); it does not
occur elsewhere in Shakespeare, but
for the plural cf. *1H6,* ii. iii. 59. For
its occurrence in Averell see Introduction, p. 30.

79. *O'erborne . . . way*] Cf. iv. v. 132
and note.

82. *holp*] See iii. i. 274 note.

83. *leads*] leaded roofs.

Com. Your temples burned in their cement, and
        Your franchises, whereon you stood, confin'd
        Into an auger's bore.

Men.   Pray now, your news?—
        You have made fair work, I fear me.—Pray, your
            news?
        If Martius should be join'd wi'th'Volscians—

Com.   If!   90
        He is their god. He leads them like a thing
        Made by some other deity than nature,
        That shapes man better; and they follow him
        Against us brats, with no less confidence
        Than boys pursuing summer butterflies,   95
        Or butchers killing flies.

Men.   You have made good work,
        You, and your apron-men; you that stood so much
        Upon the voice of occupation and
        The breath of garlic-eaters!

---

88. auger's bore] *Rowe;* Augors boare *F.*   90. wi'th'] *Alexander;* with *F.*
90–1. If . . . thing] *As Capell; one line in F.*

86. *burned . . . cement*] perhaps
calcined, burned to dust; but it
may mean 'fused together'; cf. l. 138
'burn us all into one coal'. Wilson
suggests 'into their mortar; i.e. to
the ground'. The stress is on the first
syllable of *cement,* hence the dissyl-
labic *burned.* Plutarch does not say
that Martius intended to burn Rome,
but see Introduction, p. 53.

87–8. *whereon . . . bore*] The image
of the hole made by an auger, or
boring tool, elicits a literal sense from
stood—there will not be room for
them to stand on their franchises
(King). Cf. l. 10 above, and *Mac.,*
II. iii. 120.

92. *deity . . . nature*] Cf. *Lr.,* I. ii. 1,
'Thou, Nature, art my goddess'.

96. *butchers . . . flies*] Case compares
Nashe, *Prognostication* (ed. McKerrow,
III, p. 392), 'for Butchers are like to
make greate havoc amongst flies,
and beggers on Sunneshine daies to
commit great murthers upon their
rebellious vermine'; also Dekker,

Old Fortunatus (ed. Bowers, I. ii. 162),
'would I were turn'd into a flip-flap,
and solde to the Butchers'. Cf. also
Oth., IV. ii. 67, 'as summer flies are
in the shambles'. Needlessly supposing *flies* caught from *butterflies,* Capell
proposed *sheep,* Leo *pigs,* and Hibbard *calves.* The reference to butchers
ironically courts the same kind of
contempt as *apron men* in Menenius'
follow-up.

97. *apron-men*] Cf. *Caes.,* I. i. 7,
'Where is thy leather apron and thy
rule?', and *Ant.,* v. ii. 208–9, 'Mech-
anic slaves, / With greasy aprons,
rules and hammers'. For the patrician
scorn of tradesmen, especially in
Sparta, see Introduction, p. 54.

98. *voice of occupation*] workmen's
vote.

99. *breath*] i.e. voice, vote.

garlic-eaters] Cf. *Meas.,* III. ii. 170,
'he would mouth with a beggar
though she smelt brown bread and
garlic', and *MND.,* IV. ii. 37, where
Bottom tells the actors to eat no

Com. He'll shake your Rome about your ears.

Men.   As Hercules
   Did shake down mellow fruit. You have made fair
      work!   101

Bru. But is this true, sir?

Com.   Ay, and you'll look pale
   Before you find it other. All the regions
   Do smilingly revolt, and who resists
   Are mock'd for valiant ignorance,   105
   And perish constant fools. Who is't can blame him?
   Your enemies and his find something in him.

Men. We are all undone unless
   The noble man have mercy.

Com.   Who shall ask it?
   The tribunes cannot do't for shame; the people   110
   Deserve such pity of him as the wolf
   Does of the shepherds. For his best friends, if they
   Should say, 'Be good to Rome', they charg'd him even
   As those should do that had deserv'd his hate,
   And therein show'd like enemies.

Men.   'Tis true!   115
   If he were putting to my house the brand
   That should consume it, I have not the face
   To say, 'Beseech you, cease'. You have made fair
      hands,

100–1. As . . . fruit] *As Capell; one line in F.*   104. resists] *F; resist Hanmer.*
115–16. 'Tis . . . brand] *As Pope; one line in F.*

onions or garlic. For other allusion to
stinking popular breath see III. i. 65,
III. iii. 121 and note.

100–1. *Hercules . . . fruit*] The
eleventh of Hercules' twelve labours
(referred to at IV. i. 17) was to pluck
the golden apples of the Hesperides.
But the allusion turns into hyperbole,
expressing superfluity of strength.
Cf. *Ham.*, III. ii. 185–6, 'Which now,
the fruit unripe, sticks on the tree; /
But fall unshaken when they mellow
be'.

104. *who resists*] whoever resist (see
Abbott 251).

105. *valiant ignorance*] The phrase is

used to different effect by Thersites of
Achilles, *Troil.*, III. iii. 308.

106. *constant*] loyal.

112. *For*] As for.

113–15. *charg'd . . . show'd*] subjunctive construction, 'would charge
. . . would show' (see Abbott 361). It
seems that *charge* here means 'enjoin
with a plea'; if Coriolanus' friends
were to plead with him to spare
Rome they would in that respect be
behaving as his enemies (the tribunes and plebeians who *deserv'd his
hate*) would behave.

118. *made fair hands*] i.e. you have
made a pretty mess of it; cf. *H8*,

You and your crafts! You have crafted fair!
Com.   You have brought
     A trembling upon Rome, such as was never   120
     S'incapable of help.
Both Trib.   Say not we brought it.
Men. How? Was't we? We lov'd him, but, like beasts
     And cowardly nobles, gave way unto your clusters,
     Who did hoot him out o'th'city.
Com.   But I fear
     They'll roar him in again. Tullus Aufidius,   125
     The second name of men, obeys his points
     As if he were his officer. Desperation
     Is all the policy, strength and defence,
     That Rome can make against them.

                Enter a Troop of Citizens.

Men.   Here come the clusters.
     And is Aufidius with him? You are they   130
     That made the air unwholesome when you cast
     Your stinking greasy caps in hooting at
     Coriolanus' exile. Now he's coming,
     And not a hair upon a soldier's head

---

121. *Both Trib.*] *Dyce; Tri.* | *F.*   122–4.] *As Pope;* How? . . . him, | . . .
Nobles, | . . . hoote | . . . Citty. *F.*   129. come] *F;* comes *Alexander.*

v. iv. 67, 'Y'have made a fine hand
fellows', and Tilley, H 99.

119. *crafted fair*] Unlike similar
expressions in the scene, this is
evidently a Menenius coinage.

120. *A trembling upon Rome*] Shakespeare a little exaggerates the
extremity of Roman fear and panic
at the return of Martius.

121. *S'incapable of help*] i.e. of
remedy.

122. *Was't we?*] Menenius gives an
ironical but uncertain answer to his
own question.

123. *clusters*] crowds, swarms.

125. *roar*] Cf. *1H4*, ii. iv. 250,
'and roar'd for mercy, and still run

and roar'd', and above, ii. iii 55.
Aufidius will use the word against
Martius later (v. vi. 98).

126. *second name*] i.e. second to
Coriolanus in renown.

obeys his points] 'obeys him in every
point' (Onions). But Shakespeare
also uses the verb *points* to mean
'directs' (e.g. *Wint.*, iv. iv. 518, 553)
and Wright interprets *points* here as
'directions, commands'. A 'point of
war' was a drum or trumpet signal
(see *2H4*, iv. i. 52), a usage that
gives the phrase an added cogency;
Aufidius acts like an obedient
soldier in the field.

131–2. *cast . . . caps*] Cf. iii. iii. 137.

Which will not prove a whip. As many coxcombs   135
As you threw caps up will he tumble down,
And pay you for your voices. 'Tis no matter,
If he could burn us all into one coal,
We have deserv'd it.

Citizens. Faith, we hear fearful news.

First Cit.   For mine own part,
When I said banish him, I said 'twas pity.   141

Second Cit. And so did I.

Third Cit. And so did I; and, to say the truth, so did
very many of us. That we did we did for the best,
and though we willingly consented to his banish-   145
ment, yet it was against our will.

Com. Y'are goodly things, you voices.

Men.   You have made good work,
You and your cry. Shall's to the Capitol?

Com. O, ay, what else?   *Exeunt Cominius and Menenius.*

Sic. Go masters, get you home; be not dismay'd;   150
These are a side that would be glad to have
This true which they so seem to fear. Go home,
And show no sign of fear.

First Cit. The gods be good to us! Come, masters, let's
home. I ever said we were i'th'wrong when we   155
banished him.

Second Cit. So did we all. But come, let's home.

                              Exeunt Citizens.

Bru. I do not like this news.

Sic. Nor I.

---

135. *coxcombs*] fools' heads; named
after the hood of the professional
jester. Cf. *Shr.*, II. i. 222, 'What is
your crest—a coxcomb? . . . A
combless cock, so Kate will be my
hen'.

138. *burn . . . coal*] i.e. fuse into one
cindery mass. For *coal* = cinder see
O.E.D. s.v. 2. See l. 86 note.

141.] For the suggestion that at
this point Shakespeare betrays the
plebeian cause see Rossiter, *Angel
with horns*, p. 236, and Introduction,
p. 55. The responses of plebeians,
tribunes, and patricians are well
observed.

148. *cry*] pack of hounds. See III.
iii. 120 and note.

Shall's] Shall us = shall we, as
several times in Shakespeare; see
Abbott 215.

151. *side*] faction.

Bru. Let's to the Capitol. Would half my wealth   160
　　Would buy this for a lie!
Sic.   Pray let's go.   *Exeunt.*

[SCENE VII]

Enter AUFIDIUS *with his Lieutenant.*

Auf. Do they still fly to th'Roman?
Lieu. I do not know what witchcraft's in him, but
　　Your soldiers use him as the grace 'fore meat,
　　Their talk at table and their thanks at end;
　　And you are darken'd in this action, sir,   5
　　Even by your own.
Auf.   I cannot help it now,
　　Unless, by using means, I lame the foot
　　Of our design. He bears himself more proudlier
　　Even to my person than I thought he would
　　When first I did embrace him. Yet his nature   10
　　In that's no changeling, and I must excuse
　　What cannot be amended.
Lieu.   Yet I wish, sir,
　　I mean for your particular, you had not
　　Join'd in commission with him; but either

---

161. S.D.] *F* (*Exeunt Tribunes.*).

Scene VII

SCENE VII] *Capell.*   14–16.] *As Malone;* Ioyn'd . . . borne / . . . soly. / *F.*

Scene VII] Most editors follow Theobald and set the scene in 'A Camp at a small distance from Rome'. The imminence of the attack on Rome is clear from the dialogue; a tent-structure would be appropriate but is not indicated.

5. *darken'd*] eclipsed; cf. II. i. 257.
action] military action, campaign.

6. *your own*] i.e. your own men; or, possibly, a pun on *action* ('your own deed').

7–8. *Unless . . . design*] i.e. 'except

by using such means as would cause me to impede our design on Rome'.

8. *more proudlier*] Cf. III. i. 119, 'more worthier', and for other instances, Abbott 11.

11. *changeling*] turncoat, renegade, as in *1 H 4*, v. i. 76.

13. *for your particular*] as far as you personally are concerned; cf. e.g. *Troil.*, II. ii. 9.

14. *Join'd in commission*] Cf. North, 'Thus he was joyned in commission with Tullus as generall of the Volsces' (Appendix, p. 350).

Have borne the action of yourself, or else   15
  To him had left it solely.
Auf. I understand thee well, and be thou sure
  When he shall come to his account, he knows not
  What I can urge against him. Although it seems,
  And so he thinks, and is no less apparent   20
  To th'vulgar eye, that he bears all things fairly
  And shows good husbandry for the Volscian state,
  Fights dragon-like, and does achieve as soon
  As draw his sword: yet he hath left undone
  That which shall break his neck or hazard mine   25
  Whene'er we come to our account.
Lieu. Sir, I beseech you, think you he'll carry Rome?
Auf. All places yields to him ere he sits down,
  And the nobility of Rome are his.
  The senators and patricians love him too;   30
  The tribunes are no soldiers, and their people
  Will be as rash in the repeal as hasty
  To expel him thence. I think he'll be to Rome
  As is the osprey to the fish, who takes it

---

15. Have] *F*; had *Pope*.   19. him. Although] *Capell;* him, although *F*.
34. osprey] *F* (Asprey), *Theobald*.

15. *Have*] for 'could have'. Sisson
remarks that 'shifting of construction
is a characteristic of Shakespeare's
later style'.

17–26. *I understand . . . account*]
For the 'first occasion of the Volsces
envy to Coriolanus' and for the
'secret murmurings' against him see
North, Appendix, p. 355. The
source does not, however, make it
precisely clear what, at this stage, he
has *left undone*. Cf. the vague allusion
at v. vi. 64 to 'faults he made before
the last'.

22. *good husbandry*] careful manage-
ment.

28–57.] 'I have always thought this,
in itself so beautiful speech, the least
explicable from the mood and full
intention of the speaker of any in the
whole works of Shakespeare, I
cherish the hope that I am mistaken,
and that, becoming wiser, I shall

discover some profound excellence
in that in which I now appear to
detect an imperfection' (Coleridge,
Shakespeare Criticism, ed. T. M.
Raysor, 1960, p. 81). The comment
has provoked a wide range of
responses. A strain of self-communing
soliloquy in the speech, yielding
peculiar shifts and ambiguities, makes
it an unexpected passage of dialogue
between commander and lieutenant.

28. *All places . . . down*] i.e. they
yield before he lays siege to them.
North tells of his harsh treatment of
those who resisted, but 'Such as dyd
yeld them selves willingly unto him,
he was as careful as possible might
be to defend them from hurte'
(Appendix, ρ. 352).

29–30. *nobility . . . patricians*] The
phrase 'nobility and patricians' occurs
in North too (e.g. Appendix, p. 328).

34. *osprey*] the fish-hawk (*pandion*

By sovereignty of nature. First, he was   35
A noble servant to them, but he could not
Carry his honours even. Whether 'twas pride,
Which out of daily fortune ever taints
The happy man; whether defect of judgement,
To fail in the disposing of those chances   40
Which he was lord of; or whether nature,
Not to be other than one thing, not moving
From th'casque to th'cushion, but commanding peace
Even with the same austerity and garb
As he controll'd the war; but one of these—   45
As he hath spices of them all, not all,
For I dare so far free him—made him fear'd,
So hated, and so banish'd: but he has a merit

37. 'twas] *F3*; 'was *F*.   39. defect] *F2*; detect *F*.   43. casque] *F* (Caske),
Steevens.   45. war; but] *Theobald*; warre. But *F*.   45-7. these— . . . him—]
Cam.; these / (As . . . all) . . . him, *F*.

haliaetus). Fish were supposed to yield themselves to it by turning on their backs. Langton cites Drayton, *Polyolbion*, xxv. 134-8, and Steevens cites Peele, *Battle of Alcazar* (ed. Bullen, I, p. 253), 'I will provide thee with a princely osprey, / That as she flieth over fish in pools, / The fish shall turn their glitt'ring bellies up, / And thou shalt take thy liberal choice of all'. The F form *aspray* occurs, as Case notes, in *Two Noble Kinsmen* (ed. Brooke, *Sh. Apoc.*, I. i. 150).

37. *even*] equably; cf. II. i. 222-3 and note.

38. *out of*] arising out of, by occasion of; cf. *1 H 4*, I. iii. 51.

daily fortune] 'uninterrupted train of success' (Johnson).

39. *happy*] fortunate.

40. *disposing . . . chances*] making the most of the opportunities.

41. *whether nature*] i.e. whether it was his nature.

43. *casque . . . cushion*] i.e. from the battlefield to the senate house; *casque* = helmet, and for the cushions see III. i. 100 and note. For the

general importance of contemporary discussions of the civil role of soldiers see Introduction, pp. 27, 43-4.

44. *austerity and garb*] hendiadys for austere demeanour. For *garb* = demeanour see *O.E.D.* s.v. 2.

46-7. *As . . . him*] Shakespeare may have intended Aufidius to offer a double qualification, (1) Coriolanus is only *spiced* with all these faults, not wholly afflicted by them, (2) not all, but only one of these faults made him feared and hated. The editorial punctuation allows more momentum to the main argument.

47. *free*] absolve.

48-9. *merit . . . utt'rance*] If the antecedent of *it* is the fault that Aufidius has just tried to specify (*one of these*), he means that Martius' merit will choke back any talk of his defects. But Johnson, concerned about the continuity with ll. 51-3 (see next note), supposed *it* to refer reflexively to *merit*, and *utt'rance* to mean 'boasting'. Without fully admitting Johnson's interpretation, it is possible to recognize in the shift of Aufidius'

To choke it in the utt'rance. So our virtues
Lie in th'interpretation of the time,   50
And power, unto itself most commendable,
Hath not a tomb so evident as a chair
T'extol what it hath done.
One fire drives out one fire; one nail, one nail;
Rights by rights falter, strengths by strengths do fail.
Come, let's away. When, Caius, Rome is thine,   56
Thou art poor'st of all: then shortly art thou mine.

Exeunt.

49. virtues] *F2* (Vertues); Vertue, *F.*   55. Rights . . . falter,] *Dyce;* Rights
. . . fouler *F;* Right's . . . fouler *Sisson, after Pope* (Right's by right); Rights . . .
founder *Ard¹. conj. Johnson;* Rights . . . fuller *Hibbard.*   57. Thou art] *F;*
Thou'rt *Pope, Sisson.*

argument the emergent idea that merit is destroyed by being proclaimed. The text retains F's colon after *banish'd,* but substitutes a full-stop for a colon after *utt'rance.*

51–3. *And power . . . done*] 'This is a common thought, but miserably ill expressed', says Johnson, 'The sense is, the virtue which delights to commend itself, will find the surest *tomb* in the *chair* wherein it holds forth its own commendation.' But as Coriolanus is manifestly not given to vulgar self-commendation, the point so stated seems to the audience, if not to Aufidius, not only banal but also inept. The obscurity of the speech is part of its dramatic force, as if Aufidius' thoughts are imperfectly clarified even to himself. The *chair* is a rostrum for formal oration, as in *Caes.,* III. ii. 63, where Antony is invited to 'go up into the public chair', and as specified by North for Cominius' commendation of Coriolanus (see I. ix. 19–27 note). The passage may paraphrase, 'Power, in itself most deserving of commendation, is manifestly entombed when it is publicly commemorated'; power destroys itself through the very processes of fame and defamation. The words are therefore a fuller rendering of the thought intimated in

ll. 48–9, and they anticipate the generalities about self-destruction that immediately follow.

54–5. *One fire . . . fail*] Three of the four proverbs have analogues elsewhere. For the first two cf. *Gent.,* II. iv. 188–9, 'Even as one heat another heat expels / Or as one nail by strength drives out another'; also Tilley, F 277 and N 17, *Caes.,* III. i. 172, and *Rom.,* I. ii. 45. For the fourth, Hibbard finds an analogue in Erasmus, *Adagia* (949 c), 'Fortis in alium fortiorem incidit. Dici solitum, ubi quis nimium fretus suis viribus, aliquando nanciscitur, a quo vincatur.' (The strong man meets a stronger. Usually said when a man who relies too much on his own unaided power eventually lights on one who proves too much for him.) For the third see next note.

55. *Rights . . . falter*] Dyce's *falter* for F's *fouler* seems the more probable, as Wilson observes, in view of the possibility that the copy read *faulter* or *foulter*. While the rapidity and casualness of the thought allow little scope for sustained analysis, there is rhetorical fitness in the transition from *falter* to *fail*. On the other hand, Hibbard's *fuller* aptly corresponds with *stronger*.

ACT V

[SCENE I]

Enter MENENIUS, COMINIUS; SICINIUS, BRUTUS (*the two Tribunes*), *with others.*

Men. No, I'll not go: you hear what he hath said
  Which was sometime his general, who lov'd him
  In a most dear particular. He call'd me father:
  But what o'that? Go you that banish'd him;
  A mile before his tent fall down, and knee   5
  The way into his mercy. Nay, if he coy'd
  To hear Cominius speak, I'll keep at home.
Com. He would not seem to know me.
Men.   Do you hear?
Com. Yet one time he did call me by my name.
  I urg'd our old acquaintance, and the drops   10
  That we have bled together. 'Coriolanus'
  He would not answer to; forbad all names:
  He was a kind of nothing, titleless,

ACT V

Scene I

ACT V] *F* (*Actus Quintus.*).   SCENE I] *Rowe.*   2. lov'd] *Pope;* loued *F.*
5. knee] *F;* kneele *F2.*

Scene I] Editors follow Theobald, 'A public Place in Rome'. The scene focuses no attention on its own location but powerfully evokes the scene in Martius' tent outside Rome.

1–2. *he . . . general*] i.e. Cominius.

3. *In . . . particular*] in close personal affection (see *O.E.D.*, particular 6 d).

5. *knee*] Wilson compares *More*, II. iv. 134–5, 'and your unreverent knees, / Make them your feet to kneele to be forgyven'. Pilgrims approached shrines on their knees. The physical enactment of humility

has a peculiar importance in this play (see Introduction, p. 58).

6. *coy'd*] showed reluctance (Case). *O.E.D.* (coy 4 b) gives 'disdain', quoting this instance only; but as Case says, the root-sense (from Latin *quietus*, and French *quoy*) supports Steevens's gloss, 'condescended unwillingly, with reserve, coldness'. The senses come together in *Ven.*, 112, 'my coy disdain'.

8. *would not seem to*] i.e. affected not to.

12. *forbad all names*] For the significance of the repudiation of a name see Introduction, p. 41, 53.

Till he had forg'd himself a name o'th'fire
Of burning Rome.

Men.   Why, so: you have made good work!
A pair of tribunes that have wrack'd for Rome   16
To make coals cheap: a noble memory!

Com. I minded him how royal 'twas to pardon
When it was less expected. He replied
It was a bare petition of a state   20
To one whom they had punish'd.

Men.   Very well.
Could he say less?

Com. I offer'd to awaken his regard
For's private friends. His answer to me was
He could not stay to pick them in a pile   25
Of noisome musty chaff. He said 'twas folly,
For one poor grain or two, to leave unburnt
And still to nose th'offence.

Men.   For one poor grain or two?
I am one of those; his mother, wife, his child,
And this brave fellow too: we are the grains,   30

---

14. o'th'] F (a'th'); i'th' *Johnson.*   16. wrack'd for] *F;* rack'd for *Johnson;*
reck'd for *Warburton, conj. Theobald;* sack'd fair *Hanmer;* wreck'd fair *Mason.*
21–2. Very . . . less?] *As Johnson;* one line in F.

---

14. *o'th'fire*] Johnson's *i'th'fire* is
more precise, but emendation is
needless.

16. *wrack'd for*] i.e. done for Rome
the service of wrecking it. The
construction is elliptical and possibly
intends a pun on *wrack'd* = wrecked,
brought to ruin, and *rack'd* = strained every nerve. Emendation is
plausible but needless.

17. *coals*] charcoal; cf. IV. vi. 138.
a noble memory!] a fine memorial!
Cf. IV. v. 72, V. vi. 153. The phrase
marks a sardonic moment in the
play's preoccupation with the word
noble.

19. *When . . . less*] i.e. the less it was.
20. *bare*] probably 'threadbare,
beggarly'; but 'mere' (Steevens) is
possible, suggesting that petitionary
words cannot weigh against punish-

ment, and 'barefaced' (Chambers)
has found support although it has
no Shakespearean parallel. Mason
proposed *base,* as in *H8,* v. iii. 125,
'They are too thin, and base to hide
offences' (F), but editors of *H8*
commonly read *bare.*

23. *offer'd*] ventured.

25–6. *He could . . . chaff*] For the
winnowing metaphor cf. Matthew,
iii. 12, *Mer.V.,* I. i. 115–18, and for
the sparing of a city for the sake of a
few cf. the imminent destruction of
Sodom in Genesis, xviii. 24–33,
where the few were not found. It is
hard to forget the play's earlier
preoccupation with 'musty superfluity' (I. i. 225, I. i. 16).

28. *th'offence*] i.e. the offensive
matter, the noisome chaff.

You are the musty chaff, and you are smelt
Above the moon. We must be burnt for you.
Sic. Nay, pray be patient. If you refuse your aid
In this so never-needed help, yet do not
Upbraid's with our distress. But sure, if you   35
Would be your country's pleader, your good tongue
More than the instant army we can make,
Might stop our countryman.
Men.   No, I'll not meddle.
Sic. Pray you go to him.
Men.   What should I do?
Bru. Only make trial what your love can do   40
For Rome, towards Martius.
Men.   Well, and say that Martius
Return me, as Cominius is return'd,
Unheard; what then?
But as a discontented friend, grief-shot
With his unkindness? Say't be so?
Sic.   Yet your good will   45
Must have that thanks from Rome after the measure
As you intended well.
Men.   I'll undertake't.
I think he'll hear me. Yet to bite his lip
And hum at good Cominius, much unhearts me.
He was not taken well; he had not din'd: 50
The veins unfill'd, our blood is cold, and then

41-3. Well . . . then?] *As Pope;* Well . . . mee, / . . . then? / *F.*

31-2. *smelt . . . moon*] for the
hyperbole cf. *Ham.*, III. iii. 36.

34. *In this . . . help*] i.e. in this time
when help was never so needed. The
ellipsis is arbitrary and probably
accidental.

37. *instant . . . make*] i.e. the army
we can raise on the instant, immediately.

44. *But as*] i.e. returned merely as.
grief-shot] grief-stricken; not used
elsewhere by Shakespeare, and no
other instance in *O.E.D.*

46-7. *after . . . well*] i.e. to the
extent that you meant well.

48. *bite his lip*] in anger, as in
Shr., II. i. 241, and *R3*, IV. ii. 27.

49. *hum*] an expression of hostile
dissatisfaction; cf. *Mac.*, III. vi. 42,
and below, v. iv. 21.

50. *taken well*] taken at advantage,
tackled at the right moment; cf.
MND., III. ii. 16, *Ham.*, III. iii. 80.

50-5. *din'd . . . souls*] For the possible link between this passage and
the version of the fable of the belly as
given in Holland's Livy see Introduction, p. 55, and I. i. 134-9 note.
The limits of Merenius' 'wisdom of
the belly' are about to be discovered.

We pout upon the morning, are unapt
To give or to forgive; but when we have stuff'd
These pipes and these conveyances of our blood
With wine and feeding, we have suppler souls   55
Than in our priest-like fasts. Therefore I'll watch him
Till he be dieted to my request,
And then I'll set upon him.

Bru. You know the very road into his kindness,
And cannot lose your way.

Men.   Good faith, I'll prove him,
Speed how it will. I shall ere long have knowledge   61
Of my success.   *Exit.*

Com.   He'll never hear him.

Sic.   Not?

Com. I tell you, he does sit in gold, his eye
Red as 'twould burn Rome; and his injury
The gaoler to his pity. I kneel'd before him: 65
'Twas very faintly he said 'Rise', dismiss'd me
Thus, with his speechless hand. What he would do

62. Not?] F (Not.).

54. *conveyances*] channels (*O.E.D.* s.v. 8).

55. *suppler*] Cf. *Troil.*, II. iii. 216, 'I will knead him, I'll make him supple'.

57. *dieted*] conditioned by feeding.

60. *prove*] try.

61. *Speed . . . will*] no matter how it turns out.

62. *success*] fortune (good or bad), the outcome of the attempt.

63. *sit in gold*] Cf. North, 'he was set in his chayer of state, with a marvelous and unspeakable majestie' (Appendix, p. 354).

63-4. *his eye Red*] Cf. *2H6*, III. i. 154, 'Beaufort's red sparkling eyes blab his heart's malice', and *John*, IV. ii. 163, 'With eyes as red as new-enkindled fire'. Here the metaphor is more formidable, as the symbolic fire is proleptically actual.

64. *injury*] grievance.

67-9. *What . . . conditions*] much disputed. Difficulties of phrase, movement, and syntax are resolved in the theatre if Cominius is flourishing his letter from Coriolanus and indicating its contents. If l. 69 is taken to mean 'being bound by oath to comply with conditions agreed with the Volscians' the rest presents only slight difficulty. The conditions (referred to again at v. iii. 80) determine what Coriolanus *would do* and what *he would not*. For *yield* = comply cf. *O.E.D.* s.v. 17. Of the proposed emendations, Jervis's clarifies the sense and F could be explained as a misinterpretation of a marginal note; Brooks suggests that Shakespeare may have omitted the repetitious phrase *what he would not* from a fair copy of his original draft, and made a note of the omitted words in the margin; the compositor then replaced the words to follow, instead of precede, *He . . . me*. Emendation is needless, however,

He sent in writing after me: what he would not,
Bound with an oath to yield to his conditions:
So that all hope is vain,   70
Unless his noble mother and his wife,
Who, as I hear, mean to solicit him
For mercy to his country. Therefore let's hence,
And with our fair entreaties haste them on.   *Exeunt.*

[SCENE II]

Enter MENENIUS *to the Watch or Guard.*

First Watch. Stay! Whence are you?
Second Watch.   Stand, and go back!

68.] *F;* What he would not, he sent in writing after me; *Jervis.*   69. oath . . .
conditions:] *F;* oath, not to yield to new conditions; *Hanmer;* oath. To yield to
his conditions,—*Johnson;* oath to yield no new conditions. *conj. Johnson;* oath
to yield to no conditions. *Singer;* oath to hold to no conditions. *conj. Solly.*
70–2.] *as Johnson;* So . . . Mother, | . . . him | *F.*

Scene II

SCENE II] *Rowe.*   1, 2. *First Watch, Second Watch*] *F* (1 *Wat.*, 2 *Wat.* (*then* 1, 2)).

as an actor flourishing a letter would
have no difficulty in conveying this
part of F's sense; he may appear to
indicate passages and even phrases
in the document. Other emendations
are variants on the assumption that
Coriolanus is to make no concessions
to the Romans; but in fact he does
offer conditions of a kind (see v. iii.
14). Sisson retains F substantially and
claims that 'the word *bound* suggests
not only "coupled with" but also
"binding together" the two sets'
(*New Readings*). Many have supposed
with Malone that some words have
dropped out of the text between *oath*
and *to yield.*

70–3. *So that . . . country*] The sense
is not difficult, but different accounts
have been given of the nature of the
ellipsis. Wilson glosses *Unless,* 'if it
were not for' (cf. *All's W.,* IV. i. 6),
which is apt and probable. Otherwise we may understand, 'Unless
we put hope in his noble mother'.

Scene II

Scene II] Most editors follow Theobald's location, 'The Volscian Camp',
often adding, 'before Rome'. Some,
following Capell, specify 'an ad-
vanced post' of the camp. The
problem is to determine whether the
watch are guarding the tent of Coriolanus or not. Menenius at v. iv. 22
will speak of Martius sitting 'in his
state' and we have been led to expect
a figure who sits 'in gold' (v. i. 63).
A central tent-structure could conceal the 'state', however; attendants could draw its drapes and
Coriolanus occupy it while Menenius
speaks to the guards in ll. 59–66.
Menenius is not named at this point
in Plutarch (see Introduction, p. 33)
but Shakespeare finds occasion for
the scene in North's report of the
'familiar friends' whose expectation
of 'at the least . . . a curteous welcome' was disappointed (Appendix,
p. 354).

Men. You guard like men; 'tis well. But, by your leave,
     I am an officer of state, and come
     To speak with Coriolanus.
First Watch.   From whence?
Men.   From Rome.
First Watch. You may not pass; you must return: our
          general   5
     Will no more hear from thence.
Second Watch. You'll see your Rome embrac'd with fire before
     You'll speak with Coriolanus.
Men.   Good my friends,
     If you have heard your general talk of Rome
     And of his friends there, it is lots to blanks   10
     My name hath touch'd your ears: it is Menenius.
First Watch. Be it so, go back: the virtue of your name
     Is not here passable.
Men.   I tell thee, fellow,
     Thy general is my lover. I have been
     The book of his good acts whence men have read   15
     His fame unparallel'd, haply amplified;
     For I have ever verified my friends,

3–4. I . . . Coriolanus] *As Pope; one line in* F.   5–6.] *As Pope; prose in* F.
16. haply] *Hanmer;* happely *F;* happily *F3.*   17. verified] *F;* magnified
Hanmer; varnished *Wilson, conj. Edwards.*

10. *lots to blanks*] *O.E.D.* (lot *sb.* 5)
gives 'a thousand to one'; but the
expression is disputed. Johnson understood *lots* as prizes in a lottery, but
Malone took it as lottery tickets,
quoting *Continuation of Stowe's Chronicle,* 1615, p. 1002, 'Out of which
lottery, for want of filling, by the
number of lots, there were then
taken out and thrown away three
score thousand blanks, without abat-
ing of any one prize'. The evidence
cited in *O.E.D.* suggests that *lots*
sometimes included both prize-win-
ning tickets and *blanks,* but sometimes
only winners, and it gives no other
instance of Menenius' phrase. It
may simply mean 'the chances are'.
     11–12. *touch'd . . . virtue*] For the
association of 'touch' and 'virtue'
King compares *Mac.,* IV. iii. 143.

13. *passable*] (a) tenderable as
currency, (b) acceptable as a pass-
word. For a different quibble on the
word, see *Cym.,* I. ii. 8.
     14. *lover*] friend; cf. *Caes.,* III. ii. 43,
'I slew my best lover for the good of
Rome'.
     17–19. *verified . . . suffer*] for I have
always supported my friends, of
whom he is chief, with the amplest
testimony that truth would tolerate
without slipping into falsehood.
O.E.D. (verify I c) gives only this
instance of the sense 'To support or
back up by testimony'. Wilson,
however, anticipated by Edwards,
makes a strong case for *varnished,*
citing *Ham.,* IV. vii. 132–3, 'set a
double varnish on the fame / The
Frenchman gave you'; both find a
quibble on *size* (stature, glutinous

Of whom he's chief, with all the size that verity
Would without lapsing suffer. Nay, sometimes,
Like to a bowl upon a subtle ground,   20
I have tumbled past the throw, and in his praise
Have almost stamp'd the leasing. Therefore, fellow,
I must have leave to pass.

First Watch. Faith, sir, if you had told as many lies in
his behalf as you have uttered words in your own,   25
you should not pass here; no, though it were as
virtuous to lie as to live chastely. Therefore go back.

Men. Prithee, fellow, remember my name is Menenius,
always factionary on the party of your general.

Second Watch. Howsoever you have been his liar, as you   30
say you have, I am one that, telling true under him,
must say you cannot pass. Therefore go back.

Men. Has he dined, canst thou tell? For I would not
speak with him till after dinner.

First Watch. You are a Roman, are you?   35

Men. I am as thy general is.

First Watch. Then you should hate Rome, as he does.
Can you, when you have pushed out your gates the
very defender of them, and, in a violent popular
ignorance, given your enemy your shield, think to   40
front his revenges with the easy groans of old women,

22. almost] *F* ((almost)).   36. am] *F; am, F4.*

wash); cf. *Ham.,* II. ii. 456, 'o'ersized
with coagulate gore'. Of the many
emendations proposed *varnished* is the
most plausible graphically, particularly (as Wilson observes) in the MS.
form *vernished.*

20. *subtle*] deceitful, tricky. The
green may be deceptively smooth
and fast or, as Malone says, 'arti-
ficially unlevel'.

21. *tumbled . . . throw*] bowled
beyond the intended distance, gone
too far. Another bowling metaphor
is used at III. i. 59.

22. *stamp'd the leasing*] authenticated
falsehood. Probably a coinage metaphor but possibly legal, 'set the seal

on'. For *leasing* = falsehood (O.E.
léasung) cf. *Tw.N.,* I. v. 92, the only
other Shakespearean use.

27. *lie . . . chastely*] a bawdy quibble.

29. *factionary*] 'active as a partisan'
(*O.E.D.,* giving only this instance).

30. *Howsoever*] notwithstanding.
liar] perhaps sustaining the pun in
l. 27; note F's spelling, *Lier.*

34. *after dinner*] Case quotes
Harrison, *Description of England,* 1577,
II, 6: 'With us, the nobilitie, gentrie,
and students do ordinarilie go to
dinner at eleven before noon'.

36. *I am*] F4's comma diminishes
the irony.

41. *front*] confront.

the virginal palms of your daughters, or with the
palsied intercession of such a decayed dotant as you
seem to be? Can you think to blow out the intended
fire your city is ready to flame in, with such weak   45
breath as this? No, you are deceived; therefore back
to Rome, and prepare for your execution. You are
condemned; our general has sworn you out of re-
prieve and pardon.

Men. Sirrah, if thy captain knew I were here, he would   50
use me with estimation.

First Watch. Come, my captain knows you not.

Men. I mean thy general.

First Watch. My general cares not for you. Back, I say,
go: lest I let forth your half-pint of blood. Back,   55
that's the utmost of your having. Back!

Men. Nay, but fellow, fellow—

Enter CORIOLANUS *with* AUFIDIUS.

Cor. What's the matter?

Men. Now, you companion, I'll say an errand for you;
you shall know now that I am in estimation; you   60
shall perceive that a Jack guardant cannot office me

43. dotant] *F;* dotard *F4.*   50–1.] *Prose as Pope;* Sirra . . . heere, / He . . .
estimation. / *F.*   57. fellow—] *Theobald;* Fellow. *F.*   59. errand] *F*
(arrant), *Pope.*

42. *virginal . . . daughters*] i.e.
supplicant hands of your virgin
daughters.

43. *palsied intercession*] The paralysis
of Rome itself is described by North
in terms similar to those applied by
the guard to Menenius (Appendix,
p. 355).

dotant] dotard. The form is pre-
served only from this passage in
O.E.D.

48–9. *sworn . . . pardon*] For Coriolanus' oath cf. v. i. 69 and v. iii. 80,
also North, Appendix, p. 356.

56. *that's . . . having*] probably 'all
that you can get', but possibly 'as
far as you go'. Warburton and
others have taken it as a reference to

Menenius' 'half pint of blood' and
have emended or repunctuated accordingly.

59. *companion*] fellow; cf. iv. v. 13–
14.

I'll say . . . you] i.e. 'I'll make your
report for you'. Other possibilities
include 'now you will see me deliver
my message', and 'I'll tell him a
story about you' (Wright). Gomme
thinks that F's *arrant* (a common
variant, like *arrand*) may hold a pun
on the sense 'in error, aberrant,
roguish', but its effect would be
strained and awkward.

61. *Jack guardant*] Jack in office;
cf. *R2,* v. v. 60, 'Jack of the clock',
Ant., iii. xiii. 93, and *1H6,* i. i. 175,

from my son Coriolanus. Guess but by my entertainment with him, if thou stand'st not i'th'state of hanging, or of some death more long in spectatorship and
crueller in suffering. Behold now presently, and   65
swound for what's to come upon thee. [*To Coriolanus*] The glorious gods sit in hourly synod about
thy particular prosperity, and love thee no worse
than thy old father Menenius does! O my son, my
son, thou art preparing fire for us: look thee, here's   70
water to quench it. I was hardly moved to come to
thee, but being assured none but myself could move
thee, I have been blown out of your gates with sighs,
and conjure thee to pardon Rome and thy petitionary countrymen. The good gods assuage thy wrath,   75
and turn the dregs of it upon this varlet here—this,
who, like a block, hath denied my access to thee.

Cor. Away!

Men. How! Away?

Cor. Wife, mother, child, I know not. My affairs   80
Are servanted to others. Though I owe

62. but by] *Malone;* but *F;* by *Hanmer.*   66. swound] *F* (swoond) *;* swoon *F4.*
S.D.] *Pope;* not in *F.*   73. your] *F;* our *F4.*

'Jack out of office'; *guardant =* pro-
tector, guard (cf. *1H6,* IV. vii. 9) is
also a heraldic term, which lends
piquancy to Menenius' phrase.

61–2. *office me from*] i.e. use his
petty authority to keep me from.
The verb is suggested by *Jack.*

62–3. *Guess . . . entertainment*]
Menenius clearly invites the guards
to judge their treatment from the
warmth of his reception. Emendation
is necessary and, as Malone says, it is
more probable that *by* should have
been omitted than confounded with
but.

65. *presently*] immediately. Menenius invites attention to a new 'scene',
and Martius may by now have
mounted the chair of state which is a
necessary element in the sequence of
petitionary spectacles (see headnote,
and Introduction, p. 73).

66. *swound*] swoon. F's *swoond* is

given by *O.E.D.* as a dialect form of
the old verb *swound* (= swoon, faint).
Many read *swoon,* but to do so is
strictly to emend, not to modernize.

67–8. *sit . . . prosperity*] i.e. let them
continually preside over your personal well-being.

71. *hardly moved*] with difficulty
persuaded, perhaps anticipating the
conceit about sighs.

73. *your gates*] probably correct, in
view of *thy . . . countrymen* which
shortly follows. Coriolanus may retort
the phrases upon Menenius in l. 87.

74–5. *petitionary*] suppliant, peti-
tioning. Evidently a Shakespearean
coinage (see *O.E.D.*).

77. *block*] obstruction; block-head.

81–3. *Though I . . . breasts*] i.e.
while my powers of revenge belong
to me personally, my powers of
pardon rest with the Volscians. For
owe = own cf. *Tp.,* I. ii. 454. Aside

My revenge properly, my remission lies
In Volscian breasts. That we have been familiar,
Ingrate forgetfulness shall poison rather
Than pity note how much. Therefore be gone.   85
Mine ears against your suits are stronger than
Your gates against my force. Yet, for I lov'd thee,
Take this along; I writ it for thy sake,
And would have sent it. [*Gives him a letter.*] Another
    word, Menenius,
I will not hear thee speak. This man, Aufidius,   90
Was my belov'd in Rome: yet thou behold'st.

Auf. You keep a constant temper.

Exeunt [Coriolanus and Aufidius].
The Guard and Menenius remain.

First Watch. Now, sir, is your name Menenius?

Second Watch. 'Tis a spell, you see, of much power. You
    know the way home again.   95

First Watch. Do you hear how we are shent for keeping
    your greatness back?

Second Watch. What cause do you think I have to
    swound?

Men. I neither care for th'world nor your general.   100
For such things as you, I can scarce think there's
any, y'are so slight. He that hath a will to die by

85. pity note] *Theobald*; pitty: Note *F.*   much.] much, *F*; much—*Rowe.*
89. S.D.] *Pope; not in F.*   92. S.D. *Coriolanus . . . Aufidius] Capell.*   *The . . .*
remain.] *F* (*Manet the Guard and Menenius.*).

from the dominant sense, however,
there appears to be an elusive
quibble between *owe* meaning 'in-
debted to' and *remission* meaning
'release from an obligation'. Coriolanus says that while he owes his
revenge to himself, remission from
that debt can be granted only by the
Volscians.

83–5. *That we . . . much*] i.e. ungrateful forgetfulness shall put an
end to our intimacy rather than
compassion take account of it. In its
immediate application the forgetfulness is attributed to Coriolanus,
but the general application allows its

attribution to the Romans—their
ingratitude to him occasions his to
Menenius. For *poison* = destroy,
stifle cf. *LLL.*, IV. iii. 301 (in both
texts Theobald emends to *prison*).

87. *for*] because.

91. *belov'd*] Cf. *Shr.*, I. ii. 3, 'My
best beloved and approved friend'.

92. S.D. Guard] This can be taken
to mean the two men on watch; cf.
S.D. opening the scene, and F's
Exit Watch at end of scene.

96. *shent*] told off, scolded; cf.
Tw.N., IV. ii. 100, and *Wiv.*, I. iv. 33.

99. *swound*] swoon. See above,
l. 66 note.

himself, fears it not from another: let your general
do his worst. For you, be that you are, long; and
your misery increase with your age! I say to you, 105
as I was said to, Away! *Exit.*

First Watch. A noble fellow, I warrant him.

Second Watch. The worthy fellow is our general: he's the
rock, the oak not to be wind-shaken. *Exeunt.*

[SCENE III]

Enter CORIOLANUS *and* AUFIDIUS [*with Others*].

Cor. We will before the walls of Rome tomorrow
Set down our host. My partner in this action,
You must report to th'Volscian lords how plainly
I have borne this business.

Auf. Only their ends
You have respected, stopp'd your ears against 5
The general suit of Rome: never admitted
A private whisper, no, not with such friends
That thought them sure of you.

Cor. This last old man,
Whom with a crack'd heart I have sent to Rome,
Lov'd me above the measure of a father, 10
Nay, godded me indeed. Their latest refuge

108–9.] *As F4;* The . . . Rock, / The . . . shaken. / *F.*   109. S.D. *Exeunt*] *F*
(*Exit*).

Scene III

SCENE III] *Pope.*   S.D. *with Others*] *After Capell.*   4–7. Only . . . friends] *As Capell;* Onely . . . respected, / . . . Rome: / . . . frends / *F.*

102–3. *by himself*] by his own hand.
104. *long*] for a long time.

Scene III

Scene III] Capell locates in the
'Tent of Coriolanus', but as the scene
was probably continuous with the
last it is better to suppose that the
structure serving as a tent at the
beginning of the last scene serves as
canopy to the throne in this. Paintings of the supplication scene are

instructive in this respect (see Introduction, p. 89).
2. *My . . . action*] In Plutarch's
account Aufidius stays at home (see
Appendix, p. 351).
3. *plainly*] straightforwardly.
6–7. *general . . . private*] *private* is
contrasted with *general* (i.e. 'public')
(King).
10. *measure*] Cf. *Cym.*, II. iv. 113,
and *Ant.*, I. i. 2.
11. *godded*] made a god of. Not

Was to send him; for whose old love I have
(Though I show'd sourly to him) once more offer'd
The first conditions, which they did refuse
And cannot now accept, to grace him only   15
That thought he could do more. A very little
I have yielded to. Fresh embassies and suits,
Nor from the state nor private friends, hereafter
Will I lend ear to. (*Shout within.*) Ha! what shout is
        this?
Shall I be tempted to infringe my vow   20
In the same time 'tis made? I will not.

Enter VIRGILIA, VOLUMNIA, VALERIA, *young* MARTIUS,
                with Attendants.

My wife comes foremost; then the honour'd mould
Wherein this trunk was fram'd, and in her hand
The grandchild to her blood. But out, affection!
All bond and privilege of nature break!   25
Let it be virtuous to be obstinate.
What is that curtsy worth? or those doves' eyes,

15–16. accept, . . . more. A] *F* (accept, to . . . more: A); accept. To . . . more,
a *Chambers.*   17. to] *F2*; too *F.*   19. S.D.] *Follows* this? *in F.*   21. S.D.
Attendants] *F*; *Attendants, all in mourning* | *Theobald.*   27. doves'] *Steevens*;
Doues *F*; dove's *Kittredge.*

elsewhere in Shakespeare, and aptly
coined for this play.

   latest refuge] last resource. Cf.
Tim., III. iii. 11.

   15–17. *accept . . . yielded to*] The
sense varies according to interpretation of F's colon after *more*. If this is
treated as a full stop, Coriolanus
appears to have conceded to Menenius only a renewal of the terms first
offered to Cominius; if it is treated
as a comma, he appears to have made
some extra concession. There is no
evidence elsewhere in the play of an
extra concession, and since it is often
necessary to treat the colon as a full
stop, I have done so here. The
Romans presumably cannot accept
the old terms as a point of honour,
once having refused them.

   22. *My wife . . . foremost*] Cf. North,
'his wife which came formest'
(Appendix, p. 360).

   mould] Wilson (after Maxwell)
quotes Nashe (ed. McKerrow, II,
p. 74), 'The Mould wherein thou
wert cast' (also used of mother and
child). Cf. *Wint.*, II. iii. 102. 'Mould'
is also used to mean the earth from
which man is fashioned, cf. III. ii. 103
above, and l. 29 below.

   25. *All bond . . . nature*] Cf. *Lr.*,
II. iv. 177, 'The offices of nature,
bond of childhood'.

   27. *doves' eyes*] Cf. Song of Solomon,
i. 15, iv. 1. Noble (p. 28) remarks
that the expression is 'not native to
the English'.

Which can make gods forsworn? I melt, and am not
Of stronger earth than others. My mother bows,
As if Olympus to a molehill should   30
In supplication nod; and my young boy
Hath an aspect of intercession which
Great nature cries, 'Deny not'. Let the Volsces
Plough Rome and harrow Italy; I'll never
Be such a gosling to obey instinct, but stand   35
As if a man were author of himself
And knew no other kin.

Vir.   My lord and husband!
Cor. These eyes are not the same I wore in Rome.
Vir. The sorrow that delivers us thus chang'd
Makes you think so.

Cor.   Like a dull actor now   40
I have forgot my part and I am out,
Even to a full disgrace. Best of my flesh,
Forgive my tyranny; but do not say,
For that 'Forgive our Romans'. O, a kiss
Long as my exile, sweet as my revenge!   45

36–7. As . . . kin.] *As Rowe*³; *one line in* F.   40–2. Like . . . flesh,] *As Pope;* like
. . . part, / . . . Flesh, / F.

32. *aspect of intercession*] accented
aspèct. For a less generous use of
intercession see above, v. ii. 43.

35. *gosling*] Cf. I. iv. 34.

instinct] accented *instìnct*. Shakespeare uses the word to signify the
promptings of divine and human
animal nature; Coriolanus here
speaks as if all instincts were merely
animal. Cf. *R3*, II. iii. 42, 'divine
instinct'; *2H6*, III. ii. 250, 'mere
instinct of love and loyalty'; *1H4*,
II. iv. 263, 'I was now a coward on
instinct'.

36. *author of himself*] self-begotten
(*O.E.D.*, author 2 a); cf. the different
use of 'author' in North, 'thy selfe is
thonly author' (Appendix, p. 362).

38. *eyes . . . same*] Coriolanus alludes
to his changed outlook and dispo-

sition; Virgilia affects to take him
more literally.

39. *delivers*] presents; cf. *Tw.N.*,
I. ii. 42.

40–2. *Like . . . disgrace*] Cf. *Sonn.*,
XXIII. 1–2, 'As an unperfect actor on
the stage / Who with his fear is put
besides his part'. Coriolanus presumably speaks reflectively and aside.

41. *out*] also used of an actor for-
getting his lines in *LLL.*, v. ii. 152.

43. *tyranny*] in the general sense,
'cruelty, violence'; cf. *Lr.*, III. iv. 2,
Mer.V., IV. i. 13.

44. *For that*] i.e. because I have
asked you to forgive me. As Gomme
remarks, there may be an allusion to
the Lord's prayer. Coriolanus sets
the principle aside.

Now by the jealous queen of heaven, that kiss
I carried from thee, dear; and my true lip
Hath virgin'd it e'er since. You gods! I prate,
And the most noble mother of the world
Leave unsaluted. Sink, my knee, i'th'earth: *Kneels.*   50
Of thy deep duty more impression show
Than that of common sons.

Vol.   Oh, stand up bless'd!
Whilst, with no softer cushion than the flint,
I kneel before thee, and unproperly
Show duty as mistaken all this while   55
Between the child and parent.   [*Kneels.*]

Cor.   What's this?
Your knees to me? to your corrected son?
Then let the pebbles on the hungry beach

48. prate] *Theobald;* pray *F, Hibbard.*   56. S.D.] *Rowe; not in F.*   56–7.
What's . . . son?] *After Pope* (What is); What's . . . me? / . . . Sonne? / *F.*

46. *jealous . . . heaven*] 'Juno, the
guardian of marriage, and conse-
quently the avenger of connubial
perfidy' (Johnson). Noble finds
'Queen of Heaven' in Jeremiah,
vii. 18 and xliv. 17–25, where it
probably refers to Ishtar.

48. *virgin'd*] one of the more
striking noun/verb coinages that the
play offers, see Introduction, p. 68.

prate] Hibbard retains F's *pray,*
with the argument that Coriolanus
has just sworn by Juno and may well
think he is praying, and that *prate*
is an ugly word to describe his tender greeting to Virgilia. Coriolanus,
however, appears good-naturedly to
slight the love-talk in order to
apologize to his mother, and *pray* is
not easily spoken lightly. For *prate*
cf. *Mac.,* II. i. 58.

51. *thy . . . impression*] Coriolanus
invites his knee to make a deep
impression both literally and figuratively upon the yielding earth.
Volumnia complicates the metaphor
by her reply—when she kneels to
him she kneels on flint.

54. *unproperly*] against propriety.
For the prefix *un* see Abbott 442.

55–6. *Show . . . parent*] i.e. show that
duty has all this while been mistaken
in supposing itself owed by the child
to the parent. Volumnia means by
duty its expression in the act of
kneeling. See Introduction, p. 57.

57. *corrected*] Coriolanus recognizes
that he has been rebuked by his
mother's irony.

58. *pebbles*] F's *Pibbles* was a common form and would have stood in
Shakespeare's MS.

hungry] Many, following Steevens,
gloss 'sterile, barren'; cf. *O.E.D.*
(s.v. 6) for instances of *hungry* applied
to poor soil and unstocked rivers, but
the sense is not found elsewhere in
Shakespeare. Malone supposed the
beach hungry for shipwrecks, citing
Tw.N., II. iv. 99–100, 'mine is all as
hungry as the sea, / And can digest
as much'. It may be that by an
extremity of ellipsis *hungry* is transferred to the beach from the sea (cf.
Tp., III. iii. 55, 'the never-surfeited
sea', and *Per.,* III. ii. 57, 'If the sea's

Fillip the stars. Then let the mutinous winds
Strike the proud cedars 'gainst the fiery sun,   60
Murd'ring impossibility, to make
What cannot be, slight work!

Vol.   Thou art my warrior:
I holp to frame thee. Do you know this lady?

Cor. The noble sister of Publicola,
The moon of Rome, chaste as the icicle   65
That's curdied by the frost from purest snow
And hangs on Dian's temple! Dear Valeria!

Vol. This is a poor epitome of yours,
Which by th'interpretation of full time
May show like all yourself.

Cor.   The god of soldiers,   70
With the consent of supreme Jove, inform
Thy thoughts with nobleness, that thou mayst prove
To shame unvulnerable, and stick i'th'wars

62–3. Thou . . . thee] *As Rowe; one line in F.*   63. holp] *Pope;* hope *F.*
66. curdied] *F;* curdled *Rowe;* curded *Steevens.*

stomach be o'ercharg'd with gold'). The sea's hunger is manifest on the beach as it encroaches upon the land and chafes and storms upon the pebbles (cf. *Lr.*, IV. vi. 21). A similar transference occurs in *1H6*, I. ii. 27–8, 'like lions wanting food, / Do rush upon us as their hungry prey', where *prey* = prey for their hunger. The point of Coriolanus' hyperbole is that it is the normal fate of pebbles to be dragged into the hungry sea and not lifted to the stars.

59. *Fillip*] strike against, touch. F's spelling *Fillop* occurs also in *2H4*, I. ii. 215 F; the form *fillip* (as in *Troil.*, IV. v. 45) is more common.

mutinous winds] Cf. *Tp.*, v. i. 42, 'call'd forth the mutinous winds'.

64. *sister of Publicola*] For Valeria's more conspicuous role in the embassy see North, Appendix, pp. 358–9.

65. *chaste . . . icicle*] A different Valeria is commended for her 'wyfly chastitee' in Chaucer's *Franklin's Tale* (ed. Robinson, 1453–6).

66–7. *snow . . . temple*] Cf. *Tim.*, IV. iii. 383–4, 'Whose blush doth thaw the consecrated snow / That lies on Dian's lap', *Oth.*, v. ii. 4–5, *Tp.*, IV. i. 55, *Cym.*, II. v. 13. The play resembles *Othello* in using an image of cool and exquisite purity to lend poignancy to incipient violence.

68–9. *epitome . . . time*] i.e. your son is an abridged version of yourself to be amplified in the fullness of time. Time is thought of as expounding a theme, like an orator. For a different use of 'interpretation' in relation to time cf. IV. vii. 50.

70. *god of soldiers*] Mars.

71. *inform*] imbue, inspire. Within the rhetoric of the play, however, the radical sense 'give form to' is not far away. Cf. *frame*, l. 63 above.

73. *To shame unvulnerable*] referring primarily to the battlefield virtue of courage that cannot be shamed; but the phrase has other resonances about Coriolanus' own situation (see Introduction, p. 56).

     Like a great sea-mark standing every flaw
     And saving those that eye thee!
Vol.   Your knee, sirrah.   75
Cor. That's my brave boy!
Vol. Even he, your wife, this lady and myself
     Are suitors to you.
Cor.   I beseech you, peace!
     Or, if you'd ask, remember this before:
     The thing I have forsworn to grant may never   80
     Be held by you denials. Do not bid me
     Dismiss my soldiers, or capitulate
     Again with Rome's mechanics. Tell me not
     Wherein I seem unnatural. Desire not
     T'allay my rages and revenges with   85
     Your colder reasons.
Vol.   Oh, no more, no more!
     You have said you will not grant us anything:
     For we have nothing else to ask but that
     Which you deny already. Yet we will ask,

80–1. thing . . . you denials] *F;* thing . . . your denials *F3;* thing . . . you
denial *F4;* things . . . you denials *Capell.*   84–6. Wherein . . . reasons.] *As
Pope;* Wherein . . . t'allay / . . . reasons. / *F.*

stick] stand out, stand firm, cf.
Ham., v. ii. 249.

74. *sea-mark*] a land-mark used by
sailors for taking bearings and
keeping course; cf. *Oth.*, v. ii. 271,
Sonn., cxvi. 5. For the sway of battle
compared to the sea cf. *3H6*, ii. v.
5–10.

standing] withstanding.

flaw] Dyce (*Glossary*) quotes Smith's
Sea Grammar, 1627, p. 46, 'A flaw of
wind is a gust, which is very violent
upon a sudden, but quickly endeth'.
Cf. *Per.*, iii. i. 39.

80–1. *The thing . . . denials*] i.e. that
which I have sworn not to grant may
never be regarded by you as
denial of your pleas. The thought is
cryptic because Coriolanus is trying
to have it both ways; but *thing* is
singular because it refers comprehensively to the commitment by oath
to the Volscians, and *denials* plural

either because there are several
conditions within the oath or because
several voices are pleading.

82. *capitulate*] bargain, come to
terms, cf. *1H4*, iii. ii. 120 (the only
other Shakespearean instance).

83. *mechanics*] workmen.

85. *allay*] abate. Case supposes the
metaphor to be from 'cooling and
qualifying a liquid' (cf. *Mer.V.*, ii. ii.
171, *Troil.*, iv. iv. 8, and above,
ii. i. 48); but it is not specific, and
may have a closer parallel in *H8*,
i. i. 148–9, 'If with the sap of reason
you would quench / Or but allay the
fire of passion'. The complex history
of the word is epitomized in Shakespeare's use of it—sometimes close to
'quench', sometimes to 'temper', and
sometimes to 'dilute' (see *O.E.D.*,
which traces overlapping meanings
from O.E. *alecgan*, 'to put down', and
Latin *alligare*, 'to mix').

That if you fail in our request, the blame   90
May hang upon your hardness: therefore hear us.

Cor. Aufidius, and you Volsces, mark; for we'll
Hear nought from Rome in private. Your request?

Vol. Should we be silent and not speak, our raiment
And state of bodies would bewray what life   95
We have led since thy exile. Think with thyself
How more unfortunate than all living women
Are we come hither; since that thy sight, which should
Make our eyes flow with joy, hearts dance with
         comforts,
Constrains them weep, and shake with fear and sorrow,
Making the mother, wife and child to see   101
The son, the husband and the father, tearing
His country's bowels out. And to poor we
Thine enmity's most capital. Thou barr'st us
Our prayers to the gods, which is a comfort   105
That all but we enjoy; for how can we,
Alas! how can we for our country pray,
Whereto we are bound, together with thy victory,
Whereto we are bound? Alack, or we must lose
The country, our dear nurse, or else thy person,   110

---

90. you] *F*; we *Rowe*.

93. *Hear . . . private*] At this point Coriolanus probably sits in his 'chayer of state', see North, Appendix, p. 360, and l. 131 below; also Introduction, p. 73.

94–125, 131–82.] Volumnia's great speeches are close renderings of the versions in North (Appendix, pp. 361–363).

94–5. *raiment . . . bodies*] i.e. neglected clothes and emaciated bodies.

95. *bewray*] expose, reveal; often interchangeable with *betray* in Shakespeare; here caught from North.

96. *exile*] accented *exíle*.

Think with thyself] think to yourself, reflect. North's phrase.

97. *unfortunate*] sometimes taken as evidence that Shakespeare had before him the 1612 edition of North's Plutarch; see Introduction, p. 27.

102–3. *tearing . . . out*] North has, 'besieging the walls of his native countrie'.

103. *poor we*] We is used for 'us' in *Ham.*, I. iv. 54, *Caes.*, III. i. 96 (Wright).

104. *capital*] fatal, deadly; cf. North, 'more than any mortall enemie'.

108–9. *Whereto . . . bound*] Gomme thinks the repetition the sign of a contaminated text, and suggests a copy might have read, 'Whereto: together with thy victory: / We all are bound'. But similarly symmetrical rhetoric is used to express Blanche's dilemma in *John.*, III. i. 327–36. What Gomme's version gains in smoothness it loses in symmetry and cogency.

109–10. *or . . . or*] either . . . or; cf. Abbott 136.

Our comfort in the country. We must find
An evident calamity, though we had
Our wish, which side should win: for either thou
Must as a foreign recreant be led
With manacles through our streets, or else   115
Triumphantly tread on thy country's ruin,
And bear the palm for having bravely shed
Thy wife and children's blood. For myself, son,
I purpose not to wait on fortune till
These wars determine. If I cannot persuade thee   120
Rather to show a noble grace to both parts,
Than seek the end of one, thou shalt no sooner
March to assault thy country than to tread—
Trust to't, thou shalt not—on thy mother's womb
That brought thee to this world.

Vir.   Ay, and mine,   125
That brought you forth this boy to keep your name
Living to time.

Boy.   A shall not tread on me.
I'll run away till I am bigger, but then I'll fight.

Cor. Not of a woman's tenderness to be,
Requires nor child nor woman's face to see.   130
I have sat too long.   [*Rising.*]

Voi.   Nay, go not from us thus.

---

115. through] *F;* thorough *Johnson.*   125–8. Ay . . . fight.] *After Pope* (mine too)*;* I, and . . . boy, / . . . time. / . . . away / . . . fight. / *F.*   131. S.D.] *Capell; not in F.*

112. *evident*] manifest, certain; cf. IV. vii. 52.

114. *foreign recreant*] i.e. foreign because a *renegade* (recreant) to Rome; cf. *1H6*, I. ii. 126, *Troil.*, I. iii. 287.

117. *bear the palm*] Cf. *Caes.*, I. ii. 131.

120. *determine*] are determined, come to an end.

121. *Rather . . . parts*] North has, 'rather to doe good unto both parties'. Shakespeare takes the opportunity to revisit the word *noble*, now in an auspicious phrase.

122–4. *thou shalt . . . womb*] North's

syntax is clearer: 'thou shalt no soner marche forward to assault thy countrie, but thy foot shall treade upon thy mothers wombe'. Shakespeare's parenthesis, *Trust . . . not*, is merely emphatic. For the use of *to* for connecting purposes (*to tread*) see Abbott 350 and 416.

125–8. *Ay . . . fight*] Virgilia and the young Martius do not intervene in Plutarch's account.

127. *A*] He.

129–30. *Not of . . . see*] i.e. if I am not to be as tender as a woman, I must not look at their faces. The rhyme stylizes the sentiment and detaches it from the dialogue.

If it were so that our request did tend
To save the Romans, thereby to destroy
The Volsces whom you serve, you might condemn us
As poisonous of your honour. No, our suit   135
Is that you reconcile them: while the Volsces
May say, 'This mercy we have show'd', the Romans,
'This we receiv'd'; and each in either side
Give the all-hail to thee, and cry, 'Be bless'd
For making up this peace!' Thou know'st, great son,
The end of war's uncertain, but this certain,   141
That if thou conquer Rome, the benefit
Which thou shalt thereby reap is such a name
Whose repetition will be dogg'd with curses,
Whose chronicle thus writ: 'The man was noble,   145
But with his last attempt he wip'd it out,
Destroy'd his country, and his name remains
To th'insuing age abhorr'd.' Speak to me, son:
Thou has affected the fine strains of honour,
To imitate the graces of the gods,   150
To tear with thunder the wide cheeks o'th'air,
And yet to charge thy sulphur with a bolt

141. war's] *Rowe;* Warres *F.*   149. fine] *Johnson;* fiue *F;* first *Rowe³.*   152.
charge] *Theobald;* change *F.*

139. *Give . . . hail*] For the mode of
acclaim cf. *Mac.,* I. v. 52.

141. *The end . . . uncertain*] North
has, 'though the ende of warre be
uncertaine' (Appendix, p. 362).
Anders cites the *Sententiae Pueriles,*
'Belli excitus incertus' (see Baldwin,
Shakspere's Small Latine and Lesse Greeke,
1942, I, p. 234).

143–4. *such . . . Whose*] such . . .
that its. For the construction see
Abbott 278.

145. *Whose . . . writ*] i.e. that your
name's story will thus be written.

146. *it*] probably 'his nobility', but
possibly 'his noble name'.

149. *affected*] (a) assumed (in
relation to *strains of honour*), (b)
aspired (in relation to *to imitate* etc.).
fine strains] 'The niceties, the
refinements' (Johnson). F's *fiue* is

apparently a minim error, not a
turned letter.

150–3. *To imitate . . . oak*] i.e.
Coriolanus, like Jove, will display
immense power but inflict comparatively little damage; cf. *Meas.,*
II. ii. 114–17, where the oak is
damaged and the myrtle spared. The
graces are the attributes of terror and
mercy. There is no equivalent
passage in North.

151. *tear . . . air*] Cf. *R2,* III. iii.
57, *Tp.,* I. ii. 4. The metaphor is
from Aeolian figures on maps.

152. *charge*] Theobald's reading is
generally followed. Schmidt supposed
F's *change . . . with* to mean 'exchange
with', but elsewhere Shakespeare
closely associates *sulphur* and *bolt* as
aspects of lightning (cf. *Cym.,* v. v.
240, 'The gods throw stones of

That should but rive an oak. Why dost not speak?
Think'st thou it honourable for a noble man
Still to remember wrongs? Daughter, speak you: 155
He cares not for your weeping. Speak thou, boy:
Perhaps thy childishness will move him more
Than can our reasons. There's no man in the world
More bound to's mother, yet here he lets me prate
Like one i'th'stocks. Thou hast never in thy life   160
Show'd thy dear mother any courtesy,
When she, poor hen, fond of no second brood,
Has cluck'd thee to the wars, and safely home,
Loaden with honour. Say my request's unjust,
And spurn me back; but if it be not so,   165
Thou art not honest, and the gods will plague thee
That thou restrain'st from me the duty which
To a mother's part belongs. He turns away.
Down ladies: let us shame him with our knees.
To his surname Coriolanus longs more pride   170
Than pity to our prayers. Down! an end:

154. noble man] *F2;* Nobleman *F.*   163. cluck'd] *F2;* clock'd *F.*   169. him
with] *F2;* him with him with *F.*

sulphur on me', and *Per.*, III. i. 6,
'thy nimble sulphurous flashes'). A
probable minim error.

153. *Why . . . speak?*] Cf. North,
'he held his peace a prety while, and
aunswered not a word'.

155. *Still*] always.

156. *weeping*] Cf. IV. ii. 52.

159. *bound to's mother*] Cf. North,
'No man living is more bounde to
shewe him selfe thankefull in all
partes and respects, then thy selfe'.
The audience is free to take the
phrase ironically (= tied to); cf.
Oth., III. ii. 217, 'I am bound to thee
for ever'.

160. *Like . . . stocks*] i.e. despised
and unheeded. A parochial touch.

162. *fond of*] wishing for, desirous
of; cf. *Cym.*, I. i. 37 (Case).

163. *cluck'd*] F's *clock'd* could be
retained as a legitimate archaic
form and a current dialect one (cf.
O.E.D., clock v.²). Modernization

evades any suggestion of the pun,
alleged by Gomme, on 'clocked' =
timed.

164. *Loaden*] Shakespeare uses both
this form and *laden*.

164–6. *Say . . . honest*] i.e. if he
spurns her just request he is both
dishonourable and unfilial. Shakespeare renders North's 'And therefore,
it is not only honest, but due unto me,
that without compulsion I should
obtaine my so just and reasonable
request of thee'.

167. *restrain'st*] in the legal sense,
'keep'st back, withold'st' (Case).

170. *surname Coriolanus*] The name
originally signified the conqueror of
Corioles, but Volumnia now takes
it as 'man of Corioli'; as King says
the sentiment anticipates ll. 178–80.

longs] The verb *long* is now super-
seded by the compound form *belong*
(*O.E.D.*, long v.²). Cf. *Meas.*, II. ii. 59.

171. *an end*] i.e. let's make an end.

This is the last. So, we will home to Rome
And die among our neighbours. Nay, behold's,
This boy that cannot tell what he would have,
But kneels, and holds up hands for fellowship,   175
Does reason our petition with more strength
Than thou hast to deny't. Come, let us go:
This fellow had a Volscian to his mother;
His wife is in Corioles, and his child
Like him by chance. Yet give us our dispatch: 180
I am husht until our city be afire,
And then I'll speak a little.

Cor. (*Holds her by the hand silent.*) O mother, mother!
What have you done? Behold, the heavens do ope,
The gods look down, and this unnatural scene
They laugh at. O my mother, mother! O!   185
You have won a happy victory to Rome;
But for your son, believe it, O, believe it,
Most dangerously you have with him prevail'd,
If not most mortal to him. But let it come.
Aufidius, though I cannot make true wars,   190

179. his] *F;* this *Theobald.*   181–2. I am . . . little.] *As Pope; one line in F.*

172. *So, we*] The comma in F seems to express a significant pause; but it is often omitted.

175. *kneels . . . fellowship*] It is likely that all kneel together to express their 'fellowship', anticipating North's report that at the end of her speech, 'her selfe, his wife and children, fell downe upon their knees before him'.

176. *reason*] plead for.

178. *to*] = for; cf. l. 186 below.

180. *dispatch*] dismissal.

181. *husht*] silent. The adjectival form is earlier than the participle *hush'd* that Capell substitutes for it (see *O.E.D.*, husht).

182. S.D.] This expressive direction conflates two passages from North, one from an interlude in Volumnia's speech, 'he held his peace a prety while', and the other at the end, 'holding her hard by the right hande, oh mother, sayed he, you have won a happy victory for your countrie'.

Bertram Joseph finds the gesture called *Chirothripsia* specifically related to Coriolanus and Volumnia by Bulwer; it means, 'to press hard and wring another's hand'; see Introduction, p. 60.

184. *unnatural scene*] i.e. the tableau presented by the figures. Shakespeare uses the word *scene* some forty times, invariably in a theatrical sense. For the significance of *unnatural* and the gods' laughter see Introduction, p. 58.

189. *mortal*] Cf. North, 'mortal and unhappy for your sonne'. For Shakespeare's adverbial use of the word (following *dangerously*) see Abbott 397.

But let it come] a tellingly simple tragic formulation, not found in North. See Introduction, p. 60.

190. *true wars*] i.e. war true to his undertaking.

I'll frame convenient peace. Now, good Aufidius,
Were you in my stead, would you have heard
A mother less? or granted less, Aufidius?
Auf. I was mov'd withal.
Cor.   I dare be sworn you were:
And sir, it is no little thing to make   195
Mine eyes to sweat compassion. But, good sir,
What peace you'll make, advise me. For my part,
I'll not to Rome, I'll back with you; and pray you,
Stand to me in this cause. O mother! wife!
Auf. [*Aside*] I am glad thou hast set thy mercy and thy
    honour   200
At difference in thee. Out of that I'll work
Myself a former fortune.
Cor. [*To Volumnia, Virgilia, &c.*] Ay, by and by;
But we will drink together; and you shall bear
A better witness back than words, which we,
On like conditions, will have counterseal'd.   205
Come, enter with us. Ladies, you deserve
To have a temple built you. All the swords
In Italy and her confederate arms
Could not have made this peace.   *Exeunt.*

192. stead] *F* (steed), *F4.*   200. S.D.] *Rowe; not in F.*   202. S.D. *To . . . &c.*]
Rowe; The Ladies make signs to Coriolanus. | Johnson.   202–3. Ay . . . bear] *As
Hanmer;* I by . . . together: / . . . beare / *F.*

191. *convenient*] i.e. one which
brings both parties together, 'fitting,
commodious', not merely expedient.
    196. *Mine . . . compassion*] Coriolanus is weeping. North says of him
(before Volumnia speaks), 'nature so
wrought with him, that the teares
fell from his eyes' (Appendix, p. 361).
    199. *Stand to*] stand by.
    O mother!] At this point Coriolanus joins his family. North has, 'he
spake a little apart with his mother
and wife'.
    201–2. *I'll work . . . fortune*] 'I'll

contrive to raise my fortunes to their
former heights' (Case). Cf. Coriolanus' sanguine resolution at iv. i. 32,
53.
    204. *better witness*] i.e. a formal
treaty.
    205. *like conditions*] presumably,
like those that have been proposed in
words.
    207. *temple . . . you*] For 'The temple
of Fortune built for the women' see
North, Appendix, p. 364. It is ironic
that Coriolanus should propose the
memorial. See Introduction, p. 35.

[SCENE IV]

Enter MENENIUS *and* SICINIUS.

Men. See you yond coign o'th'Capitol, yond corner-
stone?

Sic. Why, what of that?

Men. If it be possible for you to displace it with your
little finger, there is some hope the ladies of Rome,   5
especially his mother, may prevail with him. But I
say there is no hope in't; our throats are sentenced
and stay upon execution.

Sic. Is't possible that so short a time can alter the condition of a man?   10

Men. There is differency between a grub and a butterfly;
yet your butterfly was a grub. This Martius is
grown from man to dragon: he has wings: he's more
than a creeping thing.

Sic. He loved his mother dearly.   15

Men. So did he me; and he no more remembers his
mother now than an eight-year-old horse. The tart-
ness of his face sours ripe grapes. When he walks, he
moves like an engine and the ground shrinks before
his treading. He is able to pierce a corslet with his   20

Scene IV

SCENE IV] *Pope.*   I. coign] *Capell;* coin *F.*   II. differency] *F;* difference *F2.*

Scene IV

Scene IV] located by Theobald in
the 'Forum' and by Capell in 'A
public place'. It is likely that Shakespeare thought of the Capitol (l. 1)
as being visible from the market-
place.

   I. *coign*] quoin, corner-stone.

   8. *stay upon*] wait for; cf. *All's W.*,
III. v. 42.

   9–10. *condition*] character, disposition. Sicinius alludes to Coriolanus' attitude towards his mother and
his patrician friends.

   II–14.] For some comment on the
metamorphosis of Coriolanus see
Introduction, p. 51.

   II. *differency*] This is the first
instance of the form recorded in
O.E.D.

   13. *dragon*] Cf. IV. vii. 23 and IV. i.
30.

   17. *than . . . horse*] i.e. than a horse
remembers its dam. Case cites
Nashe (ed. McKerrow, III, p. 13),
'be not a horse to forget thy own
worth'.

   19. *engine*] engine of war. Case
cites *Troil.*, I. iii. 206–8, 'So that the
ram that batters down the wall, / For
the great swinge and rudeness of his
poise, / They place before his hand
that made the engine'.

   20. *corslet*] steel body-armour.

eye, talks like a knell, and his hum is a battery. He
sits in his state as a thing made for Alexander.
What he bids be done is finished with his bidding.
He wants nothing of a god but eternity, and a heaven
to throne in.   25

Sic. Yes, mercy, if you report him truly.

Men. I paint him in the character. Mark what mercy
his mother shall bring from him. There is no more
mercy in him than there is milk in a male tiger; that
shall our poor city find; and all this is long of you.   30

Sic. The gods be good unto us.

Men. No, in such a case the gods will not be good unto
us. When we banished him, we respected not them;
and, he returning to break our necks, they respect
not us.   35

Enter a Messenger.

Mess. Sir, if you'd save your life, fly to your house.
    The plebeians have got your fellow-tribune,
    And hale him up and down, all swearing, if
    The Roman ladies bring not comfort home,
    They'll give him death by inches.

21. *hum . . . battery*] For *hum*
expressing anger and contempt cf.
v. i. 49. A *battery* may be any kind of
military assault, but Shakespeare
may have siege-guns in mind (cf.
John, II. i. 462, 'He speaks plain
cannon-fire', and II. i. 382, 'battering
cannon').

22. *state*] chair of state, throne.
See v. i. 63 note, and Introduction,
p. 73.
    thing . . . Alexander] i.e. an image
made to resemble Alexander the
Great.

24. *wants*] lacks.

24–5. *nothing . . . throne in*] Noble
compares Isaiah, lviii. 15 (Geneva),
'For thus sayth hee, that is hie and
excellent, hee that inhabiteth the

eternitie whose Name is the Holy
one', and lxvi. 1, 'Thus sayth the
Lord, The heaven is my throne';
also the Prayer Book Communion,
'But thou art the same Lord, whose
property is always to have mercy'.
The analogues are a reminder that
the play has its context in Judaic/
Christian as well as pagan tradition.

27. *in the character*] to the life, as he
is.

30. *long*] 'on account of, "along of".
Now *arch.* and *dial.*' (*O.E.D.*, s.v. *a.*²).
Many emend to '*long* (= along), but
improperly.

34. *break our necks*] probably with
the stress on *our*; cf. III. iii. 30.

37. *plebeians*] accented *plèbeians*.

38. *hale*] haul.

Enter another Messenger.

Sic.   What's the news?   40

Second Mess. Good news, good news! The ladies have
          prevail'd,
     The Volscians are dislodg'd, and Martius gone.
                                        [*Exeunt Attendants.*]
     A merrier day did never yet greet Rome,
     No, not th'expulsion of the Tarquins.

Sic.   Friend,
     Art thou certain this is true? Is't most certain?   45

Second Mess. As certain as I know the sun is fire.
     Where have you lurk'd that you make doubt of it?
     Ne'er through an arch so hurried the blown tide
     As the recomforted through th'gates. Why, hark you!
                    Trumpets, hautboys, drums beat, all together.
     The trumpets, sackbuts, psalteries and fifes,   50
     Tabors and cymbals and the shouting Romans
     Make the sun dance. Hark you!   *A shout within.*

Men.   This is good news.

41, 46, 60, 62. *Second Mess.*] Dyce; *Mess. F (subst.*).   44–5. Friend . . . certain?]
After Pope (is it not); Friend . . . true? / . . . certaine. / *F.*   49. S.D. *hautboys*]
F (Hoboyes).   51. cymbals] *F (Symboles), F4.*

40. *death by inches*] apparently any form of lingering death; cf. *Cym.*, v. v. 50–2.

42. *are dislodg'd*] have withdrawn from their encampment; cf. North, 'the next morning he dislodged' (Appendix, p. 364).

46. *sun is fire*] Cf. i. iv. 39, v. iii. 60.

48. *Ne'er . . . tide*] Cf. *Lucr.*, 1667–8, 'As through an arch the violent roaring tide / Outruns the eye that doth behold his haste'. For *blown* = swollen cf. *Lr.*, iv. iv. 27, *1 H4*, iv. ii. 46; but it may also mean wind-driven.

49. S.D.] 'the loudest musical effect the theatre could provide' (G. H. Cowling, *Music on the Shakespearean Stage*, 1913, p. 55).

hautboys] reed instruments, forerunners of the modern oboe but meant for outdoor occasions, producing a high, loud note (hence the name, from French *hautbois*). E. W. Naylor, *Shakespeare and Music*, 1896, p. 175, says that their use 'always implies a certain special importance in the music, and is generally connected with a Royal banquet, masque or procession'.

50–1. *trumpets . . . cymbals*] Wright compares the instruments of Daniel, iii. 5, 'cornet, flute, harp, sackbut, psaltery, dulcimer', where the people worship the golden image set up by Nebuchadnezzar. See Introduction, p. 61.

50. *sackbuts*] bass instruments resembling the trombone.

51. *Tabors*] small drums, often played with pipes by the same performer.

52. *sun dance*] Wright compares *Tw.N.*, ii. ii. 56, 'But shall we make

I will go meet the ladies. This Volumnia
Is worth of consuls, senators, patricians,
A city full; of tribunes such as you,   55
A sea and land full. You have pray'd well today.
This morning for ten thousand of your throats
I'd not have given a doit. Hark, how they joy!

Sound still with the shouts.

Sic. First, the gods bless you for your tidings; next
    Accept my thankfulness.
Second Mess.   Sir, we have all   60
    Great cause to give great thanks.
Sic.   They are near the city?
Second Mess. Almost at point to enter.
Sic.   We'll meet them,
    And help the joy.   *Exeunt.*

[SCENE V]

Enter two Senators, with Ladies [VOLUMNIA, VIRGILIA *and*
VALERIA], *passing over the stage, with other Lords.*

First Sen. Behold our patroness, the life of Rome!
    Call all your tribes together, praise the gods,
    And make triumphant fires. Strew flowers before them;

59–60. First . . . thankfulness] *As Pope;* First . . . tydings: / . . . thankfulnesse /
F.   60–1. Sir . . . thanks] *As Capell; one line in* F.   61–3. They . . . joy] *As
Capell; prose in* F.

Scene v

SCENE v] *Dyce.*   S.D. *Lords.*] *Lords* [*and the people*]. *Ard.¹, after Capell.*
1. First Sen.] *Capell; Sena.* / F.

the welkin dance indeed?' He also
supposes an allusion to the common
belief that the sun danced on Easter
day.

  58. *doit*] Cf. I. v. 6 and note.

  62. *at point*] on the point of.

Scene v

Scene v] Some editors continue the
scene from the previous one; others
follow Capell's 'A Street near the
Gate'. Allardyce Nicoll (*Shakespeare
Survey,* 12, pp. 47–55) gives reason for

believing that the opening S.D.,
passing over the stage, required a
processional movement 'from yard to
platform to yard again'. The ladies
may be repeating the route of Coriolanus' ovation (see II. i. headnote).
If Nicoll is right the senator's speech
becomes an address to the public on
and off the stage.

  3. *triumphant fires*] North tells of the
Romans, 'wearing garlands of flowers
upon their heads, sacrificing to the
goddes, as they were wont to doe

Unshout the noise that banish'd Martius;
Repeal him with the welcome of his mother: 5
Cry, 'Welcome, ladies, welcome!'

All.   Welcome, ladies,
Welcome!   *A flourish with drums and trumpets. [Exeunt.]*

[SCENE VI]

Enter TULLUS AUFIDIUS, *with Attendants.*

Auf. Go tell the lords o'th'city I am here.
Deliver them this paper. Having read it,
Bid them repair to th'market-place, where I,
Even in theirs and in the commons' ears,
Will vouch the truth of it. Him I accuse   5
The city ports by this hath enter'd, and
Intends t'appear before the people, hoping
To purge himself with words. Dispatch.

                                    [Exeunt Attendants.]
        Enter three or four Conspirators of Aufidius's faction.
        Most welcome.

First Con. How is it with our general?
Auf.   Even so   10

4. Unshout] *F* (Vnshoot), *Rowe.*   6–7. Welcome, ladies, / Welcome!] *As Steevens (1793); one line in F.*   7. S.D. *Exeunt.*] *F2; not in F.*

Scene VI

SCENE VI] *Dyce.*   5. accuse] *Rowe;* accuse: *F.*   8. S.D. *Exeunt Attendants.*]
Malone; not in F.   10–12. Even . . . slain] *As Pope (subst.); prose in F.*

upon the newes of some great obteined victorie', but he says nothing
about fires (see Appendix, p. 364).
Bonfires, however, were a common
Elizabethan form of celebration (e.g.
at the defeat of the Armada). Case
compares *Cym.*, III. i. 32, 'rejoicing
fires'.

    5. *Repeal*] recall.

Scene VI

    Scene VI] Plutarch sets the scene in
Antium and Shakespeare appears to
follow him in alluding to Aufidius'

native town in l. 50, to the city from
which Aufidius *parted* in l. 73 (cf.
IV. iv. 1, 8), and to the *Antiates* in
l. 80. At l. 90, however, the dramatic
advantage of *Coriolanus, in Corioles*
proves irresistible, and Corioles remains the setting from then on. The
only acceptable 'location' would be
non-specific (e.g. 'A Volscian City');
but most editors follow Rowe's
'Antium', and few Singer's 'Corioli'.

    5. *Him*] He whom (see Abbott 208).

    6. *ports*] gates; cf. I. vii. 1.

As with a man by his own alms empoison'd,
And with his charity slain.

Second Con.   Most noble sir,
If you do hold the same intent wherein
You wish'd us parties, we'll deliver you
Of your great danger.

Auf.   Sir, I cannot tell.   15
We must proceed as we do find the people.

Third Con. The people will remain uncertain whilst
'Twixt you there's difference; but the fall of either
Makes the survivor heir of all.

Auf.   I know it,
And my pretext to strike at him admits   20
A good construction. I rais'd him, and I pawn'd
Mine honour for his truth; who being so heighten'd,
He water'd his new plants with dews of flattery,
Seducing so my friends; and to this end
He bow'd his nature, never known before   25
But to be rough, unswayable and free.

Third Con. Sir, his stoutness
When he did stand for consul, which he lost
By lack of stooping—

Auf.   That I would have spoke of.
Being banish'd for't, he came unto my hearth,   30
Presented to my knife his throat; I took him,

12–14. Most . . . deliver you] *As Pope;* Most . . . intent / . . . you / *F.*   29.
stooping—] *Rowe;* stooping. *F.*

---

11. *by . . . empoison'd*] destroyed by
his own benevolence. If the metaphor
is made too specific we have to
suppose that food and drink given in
charity are returned poisoned.

12. *with*] For *with* = by see Abbott
193.

14–15. *deliver . . . Of*] For the construction Case compares *John*, III. iv.
55, 'How I may be deliver'd of these
woes'.

18. *difference*] rivalry.

20. *pretext*] accented *pretèxt*.

22. *heighten'd*] i.e. raised to a
position of power and patronage.

The charges that follow have no
warrant either in the play or in the
source.

23. *plants*] i.e. those on whom he
conferred honour; cf. *Mac.*, I. iv.
28–9, 'I have begun to plant thee, and
will labour / To make thee full of
growing'.

26. *free*] free-spoken, frank.

27. *stoutness*] obstinacy, unyieldingness. See III. ii. 127 and note.

29. *That . . . of*] I would have
dealt with that (had you not interrupted).

Made him joint-servant with me, gave him way
In all his own desires; nay, let him choose
Out of my files, his projects to accomplish,
My best and freshest men; serv'd his designments   35
In mine own person; holp to reap the fame
Which he did end all his; and took some pride
To do myself this wrong: till at the last
I seem'd his follower, not partner, and
He wag'd me with his countenance, as if   40
I had been mercenary.

First Con.   So he did, my lord.
The army marvell'd at it, and in the last,
When he had carried Rome, and that we look'd
For no less spoil than glory—

Auf.   There was it:
For which my sinews shall be stretch'd upon him;   45
At a few drops of women's rheum, which are
As cheap as lies, he sold the blood and labour
Of our great action. Therefore shall he die,

---

32. joint-servant] *F;* joint servant *Sisson.*   34–5. projects . . . accomplish, . . .
men;] *F3;* projects, . . . accomplish . . . men, *F.*   44. glory—] *F3;* Glory. *F.*

---

34. *files*] i.e. the ranks and files of
Aufidius' troops.

35. *designments*] designs, purposes.
The form was fairly common, but
Shakespeare uses it elsewhere only in
Oth., II. i. 22.

36–7. *holp . . . his*] The harvesting
metaphor is probably sustained in
end, meaning 'gather in' (see *O.E.D.,*
end v.², and *E.D.D.*). In the ordinary
sense, Coriolanus may 'end by
making the crop his own'.

40–1. *wag'd . . . mercenary*] paid me
with his favour, as if I were a hire-
ling. The thought is prompted by
North, 'every man honoured Martius,
and thought he could doe all, and
that all other governours and captaines must be content with such
credit and authoritie, as he would
please to countenaunce them with'
(Appendix, p. 355). By 'countenance
with' North evidently means 'allow,
sanction', but it is hard to exclude

from Shakespeare's version a suggestion of what Johnson called 'good
looks'; Coriolanus both assumes
powers of patronage and pays with
smiles instead of wages.

42. *in the last*] at the last. Wright
compares *Ham.,* I. v. 27, 'in the best',
and *Lr.,* I. i. 191, 'in the least'.

43. *had carried*] possibly 'might
have carried' (see Abbott 361), but
probably 'had virtually carried'. For
'carry' meaning 'win by military
assault' see *O.E.D.,* s.v. 16, and
All's W., III. vii. 19.

44. *There was it*] 'That was the
thing'; cf. *1 H 4,* III. iii. 13 (Case).

45. *my sinews . . . him*] I will strain
every nerve against him. See I. i. 137
note.

46. *rheum*] used of glandular
secretions, often from eyes and nose;
for the contemptuous application of
the word to tears cf. *John,* III. i. 22
and IV. iii. 108.

And I'll renew me in his fall. But hark!

Drums and trumpets sound, with great shouts of the people.

First Con. Your native town you enter'd like a post,   50
And had no welcomes home; but he returns
Splitting the air with noise.

Second Con.   And patient fools,
Whose children he hath slain, their base throats tear
With giving him glory.

Third Con.   Therefore, at your vantage,
Ere he express himself or move the people   55
With what he would say, let him feel your sword,
Which we will second. When he lies along,
After your way his tale pronounc'd shall bury
His reasons with his body.

Auf.   Say no more.
Here come the lords.   60

Enter the Lords of the City.

All Lords. You are most welcome home.

Auf.   I have not deserv'd it.
But, worthy lords, have you with heed perus'd
What I have written to you?

All Lords.   We have.

First Lord.   And grieve to hear't.
What faults he made before the last, I think
Might have found easy fines; but there to end   65

49. S.D. *sound*] *F3*; *sounds* | *F.*   56–8. sword, ... second. When ... way]
Theobald (subst.); Sword: ... second, when ... way. *F.*   63. *All Lords.*] *F*
(*All.*).

50. *native town*] Aufidius' home
town is Antium; see note on location
of scene.

post] messenger. Aufidius merely
brought news of Coriolanus.

54. *at your vantage*] taking your
opportunity; cf. North, 'Tullus . . .
sought divers meanes to make him
out of the waye, thinking that if he
let slippe that present time, he should
never recover the like and fit occasion
againe.' (Appendix, p. 366.)

57. *lies along*] lies prostrate, stretch-
ed out.

58. *After . . . pronounc'd*] his story
told in your fashion. F's punctuation
seems indefensible but is silently
retained by Harrison.

59. *His reasons*] his account of
himself.

64. *faults . . . last*] for the offences
he is alleged to have committed see
iv. vii. 17–26.

65. *found*] suffered; cf. v. iii. 111–12,
'find | An evident calamity'.

easy fines] light penalties. A fine
could be a penalty of any kind (see
O.E.D., s.v. *sb.*[1] 8 d).

Where he was to begin, and give away
The benefit of our levies, answering us
With our own charge, making a treaty where
There was a yielding: this admits no excuse.

Auf. He approaches: you shall hear him.   70

Enter CORIOLANUS *marching with drum and colours, the Commoners
being with him.*

Cor. Hail lords, I am return'd your soldier,
No more infected with my country's love
Than when I parted hence, but still subsisting
Under your great command. You are to know
That prosperously I have attempted, and   75
With bloody passage led your wars even to
The gates of Rome. Our spoils we have brought home
Doth more than counterpoise a full third part
The charges of the action. We have made peace
With no less honour to the Antiates   80

78. Doth] *F; Do Pope.*

67. *benefit . . . levies*] the advantage conferred by the armies we had raised.

67–8. *answering . . . charge*] The phrase is obscure, but appears to have been prompted by North who reports that Martius 'was willing to geve up his charge, and would resigne it into the handes of the lordes of the Volsces, if they dyd all commaund him, as by all their commaundement he receyved it' (Appendix, p. 366). It is therefore likely that *charge* means 'authority, office' and not 'expense' (cf. *charges* in l. 79). The difficulty persists, however; for if Shakespeare had the North passage in mind he would mean that Coriolanus responded to criticism by surrendering his power to those who gave it him, which seems unlikely in view of the order of the offences alleged by the Lord (the *answering* precedes *making a treaty*). More probably Coriolanus retorts

that he acted with the authority that they themselves had charged him with. Many follow Johnson, 'rewarding us with our own expenses: making the cost of war its recompense'; Case proposes 'accounting to us with a mere return of expenses' and compares ll. 77–9 below. Johnson's version is plausible, but I find the analogue in North hard to set aside.

70. S.D.] an expressive spectacle; see Introduction, p. 19.

72. *infected*] affected, under the influence of. Not always related to disease; cf. *John,* IV. iii. 69, 'never to be infected with delight'. The suggestion of contamination is hard to exclude here, however.

73. *hence*] i.e. from Antium; see note on location of scene.

78. *more . . . part*] outweigh by more than a third.

80. *Antiates*] See note on location of scene.

Than shame to th'Romans; and we here deliver,
Subscrib'd by th'consuls and patricians,
Together with the seal o'th'senate, what
We have compounded on.

Auf.   Read it not, noble lords;
But tell the traitor in the highest degree   85
He hath abus'd your powers.

Cor. Traitor? How now!

Auf.   Ay, traitor, Martius!

Cor.   Martius!

Auf. Ay, Martius, Caius Martius! Dost thou think
I'll grace thee with that robbery, thy stol'n name
Coriolanus, in Corioles?   90
You lords and heads o'th'state, perfidiously
He has betray'd your business, and given up,
For certain drops of salt, your city Rome,
I say 'your city', to his wife and mother;
Breaking his oath and resolution, like   95
A twist of rotten silk, never admitting
Counsel o'th'war: but at his nurse's tears
He whin'd and roar'd away your victory,
That pages blush'd at him, and men of heart
Look'd wond'ring each at others.

Cor.   Hear'st thou, Mars?

85. traitor] *F;* traitor, *Theobald.*   100. others] *F;* other *Rowe.*

84. *compounded*] agreed.

85. *traitor . . . degree*] As Wright observes, the phrase appears to be used in a technical and legal sense; cf. *R3*, v. iii. 196, 'perjury, in the high'st degree', and *Tw.N.*, I. v. 50, 'Misprision in the highest degree!' The parallels help to vindicate F's punctuation, but the sense that Theobald brings out with a comma after *traitor* is still available. North reports that the conspirators cried out that 'they would not suffer a traytour to usurpe tyrannicall power over the tribe of the Volsces' (Appendix, p. 367).

93. *drops of salt*] Here and in l. 97 (*nurse's tears*) Aufidius seems to allude

to Volumnia and her party, as he does in l. 46 ('women's rheum'); but both in North and in the play it is Coriolanus who weeps. For *salt* cf. *Tp.*, I. ii. 155, *Ham.*, I. ii. 154, *Lr.*, IV. vi. 196.

96. *twist*] twisted thread.

96–7. *never . . . war*] i.e. allowing no counsel of war to be held.

98. *whin'd and roar'd*] Wilson refers back to v. iii. 185, 'O my mother, mother! O!' Aufidius' exaggeration may still warrant very conspicuous distress at the moment of Coriolanus' breakdown (see Introduction, p. 62). See also IV. vi. 125 note.

100. *each at others*] at one another.

Auf. Name not the god, thou boy of tears!

Cor.   Ha!   101

Auf. No more.

Cor. Measureless liar, thou hast made my heart
    Too great for what contains it. 'Boy'! O slave!
    Pardon me, lords, 'tis the first time that ever   105
    I was forc'd to scold. Your judgements, my grave lords,
    Must give this cur the lie; and his own notion,
    Who wears my stripes impress'd upon him, that
    Must bear my beating to his grave, shall join
    To thrust the lie unto him.

First Lord.   Peace, both, and hear me speak.

Cor. Cut me to pieces, Volsces, men and lads,   111
    Stain all your edges on me. Boy! False hound!
    If you have writ your annals true, 'tis there,
    That like an eagle in a dove-cote, I
    Flutter'd your Volscians in Corioles.   115

---

115. Flutter'd] *F* (Flatter'd), *F3*.

102. *No more*] It is uncertain whether Aufidius is seeking to provoke Coriolanus or silence him; if the first, his meaning is 'no more than a boy'.

103. *Measureless*] boundless. Perhaps anticipating the breaking of constraints in the image that follows.

103–4. *heart . . . contains it*] Cf. *Ant.*, I. i. 6–8, and IV. xiv. 40–1, 'Heart, once be stronger than thy continent, / Crack thy frail case'.

105–6. *first . . . scold*] 'In this he is much mistaken' (Case). While Coriolanus may be thought to speak with truth of his demeanour before the Volscian lords, the audience may still suppose him defective in self-knowledge.

107. *notion*] understanding, awareness (cf. *O.E.D.*, s.v. 5 a; *Mac.*, III. i. 82; *Lr.*, I. iv. 227).

108–9. *stripes . . . beating*] The terms appear consistent with the obloquy of *cur* and *False hound* (l. 112), but cf. I. viii. 12 and IV. v. 109, 122, where whipping and beating are battle-terms simply.

108. *that*] i.e. Aufidius.

110. *thrust . . . him*] i.e. retort the lie against him, compel him to answer for it.

112. *edges*] Cf. *Ant.*, II. vi. 38–9, 'To part with unhack'd edges and bear back / Our targes undinted'.

113. *there*] i.e. in the annals.

114. *eagle*] For the sovereignty of the eagle among birds cf. *3H6*, II. i. 91, *John*, v. ii. 149, and above, III. i. 138. For a specifically Roman version cf. *Cym.*, IV. ii. 349, 'Jove's bird, the Roman eagle', but the emblems seem not to be intended here.

115. *Flutter'd*] F's *Flatter'd* is probably the correct old form, resembling German, *flattern* (see *O.E.D.*, flatter *v.*²), and it might be retained in an old-spelling text; its ambiguity in a modern text is startling, however, and the fact that no other instances have been recorded after 1450 leaves wide open the possibility of a misreading or misprint.

Alone I did it. Boy!

Auf.   Why, noble lords,
Will you be put in mind of his blind fortune,
Which was your shame, by this unholy braggart,
'Fore your own eyes and ears?

All Con.   Let him die for't.

All People. Tear him to pieces! Do it presently!   120
He killed my son! My daughter! He killed my
cousin Marcus! He killed my father!

Second Lord. Peace, ho! no outrage, peace!
The man is noble, and his fame folds in
This orb o'th'earth. His last offences to us   125
Shall have judicious hearing. Stand, Aufidius,
And trouble not the peace.

Cor.   O that I had him,
With six Aufidiuses, or more, his tribe,
To use my lawful sword.

Auf.   Insolent villian!

All Con. Kill, kill, kill, kill, kill him!

> *The Conspirators draw, and kill Martius, who falls;*
> *Aufidius stands on him.*

116. Boy!] *F* (Boy.); 'Boy!' *Cam.*
Tear ... presently: / ... Cosine / ...
Pope; O ... more: / ... Sword. / *F.*
draw); *Draw both the Conspirators.* / *F.*
Coriolanus / *Malone.*

121–2. He ... father!] Prose as *Capell;*
Father. / *F.*   127–9. O ... sword.] *As*
130. S.D. *The ... draw*] *Rowe subst.* (*all*
kill] *F4; kils* / *F.*   *Martius*] *F;*

117. *blind fortune*] reckless good
luck. There is not likely to be an
allusion to the blind goddess Fortune
specific enough to justify retaining F's
capital in *Fortune;* F also has a capital
for *Braggart* in l. 118. But Fortune
features in Poussin's picture of
Coriolanus (see Introduction, p. 89),
and may have been a figure in the
façade (see Introduction, p. 73).

120–2.] North attributes the killing
of Coriolanus to the conspirators,
with 'none of the people once offering
to rescue him'; Shakespeare makes
the people more active, recovering
the clamour of the banishment.

120. *presently*] immediately.

124–5. *folds ... earth*] encompasses
the globe. For *folds in* cf. III. iii. 68.

126. *judicious*] probably in the
obsolete sense 'judicial', but both
here and in *Lr.*, III. iv. 73 (Shakespeare's only comparable use of the
word), the current sense, 'wise, of
good judgement' is available and apt
(cf. *Ham.*, III. ii. 25).

Stand] Hold off.

128. *his tribe*] i.e. the whole line of
Aufidiuses; cf. IV. ii. 24.

129. *lawful sword*] i.e. the sword of
lawful war. Coriolanus wishes himself opposed in the battlefield to
Aufidius and his kin.

130. *Kill ... kill*] The cry of soldiers
for 'no quarter!'. Case cites Cotgrave:
'*A mort, à mort*: Kill, kill; the cry of
bloudie souldiors persuing their fearefull enemies unto death'. Cf. *Lr.*,

Lords.   Hold, hold, hold, hold!

Auf. My noble masters, hear me speak.

First Lord.   O Tullus!   131

Second Lord. Thou hast done a deed whereat valour will
    weep.

Third Lord. Tread not upon him. Masters all, be quiet!
    Put up your swords.

Auf. My lords, when you shall know (as in this rage,   135
    Provok'd by him, you cannot) the great danger
    Which this man's life did owe you, you'll rejoice
    That he is thus cut off. Please it your honours
    To call me to your senate, I'll deliver
    Myself your loyal servant or endure   140
    Your heaviest censure.

First Lord.   Bear from hence his body,
    And mourn you for him. Let him be regarded
    As the most noble corse that ever herald
    Did follow to his urn.

Second Lord.   His own impatience
    Takes from Aufidius a great part of blame.   145
    Let's make the best of it.

132.] *As Steevens (1790); Thou . . . whereat / . . . weepe. / F.*   133. him. Masters all,] *After Rowe (him—Masters all); him Masters all F.*   135.] *As Pope; My Lords, / . . . Rage / F.*

IV. vi. 188, *Ven.*, 652. Also Plutarch, Life of Marcellus, where the Romans in battle cry '*Feri, Feri*: which is as much as kill, kill' (S.H.P., III, p. 66).

130. S.D. (F) both] l. 8 S.D. refers to *three or four* conspirators; for the possible textual significance of the inconsistency see Introduction, p. 23.

Martius] It appears that Shakespeare, here and at l. 154 S.D., was content to revert to the *nomen gentilicium* and (like the Volscians) discard the *cognomen*, or *agnomen* (see I. ix. 64 note).

137. *owe you*] hold in store for you. Verity glosses 'possessed for you', needlessly alleging the other common, but less usual sense of *owe*, 'own'.

139. *deliver*] render, show, prove.

143–4. *herald . . . urn*] As evidence

that the herald followed the procession at the funerals of English nobility, proclaiming their titles, Case (after Hart) cites John Nichols, *Progresses and Public Processions of Queen Elizabeth*, 1823, II, pp. 483–94, which offers a description of the funeral of Sir Philip Sidney (1587). For *urn* cf. *H5*, I. ii. 228, *Ham.*, I. iv. 49–50, 'the sepulchre / Wherein we saw thee quietly enurn'd'; the word may refer to a precise form of burial or to entombment generally. North remarks that many Volscians did not consent to Coriolanus' murder, 'for men came out of all partes to honour his bodie, and dyd honorably burie him, setting out his tombe with great store of armour and spoyles, as the tombe of a worthie persone and great captaine' (Appendix, pp. 367–8).

Auf.   My rage is gone,
And I am struck with sorrow. Take him up.
Help, three o'th'chiefest soldiers. I'll be one.
Beat thou the drum that it speak mournfully;
Trail your steel pikes. Though in this city he   150
Hath widow'd and unchilded many a one,
Which to this hour bewail the injury,
Yet he shall have a noble memory.
Assist.
        Exeunt, bearing the body of Martius. A dead march sounded.

153–4. Yet . . . Assist] *As Capell; one line in F.*   154. S.D. *Martius*] *F; Coriolanus | Malone.*

148. *one*] i.e. the fourth of the bearers; cf. *Ham.*, v. ii. 387.

150. *Trail . . . pikes*] Pikes were trailed by holding them in reverse, with the head behind the bearer. It was the usual practice at funerals, including Sir Philip Sidney's (see above, ll. 143–4 note).

151. *widow'd and unchilded*] Noble quotes Isaiah, xlvii. 9 (Geneva), 'But these two things shall come to thee suddenly on one day, the losse of children, and widow-hood, they shall come upon thee in their perfection', referring to the judgement of God upon Babylon for her unmerciful dealings. Like other Biblical echoes in the play, this one is highly suggestive without being in any way a controlled allusion. See Introduction, p. 67.

153. *memory*] memorial. See passage from North quoted above, ll. 143–4 note.

154. S.D. Martius] See above, l. 130 S.D. note.

dead march] Funeral music was rarely heard on the Elizabethan stage (see G. H. Cowling, *Music on the Shakespearian Stage*, 1913, p. 34; cf. *2 Tamb.*, III. ii, and *Tit.*, I. i).

APPENDIX

SOURCE MATERIAL

1. 'The Life of Caius Martius Coriolanus', from Plutarch's *Lives of Noble Grecians and Romanes*, 1579.
2. Extract from Camden's *Remaines of a Greater Worke, Concerning Britaine*, 1605.

The following text of the 'Life of Caius Martius Coriolanus' is from the 1928 Shakespeare Head Press reprint of the 1579 edition, and it has been checked against a copy of the original 1579 edition.[1] Since there is good reason to believe that Shakespeare used the 1595 edition, however, the 1595 readings are recorded wherever they affect the choice of word in the text; a few important 1603 and 1612 variants are also noted. The extract from Camden was first printed in its present form in the Arden edition of 1922.

THE LIFE OF CAIUS MARTIUS CORIOLANUS

THE house of the *Martians*[2] at ROME was of the number of the *Patricians*, out of the which hath sprong many noble personages: whereof *Ancus Martius* was one, king *Numaes* daughters sonne, who was king of ROME after *Tullus Hostilius*. Of the same house were *Publius*, and *Quintus*, who brought to ROME their best water they had by conducts.[3] *Censorinus*[4] also came of that familie, that was so surnamed, bicause the people had chosen him *Censor* twise.[5] Through whose persuasion they made a lawe, that no man from thenceforth might require, or enjoye the *Censorshippe* twise. *Caius Martius*, whose life we intend now to write, being left an orphan by his father, was brought up under his mother a widowe, who taught us by experience, that orphanage bringeth many discommodities to a

The familie of the Martians.

Publius and Quintus Martius, brought the water by conduits to Rome.

Censorinus lawe.

1. That in Emmanuel College, Cambridge (STC 20066).
2. II. iii. 236–43.   3. 1595, *conduites*, as at II. iii. 240.
4. See II. iii. 241, where Delius supplies a line missing from the text.
5. II. iii. 242.

childe, but doth not hinder him to become an honest man, and to excell in vertue above the common sorte: as they that are meanely borne, wrongfully doe complayne, that it is the occasion of their casting awaye, for that no man in their youth taketh any care of them to see them well brought up, and taught that were meete. This man

Coriolanus wit.

also is a good proofe to confirme some mens opinions. That a reare and excellent witte untaught, doth bring forth many good and evill things together: like as[1] a fat soile bringeth forth herbes and weedes that lieth unmanured. For this *Martius* naturall wit and great harte dyd marvelously sturre up his corage, to doe and attempt notable actes. But on the other side for lacke of education, he was so chollericke and impacient, that he would yeld to no living creature: which made him churlishe, uncivill, and altogether unfit for any mans conversation.[2] Yet men marveling much at his constancy, that he was never overcome with pleasure, nor money, and howe he would endure easely all manner of paynes & travailles: thereupon they well liked and commended his stowtnes and temperancie. But for all that, they could not be acquainted with him, as one cittizen useth to be with another in the cittie. His behaviour was so unpleasaunt to them, by reason of a certaine insolent and sterne manner he had, which bicause it was to lordly, was disliked. And to saye truely, the

The benefit of learning.

greatest benefit that learning bringeth men unto, is this: that it teacheth men that be rude and rough of nature, by compasse and rule of reason, to be civill &. curteous, and to like better the meane state, then the higher. Nowe in those dayes, valliantnes was honoured in ROME above

What this worde Virtus signifieth.

all other vertues: which they called *Virtus*, by the name of vertue selfe,[3] as including in that generall name, all other speciall vertues besides. So that *Virtus* in the Latin, was asmuche as

1. 1595 omits *as*.
2. As III. i. 318, but Martius is also said to have had 'an eloquent tongue' (see below, p. 367) and throughout the play he is capable of patrician grace.
3. 1595, *it selfe*. Cf. II. ii. 83–5.

valliantnes. But *Martius* being more inclined to the warres, then any other gentleman of his time: beganne from his Childehood to geve him self to handle weapons, and daylie dyd exercise him selfe therein. And outward he esteemed armour to no purpose, unles one were naturally armed within. Moreover he dyd so exercise his bodie to hardnes, and all kynde of activitie, that he was very swift in ronning, strong in wrestling, and mightie in griping, so that no man could ever cast him. In so much as those that would trye masteries with him for strength & nimblenes, would saye when they were overcome: that all was by reason of his naturall strength, & hardnes of warde, that never yelded to any payne or toyle he tooke apon him. The first time he went to the warres, being but a strippling, was when *Tarquine* surnamed the prowde (that had bene king of ROME, and was *Coriolanus first* driven out for his pride, after many attemptes made *going to the* by sundrie battells to come in againe, wherein he *warres.* was ever overcome) dyd come to ROME with all the ayde of the LATINES, and many other people of ITALIE:[1] even as it were to set up his whole rest apon a battell by them, who with a great and mightie armie had undertaken to put him into his Kingdome againe, not so much to pleasure him, as to overthrowe the power of the ROMAINES, whose greatnes they both feared and envied. In this battell, wherein were many hotte and sharpe encounters of either partie, *Martius* valliantly fought in the sight of the Dictator: and a RO-MAINE souldier being throwen to the ground even hard by him, *Martius* straight bestrid him, and slue the enemie with his owne handes that had before overthrowen the ROMAINE.[2] Hereupon, after the battell was wonne, the Dictator dyd not forget so noble an acte, and therefore first of all he crowned *Martius* with a garland of oken boughs.[3] For who- *Coriolanus* soever saveth the life of a ROMAINE, it is a manner *crowned with a* among them, to honour him with such a garland. *garland of oken boughes.*

1. II. ii. 87–9.
2. II. ii. 89–94. But North's Martius does not meet 'Tarquin's self'.
3. II. ii. 98.

This was, either bicause the lawe dyd this honour to the oke, in favour of the ARCADIANS, who by the oracle of *Apollo* were in very[1] olde time called eaters of akornes: or els bicause the souldiers might easely in every place come by oken boughes: or lastely, bicause they thought it very necessarie to geve him that had saved a cittizens life, a crowne of this tree to honour him, being properly dedicated unto *Jupiter*, the patron and protectour of their citties, and thought amongest other wilde trees to bring forth a profitable fruite, and of plantes to be the strongest. Moreover, men at the first beginning dyd use akornes for their bread, & honie for their drincke: and further, the oke dyd feede their beastes, and geve them birdes, by taking glue from the okes, with the which they made birdlime to catche seely birdes. They saye that *Castor*, and *Pollux*, appeared in this battell,[2] and how incontinently after the battell, men sawe them in the market place at ROME, all their horses being on a white fome: and they were the first that brought newes of the victorie, even in the same place, where remaineth at this present a temple built in the honour of them neere unto the fountaine. And this is the cause, why the daye of this victorie (which was the fiftenth of Julye) is consecrated yet to this daye unto *Castor* and *Pollux*. Moreover it is daylie seene, that honour and reputation lighting on young men before their time, and before they have no great corage by nature: the desire to winne more, dieth straight in them, which easely happeneth, the same having no deepe roote in them before. Where contrariwise, the first honour that valliant mindes doe come unto, doth quicken up their appetite, hasting them forward as with force of winde, to enterprise things of highe deserving praise. For they esteeme, not to receave reward for service done, but rather take it for a remembraunce and encoragement, to make them doe better in time to come: and be

The goodnes of the oke.

To soden honor in youth killeth further desier of fame.

---

1. 1595 omits *very*.
2. One of several marvels omitted from the play; Shakespeare used similar material in *Julius Caesar*.

ashamed also to cast their honour at their heeles, not seeking to increase it still by like deserte of worthie valliant dedes.[1] This desire being bred in Martius, he strained still to passe him selfe in manlines: & being desirous to shewe a daylie increase of his valliantnes, his noble service dyd still advaunce his fame, bringing in spoyles apon spoyles from the enemie. Whereupon, the captaines that came afterwards (for envie of them that went before) dyd contend who should most honour him, and who should beare most honorable testimonie of his valliantnes. In so much the ROMAINES having many warres and battells in those dayes, Coriolanus was at them all: and there was not a battell fought, from whence he returned not[2] without some rewarde of honour. And as for other, the only respect that made them valliant, was they hoped to have honour: but touching Martius, the only thing that made him to love honour, was the joye he sawe his mother dyd take of him.[3] For he thought nothing made him so happie and honorable, as that his mother might heare every bodie praise and commend him, that she might allwayes see him returne with a crowne upon his head, and that she might still embrace him with teares ronning downe her cheekes for joye.[4] Which desire they saye Epaminondas dyd avowe & confesse to have bene in him: as to thinke him selfe a most happie & blessed man, that his father & mother in their life time had seene the victorie he wanne in the plaine of LEVCTRES. Now as for Epaminondas, he had this good happe, to have his father and mother living, to be partakers of his joye & prosperitie. But Martius thinking all due to his mother, that had bene also due to his father if he had lived: dyd not only content him selfe to rejoyce and honour her, but at her desire tooke a wife also, by whom he had two children, and yet never left his mothers house therefore.[5] Now he being growen to great credit and authoritie in ROME for his valliantnes, it

Coriolanus noble endevour to continue well deserving.

Coriolanus and Epaminondas did both place their desire of honour alike.

The obedience of Coriolanus to his mother.

1. Cf. II. ii. 98–101.   2. 1603, *not with.*   3. I. i. 38.   4. I. iii. 16–18.
5. See I. iii headnote. There is only one child in the play.

Extremitie of userers complained of at Rome by the people.

fortuned there grewe sedition in the cittie, bicause
the Senate dyd favour the riche against the people
who dyd complaine of the sore oppression of
userers,[1] of whom they borowed money. For those
that had litle, were yet spoyled of that litle they
had by their creditours, for lacke of abilitie to
paye the userie: who offered their goodes to be
solde, to them that would geve most. And suche as
had nothing left, their bodies were layed holde of,[2]
and they were made their bonde men, notwithstanding all the woundes and cuttes they shewed,
which they had receyved in many battells, fighting
for defence of their countrie and common wealth:
of the which, the last warre they made, was against
the SABYNES, wherein they fought apon the
promise the riche men had made them,[3] that from
thenceforth they would intreate them more gently,
and also upon the worde of *Marcus Valerius* chief
of the Senate, who by authoritie of the counsell,
and in the behalfe of the riche, sayed they should
performe that they had promised. But after that
they had faithfully served in this last battell of all,
where they overcame their enemies, seeing they
were never a whit the better, nor more gently
intreated, and that the Senate would geve no eare
to them, but made as though they had forgotten
their former promise, & suffered them to be made
slaves and bonde men to their creditours, and
besides, to be turned out of all that ever they had:
they fell then even to flat rebellion and mutine, and
to sturre up daungerous tumultes within the cittie.
The ROMAINES enemies hearing of this rebellion,
dyd straight enter the territories of ROME with a
marvelous great power, spoyling and burning all
as they came.[4] Whereupon the Senate immediatly
made open proclamation by sounde of trumpet,
that all those which[5] were of lawfull age to carie
weapon, should come & enter their names into the
muster masters booke, to goe to the warres: but no

Counsellers promises make men valliant, in hope of just performance. Ingratitude, and good service unrewarded, provoketh rebellion.

1. I. i. 80–1.   2. 1595, *on.*
3. Shakespeare leaves out much here that tends to vindicate the populace.
4. This establishes the vulnerability of a disunited Rome. The 'enemies' are
identified as the Volscians in I. ii. 22–5.
5. 1595, *that.*

man obeyed their commaundement.[1] Whereupon their chief magistrates, and many of the Senate, beganne to be of divers opinions among them selves. For some thought it was reason, they should somewhat yeld to the poore peoples request, and that they should a litle qualifie the severitie of the lawe. Other held hard against that opinion, and that was *Martius* for one. For he alleaged, that the creditours losing their money they had lent, was not the worst thing that was thereby: but that the lenitie that was favored, was a beginning of disobedience, and that the prowde attempt of the communaltie, was to abolish lawe, and to bring all to confusion.[2] Therefore he sayed, if the Senate were wise, they should betimes prevent, and quenche this ill favored and worse ment beginning. The Senate met many dayes in consultation about it:[3] but in the end they concluded nothing. The poore common people seeing no redresse, gathered them selves one daye together, and one encoraging another, they all forsooke the cittie, and encamped them selves upon a hill, called at this daye[4] the holy hill, alongest the river of Tyber, offering no creature any hurte or violence,[5] or making any shewe of actuall rebellion: saving that they cried as they went up and down, that the riche men had driven them out of the cittie, and that all I TALIE through they should finde ayer, water, and ground to burie them in. Moreover, they sayed, to dwell at R OME was nothing els but to be slaine, or hurte with continuall warres, and fighting for defence of the riche mens goodes. The Senate being afeard of their departure, dyd send unto them certaine of the pleasauntest olde men, and the most acceptable to the people among them. Of those, *Menenius Agrippa* was he, who was sent for chief man of the message from the Senate.[6] He, after many good

Martius Coriolanus against the people.

The people leave the cittie and doe goe to the holy hill.

1. Martius alludes to the episode at III. i. 121–3; it is more strongly emphasized in the Weigel/Brecht version (see Introduction, p. 87).
2. III. i. 107–11. 3. I. i. 56. 4. 1595, *that daye.*
5. Shakespeare's protesters in I. i are distinctly more violent than Plutarch's (e.g. I. i. 59–60).
6. When Menenius meets the people in the play it is as a member of the senate (I. i. 56) but it is not clear that he comes formally as an emissary.

persuasions and gentle requestes made to the
people, on the behalfe of the Senate: knit up his
oration[1] in the ende, with a notable tale, in this

manner. That on a time all the members of mans
bodie, dyd rebell against the bellie,[2] complaining
of it, that it only remained in the middest of the
bodie,[3] without doing any thing, neither dyd beare
any labour[4] to the maintenaunce of the rest:
whereas all other partes and members dyd labour
paynefully, and was[5] very carefull to satisfie the
appetites and desiers of the bodie. And so the bellie,
all this notwithstanding, laughed[6] at their follie,
and sayed. It is true, I first receyve all meates[7]
that norishe mans bodie: but afterwardes I sent it
againe to the norishement of other partes of the
same.[8] Even so (quoth he) ô you, my masters and
cittizens of ROME: the reason is a like betweene
the Senate, and you. For matters being well
digested,[9] & their counsells throughly examined,
touching the benefit of the common wealth: the
Senatours are cause of the common commoditie
that commeth unto every one of you.[10] These
persuasions pacified the people, conditionally, that
the Senate would graunte there should be yerely

chosen five magistrates,[11] which they now call
Tribuni Plebis, whose office should be to defend
the poore people from violence and oppression. So
Junius Brutus, and *Sicinius Vellutus*,[12] were the first
Tribunes of the people that were chosen, who had
only bene the causers & procurers of this sedition.
Hereupon the cittie being growen againe to good
quiet and unitie, the people immediatly went to
the warres, shewing that they had a good will to
doe better then ever they dyd, and to be very willing to obey the magistrates in that they would
commaund, concerning the warres. *Martius* also,
though it liked him nothing to see the greatnes of

1. I. i. 64–162. See Introduction, pp. 38–9.   2. I. i. 95–6.
3. I. i. 97–8.   4. I. i. 100.   5. 1595, *were*.
6. I. i. 106, 108, where the belly smiles.   7. 1595, *meanes*.
8. I. i. 134–9.   9. I. i. 149.   10. I. i. 150–3.
11. North specifies five and names two; hence the memory-lapse at I. i.
214–16.
12. North and Shakespeare follow Amyot's error for *Bellutus*.

the people thus increased, considering it was to the
prejudice, and imbasing of the nobilitie,[1] and also
sawe that other noble *Patricians* were troubled as
well as him selfe: he dyd persuade the *Patricians*
to shew them selves no lesse forward and willing to
fight for their countrie, then the common people
were: and to let them knowe by their dedes and
actes, that they dyd not so much passe the people
in power and riches, as they dyd exceede them in
true nobilitie and valliantnes.[2] In the countrie of
the VOLSCES, against whom the ROMAINES
made warre at that time, there was a principall
cittie and of most fame, that was called CORIOLES,
before the which the Consul *Cominius* dyd laye
seige.[3] Wherefore all the other VOLSCES fearing
least that cittie should be taken by assault, they
came from all partes of the countrie to save it, en-
tending to geve the ROMAINES battell before the
cittie, and to geve an onset on them in two severall
places. The Consul *Cominius* understanding this,
devided his armie also in two partes, and taking
the one parte with him selfe, he marched towards
them that were drawing to the cittie, out of the
countrie:[4] and the other parte of his armie he left
in the campe with *Titus Lartius*[5] (one of the
valliantest men the ROMAINES had at that time)
to resist those that would make any salye out of the
cittie apon them. So the CORIOLANS making
small accompt of them that laye in campe
before the cittie, made a salye out apon them, in
the which at the first the CORIOLANS had the
better, and drave the ROMAINES backe againe into
the trenches of their campe.[6] But *Martius* being
there at that time, ronning out of the campe with a
fewe men with him, he slue the first enemies he
met withall, and made the rest of them staye upon
a[7] sodaine, crying out to the ROMAINES that had
turned their backes, & calling them againe to fight

The cittie of Corioles beseiged by the Consul Cominius.

Titus Lartius, a valliant Romaine.

1. I. i. 210–20.
2. This idea is assimilated into the play's account of Martius.
3. I. ii. 27–8.   4. I. iii. 96–9.
5. 1595 reads *Latius*, in the text and in the margin; see Introduction, p. 21.
6. See I. iv. 29 S.D. and I. iv. 42.   7. 1595, *the*.

with a lowde voyce.[1] For he was even such another,
as *Cato* would have a souldier and a captaine to

be: not[2] only terrible, and fierce to laye about him,
but to make the enemie afeard with the sounde of
his voyce, and grimnes of his countenaunce. Then
there flocked about him immediatly, a great
number of ROMAINES: where at the enemies were
so afeard, that they gave backe presently. But
Martius not staying so, dyd chase & followe them
to their owne gates,[3] that fled for life. And there,
perceyving that the ROMAINES retired backe, for
the great number of dartes and arrowes which
flewe about their eares from the walles of the cittie,
and that there was not one man amongest them
that durst venter him selfe to followe the flying
enemies into the cittie, for that it was full of men of
warre, very well armed, and appointed: he dyd
encorage his fellowes with wordes & dedes, crying
out to them, that fortune had opened the gates of
the cittie, more for the followers, then the flyers.[4]
But all this notwithstanding, fewe had the hartes to
followe him. Howbeit *Martius* being in the throng
emong the enemies, thrust him selfe into the gates
of the cittie, and entred the same emong them that
fled, without that any one of them durst at the
first turne their face upon him, or els offer to staye
him. But he looking about him, and seeing he was
entred the cittie with very fewe men[5] to helpe him,
and perceyving he was environned by his enemies
that gathered round about to set apon him: dyd
things then[6] as it is written, wonderfull and in-
credible, aswell for the force of his hande, as also
for the agillitie of his bodie, and with a wonderfull
corage and valliantnes, he made a lane through the
middest of them, and overthrewe also those he
layed at: that some he made ronne to the furthest
parte of the cittie, and other for feare he made
yeld them selves, and to let fall their weapons

1. See I. iii. 32–4, I. iv. 30–42.   2. I. iv. 57.
3. I. iv. 42 S.D.   4. I. iv. 44–5.
5. At I. iv. 45 Martius enters alone (cf. II. ii. 110, v. vi. 116).
6. 1595 omits *then*.

before him. By this meanes, *Lartius*[1] that was gotten out, had some leysure to bring the RO-
MAINES with more safety into the cittie. The cittie   *The cittie of*
being taken in this sorte, the most parte of the   *Corioles taken.*
souldiers beganne incontinently to spoyle, to carie
awaye, and to looke up the bootie they had wonne.
But *Martius* was marvelous angry with them, and
cried out on them,[2] that it was no time nowe to
looke after spoyle, and to ronne straggling here
and there to enriche them selves, whilest the other
Consul and their fellowe cittizens peradventure
were fighting with their enemies: and howe that
leaving the spoyle they should seeke to winde them
selves out of daunger and perill.[3] Howbeit, crie,
and saye to them what he could, very fewe of them
would hearken to him. Wherefore taking those that
willingly offered them selves to followe him, he
went out of the cittie, and tooke his waye towardes
that parte, where he understoode the rest of the
armie was: exhorting and intreating them by the
waye that followed him, not to be fainte harted,
and ofte holding up his handes to heaven, he
besought the goddes to be so[4] gracious and favor-
able unto him, that he might come in time to the
battell, and in good hower[5] to hazarde his life in
defence of his country men. Now the ROMAINES
when they were put in battell raye, and ready to
take their targettes on their armes, and to guirde
them upon their arming coates, had a custome to
make their willes at that very instant, without any
manner of writing, naming him only whom they
would make their heire, in the presence of three or
foure witnesses.[6] *Martius* came just to that reckon-   *Souldiers*
ing, whilest the souldiers were a doing after that   *testaments.*
sorte, and that the enemies were approched so
neere, as one stoode in viewe of the other. When
they sawe him at his first comming, all bloody,[7]
and in a swet, and but with a fewe men following

1. 1595, *Martius*. Cf. II. ii. 112, 'aidless came off'; but at I. iv. 62 it is Lartius
who is ready to 'fetch off' Martius.
2. I. v. 1–8; but Martius' invective does not follow North.
3. 1595, *of perill.*   4. 1595 omits *so.*   5. 1595, *a good houre.*
6. Not in the play.   7. I. vi. 21–2.

him: some thereupon beganne to be afeard. But sone after, when they sawe him ronne with a lively cheere to the Consul, and to take him by the hande, declaring howe he had taken the cittie of CORIO-LES, and that they sawe the Consul *Cominius* also kisse and embrace him:[1] then there was not a man but tooke harte againe to him, and beganne to be of a good corage, some hearing him reporte from poynte to poynte, the happy successe of this em-ployte,[2] and other also conjecturing it by seeing their gestures a farre of. Then they all beganne to call upon the Consul to marche forward, and to delaye no lenger, but to geve charge upon the enemie.[3] *Martius* asked him howe the order of their enemies battell was, & on which side they had placed their best fighting men. The Consul made him aunswer, that he thought the bandes which were in the voward of their battell, were those of the ANTIATES, whom they esteemed to be the warlikest men, and which for valliant corage would geve no place, to any of the hoste of their enemies. Then prayed *Martius*, to be set directly against them.[4] The Consul graunted him, greatly praysing his corage. Then *Martius*, when both armies came almost to joyne, advaunced him selfe a good space before his companie, and went so fiercely to geve charge on the voward that came right against him, that they could stande no lenger in his handes: he made suche a lane through them, and opened a passage into the battell of the enemies. But the two winges of either side turned one to the other, to compasse him in betweene them: which the Consul *Cominius* perceyving, he sent thither straight of the best souldiers[5] he had about him. So the battell was marvelous bloudie about *Martius*, and in a very shorte space many were slaine in the place. But in the ende the ROMAINES were so strong, that they distressed the enemies, and brake their arraye: and scattering

By Coriolanus meanes, the Volsci were overcome in battell.

---

1. Cf. I. vi. 29; Shakespeare adds the allusion to 'nuptial day'. See Introduction, p. 49.

2. I. vi. 34–45.   3. Cf. I. vi. 75 S.D.   4. I. vi. 47–62.

5. Possibly suggesting the 'certain number' at I. vi. 80.

them, made them flye. Then they prayed *Martius*
that he would retire to the campe, bicause they
sawe he was able to doe no more, he was[1] already
so wearied[2] with the great payne he had taken, and
so fainte with the great woundes he had apon him.
But *Martius* aunswered them, that it was not for
conquerours to yeld, nor to be fainte harted: and
thereupon beganne a freshe[3] to chase those that
fled, untill suche time as the armie of the enemies
was utterly overthrowen,[4] and numbers of them
slaine, and taken prisoners. The next morning
betimes, *Martius* went to the Consul, and the other
ROMAINES with him. There the Consul *Cominius*
going up to his chayer of state, in the presence of
the whole armie, gave thankes to the goddes for
so great, glorious, and prosperous a victorie:
then he spake to *Martius*, whose valliantnes
he commended beyond the moone, both for
that he him selfe sawe him doe with his eyes, as
also for that *Martius* had reported unto him.[5]
So in the ende he willed *Martius*,[6] he should choose
out of all the horses they had taken of their enemies, and of all the goodes they had wonne
(whereof there was great store) tenne[7] of every *The tenth parte*
sorte which he liked best, before any distribution *of the enemies*
should be made to other. Besides this great *goods offered*
honorable offer he had made him, he gave him in[8] *Martius for*
testimonie that he had wonne that daye the price[9] *rewarde of his*
of prowes above all other, a goodly horse with a *Cominius the*
capparison,[10] and all furniture to him: which the *Consul.*
whole armie beholding, dyd marvelously praise *Valiancie*
and commend. But *Martius* stepping forth,[11] tolde *honour in the*
the Consul, he most thanckefully accepted the gifte *fielde. Martius*
of his horse, and was a glad man besides, that his *and refusall.*

1. 1595 omits *was*.　　2. Reserved by Shakespeare until I. x. 91.
3. Shakespeare takes this opportunity to have Martius meet Aufidius (I. viii).
4. ii. ii. 120–1.　　5. I. ix. 1–11, II. ii. 82–122.　　6. 1595, *Martius, that.*
7. Shakespeare follows the marginal note, *tenth part*, at I. ix. 31–6.
8. 1595 omits *in*.
9. I.e. *prize*; the words were not then firmly distinguished.
10. See I. ix. 12, where the report makes a metaphor, and I. ix. 60–1, where it contributes to the action.
11. I. ix. 36–40. Martius' protest is much amplified by Shakespeare in I. ix. 41–52.

service had deserved his generalls commendation: and as for his other offer, which was rather a mercenary reward, then an honorable recompence, he would none of it, but was contented to have his equall parte with other souldiers. Only, this grace (sayed he) I crave, and beseeche you to graunt me. Among the VOLSCES there is an olde friende and hoste of mine, an honest wealthie man, and now a prisoner, who living before in great wealth in his owne countrie, liveth now a poore prisoner in the handes of his enemies: and yet notwithstanding all this his miserie and misfortune, it would doe me great pleasure if I could save him from this one daunger: to keepe him from being solde as a slave.[1] The souldiers hearing *Martius* wordes, made a marvelous great showte[2] among them: and they were moe[3] that wondred at his great contentation and abstinence, when they sawe so litle covetousnes in him, then they were that highely praised and extolled his valliantnes. For even they them selves, that dyd somewhat malice and envie his glorie, to see him thus honoured, & passingly praysed, dyd thincke him so muche the more worthy of an honorable recompence for his valliant service as the more carelesly he refused the great offer made him[4] for his profit: and they esteemed more the vertue that was in him, that made him refuse suche rewards, then that which made them to be offred him,[5] as unto a worthie persone. For it is farre more commendable, to use riches well, then to be valliant: and yet it is better not to desire them, then to use them well.[6] After this showte and noyse of the assembly was somewhat appeased, the Consul *Cominius* beganne to speake in this sorte. We cannot compell *Martius* to take these giftes we offer him, if he will not receave them: but we will geve him suche a rewarde for the noble service he hath done, as he

1. In the play it is 'a poor man' not 'an honest wealthie' one (I. ix. 80-9); Shakespeare adds Martius' forgetfulness.

2. At an earlier point in the play (I. ix. 40 S.D.).

3. Cf. II. iii. 124.   4. 1595, *unto him*.   5. 1595, *to him*.

6. This reflection is not offered in the play; abstention from reward is part of Martius' *virtus*.

cannot refuse. Therefore we doe order and decree, that henceforth he be called *Coriolanus*, onles his valliant acts have wonne him that name before our nomination.[1] And so ever since, he stil bare the third name of *Coriolanus*. And thereby it appeareth, that the first name the ROMAINES have, as *Caius*: was our Christian name now. The second, as *Martius*: was the name of the house and familie they came of. The third, was some addition geven, either for some acte or notable service, or for some marke on their face, or of some shape of their bodie, or els for some speciall vertue they had. Even so dyd the GRÆCIANS in olde time give additions to Princes, by reason of some notable acte worthie memorie. As when they have called some, *Soter*, and *Callinicos*: as muche to saye, saviour and conquerour. Or els for some notable apparaunt marke on ones face, or on his bodie, they have called him *Phiscon*, and *Grypos*: as ye would saye, gorebelley, and hooke nosed: or els for some vertue, as *Euergetes*, and *Phyladelphos*: to wit, a Benefactour, and lover of his brethern. Or otherwise for ones great felicitie, as *Eudæmon*: as muche to saye, as fortunate. For so was the second of the *Battes** surnamed. And some Kings have had surnames of jeast and mockery. As one of the *Antigones* that was called *Doson*, to saye, the Gever: who was ever promising, and never geving. And one of the *Ptolomees* was called *Lamyros*: to saye, conceitive. The ROMAINES use more then any other nation, to give names of mockerie in this sorte. As there was one *Metellus* surnamed *Diadematus*, the banded: bicause he caried a bande about his heade of longe time, by reason of a sore he had in his forehead. One other of his owne familie was called *Celer*: the quicke flye. Bicause a fewe dayes after the death of his father, he shewed the people the cruell fight of fensers at unrebated swordes, which they founde wonderfull for the shortnes of time. Other had their surnames derived of some accident of their birthe. As to this daye they call him *Proculeius*, that is borne, his

Martius surnamed Coriolanus by the Consul. How the Romaines came to three names.

Why the Græcians gave Kings surnames.

** These were the princes that built the cittie of Cyrene.*

Names of mockery among the Romaines.

1. 1. ix. 62–6.

father being in some farre voyage: and him *Posthumius*, that is borne after the deathe of his father. And when of two brethern twinnes, the one doth dye, and thother surviveth: they call the surviver, *Vopiscus*. Somtimes also they geve surnames derived of some marke or misfortune of the bodie. As *Sylla*, to saye, crooked nosed: *Niger*, blacke: *Rufus*, red: *Cæcus*, blinde: *Claudus*, lame. They dyd wisely in this thing to accustome men to thincke, that neither the losse of their sight, nor other such misfortunes as maye chaunce to men, are any shame or disgrace unto them, but the manner was to aunswer boldly to suche names, as if they were called by their proper names. Howbeit these matters would be better amplified in other stories then this. Now when this warre was ended, the flatterers of the people beganne to sturre up sedition againe, without any newe occasion, or just matter offered of complainte. For they dyd grounde this seconde insurrection against the Nobilitie and *Patricians*, apon the peoples miserie and misfortune, that could not but fall out, by reason of the former discorde and sedition betweene them and the Nobilitie. Bicause the most parte of the errable[1] lande within the territorie of ROME, was become heathie and barren for lacke of plowing, for that they had no time nor meane to cause corne, to be

Sedition at Rome, by reason of famine.

brought them out of other countries to sowe, by reason of their warres which made the extreme dearth they had emong them. Now those busie pratlers that sought the peoples good will, by suche flattering wordes, perceyving great scarsitie of corne to be within the cittie, and though there had bene plenty enough, yet the common people had no money to buye it:[2] they spread abroad false tales and rumours against the Nobilitie, that they in revenge of the people, had practised and procured the extreme dearthe emong them.[3] Furthermore, in the middest of this sturre, there came ambassadours to ROME from the cittie of VELITRES, that offered up their cittie to the Ro-

---

1. I.e. *earable*; 1595, *arrable*.   2. I. i. 188.   3. I. i. 15–24, 78–80.

MAINES, and prayed them they would send newe inhabitants to replenishe the same: bicause the plague had bene so extreme among them, and had killed such a number of them, as there was not left alive the tenth persone of the people that had bene there before. So the wise men of ROME beganne to thincke, that the necessitie of the VE-LITRIANS fell out in a most happy hower, and howe by this occasion it was very mete[1] in so great a scarsitie of vittailes, to disburden ROME of a great number of cittizens: and by this meanes as well to take awaye this newe sedition, and utterly to ryd it out of the cittie,[2] as also to cleare the same of many mutinous & seditious persones, being the superfluous ill humours that grevously fedde this disease.[3] Hereupon the Consuls prickt out all those by a bill, whom they intended to sende to VELITRES, to goe dwell there as in forme of a colonie: and they leavied out of all the rest that remained in the cittie of ROME, a great number to goe against the VOLSCES, hoping by the meanes of forreine warre, to pacifie their sedition at home.[4] Moreover they imagined, when the poore with the riche, and the meane sorte with the nobilitie, should by this devise be abroad in the warres, and in one campe, and in one service, & in one like daunger: that then they would be more quiet and loving together.[5] But *Sicinius* and *Brutus*, two seditious Tribunes, spake against either of these devises, and cried out apon the noble men, that under the gentle name of a colonie, they would cloke and culler the most cruell and unnaturall facte as might be: bicause they sent their poore cittizens into a sore infected cittie and pestilent ayer, full of dead bodies unburied,[6] & there also to dwell under the tuytion of a straunge god, that

Velitres made a colonie to Rome.
Two practises to remove the sedition in Rome.

Sicinius and Brutus Tribunes of the people, against both those devises.

1. 1595, *meere.*   2. 1595, *and.*
3. Cf. I. i. 224–5, 248–9. Shakespeare makes no direct use of the Velitrean episode.
4. This idea is present behind I. i. (e.g. 249–50), but the threat to Rome remains real.
5. Shakespeare may remember this notion of community in IV. vi (see Introduction, p. 55).
6. Cf. IV. v. 43, 'I'th'city of kites and crows.'

had so cruelly persecuted his people. This were (said they) even as muche, as if the Senate should hedlong cast downe the people into a most bottomles pyt. And are not yet contented to have famished some of the poore cittizens heretofore to death, and to put other of them even to the mercie of the plague: but a freshe, they have procured a voluntarie warre, to the ende they would leave behind no kynde of miserie and ill, wherewith the poore syllie people should not be plagued, and only bicause they are werie to serve the riche. The common people being set on a broyle and braverie with these wordes, would not appeare when the Consuls called their names by a bill, to prest them for the warres, neither would they be sent out to this newe colonie: in so muche as the Senate knewe not well what to saye, or doe in the matter. *Martius* then, who was now growen to great credit, and a stowte man besides, and of great reputation with the noblest men of ROME, rose up, & openly spake against these flattering Tribunes. And for the replenishing of the cittie of VELITRES, he dyd compell those that were chosen, to goe thither, and to departe the cittie, apon great penalties to him that should disobey:[1] but to the warres, the people by no meanes would be brought or constrained. So *Martius* taking his friendes and followers with him, and such as he could by fayer wordes intreate to goe with him, dyd ronne certen forreyes into the dominion of the ANTIATES, where he met with great plenty of corne,[2] and had a marvelous great spoyle, aswell of cattell, as of men he had taken prisoners, whom he brought awaye with him, and reserved nothing for him selfe. Afterwardes having brought backe againe all his men that went out with him, safe & sounde to ROME, and every man riche and loden with spoyle:[3] then the hometarriers and housedoves that kept ROME still, beganne to repent them that it was not their happe to goe with him, and so envied both them that had sped so well in this jorney, and also of malice to *Martius*,

Coriolanus offendeth the people.

Coriolanus invadeth the Antiates, and bringeth rich spoyles home.

1. III. i. 261–2.   2. I. i. 248.   3. III. iii. 4.

they spited to see his credit and estimation increase
still more and more, bicause they accompted him
to be a great hinderer of the people.[1] Shortely
after this, *Martius* stoode for the Consulshippe: and
the common people favored his sute, thinking it
would be a shame to them to denie, and refuse, the
chiefest noble man of bloude, and most worthie
persone of ROME, and specially him that had done
so great service and good to the common wealth.[2]
For the custome of ROME was at that time, that *The manner of*
suche as dyd sue for any office, should for certen *suyng for office*
dayes before be in the market place, only with a *at Rome.*
poore gowne on their backes, and without any
coate underneath, to praye the cittizens to re-
member them at the daye of election:[3] which was *Whereupon this*
thus devised, either to move the people the more, *manner of*
by requesting them in suche meane apparell, or els *devised.*
bicause they might shewe them their woundes they *suyng was so*
had gotten in the warres in the service of the
common wealth, as manifest markes and testimonie of their valliantnes. Now it is not to be
thought that the suters went thus lose in a simple
gowne in the market place, without any coate
under it, for feare, and suspition of the common
people: for offices of dignitie in the cittie were not *Offices geven*
then geven by favour or corruption. It was but of *then by desert,*
late time, and long after this, that buying and *without favour or*
selling fell out in election of officers, and that the *corruption.*
voyces of the electours were bought for money.
But after corruption had once gotten waye into the
election of offices, it hath ronne from man to man,
even to the very sentence of judges, & also emong
captaines in the warres: so as in the ende, that only
turned common wealthes into Kingdomes, by
making armes subject to money. Therefore me
thinckes he had reason that sayed: he that first
made banckets, and gave money to the common *Bankets and*
people, was the first that tooke awaye authoritie, *money geven:*
and destroyed common wealth. But this pestilence *of common-*
crept in by litle and litle, and dyd secretly winne *wealth.*
ground still, continuing a long time in ROME, *only destroyers*
before it was openly knowen and discovered. For

1. II. iii. 91–2, II. ii. 5–6, III. iii. 3.   2. II. ii. 7–36.   3. II. ii. 134–41.

no man can tell who was the first man that bought the peoples voyces for money, nor that corrupted the sentence of the judges. Howbeit at ATHENS some holde opinion, that *Anytus*, the sonne of *Anthemion*, was the first man that fedde the judges with money, about the ende of the warres of PELOPONNESVS, being accused of treason for yelding up the forte of PYLE, at that time, when the golden and unsoiled age remained yet whole in judgement at ROME. Now *Martius* following this custome, shewed many woundes and cuttes apon his bodie,[1] which he had receyved in seventeene[2] yeres service at the warres, and in many sundrie battells, being ever the formest man that dyd set out feete to fight. So that there was not a man emong the people, but was ashamed of him selfe, to refuse so valliant a man: & one of them sayed to another, we must needes chuse him Consul, there is no remedie.[3] But when the daye of election was come, and that *Martius* came to the market place with great pompe, accompanied with all the Senate, and the whole Nobilitie of the cittie about him, who sought to make him Consul,[4] with the greatest instance and intreatie they could, or ever attempted for any man or matter: then the love and good will of the common people, turned straight to an[5] hate and envie toward him, fearing to put this office of soveraine authoritie into his handes, being a man somewhat partiall toward the nobilitie, and of great credit and authoritie amongst the *Patricians*, & as one they might doubt would take away alltogether the libertie from the people. Whereupon for these considerations, they refused *Martius* in the ende,[6] and made two other that were suters, Consuls. The Senate being marvelously offended with the people, dyd accompt the

Anytus the Athenian, the first that with money corrupted the sentence of the judge, and voyces of the people.

See the fickle mindes of common people.

1. For Martius' reluctance to follow the custom see II. ii. 136–49, II. iii. 41–136, 156–206. He muses on 'custom' at II. iii. 116–20.

2. Cf. II. ii. 100, 'seventeen battles'.   3. II. iii. 1–13.

4. The same day in the play; Shakespeare apparently remembered the 'great pompe' in III. i. 1 S.D.

5. 1595 omits *an*.

6. Cf. II. iii. 153–261, where the tribunes persuade the people to 'Repent in their election'.

shame of this refusall,[1] rather to redownd to them
selves, then to *Martius*: but *Martius* tooke it in
farre worse parte then the Senate, and was out of
all pacience. For he was a man to full of passion &
choller,[2] & to muche geven to over selfe will &
opinion, as one of a highe minde and great corage,
that lacked the gravity, and affabilitie that is
gotten with judgment of learning & reason, which
only is to be looked for in a governour of state: and
that remembred not how wilfulnes is the thing of
the world, which a governour of a common wealth
for pleasing should shonne,[3] being that which
Plato called solitarines. As in the ende, all men that
are wilfully geven to a selfe opinion and obstinate
minde, & who will never yeld to others reason, but
to their owne: remaine without companie, and
forsaken of all men. For a man that will live in the
world, must nedes have patience, which lusty
bloudes make but a mocke at. So *Martius* being a
stowte man of nature, that never yelded in any
respect, as one thincking that to overcome allwayes,
and to have the upper hande in all matters, was a
token of magnanimitie, & of no base and fainte
corage, which spitteth out anger from the most
weake and passioned parte of the harte, much
like the matter of an impostume: went home to his
house, full fraighted with spite and malice against
the people, being accompanied with all the lustiest
young gentlemen, whose mindes were nobly bent
as those that came of noble race, and commonly
used for to followe and honour him. But then
specially they floct about him, & kept him companie, to his muche harme:[4] for they dyd but
kyndle and inflame[5] his choller more and more,
being sorie with him for the injurie the people
offred him, bicause he was their captaine and
leader to the warres, that taught them all marshall
discipline, and stirred up in them a noble emulation of honour and valliantnes, and yet without

*The fruites of
selfe will and
obstinacie.*

1. Cf. m. i. 67–70, 90–111. In the play Martius, however 'choleric', is clear
about the political consequences to the senate of the exertion of popular power.
2. Cf. n. iii. 196, and below, p. 342 note 2.
3. I.e. shun.   4. m. ii. 1 S.D., m. ii. 6, iv. i. 1 S.D.
5. See n. i. 251–7 and notes, for a comparable metaphor.

Great store of corne brought to Rome.

envie, praising them that deserved best. In the meane season, there came great plenty of corne to ROME, that had bene bought, parte in ITALIE, and parte was sent out of SICILE, as geven by *Gelon* the tyranne[1] of SYRACVSA: so that many stoode in great hope, that the dearthe of vittells being holpen, the civill dissention would also cease. The Senate sate in counsell apon it immediatly, the common people stoode also about the palice where the counsell was kept, gaping what resolution would fall out: persuading them selves, that the corne they had bought should be solde good cheape, and that which was geven, should be devided by the polle, without paying any pennie, and the rather, bicause certaine of the Senatours amongest them dyd so wishe and persuade the

Coriolanus oration against the insolencie of the people.

same. But *Martius* standing up on his feete, did somewhat sharpely take up those, who went about to gratifie the people therein: & called them people pleasers, and traitours to the nobilitie.[2] Moreover he sayed 'they nourished against them selves, the naughty seede and cockle, of insolencie and sedition, which had bene sowed & scattered abroade emongest the people,[3] whom they should have cut of, if they had bene wise, and have prevented their greatnes: and not to their owne destruction to have suffered the people, to stablishe a magistrate for them selves, of so great power and authoritie, as that man had, to whom they had graunted it. Who was also to be feared, bicause he obtained what he would, and dyd nothing but what he listed, neither passed for any obedience to the Consuls, but lived in all libertie, acknowledging no superiour to commaund him, saving the only heades & authours of their faction, whom he called his magistrates. Therefore sayed he, they that gave counsell, and persuaded that the corne should be geven out to the common people *gratis*, as they used to doe in citties[4] of GRÆCE, where the people had more absolute power: dyd but only nourishe their disobedience, which would breake out in the

1. 1595, *tyrant.*   2. III. i. 43–4, 112–17.   3. III. i. 67–71.
4. 1595, *the cities.*

ende, to the utter ruine and overthrowe of the
whole state.[1] For they will not thincke it is done in
recompense of their service past, sithence they
know well enough they have so ofte refused to goe
to the warres, when they were commaunded:
neither for their mutinies when they went with us,
whereby they have rebelled and forsaken their
countrie: neither for their accusations which their
flatterers have preferred unto them, and they have
receyved, and made good against the Senate:
but they will rather judge we geve and graunt
them this, as abasing our selves, and standing in
feare of them, and glad to flatter them every waye.
By this meanes, their disobedience will still growe
worse and worse: and they will never leave to
practise newe sedition, and uprores.[2] Therefore it
were a great follie for us, me thinckes to doe it:
yea, shall I saye more?[3] we should if we were wise,
take from them their Tribuneshippe, which most
manifestly is the embasing of the Consulshippe,
and the cause of the division of the cittie. The state
whereof as it standeth, is not now as it was wont to
be, but becommeth dismembred in two factions,
which mainteines allwayes civill dissention and
discorde betwene us, and will never suffer us
againe to be united into one bodie.'[4] *Martius*
dilating the matter with many such like reasons,
wanne all the young men, and almost all the riche
men to his opinion: in so much they range it out,
that he was the only man, and alone in the cittie,
who stoode out against the people, and never
flattered them. There were only a fewe olde men
that spake against him, fearing least some mischief
might fall out apon it, as in dede there followed no
great good afterward. For the Tribunes of the
people, being present at this consultation of the
Senate, when they sawe that the opinion of *Martius*
was confirmed with the more voyces, they left

1. III. i. 112–17.   2. III. i. 118–38.   3. III. i. 139.
4. Cf. III. i. 140–69; particularly, 'pluck out the multitudinous tongue'
('take from them their Tribuneshippe'), 'mangles true judgement' (cf. 'dismembred'), 'integrity which should becom't' ('to be united into one bodie'),
'these bald tribunes' (the 'Tribuneshippe').

the Senate, and went downe to the people, crying
out for helpe, and that they would assemble to
save their Tribunes. Hereupon the people ranne on
head in tumult[1] together, before whom the wordes
that *Martius* spake in the Senate were openly
reported: which the people so stomaked, that even
in that furie they were readie to flye apon the whole
Senate. But the Tribunes layed all the faulte and
burden wholy upon *Martius*, and sent their ser-
geantes[2] forthwith to arrest him, presently to
appeare in persone before the people, to aunswer
the wordes he had spoken in the Senate. *Martius*
stowtely withstoode these officers that came to
arrest him. Then the Tribunes in their owne
personnes, accompanied with the Ædiles, went to
fetche him by force, and so layed violent hands
upon him. Howbeit the noble *Patricians* gathering
together about him, made the Tribunes geve backe,
and layed it sore apon the Ædiles: so for that time,
the night parted them, and the tumult appeased.[3]
The next morning betimes,[4] the Consuls seing the
people in an uprore, ronning to the market place
out of all partes of the cittie, they were affrayed
least all the cittie would together by the eares:
wherefore assembling the Senate in all hast, they
declared how it stoode them upon, to appease the
furie of the people, with some gentle wordes,[5]
or gratefull decrees in their favour: and moreover,
like wise men they should consider, it was now no
time to stande at defence and in contention, nor
yet to fight for honour against the communaltie:
they being fallen to so great an extremitie, and
offering such imminent daunger. Wherefore they
were to consider temperately of things, and to
deliver some present and gentle pacification. The
most parte of the Senatours that were present at
this counsaill, thought this opinion best, & gave
their consents unto it. Whereupon the Consuls

*Sedition at
Rome for
Coriolanus.*

---

1. III. i. 178 S.D.   2. III. i. 171.   3. III. i. 179–251.

4. The 'rabble' returns at III. i. 261; the Patrician's 'would they were abed'
suggests that the time is evening.

5. Cf. III. ii. 59; Shakespeare in III. ii substitutes domestic persuasions for the
senate formalities.

rising out of counsaill, went to speake unto the
people as gently as they could, and they dyd pacifie
their furie and anger, purging the Senate of all the
unjust accusations layed upon them, and used
great modestie in persuading them, and also in
reproving the faultes they had committed. And as
for the rest, that touched the sale of corne: they
promised there should be no disliking offred them
in the price. So the most parte of the people being
pacified, and appearing so plainely by the great
silence and still that was among them, as yelding
to the Consuls, and liking well of their wordes:[1]
the Tribunes then of the people rose out of their
seates, and sayed. Forasmuche as the Senate
yelded unto reason, the people also for their parte,
as became them, dyd likewise geve place unto
them: but notwithstanding, they would that
Martius should come in persone to aunswer to the
articles they had devised.[2] First, whether he had
not solicited and procured the Senate to chaunge   *Articles against*
the present state of the common weale, and to take   *Coriolanus.*
the soveraine authoritie out of the peoples handes.
Next, when he was sent for by authoritie of their
officers, why he dyd contemptously resist and
disobey. Lastly, seeing he had driven and beaten
the Ædiles into the market place before all the
worlde: if in doing this, he had not done as muche
as in him laye, to raise civill warres, and to set one
cittizen against another. All this was spoken to one
of these two endes, either that *Martius* against his
nature should be constrained to humble him selfe,
and to abase his hawty and fierce minde: or els if
he continued still in his stowtnes, he should incurre
the peoples displeasure & ill will so farre, that he
should never possibly winne them againe. Which
they hoped would rather fall out so, then otherwise:[3] as in deede they gest unhappely, considering
Martius nature and disposition. So *Martius* came,
and presented him selfe, to aunswer their accusations against him, and the people held their peace,

1. Cf. III. i. 282–331 where Menenius' words have a function similar to those
of North's 'Consuls rising out of counsaill'.
2. Cf. III. i. 170–227, III. iii. 63–6, 77–83.   3. II. iii. 253–61.

and gave attentive eare, to heare what he would saye. But where they thought to have heard very humble and lowly wordes come from him, he beganne not only to use his wonted boldnes of speaking (which of it selfe was very rough and unpleasaunt, and dyd more aggravate his accusation, then purge his innocencie) but also gave him selfe in his wordes to thunder, and looke therewithall so grimly, as though he made no reckoning of the matter.[1] This stirred coales emong the people, who were in wonderfull furie at it, and their hate and malice grewe so toward him, that they could holde no lenger, beare, nor indure his bravey & careles boldnes. Whereupon *Sicinius*, the cruellest and stowtest of the Tribunes, after he had whispered a litle with his companions, dyd openly pronounce in the face of all the people, *Martius* as condemned by the Tribunes to dye. Then presently he commaunded the Ædiles to apprehend him, and carie him straight to the rocke Tarpeian, and to cast him hedlong downe the same.[2] When the Ædiles came to laye handes upon *Martius* to doe that they were commaunded, divers of the people them selves thought it to cruell, and violent a dede. The noble men also being muche troubled to see force[3] and rigour used, beganne to crie alowde, helpe *Martius*:[4] so those that layed handes of[5] him being repulsed, they compassed him in rounde emong them selves, and some of them holding up their handes to the people, besought them not to handle him thus cruelly. But neither their wordes, nor crying out could ought prevaile, the tumulte & hurly burley was so great, untill suche time as the Tribunes owne friendes & kinsemen weying with them selves the impossiblenes to convey *Martius* to execution, without great slaughter and murder of the nobilitie: dyd persuade and advise not to proceede in so violent and extraordinary a sorte, as to put such a man to death, without lawfull processe in lawe, but that they should referre the sentence of

Coriolanus stowtnes in defence of him selfe.

Sicinius the Tribune, pronounceth sentence of death upon Martius.

1. III. i. 253–8.   2. III. i. 264–5, 286–7.   3. 1595, *such force.*
4. III. i. 225.   5. 1595, *on.*

his death, to the free voyce of the people. Then *Sicinius* bethinking him self a litle, dyd aske the *Patricians*, for what cause they tooke *Martius* out of the officers handes that went to doe execution? The *Patricians* asked him againe, why they would of them selves, so cruelly and wickedly put to death, so noble and valliant a ROMAINE, as *Martius* was, and that without lawe or justice? Well, then sayed *Sicinius*, if that be the matter, let there be no more quarrell or dissention against the people: for they doe graunt your demaunde, that his cause shalbe heard according to the law.[1] Therfore sayed he to *Martius*, we doe will and charge you to appeare before the people, the third daye of our next sitting and assembly here, to make your purgation for such articles as shalbe objected against you, that by free voyce the people maye geve sentence apon you as shall please them. The noble men were glad then of the adjornment, and were muche pleased they had gotten *Martius* out of this daunger. In the meane space, before the third day of their next cession came about, the same being kept every nineth daye continually at ROME, whereupon they call it now in Latin, *Nundinæ*: there fell out warre against the ANTIATES, which gave some hope to the nobilitie, that this adjornment would come to litle effect, thinking that this warre would hold them so longe, as that the furie of the people against him would be well swaged, or utterly forgotten, by reason of the trouble of the warres.[2] But contrarie to expectation, the peace was concluded presently with the ANTIATES, and the people returned again to ROME. Then the *Patricians* assembled oftentimes together, to consult how they might stande to *Martius*, and keepe the Tribunes from occasion to cause the people to mutine againe, and rise against the nobilitie.[3] And there *Appius Clodius* (one that was taken ever as an heavy enemie to the people) dyd avowe and protest, that they would utterly abase the authoritie of the Senate, &

Coriolanus hath daye geven him to aunswer the people.

---

1. III. i. 320–31.   2. Omitted in the play.
3. Turned again to domestic persuasion in III. ii.

destroye the common weale, if they would suffer
the common people to have authoritie by voyces to
geve judgment against the nobilitie.[1] On thother
side againe, the most auncient Senatours, and
suche as were geven to favour the common people
sayed: that when the people should see they had
authoritie of life and death in their handes, they
would not be so cruell and fierce, but gentle and
civill. More also, that it was not for contempt of
nobilitie or the Senate, that they sought to have the
authoritie of justice in their handes, as a preheminence and prerogative of honour: but bicause
they feared, that them selves should be contemned
and hated of the nobilitie. So as they were persuaded, that so sone as they gave them authoritie
to judge by voyces: so sone would they leave all
envie and malice to condemne anye. *Martius*
seeing the Senate in great doubt how to resolve,
partly for the love and good will the nobilitie dyd
beare him, and partly for the feare they stoode in
of the people: asked alowde of the Tribunes,
what matter they would burden him with? The
Tribunes aunswered him, that they would shewe
howe he dyd aspire to be King, and would prove
that all his actions tended to usurpe tyrannicall
power over ROME.[2] *Martius* with that, rising up
on his feete, sayed: that thereupon he dyd willingly
offer him self to the people, to be tried apon that
accusation. And that if it were proved by him, he
had so muche as once thought of any suche matter,
that he would then refuse no kinde of punishment
they would offer him: conditionally (quoth he)
that you charge me with nothing els besides, and
that ye doe not also abuse the Senate.[3] They
promised they would not. Under these conditions
the judgement was agreed upon, and the people
assembled. And first of all the Tribunes would in
any case (whatsoever became of it) that the people
would proceede to geve their voyces by Tribes,
and not by hundreds: for by this meanes the
multitude of the poore needy people (and all suche

*Coriolanus
accused, that
he sought to be
King.*

1. Cf. Martius in III. i. 89–96.　　2. III. iii. 1–2.　　3. III. iii. 42–7.

rable as had nothing to lose, and had lesse regard of honestie before their eyes) came to be of greater force (bicause their voyces were numbred by the polle) then the noble honest cittizens, whose persones and purse dyd duetifully serve the common wealth in their warres.[1] And then when the Tribunes sawe they could not prove he went about to make him self King: they beganne to broache a freshe the former wordes that *Martius* had spoken in the Senate, in hindering the distribution of the corne at meane price unto the common people, and persuading also to take the office of Tribune-shippe from them. And for the third, they charged him a newe, that he had not made the common distribution of the spoyle he had gotten in the invading the territories of the ANTIATES: but had of his owne authoritie devided it among them, who were with him in that jorney.[2] But this matter was most straunge of all to *Martius*, looking least to have bene burdened with that, as with any matter of offence. Wherupon being burdened on the sodaine, and having no ready excuse to make even at that instant: he beganne to fall a praising of the souldiers that had served with him in that jorney. But those that were not with him, being the greater number, cried out so lowde, and made suche a noyse, that he could not be heard. To conclude when they came to tell the voyces of the Tribes,[3] there were three voyces odde, which condemned him to be banished for life.[4] After declaration of the sentence, the people made suche joye, as they never rejoyced more for any battell they had wonne upon their enemies, they were so brave & lively, and went home so jocondly from the assembly, for triumphe of this sentence.[5] The Senate againe in contrary manner were as sad and heavie, repenting them selves beyond measure, that they had not

Coriolanus banished for life.

1. III. iii. 8–11.
2. Cf. III. iii. 4–5; in the play it appears that the charges relate to the Corioli campaign, not to the forays reported by North (p. 330 above).
3. Already collected at III. iii. 11. Shakespeare makes no use of the 'three voices odd'.
4. III. iii. 93–119.
5. III. iii. 136–43. Shakespeare emphasizes the crowd's awakened malice.

rather determined to have done and suffered any
thing whatsoever, before the common people
should so arrogantly, and outrageously have
abused their authoritie. There needed no difference
of garments I warrant you, nor outward showes to
know a *Plebeian* from a *Patrician*, for they were
easely decerned by their lookes. For he that was on
the peoples side, looked cheerely on the matter:
but he that was sad, and honge downe his head,
he was sure of the noble mens side. Saving *Martius*
alone, who neither in his countenaunce, nor
in his gate, dyd ever showe him selfe abashed, or
once let fall his great corage: but he only of all
other gentlemen that were angrie at his fortune,
dyd outwardly shewe no manner of passion, nor
care at all of him selfe.[1] Not that he dyd paciently
beare and temper his good happe, in respect of
any reason he had, or by his quiet condition: but
bicause he was so caried awaye with the vehe-
mencie of anger, and desire of revenge, that he had
no sence nor feeling of the hard state he was in,
which the common people judge, not to be sorow,
although in dede it be the very same. For when
sorow (as you would saye) is set a fyre, then it is
converted into spite and malice, & driveth awaye
for that time all faintnes of harte and naturall
feare. And this is the cause why the chollericke
man[2] is so altered, and mad in his actions, as a man
set a fyre with a burning agewe: for when a mans
harte is troubled within, his pulse will beate marvelous strongly. Now that *Martius* was even in that
taking, it appeared true sone after by his doinges.
For when he was come home to his house againe,
and had taken his leave of his mother and wife,
finding them weeping, and shreeking out for
sorrowe, and had also comforted and persuaded
them to be content with his chaunce:[3] he went
immediatly to the gate of the cittie, accompanied

*Coriolanus
constant minde
in adversitie.*

*The force of
anger.*

---

1. Cf. the regulated ferocity of III. iii. 120–35; Shakespeare may have responded to the marginal note.
2. The fire and burning associated with the choleric man are assimilated into
the play (e.g. v. i. 64).
3. IV. i.

with a great number of *Patricians* that brought him thither, from whence he went on his waye with three or foure of his friendes only,[1] taking nothing with him, nor requesting any thing of any man. So he remained a fewe dayes in the countrie at his houses, turmoyled with sundry sortes and kynde of thoughtes, suche as the fyer of his choller dyd sturre up. In the ende, seeing he could revolve no waye, to take a profitable or honorable course,[2] but only was pricked forward still to be revenged of the ROMAINES: he thought to raise up some great warres against them, by their neerest neighbours. Whereupon, he thought it his best waye, first to stirre up the VOLSCES against them, knowing they were yet able enough in strength & riches to encounter them, notwithstanding their former losses they had receyved not long before, and that their power was not so muche impaired, as their malice and desire was increased, to be revenged of the ROMAINES. Now in the cittie of ANTIVM, there was one called *Tullus Aufidius*,[3] who for his riches, as also for his nobilitie and valliantnes, was honoured emong the VOLSCES as a King. *Martius* knewe very well, that *Tullus* dyd more malice and envie him, then he dyd all the ROMAINES besides: bicause that many times in battells where they met, they were ever at the encounter one against another, like lustie coragious youthes, striving in all emulation of honour, and had encountered many times together.[4] In so muche, as besides the common quarrell betweene them, there was bred a marvelous private hate one against another. Yet notwithstanding, considering that *Tullus Aufidius* was a man of a great minde, and that he above all other of the VOLSCES, most desired revenge of the ROMAINES, for the injuries they had done unto them: he dyd an acte that confirmed the true wordes of an auncient Poet, who sayed:

Tullus Aufidius, a greate persone emong the Volsces.

1. Martius goes 'alone' in IV. i. 29.
2. IV. i. 35, 'determine on some course'.
3. Named here for the first time in North.
4. Cf. I. x. 7, 'five times'.

It is a thing full harde, mans anger to withstand,
if it be stiffely bent to take an enterprise in hande.
For then most men will have, the thing that they desire,
although it cost their lives therefore, suche force hath
wicked ire.

And so dyd he. For he disguised him selfe in
suche arraye and attire, as he thought no man
could ever have knowen him for the persone he was,
seeing him in that apparell he had upon his backe:
and as *Homer* sayed of *Ulysses,*

So dyd he enter into the enemies towne.

It was even twy light when he entred the cittie
of ANTIVM, and many people met him in the
streetes, but no man knewe him.[1] So he went
directly to *Tullus Aufidius* house, and when he came
thither, he got him up straight to the chimney
harthe,[2] and sat downe, and spake not a worde to
any man, his face all muffled over. They of the
house spying him, wondered what he should be,
and yet they durst not byd him rise.[3] For ill
favoredly muffled and disguised as he was, yet
there appeared a certaine majestie in his countenance,[4] and in his silence: whereupon they went to
Tullus who was at supper,[5] to tell him of the
straunge disguising of this man. *Tullus* rose
presently from the borde, and comming towards
him, asked him what he was, and wherefore he
came. Then *Martius* unmuffled[6] him selfe, &
after he had paused a while, making no aunswer,
he sayed unto him.[7] 'If thou knowest me not yet,
Tullus, and seeing me, dost not perhappes beleeve
me to be the man I am in dede, I must of necessitie
bewraye my selfe to be that I am. I am *Caius
Martius*, who hath done to thy self particularly, and

Coriolanus disguised, goeth to Antium, a cittie of the Volsces.

Coriolanus oration to Tullus Aufidius.

1. IV. iv.   2. Cf. IV. v. 26, 80; v. vi. 30.
3. They attempt to move him in IV. v. 31–5.
4. IV. v. 61–3.   5. Followed in IV. v.   6. Cf. IV. v. 55 S.D. (Capell).
7. 'Coriolanus oration' is closely followed, IV. v. 55–8, 66–102. Among the
words used are, *great hurt and mischief, painful service, malice and displeasure, dastard
nobles* (for 'dastard nobilitie'), *extremity, hearth, spite, misery serve thy turn, prove* . . .
fortunes, to live most weary (for 'weary to live'); 'let me be banished by the people'
becomes *suffer'd me by the voice of slaves to be | Whoop'd out of Rome.* Shakespeare's
canker'd country and *spleen . . . fiends* have no counterpart in the source.

to all the VOLSCES generally, great hurte & mischief, which I cannot denie for my surname of
Coriolanus that I beare. For I never had other
benefit nor recompence, of all the true and payne-
full service I have done, and the extreme daungers
I have bene in, but this only surname: a good
memorie and witnes, of the malice and displeasure
thou showldest beare me. In deede the name only
remaineth with me: for the rest, the envie and
crueltie of the people of ROME have taken from
me, by the sufferance of the dastardly nobilitie
and magistrates, who have forsaken me, and let
me be banished by the people. This extremitie
hath now driven me to come as a poore suter, to
take thy chimney harthe, not of any hope I have
to save my life thereby. For if I had feared death,
I would not have come hither to have put my life in
hazard: but prickt forward with spite[1] and desire
I have to be revenged of them that thus have
banished me, whom now I beginne to be avenged
on, putting my persone betweene thy enemies.
Wherefore, if thou hast any harte to be wrecked of
the injuries thy enemies have done thee, spede
thee now, & let my miserie serve thy turne, and so
use it, as my service maye be a benefit to the
VOLSCES: promising thee, that I will fight with
better good will for all you, then ever[2] I dyd when
I was against you, knowing that they fight more
valliantly, who knowe the force of their enemie,
then such as have never proved it. And if it be so
that thou dare not, and that thou art wearye to
prove fortune any more: then am I also weary to
live any lenger. And it were no wisedome in thee,
to save[3] the life of him, who hath bene heretofore
thy mortall enemie, and whose service now can
nothing helpe nor pleasure thee.' *Tullus* hearing
what he sayed, was a marvelous glad man, and
taking him by the hande, he sayed unto him.
Stande up, ô *Martius*, and bee of good chere, for in
profering thy selfe unto us, thou dost us great

1. 1603, *with desire to be revenged* (omitting *spite*).
2. 1595 omits *ever*; but Shakespeare is not close at this point (IV. v. 91-3).
3. 1595, *have.*

honour: and by this meanes thou mayest hope also
of greater things, at all the VOLSCES handes.[1]
So he feasted him for that time, & entertained him
in the honorablest manner he could, talking with
him in no other matters at that present: but within
fewe dayes after, they fell to consultation together,
in what sorte they should beginne their warres.

*Great dissention
at Rome about
Martius
banishment.*

Now on thother side, the cittie of ROME was in
marvelous uprore, and discord, the nobilitie
against the communaltie, and chiefly for *Martius*
condemnation and banishment. Moreover the
priestes, the Sooth sayers, and private men also,
came and declared to the Senate certaine sightes
and wonders in the ayer, which they had seene, &
were to be considered of: amongst the which,
such a vision happened. There was a cittizen of
ROME called *Titus Latinus*, a man of meane qualitie
and condition, but otherwise an honest sober man,
geven to a quiet life, without superstition, and much
lesse to vanitie or lying. This man had a vision in
his dreame, in the which he thought that *Jupiter*
appeared unto him, and commaunded him to
signifie to the Senate, that they had caused a
very vile lewde daunser to goe before the procession: and sayed, the first time this vision had
appeared unto him, he made no reckoning of it:
and comming againe another time into his minde,
he made not muche more accompt of the matter
then before. In the ende, he sawe one of his sonnes
dye, who had the best nature and condition of all
his brethern: and sodainely he him selfe was so
taken in all his limmes, that he became lame and
impotent. Hereupon he tolde the whole circumstance of this vision before the Senate, sitting upon
his litle couche or bedde, whereon he was caried
on mens armes: and he had no sooner reported
this vision to the Senate, but he presently felt his
bodie and limmes restored again, to their former
strength and use. So raising up him self upon his
couche, he got up on his feete at that instant, and
walked home to his house, without helpe of any
man. The Senate being amazed at this matter,

1. Tullus' speech is much amplified at IV. v. 102–36.

made diligent enquierie to understand the trothe:
and in the ende they found there was such a thing.
There was one that had delivered a bondman of
his that offended him, into the hands of other
slaves and bondemen, and had commanded them
to whippe him up and down the market place,[1]
and afterwards to kill him: and as they had him in
execution, whipping him cruelly, they dyd so
martyre the poore wretch, that for the cruell
smarte and payne he felt, he turned and writhed
his bodie, in straunge and pittiefull sorte. The
procession by chaunce came by even at the same
time, and many that followed it, were hartely
moved and offended with the sight, saying: that
this was no good sight to behold, nor mete to be
met in procession time. But for all this, there was
nothing done: saving they blamed and rebuked
him, that punished his slave so cruelly. For the
ROMAINES at that time, dyd use their bondemen
very gently, bicause they them selves dyd labour
with their owne hands, and lived with them, and
emong them: and therefore they dyd use them the
more gently and familliarly. For the greatest *The Romaines*
punishment they gave a slave that had offended, *manner of*
was this. They made him carie a limmer on his *punishing their*
showlders that is fastened to the axeltree of a coche, *slaves.*
and compelled him to goe up and downe in that
sorte amongest all their neighbours. He that had
once abidden this punishement, and was seene in
that manner, was proclaimed and cried in every
market towne: so that no man would ever trust *Whereof*
him after, and they called him *Furcifer*, bicause the *Furcifer came.*
LATINES call the wodd that ronneth into the
axeltree of the coche, *Furca*, as muche to saye, as a
forke. Now when *Latinus* had made reporte to the
Senate of the vision that had happened to him,
they were devising whom this unpleasaunt daunser
should be, that went before the procession. Ther-
upon certain that stoode by, remembred the poore
slave that was so cruelly whipped through the
market place, whom they afterwardes put to death:

1. Although Shakespeare suppresses the dream episode he may remember
the whipping at IV. vi. 60–1.

and the thing that made them remember it, was the straunge and rare manner of his punishment. The priestes hereupon were repaired unto for their advise: they were wholy of opinion, that it was the whipping of the slave. So they caused the slaves master to be punished, and beganne againe a newe procession, & all other showes and sightes in honour of *Jupiter*. But hereby appeareth plainely, how king *Numa* dyd wisely ordaine all other ceremonies concerning devotion to the goddes, and specially this custome which he stablished, to bring the people to religion. For when the magistrates, bishoppes, priestes, or other religious ministers goe about any divine service, or matter of religion, an herauld ever goeth before them, crying out alowde, *Hoc age*: as to saye, doe this, or minde this. Hereby they are specially commaunded, wholy to dispose them selves to serve God, leaving all other busines and matters a side: knowing well enough, that whatsoever most men doe, they doe it as in a manner constrained unto it. But the ROMAINES dyd ever use to beginne againe their sacrifices, processions, playes, & suche like showes done in honour of the goddes, not only upon suche an occasion, but apon lighter causes then that. As when they went a procession through the cittie, and dyd carie the images of their goddes, and suche other like holy relikes upon open hallowed coches or charrets, called in LATIN *Thensæ*: one of the coche horses that drue them stoode still, and would drawe no more: and bicause also the coche man tooke the raynes of the bridle with the left hande, they ordained that the procession should be begonne againe a newe. Of later time also, they dyd renewe and beginne a sacrifice thirtie times one after another, bicause they thought still there fell out one faulte or other in the same, so holy and devout were they to the goddes. Now *Tullus* and *Martius* had secret conference with the greatest personages of the cittie of ANTIVM, declaring unto them, that now they had good time offered them to make warre with the ROMAINES, while they were in dissention one with another. They

A ceremonie instituted by king Numa, touching religion.

The superstition of the Romaines.

Thensæ.

aunswered them, they were ashamed to breake the
league, considering that they were sworne to keepe
peace for two yeres. Howbeit shortely after, the
ROMAINES gave them great occasion to make
warre with them. For on a holy daye common
playes being kept in ROME, apon some suspition,
or false reporte, they made proclamation by sound
of trumpet, that all the VOLSCES should avoyde
out of ROME before sunne set. Some thincke this
was a crafte & deceipt of *Martius*,[1] who sent one to
ROME to the Consuls, to accuse the VOLSCES
falsely, advertising them howe they had made a
conspiracie to set apon them, whilest they were
busie in seeing these games, and also to set their
cittie a fyre.[2] This open proclamation made all the
VOLSCES more offended with the ROMAINES,
then ever they were before: and *Tullus* agravating
the matter, dyd so inflame the VOLSCES against
them, that in the ende they sent their ambassadours to ROME, to summone them to deliver their
landes and townes againe, which they had taken
from them in times past, or to looke for present
warres. The ROMAINES hearing this, were marvelously netled: and made no other aunswer but
thus. If the VOLSCES be the first that beginne
warre: the ROMAINES will be the last that[3] will
ende it. Incontinently upon returne of the VOL-
SCES ambassadours, and deliverie of the RO-
MAINES aunswer: *Tullus* caused an assembly
generall to be made of the VOLSCES, and concluded to make warre apon the ROMAINES.
This done, *Tullus* dyd counsell them to take *Martius*
into their service, and not to mistrust him for the
remembraunce of any thing past, but boldely to
trust him in any matter to come: for he would doe
them more service in fighting for them, then ever
he dyd them displeasure in fighting against them.
So *Martius* was called forth, who spake so excell-
ently in the presence of them all, that he was
thought no lesse eloquent in tongue, then warlike

*The Romaines
gave the Volsces
occasion of
warres.*

*Martius
Coriolanus
craftie accusa-
tion of the
Volsces.*

1. Not in the play.
2. Not directly used in the play, but cf. IV. vi. 79, 86.
3. 1595 omits *that*.

Coriolanus chosen generall of the Volsces, with Tullus Aufidius against the Romaines.

in showe: and declared him selfe both expert in warres, and wise with valliantes.[1] Thus he was joyned in commission with *Tullus* as generall of the VOLSCES, having absolute authoritie betwene them to follow and pursue the warres. But *Martius* fearing least tract of time to bring this armie togither with all the munition and furniture of the VOLSCES, would robbe him of the meane he had to execute his purpose & intent: left order with the rulers and chief of the cittie, to assemble the

Coriolanus invadeth the territories of the Romaines.

rest of their power, and to prepare all necessary provision for the campe. Then he with the lightest souldiers he had, and that were willing to followe him, stale awaye upon the sodaine, & marched with all speede, and entred the territories of ROME, before the ROMAINES heard any newes of his comming.[2] In so much[3] the VOLSCES found such spoyle in the fields, as they had more then they could spend in their campe, and were wearie to drive and carie awaye that they had. Howbeit the gayne of the spoyle and the hurte they dyd to the ROMAINES in this invasion, was

A fine devise to make the communaltie suspect the nobilitie.

the least parte of his intent. For his chiefest purpose was, to increase still the malice and dissention between the nobilitie, and the communaltie: and to drawe that on, he was very carefull to keepe the noble mens landes and goods safe from harme and burning,[4] but spoyled all the whole countrie besides, and would suffer no man to take or hurte any thing of the noble mens.[5] This made greater sturre and broyle betweene the nobilitie and peo-

Great harte burning betwext the nobilitie and people.

ple, then was before. For the noble men fell out with the people, bicause they had so unjustly banished a man of so great valure and power. The people on thother side, accused the nobilitie, how they had procured *Martius* to make these warres, to be revenged of them: bicause it pleased them to

1. The play allows the eloquence of Martius and does not disallow his wisdom among the Volscians.
2. IV. vi. 39–40.   3. 1595, *much as.*
4. IV. vi. 79, which reports the burning but not the saving.
5. This report leaves no trace in the play, unless at IV. vii. 29, 'the nobility of Rome are his'.

see their goodes burnt and spoyled before their eyes, whilest them selves were well at ease, and dyd behold the peoples losses and misfortunes, and knowing their owne goodes safe and out of daunger: and howe the warre was not made against the noble men, that had the enemie abroad, to keepe that they had in safety.[1] Now *Martius* having done this first exploite (which made the VOLSCES bolder, and lesse fearefull of the ROMAINES) brought home all the armie againe, without losse of any man. After their whole armie (which was marvelous great, and very forward to service) was assembled in one campe: they agreed to leave parte of it for garrison in the countrie about, and the other parte should goe on, and make the warre apon the ROMAINES. So *Martius* bad *Tullus* choose, and take which of the two charges he liked best, *Tullus* made him aunswer, he knewe by experience that *Martius* was no lesse valliant then him selfe, and howe he ever had better fortune and good happe in all battells, then him selfe had. Therefore he thought it best for him to have the leading of those that should make the warres abroade: and him selfe would keepe home, to provide for the safety of the citties and of his countrie, and to furnishe the campe also of all necessary provision abroade.[2] So *Martius* being stronger then before, went first of all unto the cittie of CIRCEES, inhabited by the ROMAINES, who willingly yelded them selves, and therefore had no hurte.[3] From thence, he entred the countrie of the LATINES, imagining the ROMAINES would fight with him[4] there, to defend the LATINES, who were their confederates, and had many times sent unto the ROMAINES for their ayde. But on the one side, the people of ROME were very ill willing to goe: and on the other side the Consuls being apon their going out of their office,

---

1. In IV. vi. 81–161 the tensions spring from the common plight.
2. There is no division of roles in the play, but IV. vii makes it appear that Martius is in charge of the war upon the Romans.
3. For the willing yielding, see IV. vii. 28.   4. 1595 omits *with him*.

would not hazard them selves for so small a time:
so that the ambassadours of the LATINES returned home againe, and dyd no good. Then
Martius dyd besiege their citties, and having taken
by force the townes of the TOLERINIANS, VICA-
NIANS, PEDANIANS, and the BOLANIANS,
who made resistaunce: he sacked all their goodes,
and tooke them prisoners. Suche as dyd yeld
them selves willingly unto him, he was as carefull
as possible might be, to defend them from hurte:
and bicause they should receyve no damage by his
will, he removed his campe as farre from their
confines as he could. Afterwards, he tooke the
cittie of BOLES by assault, being about an hundred
furlonge from ROME, where he had a marvelous
great spoyle, and put every man to the sword that
was able to carie weapon. The other VOLSCES
that were appointed to remaine in garrison for
defence of their countrie, hearing his good newes,
would tary no lenger at home, but armed them
selves, and ranne to *Martius* campe, saying they
dyd acknowledge no other captaine but him.[1]
Hereupon his fame ranne through all ITALIE,
and every one praised him for a valliant captaine,
for that by chaunge of one man for another, suche
and so straunge events fell out in the state. In this
while, all went still to wracke at ROME. For, to
come into the field to fight with the enemie, they
could not abyde to heare of it, they were one so
muche against another, and full of seditious wordes,
the nobilitie against the people, and the people
against the nobilitie. Untill they had intelligence
at the length that the enemies had layed seige to
the cittie of LAVINIVM, in the which were all the
temples & images of the goddes their protectours,
and from whence came first their auncient originall,
Lavinium built for that *Æneas* at his first arrivall into ITALIE
by Æneas. dyd build that cittie. Then fell there out a marvelous sodain chaunge of minde among the people,
& farre more straunge and contrarie in the nobilitie. For the people thought, good to repeale the

---

1. The germ of IV. vii, and cf. the 'Volsces envy to Coriolanus' below.

condemnation and exile of *Martius*.[1] The Senate
assembled upon it, would in no case yeld to that.
Who either dyd it of a selfe will be to contrarie to
the peoples desire: or bicause *Martius* should not
returne through the grace and favour of the people.
Or els, bicause they were throughly angrie and
offended with him, that he would set apon the
whole, being offended but by a fewe, and in his
doings would shewe him selfe an[2] open enemie
besides unto his countrie: notwithstanding the
most parte of them tooke the wrong they had done
him, in marvelous ill parte, and as if the injurie
had bene done unto them selves. Reporte being
made of the Senates resolution, the people founde
them selves in a straight: for they could authorise
and confirme nothing by their voyces, unles it had
bene first propounded and ordeined by the Senate.
But *Martius* hearing this sturre about him, was in a
greater rage with them then before: in so muche as
he raised his seige incontinently before the cittie of
Lavinivm, and going towardes Rome, lodged
his campe within fortie furlonge of the cittie, at the
ditches called *Cluiliæ*. His incamping so neere
Rome, dyd put all the whole cittie in a wonderfull
feare: howbeit for the present time it appeased
the sedition and dissention betwixt the Nobilitie
and the people. For there was no Consul, Senatour,
nor Magistrate, that durst once contrarie the
opinion of the people, for the calling home againe
of *Martius*. When they sawe the women in a marvelous feare, ronning up and downe the cittie: the
temples of the goddes full of olde people, weeping
bitterly in their prayers to the goddes: and finally,
not a man either wise or hardie to provide for their
safetie: then they were all of opinion, that the
people had reason to call home *Martius* againe, to
reconcile them selves to him, and that the Senate
on the contrary parte, were in marvelous great
faulte to be angrie and in choller with him, when it
stoode them upon rather to have gone out and

---

1. Shakespeare does not admit such a reversal of attitudes, but the people
express dismayed regrets (IV. vi. 140–6) which prompt patrician scorn.

2. 1595, *as open*.

*The Romaines
send ambassa-
dours to
Coriolanus to
treate of peace.*

intreated him. So they all agreed together to send
ambassadours unto him, to let him understand
howe his countrymen dyd call him home againe,
and restored him to all his goodes, and besought
him to deliver them from this warre. The ambassadours that were sent, were *Martius* familliar
friendes,[1] and acquaintaunce, who looked at the
least for a curteous welcome of him, as of their
familliar friende & kynseman. Howbeit they founde
nothing lesse. For at their comming, they were
brought through the campe, to the place where he
was set in his chayer of state, with a marvelous &
an unspeakable majestie,[2] having the chiefest men
of the VOLSCES about thim: so he commaunded
them to declare openly the cause of their comming.
Which they delivered in the most humble and
lowly wordes they possiblie could devise, and with
all modest countenaunce and behaviour agreable
for the same. When they had done their message:
for the injurie they had done him, he aunswered
them very hottely, and in great choller. But as
generall of the VOLSCES, he willed them to restore
unto the VOLSCES, all their landes and citties they
had taken from them in former warres:[3] and moreover, that they should geve them the like honour
and freedome of ROME, as they had before geven
to the LATINES. For otherwise they had no other
meane to ende this warre, if they dyd not graunte
these honest and just conditions of peace. Thereupon he gave them thirtie dayes respit[4] to make
him aunswer. So the ambassadours returned
straight to ROME, and *Martius* forthwith departed
with his armie out of the territories of the RO-
MAINES. This was the first matter wherewith the

*The first
occasion of the
Volsces envy to
Coriolanus.*

VOLSCES (that most envied *Martius* glorie and
authoritie) dyd charge *Martius* with. Among those,
Tullus was chief: who though he had receyved no
private injurie or displeasure of *Martius*, yet the
common faulte and imperfection of mans nature

1. Cf. Cominius' embassy, v. i. 1–28.   2. Cf. v. i. 63, v. iv. 22.
3. For the distinction between Martius' 'great choller' about his own injuries and his careful generalship in the Volscian cause, cf. v. vi. 71–84, 105–6.
4. There is none in the play; but there are traces of these 'first conditions' at
v. iii. 14 and, possibly, v. i. 69.

wrought in him, and it grieved him to see his owne reputation bleamished, through *Martius* great fame and honour, and so him selfe to be lesse esteemed of the VOLSCES, then he was before.[1] This fell out the more, bicause every man honoured *Martius*, and thought he only could doe all, and that all other governours and captaines must be content with suche credit and authoritie, as he would please to countenaunce them with. From hence they derived all their first accusations and secret murmurings against *Martius*. For private captaines conspiring against him, were very angrie with him: and gave it out, thet the removing of the campe was a manifest treason, not of the townes, nor fortes, nor of armes, but of time and occasion, which was a losse of great importaunce, bicause it was that which in treason might both lose and binde all, and preserve the whole. Now *Martius* having geven the ROMAINES thirtie dayes respit for their aunswer, and specially bicause the warres have not accustomed to make any great chaunges, in lesse space of time then that: he thought it good yet, not to lye a sleepe and idle all the while, but went and destroyed the landes of the enemies allies, and tooke seven great citties of theirs well inhabited, and the ROMAINES durst not once put them selves into the field, to come to their ayde and helpe: they were so fainte harted, so mistrustfull, and lothe besides to make warres. In so muche as they properly ressembled the bodyes paralyticke, & losed of their limmes and members: as those which through the palsey have lost all their sence and feeling.[2] Wherefore, the time of peace expired, *Martius* being returned into the dominions of the ROMAINES againe with all his armie, they sent another ambassade[3] unto him, to praye peace, and the remove of the VOLSCES out of their countrie: that afterwardes they might with better leysure fall

Another ambassade sent to Coriolanus.

---

1. IV. vii generally expresses the Volscian 'envy'; cf. the servingman's prognostication in IV. v. 211–14, and IV. vii. 1–16.

2. The paralysis of Rome is expressed in IV. vi, V. i, and V. iv, and by the Volscian guard mocking the 'palsied intercession' of Menenius, in V. ii. 40–6.

3. Menenius in V. i and V. ii.

to suche agreementes together, as should be thought most mete and necessarie. For the Ro-MAINES were no men that would ever yeld for feare. But if he thought the VOLSCES had any grounde to demaunde reasonable articles & conditions, all that they would reasonably aske should be graunted unto, by the ROMAINES, who of them selves would willingly yeld to reason, conditionally, that they dyd laye downe armes. *Martius* to that aunswered: that as generall of the VOLSCES he would replie nothing unto it. But yet as a ROMAINE cittizen, he would counsell them to let fall their pride, and to be conformable to reason, if they were wise: and that they should returne againe within three dayes, delivering up the articles agreed upon, which he had first delivered them.[1] Or otherwise, that he would no more geve them assuraunce or safe conduite to returne againe into his campe, with suche vaine and frivolous messages. When the ambassadours were returned to ROME, and had reported *Martius* aunswer to the Senate: their cittie being in extreme daunger, and as it were in a terrible storme or tempest, they threw out (as the common proverbe sayeth) their holy ancker. For then they appointed all the bishoppes, priestes, ministers of the goddes, and keepers of holy things, and all the augures or *The priestes* soothesayers which foreshowe things to come by *and soothesayers* observation of the flying of birdes (which is an olde *sent to* auncient kynde of prophecying and divination *Coriolanus.* amongest the ROMAINES) to goe to *Martius* apparelled, as when they doe their sacrifices:[2] and first to intreate him to leave of warre, and then that he would speake to his contrymen, & conclude peace with the VOLSCES. *Martius* suffered them to come into his campe, but yet he graunted them nothing the more, neither dyd he entertaine them or speake more curteously to them, then he dyd the first time that they came unto him, saving only that he willed them to take the one of the

1. Bullough supposes these articles to be given to Menenius at v. ii. 88, but the play's context ('I writ it for thy sake') makes a personal letter more likely.
2. Not in the play.

two: either to accept peace under the first conditions offered, or els to receyve warre. When all this goodly rable[1] of superstition and priestes were returned, it was determined in counsell that none should goe out of the gates of the cittie, and that they should watche and warde upon the walles, to repulse their enemies if they came to assault them: referring them selves and all their hope to time, and fortunes uncertaine favour, not knowing otherwise howe to remedie the daunger. Now all the cittie was full of tumult, feare, and marvelous doubt what would happen: untill at the length there fell out suche a like matter, as *Homer* oftetimes sayed they would least have thought of. For in great matters, that happen seldome, *Homer* sayeth, and crieth out in this sorte,

> *The goddesse Pallas she, with her fayer glistering eyes,*
> *dyd put into his minde suche thoughts, and made him*
> *so devise.*

And in an other place:

> *But sure some god hath t'ane, out of the peoples minde,*
> *both wit and understanding eke, and have therewith*
> *assynde*
> *some other simple spirite, in steede thereof to byde,*
> *that so they might their doings all, for lacke of wit*
> *misguyde.*

And in an other place:

> *The people of them selves, did either it consider,*
> *or else some god instructed them, & so they joynde*
> *together.*

Many recken not of *Homer*, as referring matters unpossible, and fables of no likelyhoode or trothe, unto mans reason, free will, or judgement: which in deede is not his meaning. But things true and likely, he maketh to depend of our owne free wil and reason. For he oft speaketh these wordes:

> *I have thought it in my noble harte.*

1. Shakespeare uses the word only of the plebeians.

And in an other place:

Achilles angrie was, and sorie for to heare
him so to say, his heavy brest was fraught with
pensive feare.

And againe in an other place:

Bellerophon (she) could not move with her fayer tongue,
so honest and so vertuous, he was the rest among.

But in wonderous and extraordinarie thinges, which are done by secret inspirations and motions, he doth not say that God taketh away, from man his choyce and freedom of will, but that he doth move it: neither that he doth worke desire in us, but objecteth to our mindes certaine imaginations whereby we are lead to desire, and thereby doth not make this our action forced, but openeth the way to our will, and addeth thereto courage, and hope of successe.[1] For, either we must say, that the goddes meddle not with the causes and beginninges of our actions: or else what other meanes have they to helpe and further men? It is apparaunt that they handle not our bodies, nor move not our feete and handes, when there is occasion to use them: but that parte of our minde from which these motions proceede, is induced thereto, or caried away by such objectes and reasons, as God offereth unto it. Now the ROMAINE Ladies and gentlewomen did visite all the temples and goddes of the same, to make their prayers unto them: but the greatest Ladies (and more parte of them) were continuallie about the aulter of *Jupiter Capitolin*, emonge which troupe by name, was *Valeria*, *Publicolaes* owne sister. The selfe same *Publicola*, who did such notable service to the ROMAINES, both in peace and warres: and was dead also certaine yeares before, as we have declared in his life. His sister *Valeria* was greatly honoured & reverenced amonge all the ROMAINES: and did so modestlie and wiselie behave her selfe, that she did not shame nor dishonour the house she came

Valeria
Publicolaes
sister.

1. Much here might have interested the Shakespeare of *Cymbeline*, but it is ignored in *Coriolanus*.

of.[1] So she sodainely fell into such a fansie, as we
have rehearsed before, and had (by some god as I
thinke) taken holde of a noble devise.[2] Whereuppon
she rose, and thother Ladies with her, and they all
together went straight to the house of *Volumnia,*
Martius mother: and comming in to her, founde
her, and *Martius* wife her daughter in lawe set
together, and havinge her husbande *Martius*
young children in her lappe.[3] Now all the traine of
these Ladies sittinge in a ringe rounde about
her: *Valeria* first beganne to speake in this sorte
unto her. 'We Ladies, are come to visite you
Ladies (my Ladie *Volumnia* and *Virgilia*) by no
direction from the Senate, nor commaundement
of other magistrate: but through the inspiration
(as I take it) of some god above. Who havinge
taken compassion and pitie of our prayers, hath
moved us to come unto you, to intreate you in a
matter, as well beneficiall for us, as also for the
whole citizens in generall: but to your selves in
especiall (if it please you to credit me) and shall
redounde to our more fame and glorie, then the
daughters of the SABYNES obteined in former age,
when they procured lovinge peace, in stead of
hatefull warre, betwene their fathers and their
husbands. Come on good ladies, and let us goe all
together unto *Martius,* to intreate him to take
pitie uppon us, and also to reporte the trothe unto
him, howe muche you are bounde unto the citizens: who notwithstandinge they have susteined
greate hurte and losses by him, yet they have not
hetherto sought revenge apon your persons by any
discurteous usage, neither ever conceyved any
suche thought or intent against you, but doe deliver ye safe into his handes, though thereby they
looke for no better grace or clemency from him.'
When *Valeria* had spoken this unto them, all thother ladyes together with one voyce confirmed that
she had sayed. Then *Volumnia* in this sorte did
aunswer her. 'My good ladies, we are partakers

Volumnia,
Martius mother.

The wordes of
Valeria, unto
Volumnia and
Virgilia.

The aunswere of
Volumnia to the
Romaine ladies.

1. v. iii. 64–7.
2. Used by Hardy, *Coriolan,* IV. i, but not by Shakespeare (Bullough).
3. The play's only comparably domestic scene is I. iii.

with you of the common miserie and calamitie of our countrie, and yet our griefe exceedeth yours the more, by reason of our particular misfortune: to feele the losse of my sonne *Martius* former valiancie and glorie, and to see his persone environned nowe with our enemies in armes, rather to see him foorth comminge and safe kept, then of any love to defende his persone. But yet the greatest griefe of our heaped mishappes is, to see our poore countrie brought to suche extremitie, that all the hope of the safetie and preservation thereof, is nowe unfortunately cast uppon us simple women: bicause we knowe not what accompt he will make of us, sence he hath cast from him all care of his naturall countrie and common weale, which heretofore he hath holden more deere and precious, then either his mother, wife, or children. Notwithstandinge, if ye thinke we can doe good, we will willingly doe what you will have us: bringe us to him I pray you. For if we can not prevaile, we maye yet dye at his feete,[1] as humble suters for the safetie of our countrie.' Her aunswere ended, she tooke her daughter in lawe, & *Martius* children with her, and being accompanied with all the other ROMAINE ladies, they went in troupe together unto the VOLSCES campe: whome when they sawe, they of them selves did both pitie and reverence her, and there was not a man amonge them that once durst say a worde unto her. Nowe was *Martius* set then in his chayer of state, with all the honours of a generall, and when he had spied the women comming a farre of, he marveled what the matter ment: but afterwardes knowing his wife which came formest, he determined at the first to persist in his obstinate & inflexible rancker.[2] But overcomen in the ende with naturall affection, and being altogether altered to see them: his harte would not serve him to tarie their comming to his chayer, but comming

1. Cf. Hardy, *Coriolan*, IV. iii (Bullough). Not in Shakespeare; but Thomson's Volumnia threatens suicide, and Mrs Siddons retained the effect in her playing of Volumnia to Kemble's Coriolanus (see Introduction, p. 80).

2. Cf. v. iii. 22–6, 33–7, especially l. 26, 'Let it be virtuous to be obstinate'.

downe in hast, he went to meete them,[1] and first he kissed his mother, and imbraced her a pretie while, then his wife and litle children.[2] And nature so wrought with him, that the teares fell from his eyes, and he coulde not keepe him selfe from making much of them, but yeelded to the affection of his bloode, as if he had bene violently caried with the furie of a most swift running streame. After he had thus lovingly received them, and perceivinge that his mother *Volumnia* would beginne to speake to him, he called the chiefest of the counsell of the VOLSCES to heare what she would say.[3] Then she spake in this sorte.[4] 'If we helde our peace (my sonne) and determined not to speake, the state of our poore bodies, and present sight of our rayment, would easely bewray to thee what life we have led at home, since thy exile and abode abroad. But thinke now with thy selfe, howe much more unfortunatly,[5] then all the women livinge we are come hether, considering that the sight which should be most pleasaunt to all other to beholde, spitefull fortune hath made most fearefull to us: making my selfe to see my sonne, and my daughter here, her husband, besieging the walles of his native countrie.[6] So as that which is thonly comforte to all other in their adversitie and miserie, to pray unto the goddes, and to call to them for aide: is the onely thinge which plongeth us into most deepe perplexitie. For we can not (alas) together pray, both for victorie, for our countrie, and for safety of thy life also: but a worlde of grievous curses, yea more then any mortall enemie can heape uppon us, are forcibly wrapt up in our prayers. For the bitter soppe of most harde choyce is offered thy wife & children, to forgoe the one of the two: either to lose the persone of thy selfe, or the nurse of their native contrie. For my selfe (my sonne) I am determined not to tarie, till fortune in

The oration of Volumnia unto her sonne Coriolanus.

1. It is probable that Martius leaves his chair of state at v. iii. 40.
2. At v. iii. 42–7 Martius embraces his wife first.   3. v. iii. 92–3.
4. For Volumnia's oration, cf. v. iii. 94–148. Many words and phrases are retained in the opening sentences.
5. 1612, *unfortunate*; cf. v. iii. 97, and Introduction, p. 29.
6. Cf. v. iii. 102–3, 'tearing / His country's bowels out'.

my life time doe make an ende of this warre. For
If I cannot persuade thee, rather to doe good unto
both parties, then to overthrowe & destroye the
one, preferring love and nature, before the malice
& calamitie of warres: thou shalt see, my sonne,
and trust unto it, thou shalt no soner marche
forward to assault thy countrie, but thy foote shall
treade upon thy mothers wombe, that brought thee
first into this world.[1] And I maye not deferre to see
the daye, either that my sonne be led prisoner in
triumphe by his naturall country men, or that he
him selfe doe triumphe of them, and of his naturall
countrie.[2] For if it were so, that my request tended
to save thy countrie, in destroying the VOLSCES:
I must confesse, thou wouldest hardly and doubt-
fully resolve on that. For as to destroye thy naturall
countrie, it is altogether unmete and unlawfull: so
were it not just, and lesse honorable, to betraye
those that put their trust in thee. But my only
demaunde consisteth, to make a gayle deliverie of
all evills, which delivereth equall benefit and safety,
both to the one and the other, but most honorable
for the VOLSCES. For it shall appeare, that
having victorie in their handes, they have of
speciall favour graunted us singular graces: peace,
and amitie, albeit them selves have no lesse parte of
both, then we. Of which good, if so it came to
passe, thy selfe is thonly authour,[3] and so hast thou
thonly honour.[4] But if it faile, and fall out contrarie: thy selfe alone deservedly shall carie the
shamefull reproche & burden of either partie. So,
though the ende of warre be uncertaine, yet this
notwithstanding is most certaine: that if it be thy
chaunce to conquer, this benefit shalt thou reape
of thy goodly conquest, to be chronicled the plague
and destroyer of thy countrie.[5] And if fortune also
overthrowe thee, then the world will saye, that
through desire to revenge thy private injuries, thou
hast for ever undone thy good friendes, who dyd

1. These two sentences (from *For my selfe*) are closely rendered in v. iii. 118–25.

2. v. iii. 111–18.   3. Not used in the oration, but cf. v. iii. 36.

4. Cf. v. iii. 132–40, which renders North from *For if it were so.*

5. v. iii. 141–8.

most lovingly & curteously receyve thee.' *Martius* gave good eare unto his mothers wordes, without interrupting her speache at all: and after she had sayed what she would, he held his peace a prety while, and aunswered not a worde.[1] Hereupon she beganne againe to speake unto him, and sayed. 'My sonne, why doest thou not aunswer me? doest thou thinke it good altogether to geve place unto thy choller and desire of revenge, and thinkest thou it not honestie for thee to graunt thy mothers request, in so weighty a cause? doest thou take it honorable for a noble man, to remember the wronges and injuries done him:[2] and doest not in like case thinke it an honest noble mans parte, to be thankefull for the goodnes that parents doe shewe to their children, acknowledging the duety and reverence they ought to beare unto them.[3] No man living is more bounde to shewe him selfe thankefull in all partes and respects, then thy selfe: who so unnaturally sheweth all ingratitude. Moreover (my sonne) thou hast sorely taken of thy countrie, exacting grievous payments apon them, in revenge of the injuries offered thee: besides, thou hast not hitherto shewed thy poore mother any curtesie.[4] And therefore, it is not only honest, but due unto me, that without compulsion I should obtaine my so just and reasonable request of thee. But since by reason I cannot persuade thee to it, to what purpose doe I deferre my last hope?'[5] And with these wordes, her selfe, his wife and children, fell downe upon their knees before him. *Martius* seeing that, could refraine no lenger, but went straight and lifte her up, crying out: *Coriolanus* Oh mother, what have you done to me? And *compassion of* holding her hard by the right hande,[6] oh mother, *his mother.* sayed he, you have wonne a happy victorie for your countrie, but mortall and unhappy for your sonne:[7] for I see my self vanquished by you alone. These wordes being spoken openly, he spake a litle a

1. v. iii. 148. 2. v. iii. 148–55.
3. Cf. v. iii. 155–8, where Volumnia invites Virgilia and the boy to speak.
4. v. iii. 158–61. 5. Amplified in v. iii. 162–82.
6. v. iii. 182 S.D. 7. v. iii. 182–3, 185–9.

parte with his mother and wife, and then let them
returne againe to ROME, for so they dyd request
him:[1] & so remaining in campe that night, the
next morning he dislodged,[2] and marched home-
wardes into the VOLSCES countrie againe, who
were not all of one minde, nor all alike contented. For some misliked him, and that he had
done. Other being well pleased that peace should
be made, sayed: that neither the one, nor the other,
deserved blame nor reproche. Other, though they
misliked that was done, dyd not thincke him an ill
man for that he dyd, but sayed: he was not to be
blamed, though he yelded to suche a forcible
extremitie. Howbeit no man contraried his departure, but all obeyed his commaundement,
more for respect of his worthines and valiancie,
then for feare of his authoritie. Now the cittizens of
ROME plainely shewed, in what feare and daunger
their cittie stoode of this warre, when they were
delivered. For so sone as the watche upon the
walles of the cittie perceyved the VOLSCES
campe to remove, there was not a temple in the
cittie but was presently set open, and full of men,
wearing garlands of flowers upon their heads,
sacrificing to the goddes, as they were wont to doe
upon the newes of some great obteined victorie.
And this common joye was yet more manifestly
shewed, by the honorable curtesies the whole
Senate, and people dyd bestowe on their ladyes.[3]
For they were all throughly persuaded, and dyd
certenly beleeve, that the ladyes only were cause
of the saving of the cittie, and delivering them
selves from the instant daunger of the warre.
Whereupon the Senate ordeined, that the magistrates to gratifie and honour these ladyes, should
graunte them all that they would require. And they
only requested that they would build a temple of
Fortune of the women, for the building whereof they
offered them selves to defraye the whole charge of
the sacrifices, and other ceremonies belonging to
the service of the goddes. Nevertheles, the Senate
commending their good will and forwardnes,

Coriolanus withdraweth his armie from Rome.

The temple of Fortune built for the women.

1. v. iii. 202–9.   2. v. iv. 42.   3. v. iv. 40—v. v. 7.

ordeined, that the temple and image should be made at the common charge of the cittie.[1] Notwithstanding that, the ladyes gathered money emong them, and made with the same a second image of *Fortune*, which the ROMAINES saye dyd speake as they offred her up in the temple, and dyd set her in her place: and they affirme, that she spake these wordes. Ladyes, ye have devoutely offered me up. Moreover, that she spake that twise together, making us to beleeve things that never were, and are not to be credited. For to see images that seeme to sweate or weepe,[2] or to put forth any humour red or blowdie, it is not a thing unpossible. For wodde and stone doe commonly receyve certaine moysture, whereof is ingendred an humour, which doe yeld of them selves, or doe take of the ayer, many sortes and kyndes of spottes and cullers: by which signes and tokens it is not amisse we thincke, that the goddes sometimes doe warne men of things to come. And it is possible also, that these images and statues doe somtimes put forth soundes, like unto sighes or mourning, when in the middest or bottome of the same, there is made some violent separation, or breaking a sonder of things, blowen or devised therein: but that a bodie which hath neither life nor soule, should have any direct or exquisite worde formed in it by expresse voyce, that is altogether unpossible. For the soule, nor god him selfe can distinctly speake without a bodie, having necessarie organes and instrumentes mete for the partes of the same, to forme and utter distinct wordes. But where stories many times doe force us to beleeve a thing reported to be true, by many grave testimonies: there we must saye, that it is some passion contrarie to our five naturall sences, which being begotten in the imaginative parte or understanding, draweth an opinion unto it selfe, even as we doe in our sleeping. For many times we thinke we heare, that we do not heare: & we imagine we see, that we see not. Yet notwithstanding, such as are godly bent, and zealously

The image of Fortune spake to the ladyes at Rome.

Of the sweating and voyces of images.

1. v. iii. 206–7.   2. Cf. v. iii. 196.

geven to thinke apon heavenly things, so as they can no waye be drawen from beleeving that which is spoken of them, they have this reason to grounde the foundation of their beleefe upon. That is, the

omnipotencie of God[1] which is wonderfull, and hath no manner of resemblaunce or likelines of proportion unto ours, but is altogether contrarie as touching our nature, our moving, our arte, and our force: and therefore if he doe any thing unpossible to us, or doe bring forth and devise things, without mans common reache and understanding, we must not therefore thinke it unpossible at all. For if in other things he is farre contrarie to us, muche more in his workes and secret operations, he farre passeth all the rest: but the most parte of goddes doings, as *Heraclitus* sayeth, for lacke of faith, are hidden and unknowen unto us. Now when *Martius* was returned againe into the cittie of ANTIVM from his voyage, *Tullus* that

hated and could no lenger abide him for the feare he had of his authoritie: sought divers meanes to make him out of the waye,[2] thinking that[3] if he let slippe that present time, he should never recover the like and fit occasion againe. Wherefore *Tullus* having procured many other of his confederacy, required *Martius* might be deposed from his estate, to render up accompt to the VOLSCES of his charge and government.[4] *Martius* fearing to become a private man againe under *Tullus* being generall (whose authoritie was greater otherwise, then any other emong all the VOLSCES) aunswered: he was willing to geve up his charge, and would resigne it into the handes of the lordes of the VOLSCES, if they dyd all commaund him, as by all their commaundement he receyved it. And moreover, that he would not refuse even at that present to geve up an accompt unto the people, if they would tarie the hearing of it. The people hereupon called a common counsaill, in which assembly there were certen oratours appointed,

---

1. Plutarch's pious marvellings are not assimilated into the play.
2. v. vi. 1–59, anticipated in IV. vii. 25–6.
3. 1595 omits *that.*   4. Cf. IV. vii. 25–6, v. vi. 71–84.

that stirred up the common people against him.[1] and when they had tolde their tales, *Martius* rose up to make them aunswer. Now, notwithstanding the mutinous people made a marvelous great noyse, yet when they sawe him, for the reverence they bare unto his valliantnes, they quieted them selves, and gave still audience to alledge with leysure what he could for his purgation. Moreover, the honestest men of the ANTIATES, and who most rejoyced in peace, shewed by their countenaunce that they would heare him willingly, and judge also according to their conscience. Where upon *Tullus* fearing that if he dyd let him speake, he would prove his innocencie to the people, bicause emongest other things he had an eloquent tongue,[2] besides that the first good service he had done to the people of the VOLSCES, dyd winne him more favour, then these last accusations could purchase him displeasure: & furthermore, the offence they layed to his charge, was a testimonie of the good will they ought him, for they would never have thought he had done them wrong for that they tooke not the cittie of ROME, if they had not bene very neere taking of it, by meanes of his approche and conduction.[3] For these causes *Tullus* thought he might no lenger delaye his pretence and enterprise, neither to tarie for the mutining and rising of the common people against him: wherefore, those that were of the conspiracie, beganne to crie out that he was not to be heard, nor that they would not suffer a traytour[4] to usurpe tyrannicall power over the tribe of the VOLSCES, who would not yeld up his estate and authoritie. And in saying these wordes, they all fell upon him, and killed him in the market place, none of the people once offering to rescue him.[5] Howbeit it is a clere case, that this murder was not generally consented unto, of the most parte of the VOLSCES,[6] for men came out of all partes to honour his bodie, and dyd

Coriolanus murdered in the cittie of Antium.

1. There is popular acclaim but no popular conspiracy in the play (v. vi. 49–52).
2. v. vi. 55–6.   3. As Martius implies, v. vi. 74–84.   4. v. vi. 85–7.
5. v. vi. 119–30.   6. v. vi. 132–41, 144–53.

*Coriolanus
funeralles.*

honorably burie him,[1] setting out his tombe with
great store of armour and spoyles, as the tombe of a
worthie persone and great captaine. The Romaines understanding of his death, shewed no
other honour or malice, saving that they graunted
the ladyes the request they made: that they
might mourne tenne moneths for him, and that

*The time of
mourning
appointed by
Numa.*

was the full time they used to weare blackes for
the death of their fathers, brethern, or husbands,
according to *Numa Pompilius* order, who stablished
the same, as we have enlarged more amplie in the
description of his life. Now *Martius* being dead, the
whole state of the Volsces hartely wished him
alive againe. For first of all they fell out with the
Æqves (who were their friendes and confederates) touching preheminence and place: &
this quarrell grew on so farre betwene them, that
frayes & murders fell out apon it one with another.
After that, the Romaines overcame them in

*Tullus Aufidius
slaine in battell.*

battell, in which *Tullus* was slaine in the field, and
the flower of all their force was put to the swordе:
so that they were compelled to accept most shamefull conditions of peace, in yelding them selves
subject unto the conquerers, and promising to be
obedient at their commandement.

I. v. vi. 149–54 S.D.

EXTRACT FROM CAMDEN'S 'REMAINES OF A
GREATER WORKE, CONCERNING BRIT-
AINE,' ETC., 1605. GRAVE SPEECHES, AND
WITTIE APOTHEGMES OF WOORTHIE
PERSONAGES OF THIS REALME IN FORM-
ER TIMES,[1] pp. 198, 199.

POPE *Adrian* the fourth an English man borne, of the familie
of *Breakespeare* in *Middlesex*, a man commended for converting
Norway to christianity, before his Papacie, but noted in his
Papacie, for vsing the Emperour *Fredericke* the second as his
Page, in holding his stirroppe, demaunded of *John* of *Sarisbury*
his countryman what opinion the world had of the Church of
Rome, and of him, who answered: *The Church of Rome which
should be a mother, is now a stepmother, wherein sit both Scribes and
Pharises; and as for your selfe, whenas you are a father, why doe you
expect pensions from your children?* etc. Adrian smiled, and after some
excuses tolde him this tale, which albeit it may seeme long, and
us not vnlike that of *Menenius Agrippa* in *Livie*, yet give it the reading, and happly you may learne somwhat by it. *All the members
of the body conspired against the stomacke, as against the swallowing gulfe
of all their labors; for whereas the eies beheld, the eares heard, the handes
labored, the feete traveled, the tongue spake, and all partes performed
their functions, onely the stomacke lay ydle and consumed all. Hereuppon
they ioyantly agreed al to forbeare their labors, and to pine away their
lasie and publike enemy. One day passed over, the second followed very
tedious, but the third day was so grievous to them all, that they called a
common Counsel; The eyes waxed dimme, the feete could not support the
body, the armes waxed lasie, the tongue faltered, and could not lay open
the matter; Therefore they all with one accord desired the advise of the
Heart. There Reason layd open before them, that hee against whome they
had proclaimed warres, was the cause of all this their misery: For he as
their common steward, when his allowances were withdrawne, of necessitie
withdrew theirs fro them, as not receiving that he might allow. Therefore
it were a farre better course to supply him, than that the limbs should faint
with hunger. So by the perswasion of Reason, the stomacke was served, the
limbes comforted, and peace re-established. Even so it fareth with the*

1. For discussion of Camden's contribution to Shakespeare's version of the
fable of the belly (I. i. 95–154), see Introduction, p. 29. Camden follows John
of Salisbury, *Policraticus*, VI, 24.

bodies of Common-weales; for albeit the Princes gather much, yet not so much for themselves, as for others: So that if they want, they cannot supply the want of others; therefore do not repine at Princes heerein, but respect the common good of the whole publike estate.